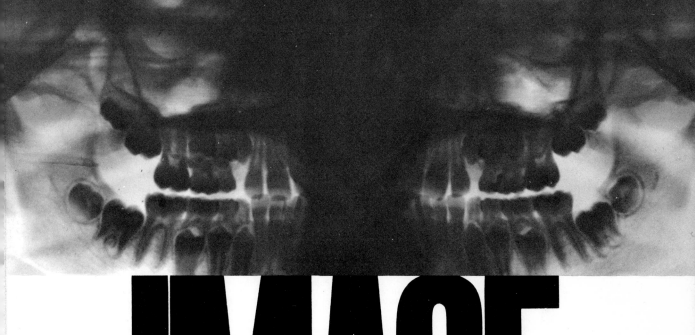

IMAGE

REFLECTIONS ON LANGUAGE

CLARK McKOWEN

DIABLO VALLEY COLLEGE

DESIGNER: GLENN BROUGH

D1285604

THE MACMILLAN COMPANY, NEW YORK

acknowledgments:

ALYESHMERNI and TAUBR, word game, pp. 234-35. From *Working with Aspects of Language* by Mansoor Alyeshmerni and Paul Taubr. Copyright © 1970 by Harcourt Brace Jovanovich, Inc. and reprinted with their permission. HANS ARP, photograph of sculpture, "Pistil." Reprinted by permission of The St. Louis Art Museum. LES BARRY, photograph, p. 157. Reprinted by permission of Les Barry. BASHO, "No oil to read by . . . ," translated by Peter Beilenson. From *Japanese Haiku*. Reprinted by permission of Peter Pauper Press. THE BEATLES, "Lucy in the Sky with Diamonds," by The Beatles. Copyright © 1967 by Northern Songs, Ltd. Used by permission. All rights reserved. RUTH BERNARD, photographs, pp. 141, 190, 254, 265. Reprinted by permission of Ruth Bernard. Excerpt from "Influencing the Image," by Ruth Bernard. Reprinted from *Aperature*. MORRIS BISHOP, "The Naughty Preposition." From *A Bowl of Bishop* by Morris Bishop. Copyright © 1954 by Morris Bishop. Reprinted by permission of the publisher, The Dial Press. Originally appeared in *The New Yorker* Magazine. ROBERT BLY, "Watching Television," from *The Light Around the Body* by Robert Bly. Copyright © 1963 by Robert Bly. By permission of Harper & Row, Publishers, Inc. GIOVANI BOLOGNA, "Rape of the Sabines." Reprinted by permission of Victoria and Albert Museum. JAMES BOSWELL, excerpts from *Boswell's London Journal, 1762-1763,* edited by Frederick A. Pottle. Copyright © 1950 by Yale University. Used with permission of McGraw-Hill Book Company. RICHARD BRAUTIGAN, "The Kool-Aid Wino." From *Trout Fishing in America*, by Richard Brautigan. Copyright © 1967 by Richard Brautigan. A Seymore Lawrence Book/Delacorte Press. Reprinted by permission of the publisher. "Nice Ass," from *Rommel Drives on Deep into Egypt* by Richard Brautigan. Copyright © 1970 by Richard Brautigan. A Seymour Lawrence Book/Delacorte Press. Reprinted by permission of the publisher. "Oranges," from *The Pill Versus the Springhill Mine Disaster* by Richard Brautigan. Copyright © 1968 by Richard Brautigan. A Seymour Lawrence Book/Delacorte Press. Reprinted by permission of the publisher. GLENN BROUGHER, drawings, pp. 8, 16, 348, 354. Reprinted by permission of Glenn Brougher. MELINDA BROUGHER, drawing, p. 215. Reprinted by permission of Melinda Brougher. GORDON BROWN, excerpts from journal. Reprinted by permission of Gordon Brown. BROWN and OLMSTED, tripset, p. 113. From *Language and Literature,* by Wentworth K. Brown and Sterling P. Olmsted. Reprinted by permission of Harcourt Brace Jovanovich, Inc. PETER BRUGEL, "Children's Games." Reprinted by permission of Kunsthistorisches Museum of Vienna. NIGEL CALDER, excerpts from *Violent Universe,* by Nigel Calder. Copyright © 1969 by Nigel Calder. Reprinted by permission of The Viking Press, Inc. ALBERT CAMUS, excerpts from *The Myth of Sisyphus,* by Albert Camus. Copyright © 1955 by Alfred A. Knopf, Inc. Reprinted by permission of the publisher. DON CARPENTER, "One of Those Big-City Girls" from *The Murder of the Frogs and Other Stories.* Copyright © 1969 by Don Carpenter. Reprinted by permission of Harcourt Brace Jovanovich, Inc. ERNST CASSIRER, excerpts from *Language and Myth,* translated by Susanne K. Langer. Dover Edition, 1946, pp. 33, 81, 99. Reprinted by permission of Yale University Press. CARLOS CASTANEDA, excerpts from *The Teachings of Don Juan,* by Carlos Castaneda. University of California Press, 1968. Reprinted by permission of the publisher. CAVAFY, "Waiting for the Barbarians." Reprinted from *The Complete Poems of Cavafy,* translated by Rae Dalven by permission of Harcourt Brace Jovanovich, Inc. Copyright © 1949 by Rae Dalven. COURTNEY B. CAZDEN, excerpts from "Suggestions from Studies of Early Language Acquisition," by Courtney B. Cazden. Reprinted by permission of Courtney B. Cazden and the Association for Childhood Education International, 3615 Wisconsin Avenue, N.W., Washington, D.C. Copyright © 1969 by the Association. MARC CHAGALL, "The Violinist." Reprinted by permission of the Stedlijk Museum. G. K. CHESTERTON, "Gold Leaves." From *The Collected Poems of G. K. Chesterton.* Reprinted by permission of Dodd, Mead & Company, and A. P. Watt & Son, Ltd. ERIC CHEYFITS, "The Otter's Song to Us." Reprinted by permission of *Esquire* Magazine. Copyright © 1972 by Esquire, Inc. WILLIAM CHILDRESS, "The Dreamer," used by permission of the author. Copyright © March 1966 by Harper's, a division of Minneapolis Star and Tribune Company. NOAM CHOMSKY, excerpts condensed from "Chomsky is difficult to please. Chomsky is easy to please. Chomsky is certain to please," by Israel Shenker. Copyright © 1971 by American Heritage Publishing Co., Inc. Reprinted by permission from *Horizon* Magazine, Spring 1971. CHARLES CHUTZ, excerpts from journal. Reprinted by permission of Charles Chutz. PAT CLITES, drawing, p. 200. Reprinted by permission of Pat Clites. LEONARD COHEN, "The first thing I do . . . ," "Dead Song," "Beneath My Hands." From *Selected Poems 1956-1968* by Leonard Cohen. Copyright © 1961 in all countries of the International Copyright Union by McClelland and Stewart Ltd., Toronto. All rights reserved. Reprinted by permission of The Viking Press, Inc. JOHN COLLIER, "Thus I Refute Beelzy." Copyright © 1940, 1967 by John Collier. Reprinted by permission of the Harold Matson Company, Inc. CHARLES DEMUTH, "I Saw the Figure 5 in Gold." Reprinted by permission of The Metropolitan Museum of Art. EMILY DICKINSON, "A Word," from *Complete Poems of Emily Dickinson,* Thomas H. Johnson, editor, Little, Brown and Company. JOAN DIDION, excerpt from "A Problem of Making Connections," by Joan Didion. Reprinted by permission of William Morris Agency, Inc. Copyright © 1969 by Joan Didion. RICHARD EBERHART, "If I Could Only Live. . . ." From *Collected Poems 1930-1960* by Richard Eberhart. Copyright © 1960 by Richard Eberhart. Reprinted by permission of Oxford University Press, Inc. ELLIOT ERWITT, photographs, pp. 104, 110. Reprinted by permission of Elliot Erwitt. M. C. ESCHER, "Drawing Hands," "Reptiles," and "Belvedere," by M. C. Escher. Reprinted by permission of the Escher Foundation—Haags Gemeentemuseum—The Hague. LAWRENCE FERLINGHETTI, "Constantly risking absurdity," "Don't let that horse. . . ." From *A Coney Island of the Mind.* Copyright © 1958 by Lawrence Ferlinghetti. Reprinted by permission of New Directions Publishing Corporation. E. M. FORSTER, excerpts from *A Passage to India* by E. M. Forster. Copyright © 1924 by Harcourt Brace Jovanovich, Inc.; copyright © 1952, by E. M. Forster. Reprinted by permission of Harcourt Brace Jovanovich, Inc., and Edward Arnold (Publishers) Ltd. JOHN FOWLES, excerpts from *The Magus* by John Fowles. Copyright © 1965 by John Fowles. Reprinted by permission of Little, Brown and Company. PETER FREUCHEN, excerpts from *Peter Freuchen's Book of the Eskimos,* edited by Dagmar Freuchen. Copyright © 1961 by the Peter Freuchen Estate. Reprinted by permission of The World Publishing Company. ROBERT FROST, "Neither Out Far Nor In Deep," "It Takes All Sorts . . . ," "For Once, Then, Something," "To Earthward." From *The Poetry of Robert Frost,* edited by Edward Connery Lathem. Copyright © 1923, 1969 by Holt, Rinehart and Winston, Inc. Copyright © 1964 by Lesley Frost Ballantine. Reprinted by permission of Holt, Rinehart and Winston, Inc. Excerpts from *Robert Frost: The Years of Triumph, 1915-1938* by Lawrance Thompson. Copyright © 1970 by Lawrance Thompson. Reprinted by permission of Holt, Rinehart and Winston, Inc. Excerpts from *Selected Letters of Robert Frost,* edited by Lawrance Thompson. Copyright © 1964 by Holt, Rinehart and Winston, Inc. Reprinted by permission of the Estate of Robert Frost and Holt, Rinehart and Winston, Inc. Excerpts from *The Letters of Robert Frost to Louis Untermeyer.* Copyright © 1963 by Holt, Rinehart and Winston, Inc. Reprinted by permission of Holt, Rinehart and Winston, Inc. R. BUCKMINSTER FULLER, excerpts from *I Seem To Be a Verb* by R. Buckminster Fuller with Jerome Agel and Quentin Fiore. Copyright © 1970 by Bantam Books, Inc. JOHN FURNIVAL, drawing, p. 255. Reprinted by permission of John Furnival. GORDON GALLUP, "Ten-Minute Comfort Stop." Condensed and reprinted from *Psychology Today* Magazine, March 1971. Copyright © Communications/Research/Machines, Inc. LAMBERT W. GARDINER, excerpts from *Psychology: A Story of a Search.* Copyright © 1970 by Wadsworth Publishing Company, Inc. Reprinted with permission of the publisher, Brooks/Cole Publishing Company, Monterey, California. SHIRLEY ANN GRAU, excerpt from *The Condor Passes.* Copyright © 1971 by Alfred A. Knopf, Inc. Reprinted by permission of the publisher. ROBERT GRAVES, "Warning to Children." From *Collected Poems 1965.* Reprinted by permission of Robert Graves. HANNAH GREEN, excerpts from *I Never Promised You a Rose Garden.* Copyright © 1964 by Hannah Green. Reprinted by permission of Holt, Rinehart and Winston, Inc. GRAHAM GREENE, "The Destructors." From *21 Stories by Graham Greene.* Copyright © 1954 by Graham Greene. Reprinted by permission of The Viking Press, Inc. NAT GREENWOOD, cartoon, p. 179. From the *San Francisco Chronicle,* March 22, 1970. Reprinted by permission of Adcox Associates. EUGENE GUILLEVIC, "In the Cave of Ice." From *Selected Poems,* translated by Denise Levertov. Copyright © 1960 by Denise Levertov Goodman and Eugene Guillevic. Reprinted by permission of New Directions Publishing Corporation. "News Item," "Yes . . . Rivers," by Eugene Guillevic, translated by Teo Savory. Copyright © 1968 by Teo Savory. Reprinted by permission of Unicorn Press. TERRY HAMMERMASTER, drawing, p. 176. Reprinted by permission of Terry Hammermaster. MAL HANCOCK, cartoons, pp. 311, 355. Reprinted by permission of Washington Star Syndicate, 444 Madison Avenue, New York, New York 10022. MIKE HARRISON, excerpts from journal. Reprinted by permission of Mike Harrison. PIET HEIN, drawings and excerpt from *Grooks I.* Copyrighted © 1966 by The M.I.T. Press. HAROLD G. HENDERSON, haikus, pp. 159, 168, 171. From *An Introduction to Haiku* by Harold G. Henderson. Copyright © 1958 by Harold G.

and the entire human race . . . .

Tell me, good Brutus, can you see your face?
No, Cassius; for the eye sees not itself / But by reflection, by some other things.

PRE FACE

Who were you before your mother conceived you ?

Introduction

Get the olive out of the cocktail glass:

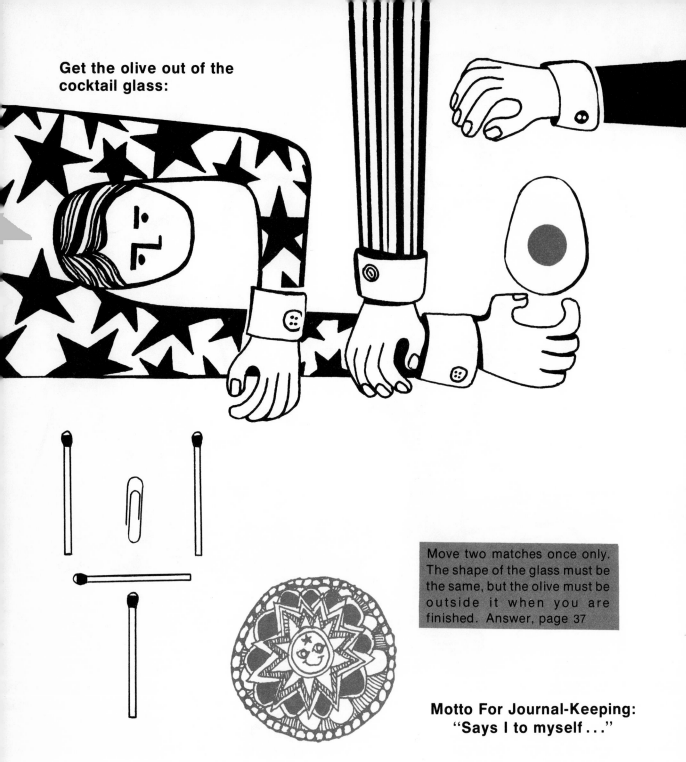

Move two matches once only. The shape of the glass must be the same, but the olive must be outside it when you are finished. Answer, page 37

Motto For Journal-Keeping:
"Says I to myself..."

10

In the space provided list everything which should not be included in·an English course.

The Space Provided

Warning to Children

Children, if you dare to think
Of the greatness, rareness, muchness,
Fewness of this precious only
Endless world in which you say
You live, you think of things like this:
Blocks of slate enclosing dappled
Red and green, enclosing tawny
Yellow nets, enclosing white
And black acres of dominoes,
Where a neat brown paper parcel
Tempts you to untie the string.
In the parcel a small island,
On the island a large tree,
On the tree a husky fruit.
Strip the husk and cut the rind off:
In the centre you will see
Blocks of slate enclosed by dappled
Red and green, enclosed by tawny
Yellow nets, enclosed by white
And black acres of dominoes,
Where the same brown paper parcel—
Children, leave the string untied!
For who dares undo the parcel
Finds himself at once inside it,
On the island, in the fruit,
Blocks of slate about his head,
Finds himself enclosed by dappled
Green and red, enclosed by yellow
Tawny nets, enclosed by black
And white acres of dominoes,
But the same brown paper parcel
Still untied upon his knee.
And, if he then should dare to think
Of the fewness, muchness, rareness,
Greatness of this endless only
Precious world in which he says
He lives—he then unties the string.

Diagnostic USAGE Quiz
Which is correct
A. *I came* **into** *the world,*
        or
B. *I came* **out of** *the world?*

umbilical cord

12

that reminds me..

Thinking about reflections, mirrors. A mirror does not give me the image the world sees. It's backwards. You can arrange a series of mirrors so that you can see your self as others see you. Still, it is a reflection even so. The eye cannot see itself except by reflection. Language as a mirror. Does the analogy work? I (the culture womb first) throw out language. It bounces off things, reflects off, and comes back to my self. Then it sees things. *But by reflection.* It does not see the thing it bounced off, because the waves come out from me, hit the object, bend a full 180 degrees and come back. Nothing out there comes back, only my own emanations. In this sense, I am sending radar probes out into the world. Is language then a probe? If so, it can never actually give me the thing probed but only a reflection, and we have seen that mirrors are not accurate, even when they are so arranged as to give us what other people have seen, for what they see is a reflection, too. But these waves we send out, aren't they things in themselves? In that sense a word is not *about* something; it *is* something. A word is not a probe. It is a *word*. Realizing this, I can work directly with what I have: words themselves, as things, as the only things I have. Words. In all shapes and sizes and arrangements. And what do I use them for? To see something. What? Me. Somehow, through these things that come out of me, to see me. They *are* me. But what is that?

Figure out how to arrange mirrors so that you do not get the ordinary mirror image but a reversal of that.

Words as mirror images. If so, what to do about that.

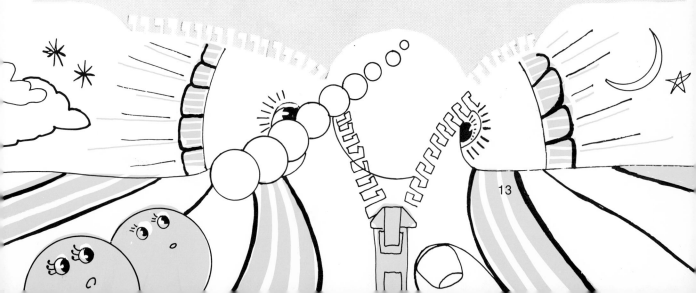

13

Daddy's shaving the windows

I love bolana sandwiches

I'm going thonging

Crick or Creek

She has curly teeth

onward Christian soldiers, marching on to Ward's

I'm wearing my muffins

I'll fist you!

They'll beat me to a pump

what's a Filosofer?

C O L D

Touch me
I'm not hot or cold
I'm this shape   C
I'm this shape   O
I'm this shape   L
I'm this shape   D
I'm letters
    Let's pretend

Let's pretend I am
    the letters
forming instantly on
    the page.
My entire self is
    not more than:

Take an ego to Lunch this week

14

alfred

I'm out and loose

ALFRED

ALFRED

wandering

surprising my self

alfr

ed

I could just

alfred

ALFRED

RRRR   RRRRRRR

or I could just

SJ all day,

ALFRED

SJ   alfred   alf

red

R   RRRRRRRRR   R   R

RRR   R   R   R   R   R

ALFREL

SJ   SJ   SJ   SJ

SJ   SJ   SJ   SJ

SJ   SJ   SJ   SJ   SJ

SJ   SJ   SJ   SJ   SJ

SJ   SJ   SJ   SJ

SJSJSJSJSJSJSJSJSJSJSJSJ

)

alfred

) ALFRED

SJ   alfred

15

HEART-WOOD

Words, our own or another's, can never be more than a commentary upon living experience. Reading can never be substituted for living. What do I understand about a tree? I have climbed into the branches and felt the trunk sway in the winds, and I have hidden among the leaves like an apple. I have lain among the branches and ridden them like another bough, and I have torn the skin of my hands and the cloth of my trousers climbing up and down the harsh bark. I have peeled away the skin of the willow and fondled the white sweet wood, and my ax has bitten through the pure fibers, and my saw laid bare the yearly rings and the heart-wood. Through the microscope I have copied out the traceries of the cells, and I have shaken out the rootlets like hair upon my hand; and I have chewed the gum and curled my tongue around the syrup, and shredded the wood fibers with my teeth. I have lain among the autumn leaves and my nostrils drank the smoke of their sacrifice. I have planed the yellow lumber and driven in the nails, and polished the smooth driftwood with my palm.

Within me now there is a graininess, a leafiness, a confluence of roots and branches, forests above and afar off, and a light soil made of a thousand years of their decay, and this whisper, this memory of fingers and nostrils, the fragile leaf-budding shivering within my eyes. What is my understanding of trees if it is not this reality lying behind these poor names? So do the lips, the tongue, the ears and eyes and fingers gather their voices and speak inwardly to the understanding. If I am wise I do not try to take another into that strange, placeless place of my thoughts, but I lead him to the forest and lose him among the trees, until he finds the trees within himself, and finds himself within the trees.

THE FRAME
EFFECT

Phase One
Take a walk. Bring back something which under ordinary circumstances would be most insignificant to you.

Phase Two
Save this object. Without altering it in any way, present it as *itself* so that it becomes significant. Do this on three successive days in three distinct ways.

Phase Three
Keep this object someplace where you will see it everyday for at least a month.

PEBBLES OR PONDS

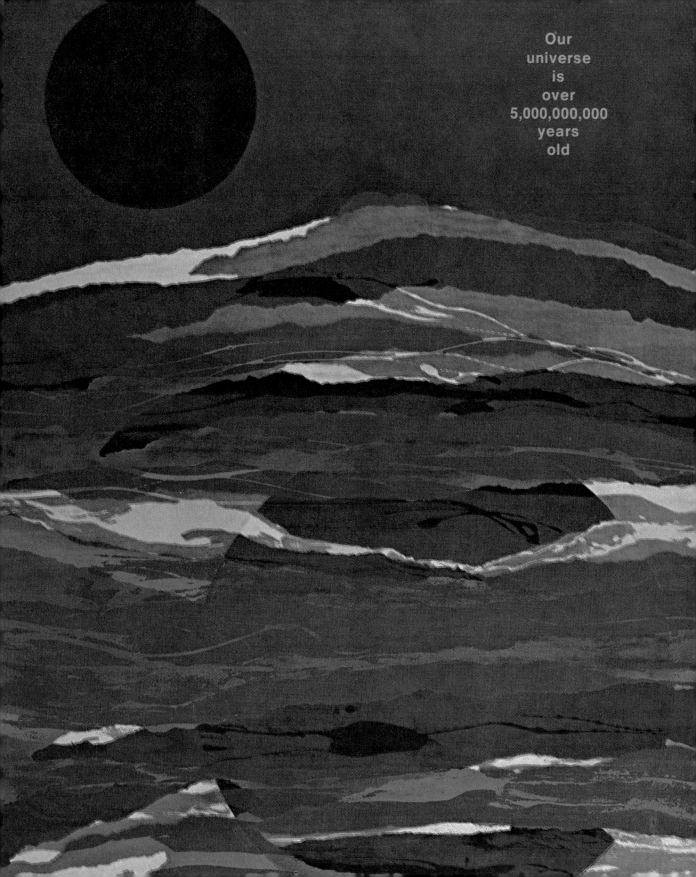

Our
universe
is
over
5,000,000,000
years
old

9

10

8

7

6

4

5

3

1

2

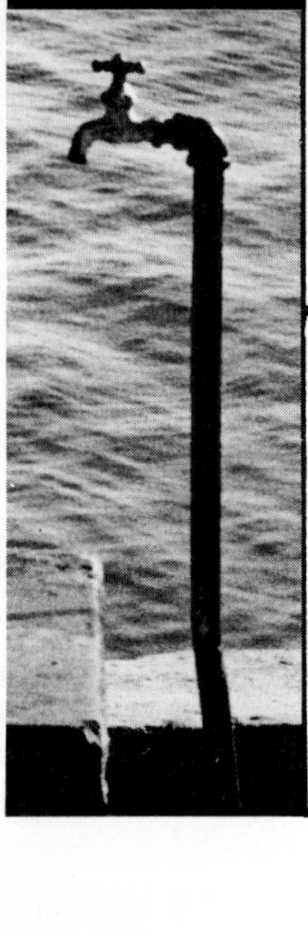

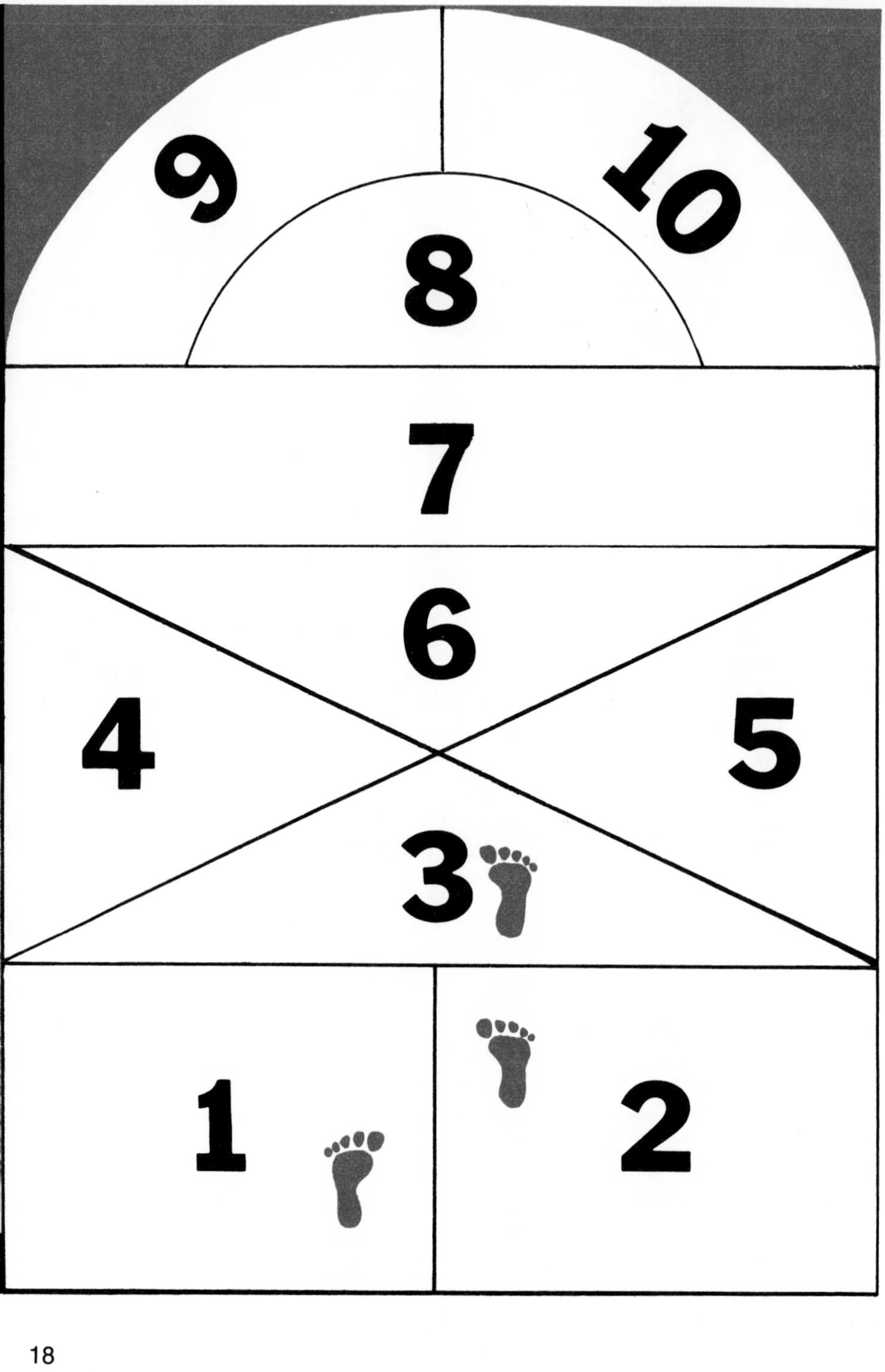

The belly button is a Mobius strip.
T or F ?

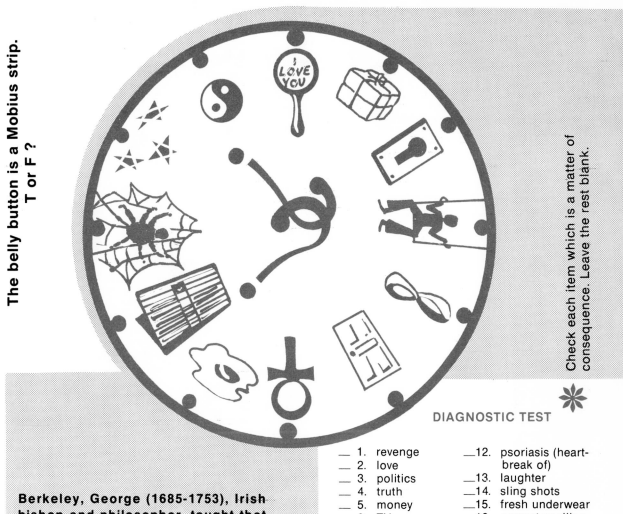

Check each item which is a matter of consequence. Leave the rest blank.

DIAGNOSTIC TEST

Berkeley, George (1685-1753), Irish bishop and philosopher, taught that material things exist only because we perceive them. And how are you, Elwood P. Dowd?

— 1. revenge
— 2. love
— 3. politics
— 4. truth
— 5. money
— 6. TV
— 7. conversation
— 8. BS
— 9. solitude
—10. space travel
—11. constipation

—12. psoriasis (heart-break of)
—13. laughter
—14. sling shots
—15. fresh underwear
—16. correct spelling
—17. vitamins
—18. garbage
—19. fleas
—20. war
—21. Timothy Leary

(Answers on page 485)

19

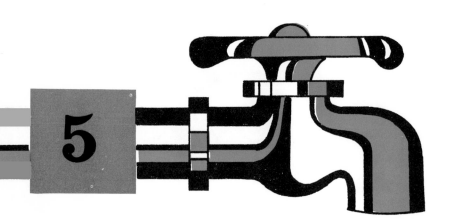

REAL-LY*

I said, "You've got to realize this,
real-ize." She thought I said "real-
eyes." I wonder (wonder,
w o n d e r) how often that happens
in a day.

You've got to real-eyes
this.
real-ize
When you haven't real-eyesd
it,
it's not r e a l.

Problem:
When it's not r e a l,
what *is* it?

REAL eyes

real EYES (mascara)

Assignment:
Real-eyes
   1. a flower,
   2. your hand,
   3. a liver spot.

  * (*-ly* [fr. OE -līc] like)

THE KOOL-AID WINO

When I was a child I had a friend who became a Kool-Aid wino as
the result of a rupture. He was a member of a very large and poor
German family. All the older children in the family had to work in
the fields during the summer, picking beans for two-and-one-half cents
a pound to keep the family going. Everyone worked except my friend
who couldn't because he was ruptured. There was no money for an
operation. There wasn't even enough money to buy him a truss. So
he stayed home and became a Kool-Aid wino.

  One morning in August I went over to his house. He was still in
bed. He looked up at me from underneath a tattered revolution of
old blankets. He had never slept under a sheet in his life.

  "Did you bring the nickel you promised?" he asked.

  "Yeah," I said. "It's here in my pocket."

  "Good."

  He hopped out of bed and he was already dressed. He had told
me once that he never took off his clothes when he went to bed.

  "Why bother?" he had said. "You're only going to get up, anyway.
Be prepared for it. You're not fooling anyone by taking your clothes
off when you go to bed."

  He went into the kitchen, stepping around the littlest children, whose
wet diapers were in various stages of anarchy. He made his breakfast:
a slice of homemade bread covered with Karo syrup and peanut butter.

  "Let's go," he said.

  We left the house with him still eating the sandwich. The store was
three blocks away, on the other side of a field covered with heavy
yellow grass. There were many pheasants in the field. Fat with summer
they barely flew away when we came up to them.

  "Hello," said the grocer. He was bald with a red birthmark on his
head. The birthmark looked just like an old car parked on his
head. He automatically reached for a package of grape Kool-Aid and put
it on the counter.

20

"Five cents."

"He's got it," my friend said.

I reached into my pocket and gave the nickel to the grocer. He nodded and the old red car wobbled back and forth on the road as if the driver were having an epileptic seizure.

We left.

My friend led the way across the field. One of the pheasants didn't even bother to fly. He ran across the field in front of us like a feathered pig.

When we got back to my friend's house the ceremony began. To him the making of Kool-Aid was a romance and a ceremony. It had to be performed in an exact manner and with dignity.

First he got a gallon jar and we went around to the side of the house where the water spigot thrust itself out of the ground like the finger of a saint, surrounded by a mud puddle.

He opened the Kool-Aid and dumped it into the jar. Putting the jar under the spigot, he turned the water on. The water spit, splashed and guzzled out of the spigot.

He was careful to see that the jar did not overflow and the precious Kool-Aid spill out onto the ground. When the jar was full he turned the water off with a sudden but delicate motion like a famous brain surgeon removing a disordered portion of the imagination. Then he screwed the lid tightly onto the top of the jar and gave it a good shake.

The first part of the ceremony was over.

Like the inspired priest of an exotic cult, he had performed the first part of the ceremony well.

His mother came around the side of the house and said in a voice filled with sand and string, "When are you going to do the dishes? . . . Huh?"

"Soon," he said.

"Well, you better," she said.

When she left, it was as if she had never been there at all. The second part of the ceremony began with him carrying the jar very carefully to an abandoned chicken house in the back. "The dishes can wait," he said to me. Bertrand Russell could not have stated it better.

He opened the chicken house door and we went in. The place was littered with half-rotten comic books. They were like fruit under a tree. In the corner was an old mattress and beside the mattress were four quart jars. He took the gallon jar over to them, and filled them carefully not spilling a drop. He screwed their caps on tightly and was now ready for a day's drinking.

You're supposed to make only two quarts of Kool-Aid from a package, but he always made a gallon, so his Kool-Aid was a mere shadow of its desired potency. And you're supposed to add a cup of sugar to every package of Kool-Aid, but he never put any sugar in his Kool-Aid because there wasn't any sugar to put in it.

He created his own Kool-Aid reality and was able to illuminate himself by it.

NEITHER OUT FAR
NOR IN DEEP

The people along the sand
All turn and look one way.
They turn their back on the land.
They look at the sea all day.

As long as it takes to pass
A ship keeps raising its hull;
The wetter ground like glass
Reflects a standing gull.

The land may vary more;
But wherever the truth may be—
The water comes ashore,
And the people look at the sea.

They cannot look out far.
They cannot look in deep.
But when was that ever a bar
To any watch they keep?

We *watch* TV.
We go to see a movie.
Does that make any
difference?

Are you satisfied with the way this passage ends?
How would Hitchcock end it?
   Lewis Carroll?
   Disney?
   A soap opera?
   You?
Try it each way, compare results with others, reflect.

True or False: 1. A story (this story) is a persona for the author. 2. It is always more about him than about his subject.

? ! ? ! ? ! ?

What is real
asked the rabbit one day
when they were lying
side by side
Does it mean having things that buzz in side you
and a stuck out handle
Real isn't how you're made
said the skin horse
It's a thing that happens to you
when a child loves you for a long long time
Not just to play with, but really loves you
then you become real
Does it hurt? asked the rabbit
Sometimes when you are real you don't mind being hurt
Does it happen all at once, like being wound up
or bit by bit
It doesn't happen all at once you become. It takes a long time
That's why it doesn't often happen
to people who break easily or have sharp edges
or have to be carefully kept. Generally by the time
you are real most of your hair has been loved off
and your eyes drop out and you get loose at the joints
But these things don't matter at all because once you are Real
you can't be ugly, except to people
who don't understand.

EXPERIENCE—THAT DRUG!

22

FIND SOMETHING UGLY.   REAL-EYES IT.   DEFINE UGLY.

(Take as long as you need.)

UNE MAGNIFIQUE IMAGE

"My last class lets out at 2:50."
John Millan,
Diablo Valley College
January 12, 1974

Lorsque j'avais six ans j'ai vu, une fois, une magnifique image, dans un livre sur la Forêt Vierge qui s'appelait "Histoires Vécues." Ça représentait un serpent boa qui avalait un fauve. Voilà la copie du dessin.

On disait dans le livre: "Les serpents boas avalent leur proie toute entière, sans la mâcher. Ensuite ils ne peuvent plus bouger et ils dorment pendant les six mois de leur digestion."

J'ai alors beaucoup réfléchi sur les aventures de la jungle et, à mon tour, j'ai réussi, avec un crayon de couleur, à tracer mon premier dessin. Mon dessin numéro 1. Il était comme ça:

Once when I was six years old I saw a magnificent picture in a book, called *True Stories from Nature,* about the primeval forest. It was a picture of a boa constrictor in the act of swallowing an animal. Here is a copy of the drawing.

In the book it said: "Boa constrictors swallow their prey whole, without chewing it. After that they are not able to move, and they sleep through the six months that they need for digestion."

I pondered deeply, then, over the adventures of the jungle. And after some work with a colored pencil I succeeded in making my first drawing. My Drawing Number One. It looked like this:

**WHO
ARE
YOU
?**

I showed my masterpiece to the grown-ups, and asked them whether the drawing frightened them.

But they answered: "Frighten? Why should any one be frightened by a hat?"

23

My drawing was not a picture of a hat. It was a picture of a boa constrictor digesting an elephant. But since the grown-ups were not able to understand it, I made another drawing. I drew the inside of the boa constrictor, so that the grown-ups could see it clearly. They always need to have things explained. My Drawing Number Two looked like this:

Whenever I met one of them who seemed to me at all clear-sighted, I tried the experiment of showing him my Drawing Number One, which I have always kept. I would try to find out, so, if this was a person of true understanding. But, whoever it was, he, or she, would always say:

"That is a hat."

Then I would never talk to that person about boa constrictors, or primeval forests, or stars. I would bring myself down to his level. I would talk to him about bridge, and golf, and politics, and neckties. And the grown-up would be greatly pleased to have met such a sensible man.

Haven't you forgotten something?

DOWN OUT OF A TREE AND LOOKED AROUND AND WONDERED WHAT HE WAS DOING HERE. *The Centaur*

The grown-ups' response, this time, was to advise me to lay aside my drawings of boa constrictors, whether from the inside or the outside, and devote myself instead to geography, history, arithmetic and grammar. That is why, at the age of six, I gave up what might have been a magnificent career as a painter. I had been disheartened by the failure of my Drawing Number One and my Drawing Number Two. Grown-ups never understand anything by themselves, and it is tiresome for children to be always and forever explaining things to them.

So then I chose another profession, and learned to pilot airplanes. I have flown a little over all parts of the world, and it is true that geography has been very useful to me. At a glance I can distinguish China from Arizona. If one gets lost in the night, such knowledge is valuable.

In the course of this life I have had a great many encounters with a great many people who have been concerned with matters of consequence. I have lived a great deal among grown-ups. I have seen them intimately, close at hand. And that hasn't much improved my opinion of them.

REVIEW QUIZ

List ten matters which are NOT of consequence:

1._____
2._____
3._____
4._____
5._____
6._____
7._____
8._____
9._____
10._____

Correct answers in the space provided

page II

24

 RELA^TIONSHIP

*Maybe that's it →
there's a RELationship
between people and
we, they can't see
each other through it.*

Out from the dirt in my hand
A plant pushes to be free.
But the roots grow down; I can't
  tell
What is plant, what is me.

*Waltuh, Waltuh, Wiuhlflowuh,
Growin' up so high;
So we are all young ladies,
An' we are ready to die.*

YOUR POEM, MAN . . .

*unless there's one thing seen
suddenly against another–a parsnip
sprouting for a President, or
hailstones melting in an ashtray–
nothing really happens. It takes
surprise and wild connections,
doesn't it? A walrus chewing
on a ballpoint pen. Two blue tail-
lights on Tyrannosaurus Rex. Green
cheese teeth. Maybe what we wanted
least. Or most. Some unexpected
pleats. Words that never knew
each other till right now. Plug us
into the wrong socket and see
what blows–or what lights up.
Try*
      untried
           circuitry,
new
      fuses.
*Tell it like it never really was,
man,
and maybe we can see it
like it is.*

RELATIONSHIP

**GETTING IN THE WAY
OF KNOWING
EACH OTHER?**

25

RELATIONSHIP

**All grown-ups were once children—
although few of them remember it.**

Find a local instance of universal energy systems. Hint: use a mirror.

A child of seven is excited by being
told that Tommy opened a door and saw
a dragon. But a child of three is excited by being told that Tommy opened
a door. Boys like romantic tales; but
babies like realistic tales—because
they find them romantic. In fact, a
baby is about the only person, I should
think, to whom a modern realistic novel
could be read without boring him.

Would it be good if we knew all the answers? I think it would dash the hopes of as many people as it overjoyed. I bet there are no answers to a good portion of it. Just think about that! NO answer to something. Doesn't that blow your body off? I know for a fact that there is NO answer. I'm just kidding you, of course, but if I did, I'd really be smart. As a last resort, famous people would consult me for the answers to many a fantastic question and in too many instances I would just have to explain to them that I'm the only one that knows for sure–that there is NO ANSWER. I would probably have to try and cheer them up as best I could before I let them leave my office.

A student

BE-KIND-TO-RHOMBENCEPHALONS WEEK

"Who are you?" said the Caterpillar.

This was not an encouraging opening for a conversation. Alice replied, rather shyly, "I—I hardly know, Sir, just at present—at least I know who I *was* when I got up this morning, but I think I must have been changed several times since then."

"What do you mean by that?" said the Caterpillar sternly. "Explain yourself!"

"I can't explain *myself,* I'm afraid, Sir," said Alice, "because I'm not myself, you see."

"I don't see," said the Caterpillar.

"I'm afraid I can't put it more clearly," Alice replied, very politely, "for I can't understand it myself, to begin with; and being so many different sizes in a day is very confusing."

"It isn't," said the Caterpillar.

Haven't you forgotten something?

Thus I refute Beelzy

"There goes the tea bell," said Mrs. Carter. "I hope Simon hears it."

They looked out from the window of the drawing-room. The long garden, agreeably neglected, ended in a waste plot. Here a little summer-house was passing close by beauty on its way to complete decay. This was Simon's retreat: it was almost completely screened by the tangled branches of the apple tree and the pear tree, planted too close together, as they always are in suburban gardens. They caught a glimpse of him now and then, as he strutted up and down, mouthing and gesticulating, performing all the solemn mumbo-jumbo of small boys who spend long afternoons at the forgotten ends of long gardens.

"There he is, bless him," said Betty.

"Playing his game," said Mrs. Carter. "He won't play with the other children any more. And if I go down there—the temper! And comes in tired out."

"He doesn't have his sleep in the afternoons?" asked Betty.

"You know what Big Simon's ideas are," said Mrs. Carter. "'Let him choose for himself,' he says. That's what he chooses, and he comes in as white as a sheet."

"Look. He's heard the bell," said Betty. The expression was justified, though the bell had ceased ringing a full minute ago. Small Simon stopped in his parade exactly as if its tinny dingle had at that moment reached his ear. They watched him perform certain ritual sweeps and scratchings with his little stick, and come lagging over the hot and flaggy grass towards the house.

Mrs. Carter led the way down to the play-room, or garden-room, which was also the tea-room for hot days. It had been the huge scullery of this tall Georgian house. Now the walls were cream-washed, there was coarse blue net in the windows, canvas-covered armchairs on the stone floor, and a reproduction of Van Gogh's *Sunflowers* over the mantelpiece.

Small Simon came drifting, and accorded Betty a perfunctory greeting. His face was an almost perfect triangle, pointed at the chin, and he was paler than he should have been. "The little elf-child!" cried Betty.

Simon looked at her. "No," said he.

At that moment the door opened, and Mr. Carter came in, rubbing his hands. He was a dentist, and washed them before and after everything he did. "You!" said his wife. "Home already!"

"Not unwelcome, I hope," said Mr. Carter, nodding to Betty. "Two people cancelled their appointments: I decided to come home. I said, I hope I am not unwelcome."

"Silly!" said his wife. "Of course not."

"Small Simon seems doubtful," continued Mr. Carter. "Small Simon, are you sorry to see me at tea with you?"

"No, Daddy."

"No, what?"

"No, Big Simon."

"That's right. Big Simon and Small Simon. That sounds more like friends, doesn't it? At one time little boys had to call their father 'sir.' If they forgot—a good spanking. On the bottom, Small Simon! On the bottom!" said Mr. Carter, washing his hands once more with his invisible soap and water.

The little boy turned crimson with shame or rage.

"But now, you see," said Betty, to help, "you can call your father whatever you like."

"And what," asked Mr. Carter, "has Small Simon been doing this afternoon? While Big Simon has been at work."

"Nothing," muttered his son.

"Then you have been bored," said Mr. Carter. "Learn from experience, Small Simon. Tomorrow, do something amusing, and you will not be bored. I want him to learn from experience, Betty. That is my way, the new way."

"I have learned," said the boy, speaking like an old, tired man, as little boys so often do.

"Que la terre est petite à qui la voit des cieux!"

"Are there any more questions?"
Joseph Alioto
San Francisco Press Club
December 12, 1968

"It would hardly seem so," said Mr. Carter, "if you sit on your behind all the afternoon, doing nothing. Had *my* father caught me doing nothing, I should not have sat very comfortably."

"He played," said Mrs. Carter.

"A bit," said the boy, shifting on his chair.

"Too much," said Mrs. Carter. "He comes in all nervy and dazed. He ought to have his rest."

"He is six," said her husband. "He is a reasonable being. He must choose for himself. But what game is this, Small Simon, that is worth getting nervy and dazed over? There are very few games as good as all that."

"It's nothing," said the boy.

"Oh, come," said his father. "We are friends, are we not? You can tell me. I was a Small Simon once, just like you, and played the same games you play. Of course there were no aeroplanes in those days. With whom do you play this fine game? Come on, we must all answer civil questions, or the world would never go around. With whom do you play?"

"Mr. Beelzy," said the boy, unable to resist.

"Mr. Beelzy?" said his father, raising his eyebrows inquiringly at his wife.

"It's a game he makes up!" said she.

"Not makes up!" cried the boy. "Fool!"

"That is telling stories," said his mother. "And rude as well. We had better talk of something different."

"No wonder he is rude," said Mr. Carter, "if you say he tells lies, and then insist on changing the subject. He tells you his fantasy: you implant a guilt feeling. What can you expect? A defense mechanism. Then you get a real lie."

"Like in *These Three*," said Betty. "Only different, of course. *She* was an unblushing little liar."

"I would have made her blush," said Mr. Carter, "in the proper part of her anatomy. But Small Simon is in the fantasy stage. Are you not, Small Simon? You just make things up."

"No, I don't," said the boy.

"You do," said his father. "And because you do, it is not too late to reason with you. There is no harm in a fantasy, old chap. There is no harm in a bit of make-believe. Only you have to know the difference between day dreams and real things, or your brain will never grow. It will never be the brain of a Big Simon. So come on. Let us hear about this Mr. Beelzy of yours. Come on. What is he like?"

"He isn't like anything," said the boy.

"Like nothing on earth?" said his father. "That's a terrible fellow."

"I'm not frightened of him," said the child, smiling. "Not a bit."

"I should hope not," said his father. "If you were, you would be frightening yourself. I am always telling people, older people than you are, that they are just frightening themselves. Is he a funny man? Is he a giant?"

"Sometimes he is," said the little boy.

"Sometimes one thing, sometimes another," said his father. "Sounds pretty vague. Why can't you tell us just what he's like?"

"I love him," said the small boy. "He loves me."

"That's a big word," said Mr. Carter. "That might be better kept for real things, like Big Simon and Small Simon."

"He is real," said the boy, passionately. "He's not a fool. He's real."

"Listen," said his father. "When you go down the garden there's nobody there. Is there?"

"No," said the boy.

"Then you think of him, inside your head, and he comes."

"No," said Small Simon. "I have to do something with my stick."

"That doesn't matter."

"Yes, it does."

"Small Simon, you are being obstinate," said Mr. Carter. "I am trying to explain something to you. I have been longer in the world than you have, so naturally I am older and wiser. I am explaining that Mr. Beelzy is a fantasy of yours. Do you hear? Do you understand?"

"Yes, Daddy."

"He is a game. He is a let's-pretend."

The little boy looked down at his plate, smiling resignedly.

"I hope you are listening to me," said his father. "All you have to do is to say, 'I have been playing a game of let's-pretend. With someone I make up, called Mr. Beelzy.' Then no one will say you tell lies, and you will know the difference between dreams and reality. Mr. Beelzy is a day dream."

The little boy still stared at his plate.

"He is sometimes there and sometimes not there," pursued Mr. Carter. "Sometimes he's like one thing, sometimes another. You can't really see him. Not as you see me. I am real. You can't touch him. You can touch me. I can touch you." Mr. Carter stretched out his big, white, dentist's hand, and took his little son by the shoulder. He stopped speaking for a moment and tightened his hand. The little boy sank his head still lower.

"Now you know the difference," said Mr. Carter, "between a pretend and a real thing. You and I are one thing; he is another. Which is the pretend? Come on. Answer me. What is the pretend?"

"Big Simon and Small Simon," said the little boy.

"Don't!" cried Betty, and at once put her hand over her mouth, for why should a visitor cry "Don't!" when a father is explaining things in a scientific and modern way?

"Well, my boy," said Mr. Carter, "I have said you must be allowed to learn from experience. Go upstairs. Right up to your room. You shall learn whether it is better to reason, or to be perverse and obstinate. Go up. I shall follow you."

"You are not going to beat the child?" cried Mrs. Carter.

"No," said the little boy. "Mr. Beelzy won't let him."

30

"Go on up with you!" shouted his father.

Small Simon stopped at the door. "He said he wouldn't let anyone hurt me," he whimpered. "He said he'd come like a lion, with wings on, and eat them up."

"You'll learn how real he is!" shouted his father after him. "If you can't learn it at one end, you shall learn it at the other. I'll have your breeches down. I shall finish my cup of tea first, however," said he to the two women.

Neither of them spoke. Mr. Carter finished his tea, and unhurriedly left the room, washing his hands with his invisible soap and water.

Mrs. Carter said nothing. Betty could think of nothing to say. She wanted to be talking: she was afraid of what they might hear.

Suddenly it came. It seemed to tear the air apart. "Good God!" she cried. "What was that? He's hurt him." She sprang out of her chair, her silly eyes flashing behind her glasses. "I'm going up there!" she cried, trembling.

"Yes, let us go up," said Mrs. Carter. "Let us go up. That was not Small Simon."

It was on the second-floor landing that they found the shoe, with the man's foot still in it, like that last morsel of a mouse which sometimes falls from the jaws of a hasty cat.

like it
never
really was

giviak

-IZE GAME

I can see now why it is said that it takes a long time to "solve" a koan (to open one's "eyes"). It seems first to become like a mirror in which you see yourself reflected (I bounce back and forth between the koan and myself). Until the self is clear and familiar you will not see the koan, only reflections...This suggests that it must be true that no one but you can solve the koan on which you are working. That is, it would do no good to be told the answer, because in a sense you are working on yourself to get the answer...On the other hand, I cannot see how the answer makes much difference. It seems to be the process of getting it that counts.

WHO
WERE...

1. real eyes, 2. polar eyes, 3. tender eyes, 4. legal eyes, 5. general eyes, 6. vandal eyes, 7. pasture eyes, 8. victim eyes, 9. standard eyes, 10. brutal eyes, 11. canon eyes, 12. sterile eyes

getting There is all the Fun.

see; saw; scene...

YOU...

Feed an ego
and starve
a
fever

Continue probing in
your journal.

the experience, if
possible. Change round and discuss
After group
large group

ers become the speakers, if
other listener hears.
If stymied, he may let the speaker
other listener let the listen-
The he speak.
know or days later
react days
Several

listener to say one thing
The speaker and listener must
listen. speaker must throughout
talk. speaker must try the
Work for half an hour to find game.
Persona Game and have one person
talk in pairs an hour about someone other

32

wake up, stupid

by Mark Harris

umbilical cord

Composition lesson:
To carve an Indian, take a piece of rock and cut away anything that doesn't look like an Indian.

When we try to pick out anything by itself, we find it hitched to everything else in the universe.

33

Test your self

WHO ARE YOU

Stubbing his toe on a rock one dark evening, Samuel Johnson remarked to his companion, "Thus I refute Berkeley." He was English, of course.

Place a check beside each item which you are not.

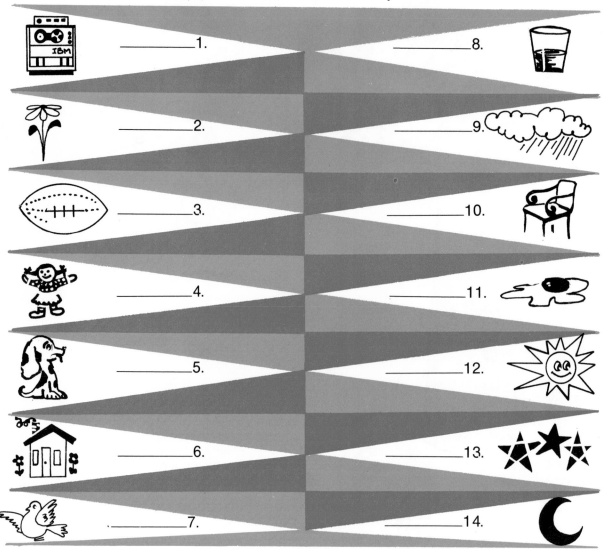

1. _____
2. _____
3. _____
4. _____
5. _____
6. _____
7. _____
8. _____
9. _____
10. _____
11. _____
12. _____
13. _____
14. _____

walter wildflower.

Hint: "It is a question of universes."

34

"The Seals can handle anybody
if they play up to their
capabilities."

Steve Swenson, Matzatlan,
January 30, 1971

Going up to Cambridge, sixty years
ago, one of our most eminent of
modern philosophers, then a callow
freshman, was greeted at the gate of
Trinity by the college porter.
"And pray, sir," that functionary
inquired with old-world politeness,
"who might you be?" Who *might* he
be? Gulf below metaphysical gulf
yawned at the young man's feet.
Who might anybody be?

. . . before my mother conceived
me?
Was I a Ford?

True or False: Where I am is
who I am.

Oh ain't I a dandy,
Oh ain't I a pet?
I walk in the rain
And I never get wet.
The girls, they all love me;
I hear them all say,
"Here comes Fritz Pumpernickle
From Latrobe, PA."

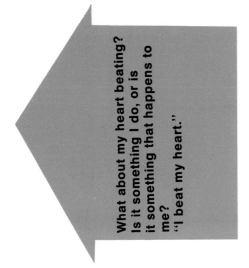

What about my heart beating?
Is it something I do, or is
it something that happens to
me?
"I beat my heart."

Charades

One person be a TV.
Some others be TV "watchers."
 (Watchers?)
Others watch the charade.
Then all talk about it.
- - - -
Try being a bicycle, a pencil,
 a tree, or be water, air, the
 universe.

35

THERE WAS A CHILD WENT FORTH

There was a child went forth every day,
And the first object he look'd upon, that object he became,
And that object became part of him for the day or a certain part of the day,
Or for many years or stretching cycles of years.

The early lilacs became part of this child,
And grass and white and red morning glories, and white and red clover, and
    the song of the phoebe-bird.
And the Third-month lambs and the sow's pink-faint-litter, and the mare's
    foal and the cow's calf,
And the noisy brood of the barnyard or by the mire of the pond-side,
And the fish suspending themselves so curiously below there, and the
    beautiful curious liquid,
And the water-plants with their graceful flat heads, all became part of him.

The field-sprouts of Fourth-month and Fifth-month became part of him,
Winter-grain sprouts and those of the light-yellow corn, and the esculent
    roots of the garden,
And the apple-trees cover'd with blossoms and the fruit afterward, and
    woodberries, and the commonest weeds by the road,
And the old drunkard staggering home from the outhouse of the tavern
    whence he had lately risen,
And the schoolmistress that pass'd on her way to the school.
And the friendly boys that pass'd and the quarrelsome boys,
And the tidy and fresh-cheek'd girls, and the barefoot negro boy and girl,
And all the changes of city and country wherever he went.

His own parents, he that had father'd him and she that had conceiv'd him
    in her womb and birth'd him,
They gave this child more of themselves than that,
They gave him afterward every day, they became part of him.

The mother at home quietly placing the dishes on the supper-table,
The mother with mild words, clean her cap and gown, a wholesome odour
    falling off her person and clothes as she walks by,
The father, strong, self-sufficient, manly, mean, anger'd, unjust.
The blow, the quick loud word, the tight bargain, the crafty lure,
The family usages, the language, the company, the furniture, the yearning
    and swelling heart,
Affection that will not be gainsay'd, the sense of what is real, the thought
    if after all it should prove unreal,
The doubts of day-time and the doubts of night-time, the curious whether
    and how,

36

Whether that which appears so is so, or is it all flashes and specks?

Men and women crowding fast in the streets; if they are not flashes and specks, what are they?

The streets themselves and the facades of houses, and goods in the windows,

Vehicles, teams, the heavy-plank'd wharves, the huge crossing at the ferries,

The village on the highland seen from afar at sunset, the river between,

Shadows, aureola and mist, the light falling on roofs and gables of white or brown two miles off,

The schooner near-by sleepily dropping down the tide, the little boat slack-tow'd astern,

The hurrying tumbling waves, quick-broken crests, slapping,

The strata of colour'd clouds, the long bar of maroon-tint away solitary by itself, the spread of purity it lies motionless in,

The horizon's edge, the flying sea-crow, the fragrance of salt marsh and shore mud,

These became part of that child who went forth every day, and who now goes, and will always go forth every day.

STOP

CLASSROOM INVENTORY

Solution to Matchstick Game, P. 10
"Every wall is a door."

37

"A CLASSROOM
IS WHERE EVERYTHING
ISN'T."

"Usually when we're invited into a classroom the first thing we do is ask people what they need that they don't have."

I want a place of my own.

me TOO!

me too

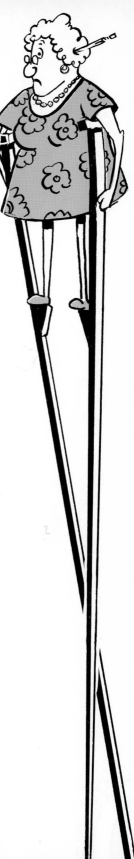

That reminds me . . . .

Rosann was teaching temporarily in a parochial elementary school. She took the kids on a trip through an overgrown empty field across from the school. She gave the kids paper bags and told them they were allowed to bring back things they found in the field. Before they had gone very far she had to set a limit because their bags were overflowing. "No more than ten things each," she had to say. But they kept begging, so she upped it to fifteen.

Thinking about the experience later, she remarked to her husband that she couldn't get over the sharp contrast between the apathy in class and the vitality, curiosity, inquisitiveness, and intensity out in the field. "Don't you know why," he said, "It's because a classroom is where everything isn't."

Everything is the same. It's boring.

if I only had a soft quiet place for a small group to work on reading.

everything is HARD.

List three things you have never seen in a classroom which should be there. Collate, reflect.

True or False: Classroom **language** is where everything isn't.

there's no place to be alone.

NAME GAME

Participants: Seven or eight, maximum.

Select one person. Write the letters of his name in a vertical column. The individual selected writes his own name. Then without discussion make up a word to go with each letter. The word should reveal the essence of the individual rather than merely describe his physical appearance.

Example:

S alty
T etanus
E arwig
V elvet
E ternity

Explore each person's answers and his reasons for choosing them. Then go on to the next person until all have been completed.

The personality is the prison of the immortal soul.

42

Where I live:

"Where do you live?" he asked. With a sudden shock I realized that this was a problem I had been confusedly thinking about for years. "Where do you live?" I handed him a card. But, needless to say, my address was not the answer to the riddle...

It wasn't a question of streets or cities, not even of countries or continents; it was a question of universes...

For what we are, what we know or think we know we are, determines where we live. Home, in a word, is homemade. Out of the raw material of given experience each of us constructs his own particular universe...

For the great majority of animals, the most conspicuous features of every human universe are simply not there. Sun, moon and stars, the sea and the dry land, all the wealth of vegetation and the countless things that swim, crawl, fly and run—the worlds, in which all but a very few species live, contain nothing that remotely resembles such objects...

The nature of any island universe depends on the nature of the individual inhabiting it...

All human worlds are more brightly colored than those inhabited by dogs. But not so deliciously smelly. All human worlds contain much greater extensions of space than does the world of the bees. To make up for this, the bees' world contains things which exist in no human world, such as two kinds of light, polarized and unpolarized, and objects whose color is ultraviolet....

Finding the center of a universe is a problem in

  a. geometry,
  b. theology,
  c. psychology,
  d. geography,
  e. logic,
  f. language,
  g. kissing.

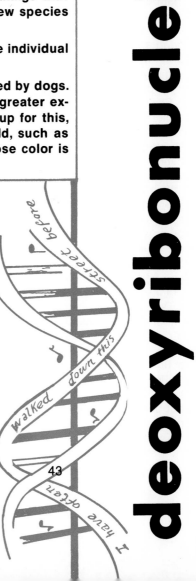

street before

walked down this

I have often

43

deoxyribonucleic acid

(title)

The weeks passed in aimless wandering. For the children, the lapse of time acquired once more the texture of a dream: things ceased happening: every inch of the schooner was now as familiar to them as the *Clorinda* had been, or Ferndale: they settled down quietly to grow, as they had done at Ferndale, and as they would have done, had there been time, on the *Clorinda*.

And then an event did occur, to Emily, of considerable importance. She suddenly realised who she was.

There is little reason that one can see why it should not have happened to her five years earlier, or even five later; and none why it should have come that particular afternoon.

She had been playing houses in a nook right in the bows, behind the windlass (on which she had hung a devil's-claw as a doorknocker); and tiring of it was walking rather aimlessly aft, thinking vaguely about some bees and a fairy queen, when it suddenly flashed into her mind that she was *she.*

She stopped dead, and began looking over all of her person which came within the range of her eyes. She could not see much, except a fore-shortened view of the front of her frock, and her hands when she lifted them for inspection; but it was enough for her to form a rough idea of the little body she suddenly realised to be hers.

She began to laugh, rather mockingly. "Well!" she thought, in effect: "Fancy *you,* of all people, going and getting caught like this!—You can't get out of it now, not for a very long time: you'll have to go through with being a child, and growing up, and getting old, before you'll be quit of this mad prank!"

Determined to avoid any interruption of this highly important occasion, she began to climb the ratlines, on her way to her favourite perch at the masthead. Each time she moved an arm or a leg in this simple action, however, it struck her with fresh amazement to find them obeying her so readily. Memory told her, of course, that they had always done so before: but before, she had never realised how surprising this was.

Once settled on her perch, she began examining the skin of her hands with the utmost care: for it was *hers.* She slipped a shoulder out of the top of her frock; and having peeped in to make sure she really was continuous under her clothes, she shrugged it up to touch her cheek. The contact of her face and the warm bare hollow of her shoulder gave her a comfortable thrill, as if it was the caress of some kind friend. But whether the feeling came to her through her cheek or her shoulder, which was the caresser and which the caressed, that no analysis could tell her.

Once fully convinced of this astonishing fact, that she was now Emily Bas-Thornton (why she inserted the "now" she did not know, for she certainly imagined no transmigrational nonsense of having been anyone else before), she began seriously to reckon its implications.

First, what agency had so ordered it that out of all the people in the world who she might have been, she was this particular one, this Emily; born in such-and-such a year out of all the years in Time, and encased in this particular rather pleasing little casket of flesh? Had she chosen herself, or had God done it?

At this, another consideration: who was God? She had heard a terrible lot about Him, always: but the question of His identity had been left vague, as much taken for granted as her own. Wasn't she perhaps God herself? Was it that she was trying to remember? However, the more she tried, the more it eluded her. (How absurd, to disremember such an important point as whether one was God or not!) So she let it slide: perhaps it would come back to her later.

Secondly, why had all this not occurred to her before? She had been alive for over ten years, now, and it had never once entered her head. She felt like a man who suddenly remembers at eleven o'clock at night, sitting in his own arm-chair, that he had accepted an invitation to go out to dinner that night. There is no reason for him to remember it now; but there seems equally little why he should not have remembered it in time to keep his engagement. How could he have sat there all the evening without being disturbed by the

*pas-sage—The process of passing from one state, condition, or stage to another.

slightest misgiving? How could Emily have gone on being Emily for ten years without once noticing this apparently obvious fact?

It must not be supposed that she argued it all out in this ordered but rather long-winded fashion. Each consideration came to her in a momentary flash, quite innocent of words; and in between her mind lazed along, either thinking of nothing or returning to her bees and the fairy queen. If one added up the total of her periods of conscious thought, it would probably reach something between four and five seconds; nearer five, perhaps; but it was spread out over the best part of an hour.

Well then, granted she was Emily, what were the consequences, besides enclosure in that particular little body (which now began on its own account to be aware of a sort of unlocated itch, most probably somewhere on the right thigh), and lodgement behind a particular pair of eyes?

It implied a whole series of circumstances. In the first place, there was her family, a number of brothers and sisters from whom, before, she had never entirely dissociated herself; but now she got such a sudden feeling of being a discrete person that they seemed as separate from her as the ship itself. However, willy-nilly she was almost as tied to them as she was to her body. And then there was this voyage, this ship, this mast round which she had wound her legs. She began to examine it with almost as vivid an illumination as she had studied the skin of her hands. And when she came down from the mast, what would she find at the bottom? There would be Jonsen, and Otto, and the crew, the whole fabric of a daily life which up to now she had accepted as it came, but which now seemed vaguely disquieting. What was going to happen? Were there disasters running about loose, disasters which her rash marriage to the body of Emily Thornton made her vulnerable to?

A sudden terror struck her: did anyone know? (Know, I mean, that she was someone in particular, Emily—perhaps even God—not just any little girl.) She could not tell why, but the idea terrified her. It would be bad enough if they should discover she was a particular person—but if they should discover she was God! At all costs she must hide *that* from them.—But suppose they knew already, had simply been hiding it from her (as guardians might from an infant king)? In that case, as in the other, the only thing to do was to continue to behave as if she did not know, and so outwit them.

But if she was God, why not turn all the sailors into white mice, or strike Margaret blind, or cure somebody, or do some other Godlike act of the kind? Why should she hide it? She never really asked herself why: but instinct prompted her strongly of the necessity. Of course, there was the element of doubt (suppose she had made a mistake, and the miracle missed fire): but more largely it was the feeling that she would be able to deal with the situation so much better when she was a little older. Once she had declared herself, there would be no turning back; it was much better to keep her godhead up her sleeve, for the present.

Grown-ups embark on a life of deception with considerable misgiving, and generally fail. But not so children. A child can hide the most appalling secret without the least effort, and is practically secure against detection. Parents, finding that they see through their child in so many places the child does not know of, seldom realise that, if there is some point the child really gives his mind to hiding, their chances are nil.

So Emily had no misgivings when she determined to preserve her secret, and needed have none.

Down below on the deck the smaller children were repeatedly crowding themselves into a huge coil of rope, feigning sleep and then suddenly leaping out with yelps of panic and dancing round it in consternation and dismay. Emily watched them with that impersonal attention one gives to a kaleidoscope. Presently Harry spied her, and give a hail.

"Emilee-ee! Come down and play House-on-fire!"

At that, her normal interests momentarily revived. Her stomach as it were leaped within her sympathetically toward the game. But it died in her as suddenly: and not only died, but she did not even feel disposed to waste her noble voice on them. She continued to stare without making any reply whatever.

"Come on!" shouted Edward.

"Come and play!" shouted Laura. "Don't be a pig!"

Then in the ensuing stillness Rachel's voice floated up:

"Don't call her, Laura, we don't really want her."

Which came first, the umbilicus or the navel?

beauty

Take off your personality and let's have a look at you.

But Aeore said passionately, "We are naked and have nothing! Therefore we must decorate ourselves, for if we did not, how are we to be told from animals?"

There it was. The unbearable thing was not the fear that the Great Spirit had foresaken man, nor even that in granting awareness of death, He had made man's hope ridiculous, but that from the beginning He had made no real distinction between the mindless animals and mankind.

"Thus I refute Berkeley."
R.R., University of
California Board of
Regents meeting, May 12, 1970

46

HOME IS HOMEMADE

But now a great thing in the street
Seems any human nod,
Where move in strange democracy
The million masks of God.

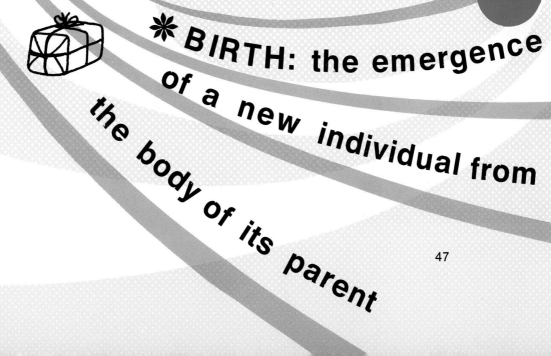

*BIRTH: the emergence of a new individual from the body of its parent

WE'RE DRUIDS

Nowadays, when a person lives somewhere, in a neighborhood, the place is not certified for him. More than likely he will live there sadly and the emptiness which is inside him will expand until it evacuates the entire neighborhood. But if he sees a movie which shows his very neighborhood, it becomes possible for him to live, for a time at least, as a person who is Somewhere and not Anywhere.

. . . . and down in the atom is
a strange discontinuity.

What is the nature of physical reality? We ourselves live in an electromagnetic world. Everyday materials, including the tissues of the human body, are held together by the electromagnetic forces that operate between atoms.

"Is that anywhere near Whirlywood Connecticut?"

H O M E

I S

H O M E M A D E

True or False:
Everyday sentences are held together by electromagnetic forces that operate between atoms.

The force that holds a sentence together is, like the self, intangible.

IMAGE

48

WHERE I LIVE

NOT VERY LONG AGO, an encyclopedia salesman stopped by America's oldest library building, which is the lovely Sturgis Library in Barnstable Village, on Cape Cod's north shore. And he pointed out to the easily alarmed librarian that the library's most recent general reference work was a 1938 *Britannica,* backstopped by a 1910 *Americana.* He said many important things had happened since 1938, naming, among others, penicillin and Hitler's invasion of Poland.

He was advised to take his astonishment to some of the library's directors. He was given their names and addresses. There was a Cabot on the list—and a Lowell and a Kittredge, and some others. The librarian told him that he had a chance of catching several directors all.at once, if he would go to the Barnstable Yacht Club. So he went down the narrow yacht club road, nearly broke his neck as he hit a series of terrific bumps put in the road to discourage speeders, to kill them, if possible.

He wanted a martini, wondered if a nonmember could get service at the bar. He was appalled to discover that the club was nothing but a shack fourteen feet wide and thirty feet long, a touch of the Ozarks in Massachusetts. It contained an hilariously warped ping-pong table, a wire lost-and-found basket with sandy, fragrant contents, and an upright piano that had been under a leak in the roof for years.

There wasn't any bar, any telephone, any electricity. There weren't any members there, either. To cap it all, there wasn't a drop of water in the harbor. The tide, which can be as great as fourteen feet, was utterly out. And the so-called yachts, antique wooden Rhodes 18's, *Beetlecats,* and a couple of *Boston Whalers,* were resting on the bluish-brown glurp of the emptied harbor's floor. Clouds of gulls and terns were yelling about all that glurp, and about all the good things in it they were finding to eat.

A few men were out there, too, digging clams as fat as partridges from the rim of Sandy Neck, the ten-mile-long sand finger that separates the harbor from the ice-cold bay. And ducks and geese and herons and other waterfowl were out there, too,

teemingly, in the great salt marsh that bounds the harbor on the west. And, near the harbor's narrow mouth, a yawl from Marblehead with a six-foot keel lay on her side, waiting for the water to come back in again. She should never have come to Barnstable Village, not with a keel like that.

The salesman, very depressed, insensitive to the barbarous beauty all around him, went to lunch. Since he was in the seat of the most booming county in New England, Barnstable County, and since the boom was a tourist boom, he had reason to expect something mildly voluptuous in the way of a place to eat. What he had to settle for, though, was a chromium stool at a formica counter in an aggressively un-cute, un-colonial institution called the Barnstable News Store, another Ozarks touch, an Ozarks department store. The motto of the place: "If it's any good, we've got it. If it's no good, we've sold it."

After lunch, he went trustee-hunting again, was told to try the village museum, which is in the old brick Customs House. The building itself is a memorial to long-gone days when the harbor was used by fair-sized ships, before it filled up with all that bluish-brown glurp. There was no trustee there, and the exhibits were excruciatingly boring. The salesman found himself strangling on apathy, an affliction epidemic among casual visitors to Barnstable Village.

He took the customary cure, which was to jump into his car and roar off toward the cocktail lounges, motor courts, bowling alleys, gift shoppes, and pizzerias of Hyannis, the commercial heart of Cape Cod. He there worked off his frustrations on a miniature golf course called Playland. At that time, that particular course had a pathetic, maddening feature typical of the random butchery of the Cape's south shore. The course was built on the lawn of what had once been an American Legion Post—and, right in the middle of the cunning little bridges and granulated cork fairways was a Sherman tank, set there in simpler and less enterprising days as a memorial to the veterans of World War Two.

The memorial has since been moved, but it is still on the south side, where it is bound to be engulfed by indignities again.

The dignity of the tank would be a lot safer in Barnstable Village, but the village would never accept it. It has a policy of never accepting anything. As a happy consequence, it changes about as fast as the rules of chess.

The biggest change in recent years has taken place at the polls. Until six years ago, the Democratic poll watchers and the Republican poll watchers were all Republicans. Now the Democratic poll watchers are Democrats. The consequences of this revolution have not been nearly as awful as expected—so far.

Another break with the past has to do with the treasury of the local amateur theatrical society, the Barnstable Comedy Club. The club had a treasurer who, once a month for thirty years, angrily refused to say what the balance was, for fear that the club would spend it foolishly. He resigned last year. The new treasurer announced a balance of four hundred dollars and some odd cents, and the membership blew it all on a new curtain the color of spoiled salmon. This ptomaine curtain, incidentally, made its debut during a production of *The Caine Mutiny Court Martial* in which Captain Queeg did *not*

nervously rattle steel balls in his hand. The balls were eliminated on the theory that they were suggestive.

Another big change took place about sixty years ago, when it was discovered that tuna were good to eat. Barnstable fishermen used to call them "horse mackerel," and curse whenever they caught one. Still cursing, they would chop it up and throw it back into the bay as a warning to other horse mackerel. Out of courage or plain stupidity, the tuna did not go away, and now make possible a post-Labor Day festival called the Barnstable Tuna Derby. Sportsmen with reels as big as courthouse clocks come from all over the Eastern seaboard for the event, the villagers are always mystified as to what brought them. And nobody ever catches anything.

Another discovery that still lies in the future for the villagers to make and to learn to live with is that mussels can be eaten without causing instant death. Barnstable Harbor is in places clogged with them. They are never disturbed. One reason for their being ignored, perhaps, is that the harbor abounds in two other delicacies far simpler to prepare—striped bass and clams. To get clams, one can scratch almost anywhere when the tide is out. To get bass, one follows the birds, looks for cone-shaped formations of them, casts his lure to the place where the cone points. Bass will be feeding there.

As for what else the future holds: Few Cape villages have much chance of coming through the present greedy, tasteless boom with their souls intact. H. L. Mencken once said something to the effect that "Nobody ever went broke overestimating the vulgarity of the American people," and fortunes now being made out of the vulgarization of the Cape surely bear this out. The soul of Barnstable Village just might survive.

For one thing, it is not a hollow village, with everything for rent, with half of the houses empty in the winter. Most of the people live there all year round, and most of them aren't old, and most of them work —as carpenters, salesmen, masons, architects, teachers, writers, and what have you. It is a class-

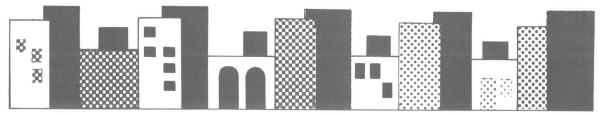

less society, a sometimes affectionate and sentimental one.

And these full houses, often riddled by termites and dry rot, but good, probably, for a few hundred years more, have been built chockablock along Main Street since the end of the Civil War. Developers find very little room in which to work their pious depredations. There is a seeming vast green meadow to the west, but this is salt marsh, the bluish-brown glurp capped by a mat of salt hay. It was this natural hay, by the way, that tempted settlers down from Plymouth in 1639. The marsh, laced by deep creeks that can be explored by small boats, can never be built upon by anyone sane. It goes underwater at every moon tide, and is capable of supporting a man and his dog, and not much more.

Speculators and developers got very excited for a while about the possibility of improving Sandy Neck, the long, slender barrier of spectacular dunes that bounds the harbor on the north. There are grotesque forests of dead trees out there, trees suffocated by sand, then unburied again. And the outer beach, for all practical purposes infinite, puts the beach of Acapulco to shame. Surprisingly, too, fresh water can be had out there from quite shallow wells. But the local government, thank God, is buying up all of Sandy Neck but the tip, at the harbor mouth, and is making it a public park to be kept unimproved forever.

There is a tiny settlement on the tip of the neck the tip that the government is not taking over. It is clustered around the abandoned lighthouse, a lighthouse that was once needed when there was water enough around to let big ships come and go. The bleached and tacky settlement can be reached only by boat or beach buggy. There is no electricity there, no telephone. It is a private resort. Less than a mile from Barnstable Village, the tip of the neck is where many villagers go when they need a vacation.

And all of the anachronistic, mildly xenophobic, charming queernesses of Barnstable Village might entitle it to the epithet, "Last Stronghold of the True Cape Codders," if it weren't for one thing: Hardly anyone in the village was born on Cape Cod. Just as petrified wood is formed by minerals slowly replacing organic materials, so has the present-day petrified Barnstable been formed by persons from Evanston and Louisville and Boston and Pittsburgh and God-only-knows-where-else, slowly replacing authentic rural Yankees.

If the real Cape Codders could rise from their churchyard graves, cast aside their beautifully lettered slate headstones, and attend a meeting of the Barnstable Village Civic Association, they would approve of the proceedings. Every proposal that has ever come before the organization has been hotly debated and voted down, except that a new siren be bought for the rescue truck. The siren goes *bweep-bweep-bweep* instead of *rowrrr,* and is guaranteed to be audible at a distance of three

CALL IT SLEEP

"Do you know where you are now?"
He looked around at the twilit street. "We went a lot of blocks," he said tentatively.
"Yes. But that street, that next one?"
He shook his head. In the thickening gloom, the street ahead looked as alien as any he had passed.
"That's Boddeh Street," she informed him. "Your school is that way, further off. But it's too dark to see. Now two—three blocks that way—" She pointed to the left—"is where we live."
"That way, Mama?" He stared incredulously.
"This way!" He pointed to the right. "This way is my school."
"That's why you were lost! It's the other way."
"O-o-h!" A new wonder dragged him to a halt.
"It—it's turning, Mama! It's turning round—back."
"What?" Her tone was amused. "The street?"
"Yes! They stopped! Just now! The school—The school is over there now!"
"So it is. The streets turn, but you—not you! Little God!" Chuckling, she stooped, kissed him.

MOM!

emergencee

51

miles.

The library, incidentally, now has a new *Britannica,* and a new *Americana,* too, purchases it made effortlessly, since it has money coming out of its ears. But so far, the school marks of the children and the conversation of the adults have not conspicuously improved.

Since the village exists for itself, and not for passersby, and since it specializes in hastening tourists on to paradises elsewhere, visitors play hell finding anything to like about it. For a quick sample of how good it can be, a visitor might stop off at St. Mary's Church on Main Street, which has, unadvertised anywhere, the most enchanting church garden in America. The garden is the work of one man, Robert Nicholson, an Episcopalian minister, a good man who died young.

At a village cocktail party one time—and the villagers *do* drink a lot—Father Nicholson was talking to a Roman Catholic and a Jew, trying to find a word to describe the underlying spiritual unity of Barnstable. He found one. "We're Druids," he said.

Barnstable is a mirror. Reflect on it.

world through
my door
how wide
house how tiny
From outside

MEETS YOUR FOOTSTEP IS AN ACT OF FAITH.

the million masks of God

And once again when the river swelled during the rainy season and roared loudly, Siddhartha said: "Is it not true, my friend, that the river has very many voices? Has it not the voice of a king, of a warrior, of a bull, of a nightbird, of a pregnant woman and a sighing man, and a thousand other voices?"

"It is so," nodded Vasudeva, "the voices of all living creatures are in its voice."

"And do you know," continued Siddhartha, "what word it pronounces when one is successful in hearing all its ten thousands voices at the same time?"

Vasudeva laughed joyously; he bent towards Siddhartha and whispered the holy Om in his ear. And this was just what Siddhartha had heard.

...sometimes you see what Wordsworth called "intimations of immortality." Tennyson used to have this experience when he sometimes sat and said his own name to himself. He sat there and said, "Alfred, Alfred." And he got the funny feeling, "Really Alfred? Who *are* you?" And then suddenly it came over him; he suddenly knew that he was the eternal ground of the world, in disguise as Alfred Tennyson."

ANKH

**Alfred Korzybski,
the first no-Count
Count, rumored to
have been Alfred
Tennyson, or whatever.**

"Whatever you say
a thing is,
it isn't."

**The water from a sparkling
mountain brook has been
urine millions of times
during the course
of evolution
of life on
Earth.**

53

Rebecca. I never told you about that letter Jane Crofut got from her minister when she was sick. The minister of her church in the town she was in before she came here. He wrote Jane a letter and on the envelope the address was like this. It said: Jane Crofut, The Crofut Farm, Grover's Corners, Button County, New Hampshire, United States of America.

George. What's funny about that?

Rebecca. But listen, it's not finished: the United States of America, Continent of North America, Western Hemisphere, the Earth, the Solar System, the Universe, the Mind of God—that's what it said on the envelope.

George. What do you know!

Rebecca. And the postman brought it just the same.

There is a relative world and an absolute one. However, I finally came to realize that they are one.

DO YOU

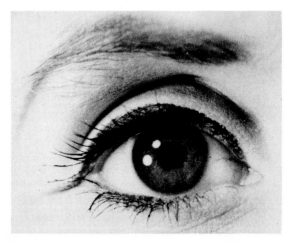

"I was wondering if my self might be floating around in there anywhere?"

WHO YOU ARE ?

54

Well, ya gotta have something to hang things on.

THE FUTURE: MEMORY INVERTED

A relationship

between
two people

"Whirlywood, Connecticut"
"Is that anywhere near
Whirlywood, Connecticut?"
"That's where I live!"
"You have no idea how clear
that makes everything."
—A Perfect Day for
Bananafish

55

Images of Time

Thinking about space-time. One thing. (One no-thing.) Let's look at something that fills space; say, this paper theater ticket I am holding. A solid object. It has three dimensions. But has it a fourth? It has length and width, and even thickness, though very little by our measurements. So it is a solid. Yes. But is it also going on *in time?* It looks steady enough. But *looks* steady (mirrors steadiness) is not enough. We know that it is composed of atoms and that they are moving and that the electrons within them are in motion. Something going on. So the three dimensions we "see" are a process, something going on, and on, and on—through a duration of *time.* Thus, it is instants of *time* we "see" when we see a "solid" piece of paper. Do we see paper? No, we see "papering," process, duration, *time.* Because our eyes are unable to keep up with it, we see chunks of time as though they were stationary. The theater ticket, then, is a chunk of time. This is quite clear when we observe the ticket after a year or two; it has grown old, we note. But this growing old has been going on all along; we just couldn't detect it. So what we see before our eyes depends as much on *when* as on *what.* Or another way to put it is What *is* when. What = When.

Think of a photograph. All photographs are *time* exposures. Each describes (gives the boundaries of) a discrete parcel of time. Consider the way that the image was created on the photographic film. The light from the subject began hitting the film at one point in time and continued pelting the film for a predetermined span and then was cut off. If we wished, we could divide the same parcel of time into, say, 100 sub-parcels, and studying carefully, we would see that each photograph was different. And we could subdivide each of those into one hundred more with the same results and so on. Thus, the solid world slips away, and everything is seen to be in motion. The solid world is a convenient frame of reference, but it is possible for us only because of the crudity of our sensorium. To mistake this "solid" world for the whole story is to be out of touch with our own nature. "For the eye sees not itself but by reflection, by some other things." Who I am is when I am.

All solids, then, are 3-D movies. We could not have a solid at all without duration, a time span. Solids are possible *only* through MOVEMENT. Through movement. Think of that: solids *could not exist* if there were no movement, no time. Like a laser-beam hologram. Pretty much the same thing: process. Or to get some idea of how it works, try time-delay photography. When we take one still of a living plant, say every three hours, and then run these through a movie projector, we see clearly that the plant is very much "alive," that it is in motion. We could show the same thing with a theater ticket . . . if we had time! Or with a rock. Or oneself. Because I *am* not. I am not a who. Or a what. Maybe *human being* captures it. The three dimensions of a solid (human), plus the motion (being) which denies it! I am a human (noun) being (verb). That will have to do until I can show that both these terms are hardly enough to describe what is going on in the space-time called *me.*

We have heard that time is a dimension of space, but in the regard we have been exploring, length-width-thickness is a dimension of time!

LABEL:
Time-delay
solid

56

THE BEST BUTTER

"What day of the month is it?" the Hatter said, turning to Alice. He had taken his watch out of his pocket, and was looking at it uneasily, shaking it every now and then and holding it to his ear.

Alice considered a little, and then said, "The fourth."

"Two days wrong!" sighed the Hatter. "I told you butter wouldn't suit the works!" he added, looking angrily at the March Hare.

"It was the *best* butter," the March Hare meekly replied.

"Yes, but some crumbs must have got in as well," the Hatter grumbled. "You shouldn't have put it in with the bread knife."

The March Hare took the watch and looked at it gloomily. Then he dipped into his cup of tea, and looked at it again. But he could think of nothing better to say than his first remark, "It was the *best* butter, you know."

Alice had been looking over his shoulder with some curiosity. "What a funny watch!" she remarked. "It tells the day of the month, and doesn't tell what o'clock it is!"

"Why should it?" muttered the Hatter. "Does *your* watch tell what year it is?"

"Of course not," Alice replied very readily, "but that's because it stays the same year for such a long time together."

"Which is just the case with *mine*," said the Hatter . . . .

Do you think I was born yesterday?

No.

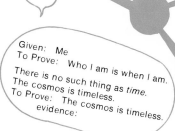

Given: Me
To Prove: Who I am is when I am.
There is no such thing as *time*.
The cosmos is timeless.
To Prove: The cosmos is timeless.
evidence:

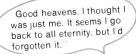

Good heavens, I thought I was just me. It seems I go back to all eternity, but I'd forgotten it.

Huh, I wouldn't give him the time of day.

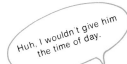

"My time is your time"

WHAT T I M E *IS* IT, ANYWAY?

I know what time it is.

You're IT

Even pure organic food is but dung, reprocessed by plants and the community of life in the soil.

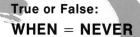

IT?

True or False:
WHEN = NEVER

57

Bed time

what actor?

THYME
is
of the
ESSENCE

If you have all the time in the world, what do you have?

what movie ?

"In Italy for 30 years under the Borgias, they had warfare, terror, murder, bloodshed—they produced Michaelangelo, Leonardo da Vinci, the Renaissance. In Switzerland they had brotherly love, 500 years of peace and what did they produce—the cuckoo clock."

Most people say there *is* a future. But how do we "know" this? Isn't the *idea* that there is a future based on a series of events that happened in the "past"? That is, the sun came up, then it came up again, then it came up again. So we deduced that it *will* come up. (Actually, we also deduce that it *did* come up, since we are never really there at the time: It takes a particle of time for events to register on our brains.) We took the past and said, "These things *did* happen: therefore these other events *will* happen." Thus, we can see that in this sense, the future is really the past turned around and pointed the other way. Memory inverted.

Problem: Create a clock suitable for measuring eternity.

58

WHEN WE ELIMINATE TIME,

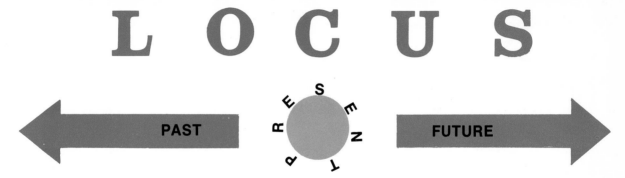

L O C U S

"How can we kill time without injuring eternity?" (Thoreau) Let's see. Conventionally in Western cultures there is the past, there is the future, and in between there is the present.

If you try to get anyone to say precisely *when* now is, things come undone. (Neat brown paper parcel.) In our minds *now* is elastic. It can refer to this eon, this century, this decade, this moment. But how big is a moment? If we want to live in the present, just how big *is* that? If we examine it, we see that physically, it does not exist, because no matter how fine our measurement, we can always imagine it smaller yet, until we get down to nothing at all.

Then, what time do we live in? The answer might appear to be "the past." Thus, when a pin pricks my finger, I am not aware of it until a particle of time afterwards, the time it takes the impulse to be transmitted to awareness centers in my brain. Whatever I am aware of already happened. So I always live in a world which was, not which is. *Was* is all there is. But what I "presently" perceive happens *after* it already happened, even this "present" thought. I can never be "right on." Even what I think *is* going on is not actually the past but an image of it, an interpretation. That interpretation is what the past became when my mind got the signals from the nerve endings.

Thus, when we reach out to touch the past, it isn't physically there. Nor is the future. (See page 58.) We can erase future; we can erase past. What's left? Only that thin, actually dimensionless, threshold called *the present*. There is no was; there is no will be; and there is no is. This whole mirage seems to be pressed against that zero-thick plane of the present, never able to get beyond it or anywhere else—because there *is* nowhere to go. It looks as though we are moving at fantastic speeds, but nothing is happening. We are in eternity already; nothing (no thing) is going on. We are at rest:

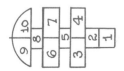

If we get going fast enough, we come to rest. Suppose I want to get from A to B. I speed up and really get going. I reach the speed of light. Wow! I invent something to cut that time in half. And so on. When would I have reached the optimum time? When I had cut the time down to zero, so that I would be there already, so that I wouldn't have to leave at all.

"How long ya gonna stay?" "$1000."

In eternity, that is the case. Time is only for when you think you're not there. But when you are there you have killed time. That is, it no longer is a factor to consider. When we begin to live in eternity, we begin to see that we can never be anywhere but where we are. We're always "there." I am where I am, and no matter how fast I travel, I can never get anywhere else. To realize this is to free ourselves from the hold time has on our minds.

WE ELIMINATE SPACE— WHICH IS A DIMENSION OF TIME. WHAT IS LEFT

Do everything at half speed for about half an hour.
Compare observations with others. Reflect.
Try to get the feel of rock time, leaf time, fly time, planet time.

59

and one clock
stopped ——
and knew the
meaning of time.

LIFE CAN
ONLY BE UNDER
STOOD BACKWARDS
BUT IT MUST BE
LIVED FORWARDS.
Kierkegaard
I LOVE YOU

TIME IS A
BOX I
LIVE IN

ETERNITY:
make something
out of no thing.

OUT OF TIME
A holiday thought

My old clock used to tell the time
and subdivide diurnity;
but now it's lost both hands and chime
and only tells eternity.

"Gotta make
the morning
last"

60

SHLOCK CLOCK

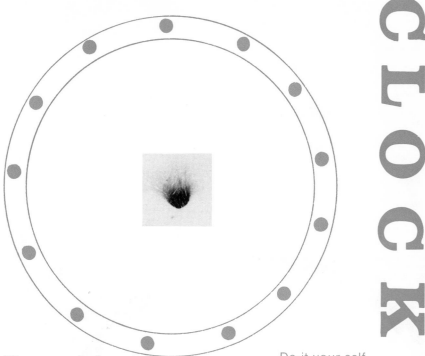

ALLATONCE: Find fifteen words from this chapter hidden here. Start anywhere and move to any adjoining letter. You may use any letter more than once, but do not use it consecutively. Thus, for "cook" you would have to have two adjoining o's.

Do-it-your-self
Model on p 19

C	I	B	M	H	C	T
U	R	O	K	O	S	O
S	T	N	A	L	P	G
R	E	C	Y	I	E	S
S	P	A	T	C	M	P
O	N	I	H	Y	A	O
D	M	R	L	W	O	D

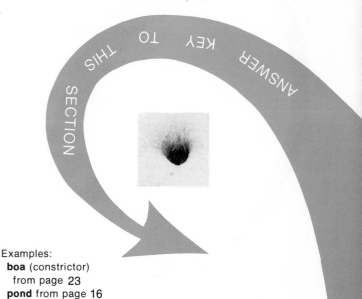

ANSWER KEY TO THIS SECTION

Examples:
boa (constrictor)
   from page **23**
pond from page 16

61

Answers on next page.

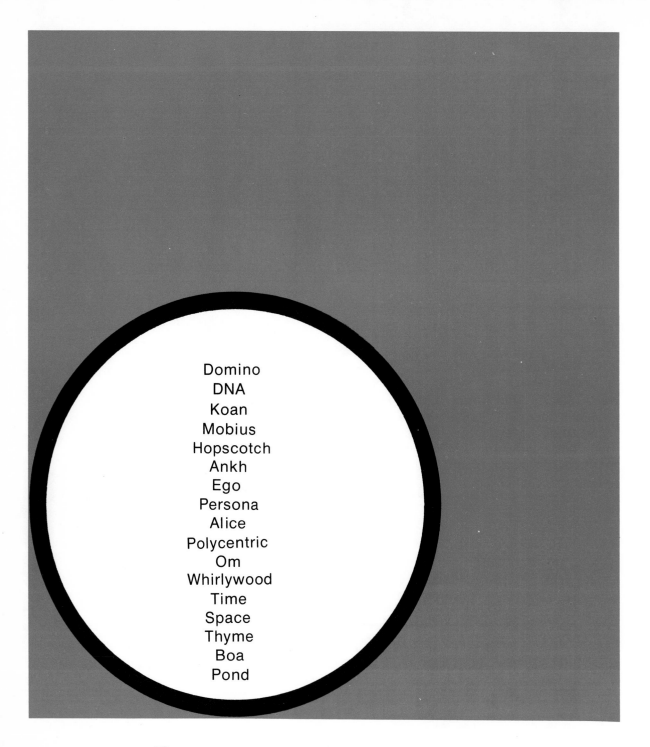

Domino
DNA
Koan
Mobius
Hopscotch
Ankh
Ego
Persona
Alice
Polycentric
Om
Whirlywood
Time
Space
Thyme
Boa
Pond

Answers for page 61

HOW ARE YOU?*

5 *Ontologically speaking, of course.

IMAGE

Problem-solver

Problems are solved, not by giving new information, but by arranging what we have always known.

Select some problem you would like to explore and solve or a situation for which you would like to discover a fresh angle of vision. You can play this game alone or with a group.

Use dice to arrive at a page number in IMAGE. You need a three-digit number. The left-hand digit may be 0 through 3; the middle digit, 0 through 9, and the right-hand digit, 0 through 9 except in the 380's where it can only go up through 4.

1. *The left-hand digit:* Throw only one die. Let 4 be your 0. Discard 5's and 6's. Thus, you roll and get a 6. Roll again. You get 4. Your left-hand digit is 0.

0

2. *The middle digit:* Roll both dice. 10 is your 0. 11 is your 1. Discard 12's. The toss comes up 5. That is your middle digit.

0 5

3. *The right-hand digit:* Since the page is in the 50's, you use both dice and go from 0 through 9. The toss comes up 12. Roll again. It comes up 10, so your digit is 0.

0 5 0

Your page is 50.

THEN, turn to this page and allow it to interplay with the problem or situation you posed. You will discover a solution or a fresh way to consider the situation.

*For the right-hand digit in 3 8 , toss only one die and let 5 equal 0. Discard 6.

64   *Example: As your first problem, find out why this process works.*

Man's mind is like some vast electronic brain, capable of the most extraordinary feats. And yet unfortunately, man does not know how to operate it. Every morning when he wakes up, man crosses to the control panel of that vast brain, and proceeds to turn knobs and press buttons. And yet this is the absurdity: with the immense machine at his disposal, he knows only how to make it do the simplest things, to deal with the most obvious, everyday problems. It is true that there are certain men whom we call men of genius, who can make it do far more exciting things: write symphonies and poems, discover mathematical laws. And then there are a few men who are perhaps the most important of all: men who use this machine *to explore its own capabilities.* They use the machine to find out what they can do with the machine. They know that it is capable of creating the Jupiter symphony and *Faust* and *The Critique of Pure Reason* and multi-dimensional geometry. Yet in a sense, these works have been achieved by accident, or, at least, by instinct. Well, many great scientific discoveries have been stumbled on by accident; but when they have been discovered, the scientist's first task is to learn the hidden laws that govern them. And this electronic brain is the greatest of all mysteries, for to know its secret would turn man into a god. So to what better purpose can consciousness be employed than to explore the laws of consciousness? And this is the meaning of the word 'phenomenology,' perhaps the most important single word in the vocabulary of the human race.

MIND

JOURNAL

1. "I could not think of anything to write in my journal. So I started writing, and ideas began to pop up and form. If I just sit and think of what I want to write, I get nowhere. I must be writing for ideas to flow."

ZAZEN

2. "You cannot sit down and say, 'Now we work.' But you can be regular in your habits; do this sort of thing day after day, day after day. Some days you will listen, some you will not. But be regular. That is one way to try without trying."

LIFE

3. "As I was sitting here trying to read two chapters in a music book, I found myself falling asleep. So I put the book down and thought I would wind things up for the night. Then I figured I should write a few notes down in my journal and in writing about something I felt involved in I began to wake up. To be interested in the subject, getting the feel of what you want to say and feeling stimulated to write it down means a lot."

List the twelve words which are in your opinion the most persuasive in the English language. Tally your answers with your classmates' to see if you listed any in common. See if you can convince each other and come up with a list you all will accept.

1. _____   7. _____

2. _____   8. _____

3. _____   9. _____

4. _____   10. _____

5. _____   11. _____

6. _____   12. _____

(A Yale research team's list is on page 128 You can use it to cheat, or wait and look at it last.)

I wished to live deliberately, to front only the essential facts of life, and see if I could not learn what it had to teach, and not, when I came to die, discover that I had not lived. I did not wish to live what was not life, living is so dear; nor did I wish to practise resignation, unless it was quite necessary. I wanted to live deep and suck out all the marrow of life, to live so sturdily and Spartan-like as to put to rout all that was not life, to cut a broad swath and shave close, to drive life into a corner, and reduce it to its lowest terms, and, if it proved to be mean, why then to get the whole and genuine meanness of it, and publish its meanness to the world; or if it were sublime, to know it by experience, and be able to give a true account of it in my next excursion. For most men, it appears to me, are in a strange uncertainty about it, whether it is of the devil or of God, and have *somewhat hastily* concluded that it is the chief end of man here to "glorify God and enjoy Him forever."

Genuine Pennsylvania Dornick

Crack this code and win a karma repair kit. If you are a *pisces* or a *scorpio,* send us a boxtop for a magic ring.

An Important Secret Message From the Sponsors.

D N A

N B

66

"The riddle does not exist. Everything that can be said can be said clearly."

how you are?

Sarah, a chimpanzee at the University of California at Santa Barbara, has a vocabulary of about 130 plastic symbols that stand for actions, names, and abstract ideas. Besides remembering the shapes that mean such things as *banana, chocolate,* and *apple,* Sarah knows the shapes that stand for *give* and *take* and the names of her human teacher and attendants.

David Premack, professor of psychology, who is Sarah's instructor, believes that it is a mistake to think that language must be limited to a system of sounds. Thus, although the vocal cords, larynx, tongue and lips of chimpanzees are not suited for speech, he feels Sarah has demonstrated that a visual symbol system can be substituted. Just as human beings read symbols that have no association with sound—pointing arrows, red, yellow and green traffic lights—so too can a chimpanzee.

Sarah knows her own name and the symbols for *bad* and *good,* and she is able to make the value judgment these symbols imply. *Good* is something her teacher likes; *bad* is what he disapproves of, quite analogous to human acculturation.

Sarah also knows that the way in which words are assembled to express an idea must make sense. Her sentences observe language rules no less than human sentences do. She writes sentences by arranging plastic chips, which have steel backing, on a magnetized board. The teacher arranges plastic "red on green." Sarah reads it, and puts a red card on a green card. When the instruction is reversed, she puts the green card on the red one. She performs just as well with a trainer who doesn't know her language as she does with one who does.

The plastic chips are colored, but those which stand for colors are not colored in accordance with their meaning. The word for red is a gray plastic chip. The word for green is a white one. When Mary Morgan, one of Sarah's teachers, writes the conditional instruction "If Sarah take red, then Mary give Sarah chocolate," Sarah chooses a red object from among several objects of various colors in order to get the chocolate. But when Mary Morgan writes "If Sarah take green, Mary no give Sarah chocolate," then Sarah carefully avoids the green and chooses another instead.

Professor Premack feels that this understanding of the "if . . . then" concept, the conditional mood, is proof that Sarah has not merely learned tricks but has actually learned language. He thinks his research shows that we need a more general theory of language than we have had, a theory that does not necessarily assume that human language is the only kind.

Some psycholinguists think human beings are genetically programmed for language and that all the natural languages of man are basically the same. It is the individual forms, such as English, that are learned from experience. These theorists will have to say either that what Sarah does isn't language or that there may be degrees of language among man's close evolutionary relatives.

run – jump – skip along

WHEN CHANCE BECOMES PROVIDENCE, IT CEASES TO BE ABSURD

When I ask you a question, I'd like to know how you think and I am interested, but I hope you will realize that the question occurs to me as one you might like to ask yourself.

Define chaos.

Define order.

Here lies
Frank
Pixley
. . .
as usual

True or false:
Man is the cryptographer
of the void?

whose woulds
these are I
think I know . . .

Here lies John Bun,
He was killed by a gun,
His name was not Bun,
   but Wood,
But Wood would not rhyme
   with gun,
But Bun would.*

67

*See also "On My First Daughter" page 72

HOW

AM I? *

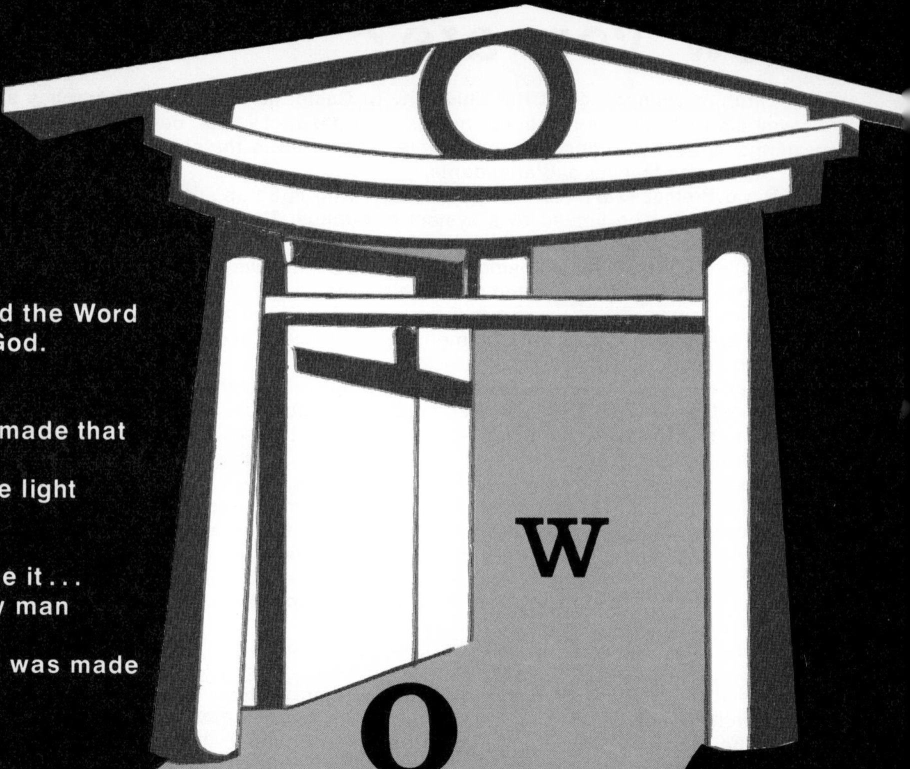

In the beginning was the Word, and the Word
was with God, and the Word was God.
He was in the beginning with God;
all things were made through him,
and without him was not anything made that
was made.
In him was life, and the life was the light
of men.
The light shines in the darkness,
and the darkness has not overcome it...
The true light that enlightens every man
was coming into the world.
He was in the world, and the world was made
through him,
Yet the world knew him not...
And the Word became flesh
and dwelt among us,
full of grace and truth;
we have beheld his glory...

W

O

R

D

68

Hint:* Check the
etymology of *Buddha.*

The first thing I do when I
wake up in the morning is to
see if I'm in a state of grace.
Being in a state of grace enables
me to ride out the chaos. To
try to control it is arrogant.
If I'm not in a state of grace,
I try to go back to bed.

Have you found the secret door
To let you down to the earth's
deep core?

ATOMIC FISSION

IMAGE
5

In a certain sense, universal mind and universal space-time are coincidental, as Whitehead understood. Mind is not really 'inside' us in the same sense that our intestines are. Our individuality is a kind of eddy in the sea of mind, a reflection of the total identity of the universal humanity.

All the galaxies must have begun at one place about five billion years ago; all the billions and trillions and quadrillions squared and squared again of tons of matter in the universe were compressed into a ball of the maximum possible density, the density within the nucleus of the atom; one cubic centimeter of this primeval egg weighed two hundred and fifty tons.

"a moment is the size of the universe. Every-thing is there allatonce, allatonce."

JUNGER THAN SPRINGTIME

If a handful of matches is thrown to the floor, they form the pattern characteristic of that moment.

Arrange six kitchen matches so that each one touches every other one firmly. You can skip trying to arrange them like the spokes of a wheel. The thickness of the ends prevents the solution.

Wait a minute...

COINCIDENCE IS AN EASTERN PREJUDICE.

Why synchronicity works: When we have only our own mind set or those of others who share our own frame of reference, we tend to channel our thinking narrowly. When we introduce a chance element into our considerations and allow it to be significant, it often breaks through our rigid thought patterns and opens a door to new and unexpected possibilities. The secret is to *allow* the game to work, to go *with* it. The more you are willing to trust the method the more successful you will be in solving your problem.

Am I a concept?

Reality (spacetime) is a psychophysical structure. It depends as much on the observer as on the observed, which after all are inseparable. Does this make any difference?

MICHAEL HAS LOST HIS PARENTS. WOULD THEY PLEASE

Truth = Prejudice.
True or false?

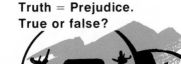

Truth is like Euclidian geometry. It only works in a defined frame of reference.

Nevertheless, the consuming hunger of the uncritical mind for what it imagines to be certainty or finality impels it to feast upon shadows.
E.T.B.

Little Willie, mad as hell,
Threw his sister down the
    well.
Mother said, when drawing
    water,
"It's so hard to raise a
    daughter."

ELEVANCE. THE VALUE OF IRRELEVANCE.

DON'T LOOK FOR YOUR ANSWER TOO SOON OR YOU

pars pro toto

CAUSALITY IS A WESTERN PREJUDICE.

Feeling becomes knowledge *indefinite infinite language* **through language. T or F?**

I *must*, before I die, find *some* way to say the essential thing that is in me, that I have never said yet—a thing that is not love or hate or pity or scorn, but the very breath of life, fierce and coming from far away, bringing into human life the vastness and the fearful passionless force of non-human things . . .

—A garden variety cryptographer

IS THERE ANY WORD FROM THE LORD?

When thought is closed
in caves,
then love shall show
its roots
in deepest hell.

Syllogism:
A. **To abstract is to be.**
B. **To relate is to be.**
Show that A can only be true if B is true also.
How can I NOT be?

Every finite particle is a sample of the in-finite.

flutterbies: **Frisian word for butterflies.**

DOWN OUT OF A TREE AND LOOKED AROUND AND WONDERED

Vocabulary Drill

hope

"For the mass of human evils swarming in Pandora's box, the Greeks brought out *hope* at the very last as the most terrible of all. I don't know of any symbol more moving. For hope, contrary to popular belief is tantamount to *resignation*. And to live is not to be resigned."

hope = resignation
Is this definition a matter of consequence?

ON MY FIRST DAUGHTER

Here lies, to each her parents' ruth,
Mary, the daughter of their youth;
Yet all heaven's gifts being heaven's due,
It makes the father less to rue.
At six months' end she parted hence
With safety of her innocence;
Whose soul heaven's queen, whose name she bears,
In comfort of her mother's tears,
Hath placed amongst her virgin-train:
Where while that severed doth remain,
This grave partakes the fleshly birth,
Which cover lightly, gentle earth!

*See also "Here Lies John Bun," page 67 . When is a pun not a pun?

In this act of appellation, man takes possession of the world both physically and intellectually — subjects it to his knowledge and his rule. This special feature reveals that fundamental character and spiritual achievement of pure monotheism of which Goethe remarked that it is always uplifting because the belief in the one and only God makes man *aware of his own inner unity. This unity, however, cannot be discovered except as it reveals itself in outward form by virtue of the concrete structures of language and myth, in which it is embodied,* and from which *it is afterward* regained by the process of logical reflection.

The book isolated the reader in silence and helped create the Western 'I.'

Not all that is plausible is true.

psychophysical story

Get a long strip of paper about two inches wide. The first person writes any sentence he wishes. The second person must add a sentence to go with the first. He then folds over the first sentence. The third person continues the story, folds the paper so that only his own sentence is showing and passes it on. When the story is finished, have someone read it to the group.

When you are finished, take the following test.

PUN
CUSHION

TEST

Choose the correct answer:
a. The story is an umbilical cord.
b. Life is like that.
c. All meaning can be summed up in the phrase, "That reminds me..."
d. If each person wrote a random sentence without seeing the preceding one, the story would still be meaningful.
e. The principle on which the story was written is that of causality.
f. The story is based on coincidence.
g. You are a wonderful human being.
h. None of the above.
i. All of the above.

Think *The Reader's Digest* could use it?

A	D	G
B	E	H
C	F	I

S
T   U
V

J	M	P
K	N	Q
L	O	R

W
X   Y
Z

72

I was in a cul-de-sac last night.

Wouldn't your electric blanket work?

Drinking Coffee

The gifted and intelligent Chinese never developed "science" as we in the West know it. Our science is based on cause and effect (causality). It is interested in sequence, in *why:* "This happened *because* this happened before it." A natural law is derived from the jumble of events surrounding the occurrence being observed. However, we need a scrupulously controlled laboratory to prove our "law" and to make predictability possible.

In the natural world, on the other hand, every process is interfered with by chance. The event which absolutely conforms to a specific law *is an exception.*

From the jumble of events, the Western scientist might derive the "law" that every quartz crystal is a hexagonal prism. But the Chinese thinker finds the uniqueness of each individual crystal more noteworthy. The *actual* form, the immediate crystal, here and now, before one's eyes, is more remarkable than the ideal form imagined by the Western scientist. In this sense, one can see that it is the Western scientist who is mystic, who is enamored of dreams, and the Chinese sage who is the realist.

So when you shoot, it's as if you collect a lot of stuff you have to sort later?
Godard: No, it isn't. It's not just a 'lot of stuff.' If it's a 'collection,' it's a collection that always has a particular end in view, a definite aim. And it isn't just any movie: it's always a particular movie. You collect only the stuff that can meet your needs.

In the ancient Chinese view, the configuration formed by chance events at the moment of observation is significant, the coincidence itself and not the hypothetical reasons imagined to account for it. Rather than sift, weigh, select, classify, and isolate, the Chinese accepts the entire moment and every tiny, nonsensical detail because they are all part of the observed event. Rather than fight the chance nature of events, he invites chance into his observation and flows with it.

One can take an interest in how things evolved out of each other, or one can take a look at how things somehow happen to have fallen together *coincidentally,* that is to say, he can look at a configuration of data as being in itself significant, regardless of *how* it came to be there. That I scratch my nose as I say hello to you is part of the hello, is it not? To be willing to accept and see *all* the details of each moment-painting of my life is to wake up to the wonder and power of chance. One sees that his state of mind as he tosses the coins, the flickering of the light, and the butterfly at the window all go together to make up a subjective-objective psychophysical world, an allatonce miracle of synchronous events.

Thinking = selective noticing.

73

But wherever the truth maybe →
The water comes ashore
And the people look at the sea...

GETTING THERE

PARALANGUAGE

I do not claim that I can tell a story as it ought to be told, I only claim to know how a story ought to be told, for I have been almost daily in the company of the most expert story-tellers for many years.

There are several kinds of stories, but only one difficult kind—the humorous. I will talk mainly about that one. The humorous story is American, the comic story is English, the witty story is French. The humorous story depends for its effect upon the *manner* of the telling; the comic story and the witty story upon the *matter*.

The humorous story may be spun out to great length, and may wander around as much as it pleases, and arrive nowhere in particular; but the comic and witty stories must be brief and end with a point. The humorous story bubbles gently along, the others burst.

The humorous story is strictly a work of art—high and delicate art—and only an artist can tell it; but no art is necessary in telling the comic and the witty story; anybody can do it. The art of telling a humorous story—understand, I mean by word of mouth, not print—was created in America, and has remained at home.

The humorous story is told gravely; the teller does his best to conceal the fact that he even dimly suspects that there is anything funny about it; but the teller of the comic story tells you beforehand that it is one of the funniest things he has ever heard, then tells it with eager delight, and is the first person to laugh when he gets through. And sometimes, if he has had good success, he is so glad and happy that he will repeat the "nub" of it and glance around from face to face, collecting applause, and then repeat it again. It is a pathetic thing to see.

Very often, of course, the rambling and disjointed humorous story finishes with a nub, point, snapper, or whatever you like to call it. Then the listener must be alert, for in many cases the teller will divert attention from that nub by dropping it in a carefully casual and indifferent way, with the pretense that

he does not know it is a nub.

Artemus Ward used that trick a good deal; then when the belated audience presently caught the joke he would look up with innocent surprise, as if wondering what they had found to laugh at. Dan Setchell used it before him, Nye and Riley and others use it to-day.

But the teller of the comic story does not slur the nub; he shouts it at you—every time. And when he prints it, in England, France, Germany, and Italy, he italicizes it, puts some whooping exclamation-points after it, and sometimes explains it in a parenthesis. All of which is very depressing, and makes one want to renounce joking and lead a better life.

Let me set down an instance of the comic method, using an anecdote which has been popular all over the world for twelve or fifteen hundred years. The teller tells it in this way:

THE WOUNDED SOLDIER

In the course of a certain battle a soldier whose leg had been shot off appealed to another soldier who was hurrying by to carry him to the rear, informing him at the same time of the loss which he had sustained; whereupon the generous son of Mars, shouldering the unfortunate, proceeded to carry out his desire. The bullets and cannon-balls were flying in all directions, and presently one of the latter took the wounded man's head off—without, however, his deliverer being aware of it. In no long time he was hailed by an officer, who said:

"Where are you going with that carcass?"

"To the rear, sir—he's lost his leg!"

"His leg, forsooth?" responded the astonished officer, "you mean his head, you booby."

Whereupon the soldier dispossessed himself of his burden, and stood looking down upon it in great perplexity. At length he said:

"It is true, sir, just as you have said." Then after a pause he added, *"But he* told *me* IT WAS HIS LEG!!!!!"

74

KINESICS

Here the narrator bursts into explosion after explosion of thunderous horse-laughter, repeating that nub from time to time through his gaspings and shriekings and suffocatings.

It takes only a minute and a half to tell that in its comic-story form; and isn't worth the telling, after all. Put into the humorous-story form it takes ten minutes, and is about the funniest thing I have ever listened to—as James Whitcomb Riley tells it.

He tells it in the character of a dull-witted old farmer who has just heard it for the first time, thinks it is unspeakably funny, and is trying to repeat it to a neighbor. But he can't remember it; so he gets all mixed up and wanders helplessly round and round, putting in tedious details that don't belong in the tale and only retard it; taking them out conscientiously and putting in others that are just as useless; making minor mistakes now and then and stopping to correct them and explain how he came to make them; remembering things which he forgot to put in in their proper place and going back to put them in there; stopping his narrative a good while in order to try to recall the name of the soldier that was hurt, and finally remembering that the soldier's name was not mentioned, and remarking placidly that the name is of no real importance, anyway—better, of course, if one knew it, but not essential, after all—and so on, and so on, and so on.

The teller is innocent and happy and pleased with himself, and has to stop every little while to hold himself in and keep from laughing outright; and does hold in, but his body quakes in a jelly-like way with interior chuckles; and at the end of the ten minutes the audience have laughed until they are exhausted, and the tears a running down their faces.

The simplicity and innocence and sincerity and unconsciousness of the old farmer are perfectly simulated, and the result is a performance which is thoroughly charming and delicious. This is art—and fine and beautiful, and only a master can compass it; but a machine could tell the other story.

To string incongruities and absurdities together in a wandering and sometimes purposeless way, and seem innocently unaware that they are absurdities, is the basis of the American art, if my position is correct. Another feature is the slurring of the point. A third is the dropping of a studied remark apparently without knowing it, as if one were thinking aloud. The fourth and last is the pause.

Artemus Ward dealt in numbers three and four a good deal. He would begin to tell with great animation something which he seemed to think was wonderful; then lose confidence, and after an apparently absent-minded pause add an incongruous remark in a soliloquizing way; and that was the remark intended to explode the mine—and it did.

For instance, he would say eagerly, excitedly, "I once knew a man in New Zealand who hadn't a tooth in his head"—here his animation would die out; a silent, reflective pause would follow, then he would say dreamily, and as if to himself, "and yet that man could beat a drum better than any man I ever saw."

The pause is an exceedingly important feature in any kind of story, and a frequently recurring feature, too. It is a dainty thing, and delicate, and also uncertain and treacherous; for it must be exactly the right length—no more and no less—or it fails of its purpose and makes trouble. If the pause is too short the impressive point is passed and the audience have had time to divine that a surprise is intended and then you can't surprise them, of course . . .

. . . is all the fur

Complete this story:

THE SOLDIER'S LAST REQUEST

I once saw a cavalry soldier shot for desertion. He was seated *astride* his coffin, a black bandage about his eyes, his arms bound behind his back. The officer of the firing squad gave the command "Ready aim!" and a dozen loaded carbines were leveled at his breast. We heard him call out, up went the guns and the officer was seen to step forward and bend his ear to the man's lips. Then the officer stepped back, repeated the command, and a second later the poor fellow was a thing of shreds and patches. "What did he say to you?" I afterward asked the officer.

75

You mean it's not finished the way it is?

macronic verse

5

Each student must create a line which he considers to be poetic.

List all the lines on the chalkboard.

Then, in small groups, make up a poem using all the lines. Use whatever punctuation you wish between the lines, but do not add any within the lines.

Read each poem aloud and select a winner. Reflect on your considerations in creating your line and on the groups' in creating the poems.

(Macronic verse was invented by Robert Norton of Diablo Valley College.)

Say the plural of
bik,
wug,
gutch.
What rules do you follow to form the plurals of words in *spoken* English?

WHEN YOU RANG THE BELL THIS MORNING WE HIDED IN THE BEDROOM...

words

In a huge auditorium in Russia Boris Pasternak was to read aloud from his own works. He started a long poem, but dropped a sheet of paper and paused. As he reached down to pick it up, a voice in the audience spoke the next phrase, then another voice picked it up and another until all the voices rolled in unison and the entire hall echoed with the lyrics. Pasternak, the pages in his hands, his hands at his sides, stood quite still.

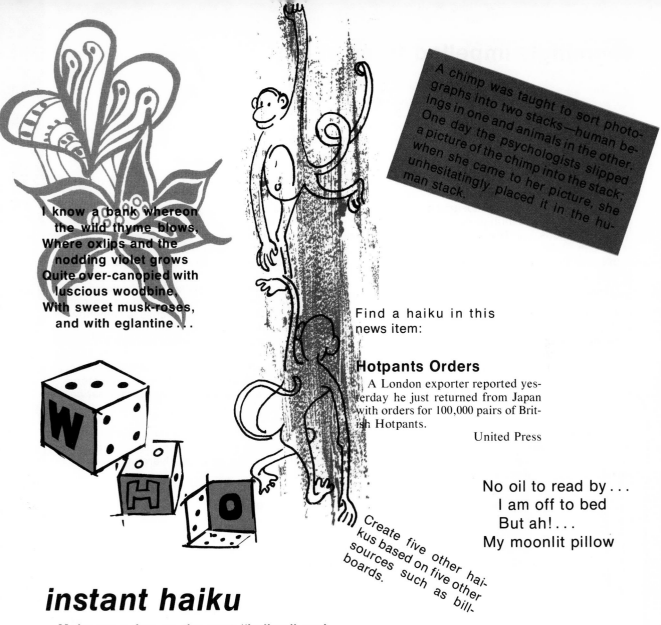

I know a bank whereon
the wild thyme blows,
Where oxlips and the
nodding violet grows
Quite over-canopied with
luscious woodbine,
With sweet musk-roses,
and with eglantine . . .

A chimp was taught to sort photographs into two stacks—human beings in one and animals in the other. One day the psychologists slipped a picture of the chimp into the stack; when she came to her picture, she unhesitatingly placed it in the human stack.

Find a haiku in this news item:

Hotpants Orders

A London exporter reported yesterday he just returned from Japan with orders for 100,000 pairs of British Hotpants.

United Press

No oil to read by . . .
I am off to bed
But ah! . . .
My moonlit pillow

Create five other haikus based on five other sources such as billboards.

instant haiku

Make up a few on-the-spot "haikus" and put them on the chalkboard as you go.

Then, work together to polish them.

Do not try to follow too precisely the traditional haiku form. Instead, decide what is essential and what could be left out, where words or phrases could go, what words should be substituted. Reflect.

Journal helpful hint:

"How can I know what I think until I see what I say?"

seemingly impelled from within

The following has been abridged and occasionally altered for continuity. The original ("Suggestions from Studies of Early Language Acauisition," CHILDHOOD EDUCATION MAGAZINE, December 1969) contains supporting evidence and source information as well as further comments on the implications of these studies.

When we say that a child has learned his native language by the time he has entered first grade, what do we mean he has learned? ... The only adequate explanation for what we call "knowing a language" is that the child learns a limited set of rules. On the basis of these rules he can produce and comprehend an infinite set of sentences. This set of rules, called a grammar, ... is not known in any conscious way. The grammar is known nonconsciously ... as a kind of tacit knowledge....Few of us can state the rules for adding /s/ or /z/ or /iz/ sounds to form plural nouns. Yet if asked to supply the plurals for nonsense syllables such as *bik* or *wug* or *gutch,* all who are native speakers of English could do so with ease....

While children are learning to form noun and verb endings, at a certain period in their development they will say *foots* instead of *feet, goed* instead of *went, mines* instead of *mine.* Children do not hear *foots* or *goed* or *mines.* These words are overgeneralizations of rules that each child is somehow extracting from the language he does hear. He hears *his, hers,* and *ours, yours* and *theirs;* and he hypothesizes that the first person singular of *mine* should be *mines.* Human beings are pattern and rule-discovering animals as these overgeneralizations ... show....

In learning how to ask a question, children will say, *Why I can't go?,* neglecting temporarily to reverse the auxiliary and pronoun. And their answer to the question, *What are you doing?,* will temporarily be, *I am doing dancing.* If the answer to *What are you eating?* takes the form, *I am eating X,* the child hypothesizes that the answer to *What are you doing?* is, *I am doing X-ing.* Only later does he learn that answers with *doing* require the exceptional form *I am X-ing.*

In a general way, the commonsense view that children imitate the language they hear around them must be true. A child in an English-speaking home grows up to speak English, not French or Hindi or some language of his own. But in the fine details of the language-learning process, imitation cannot be the whole answer, as the above examples show.

Sometimes...the child's rule system can be dramatically impervious to external alteration:

> *My teacher holded the baby rabbits and we patted them.*
> *Did you say your teacher held the baby rabbits?*
> *Yes.*
> *What did you say she did?*
> *She holded the baby rabbits and we patted them.*
> *Did you say she held them tightly?*
> *No. She holded them loosely.*

> (Conversation with four-year-old child, reported by Jean Berko Gleason)

... In another study, Gleason asked first- second- and third-grade children to give irregular plural nouns or past tense verbs after she had supplied the correct forms as she asked the question. "In the case of the verbs, they were shown a bell that could ring and told that yesterday it rang; then they were asked what the bell did yesterday." Even under these conditions, only 50 per cent of the first-graders (7 out of 14) said *rang;* 6 said *ringed* and one said *rung.* Gleason concludes:

> In listening to us, the children attended to the sense of what we said, and not the form. And the plurals and past tenses they offered were products of their own linguistic systems, and not imitations of us.

When sophisticated parents try deliberately to teach a child a form that does not fit his present rule system, the same filtering process occurs. The following conversation took place when a psychologist tried to correct an immaturity in her daughter's speech:

C. *Nobody don't like me*
M. *No, say "Nobody likes me."*
C. *Nobody don't like me*
   (eight repetitions of this dialogue)
M. *No. Now listen carefully; say "Nobody likes me."*
C. *Oh! Nobody don't likes me!*

It happens that irregular verbs such as *went* and *came* are among the most common verbs in English. Children usually learn the irregular forms first, evidently as isolated vocabulary words, and later start constructing their own overgeneralizations *goed* and *comed* .... Finally they achieve the mature pattern of rule plus exceptions. Stages on the way to the child's acquisition of mature behavior may look for the moment like regressions, like new errors in terms of adult standards, and yet be significant evidence of intellectual work and linguistic progress.

With a very few pathological exceptions, all children learn to speak the language of their parents and home community. They do so with such speed and ease, at an age when other seemingly simpler learnings such as identification of colors are absent, that one wonders how the environment helps the process along .... So far no evidence exists to show that either correction or reinforcement of the learning of grammar occurs with sufficient frequency to be a potent force ....

Brown and his colleagues have found corrections of mis-statements of fact but not correction of immature grammatical forms in hundreds of hours of recordings of three children ... and their parents. Horner found only correction of "bad language" (*pee pee*) in her study of conversation between parents and two three-year-old lower-class children. Finally, students recording the acquisition of language in such farflung areas of the world as India, California and Samoa report the same lack of correction .... Analyzing parent-child conversations, Bellugi-Klima concludes:

> The mother and child are concerned with daily activities, not grammatical instruction. Adam breaks something, looks for a nail to repair it with, finally throws pencils and nails around the room. He pulls his favorite animals in a toy wagon, fiddles with the television set; and tries to put together a puzzle. His mother is concerned primarily with modifying his behavior. She gives him information about the world around him and corrects facts. Neither of the two seems overtly concerned with the problems that we shall pursue so avidly: the acquisition of syntax.

In modifying behavior, supplying information about the world and correcting facts, mothers of young children do seem to use simpler language than they address to other adults .... Presumably, as the child's utterances become longer and more complex, so do the mother's. Other than this simplification, there is no sequencing of what the child has to learn. He is offered a cafeteria, not a carefully prescribed diet. And, seemingly impelled from within, he participates in the give-and-take of conversation as best he can from the very beginning, in the process takes what he needs to build his own language system and practices new forms to himself, often at bedtime. As far as we can tell now, all that the child needs is exposure to well-formed sentences in the context of conversation that is meaningful and sufficiently personally important to command attention ....

The foregoing picture of how children learn their native language *before* school is fairly certain, though still incomplete. Implications for how to help children continue their learning *in* school are far less certain—indeed, are controversial in the extreme—and evidence on which the controversy might be resolved is insufficient. The most obvious implication is that teachers should act the way parents have acted: talk with children about topics of mutual interest in the context of the child's ongoing work and play. This recommendation is made by many people in early childhood education in this country and in infant schools in England .... Controversy arises because so far experimental comparison of various preschool programs that focus on language development have failed to demonstrate the effectiveness of those programs based on the above philosophy ....

79

pattern-discovering animals

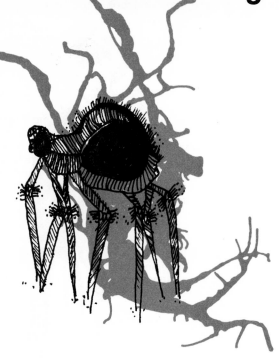

THEY'RE TAXING *THAT* NOW?

back-formation

Native speakers follow analogical principles in language development and fit new forms into patterns they imagine to exist. Thus, Middle English borrowed the Old French *cherise* and made it *cheris.* That sounded like a plural in their language, so they dropped the /z/ sound, and we now have *cherry* for the singular and *cherries* for the plural.

Grovelling was once, not a participle as the *ing* usually indicates in English, but an adverb meaning "face downwards" and was a member of a group of adverbs such as *sideling, darkling, backling* and *headling,* most of which are now obsolete. *Grovelling,* by analogy, belongs with *headlong* and *sidelong* rather than with *running* and *jumping.* However, the latter analogy was hit upon, and speakers created the verb *grovel* (without which bureaucracy could not function). Check your dictionary concerning

to peddle,
to butch,
and
to burgle.

Supply a word. Your opponent must supply the most farfetched word he can think of to go with it. Then you must find a connection between the two words. If you do, you win the round. Then it is his turn, and you try to stump him.

Thus:

> "Rose petal"
> "Stings"
> "Because it hurts me to think it will wither."

**All the world's a code
And men and women mere cryptographers.**

Is there any void from the Lord?

The fact, you see, is this. Once you have got the *knack* of using the mind properly, everything follows easily. It is a matter of breaking a habit that human beings have acquired over millions of years; of giving all their attention to the outside world, and thinking of 'imagination' as a kind of escapism, instead of recognizing that it is a brief excursion into the great unknown countries of the mind. You had to get used to thinking how your mind worked. Not just your 'mind' in the ordinary sense, but your feelings and perceptions as well. I found that by far the most difficult thing, to begin with, was to realize that *'feeling' is just another form of perception.* We tend to keep them in separate compartments. I look at a man, and I 'see' him; that is objective. A child looks at him and says: 'Ooh, what a horrid man.' The child *feels* about him, and we say that is 'subjective.' We are unaware of how stupid these classifications are, and how much they confuse our thinking. In a sense, the child's feeling is also a 'perception.' But in a far more important sense, our 'seeing' is also a feeling.

Think for a moment of what happens if you are trying to adjust a pair of binoculars. You turn the little wheel, and everything is a blur. Suddenly, a single extra turn makes everything become clear and sharp. Now think what happens if someone says to you: 'Old So-and-so died last night.' Usually, your mind is so full of other things that you don't feel anything at all—or rather, your feeling is *indistinct*, blurred, just as if the binoculars are out of focus. Perhaps weeks later, you are sitting quietly in your room reading, when something reminds you of old So-and-so who died, and quite suddenly you feel acute grief for a moment. The feeling has come into focus. What more is necessary to convince us that feeling and perception are basically the same thing?

Here is a diamond to show at tea:
The word *extra* came from the word *extraordinary.* Newspapers used to put out "extra" editions. See how our minds work?

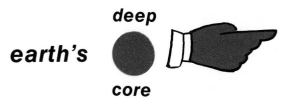

deep

earth's

core

That letter which takes the most time to write in l o n g h a n d is "k"

1. a juxtaposition of elements creating a unique form in nature.
2. a phallic symbol.
3. a pencil.
4. a tool for performing a unique form of communication.
5. a symbol of literacy and superiority.
6. a one-toothed comb.
7. a delicious chewable thing.
8. a dropable flirtation device.
9. a miniature javelin.
10. an insurance policy against cosmic destruction.
11. an infinity.

definition

Define *teacher*

Assignment:
Make 5 meaningful in a verbal-visual collage

for poets:

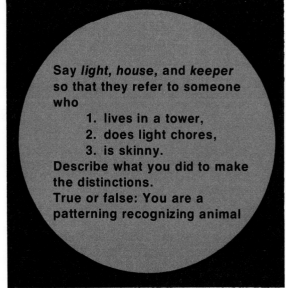

Say *light, house,* and *keeper* so that they refer to someone who
1. lives in a tower,
2. does light chores,
3. is skinny.
Describe what you did to make the distinctions.
True or false: You are a patterning recognizing animal

THE FIRST BOOKS WERE VISUAL AIDS.

SPEECH ● ● ● ● ● ● ●

In the beginning was the Word, and the Word
    was with God, and the Word was God.
The same was in the beginning with God.
All things were made by him; and without
    him was not any thing made that was made.
In him was life; and the life was the light
    of men.
And the light shineth in darkness; and the
    darkness comprehended it not...
That was the true Light, which lighteth
    every man that cometh into the world.
He was in the world, and the world was
    made by him and the world knew him not...
And the Word was made flesh, and dwelt among us,
    (and we beheld his glory, and the glory as
    of the only begotten of the Father,) full of
    grace and truth....

●

The above is the King James version
(1611). The passage on page 68 is the
revised standard version (1952). Note
the differences. Reflect.

I hate abstracts.

Because they haven't
been abstracted *enough*?

I am an abstract. T or F?

The more you abstract some-thing out of the
in-finite the more defined (finite) it becomes.
Thus, an "abstract" painting isn't very abstract.

light: undifferentiated total experience.

CHUTZPA

The movie is a ditto device.

a. the anesthesia of language
b. cross between a crow and a raven
c. a mental bruise
d. a plant whose virtue has not yet been discovered
e. cross between a crow and a mule
f. a tongue which never takes its tongue out of its cheek

___ 1. double agent
___ 2. plumber
___ 3. specimen
___ 4. plagiarism
___ 5. reality
___ 6. marriage
___ 7. graffiti
___ 8. trouble maker
___ 9. euphemism
___10. neurotic
___11. Yiddish
___12. weed
___13. memory
___14. delight
___15. craven
___16. cruel
___17. null
___18. Esprit de Corps

g. an Italian astronaut
h. an Italian opera singer
i. self-taut
j. the triumph of hope over experience
k. a sphere having an infinite radius and a center at every point
l. drain surgeon
m. takes 20%
n. multiple meanings in one form
o. intelligent, well-informed and well-versed in his rights
p. French decorator
q. a four-letter void
r. same as entity
s. Margaret Truman
t. for most people what passes for thought.

If you answered all the above correctly, you would best be suited to be a. a high school principal, b. a poet, c. a chemist, d. a salesman, e. a hooker, f. Vice President of the United States?

Select ten words and create your own metaphors for them. Make a multiple-choice test and trade with other students. Sell the best ones to your school newspaper. Expel any member of the class who uses cliche' definitions.

My Ocean View Is a Euphemism

"I bought this beach house so that I could look out my windows and see the ocean spreading around me, beautiful, peaceful, serene. When I think of what the ocean really is, I realize that that view is a euphemism."

Sir Winston Churchill, when a legislator, was once reprimanded for using the word lie. He substituted a "terminological inexactitude."

"Every scientist trails his history into every research project."

Well, Mr. Kraatz, let's hear your euphemism on the subject.

83

True or false: Reality is a euphemism.

NOBLESSE OBLIGE

How to Talk Ozark *1957*

There are indications in the current exposés of life on Madison Avenue that the men in the so-called communications industry have discovered that certain American dialects are more effective than others — both for communicating, and, more important, as tools for getting ahead in the world. In one current best-selling novel some of the characters—having observed that their confreres from the South and the Middle West are getting most of the breaks—are astute enough to try to cancel what is clearly the outlanders' main advantage by imitating their manner of speaking.

As one who has made the dialect shift in reverse, I would be less than charitable not to offer some guidance to those going the other way, particularly since I may be one of a very few willing or able to do so. The late H. L. Mencken once suggested that I expand for publication a letter I had written to him about my linguistic climb from Ozark dialect to standard English. He said that a person who could write, in formal English, about an "illiterate dialect"—from the point of view of one to whom it was a native tongue—was something of a rarity.

Most people who speak such a dialect have unconsciously acquired along with it a feeling that speech should absolutely never be tampered with. The Ozarker's exceptionally strong aversion to any modification of his speech habits has made his dialect one of the greatest repositories of archaic and obsolete English known to modern linguists. They consider it the most pristine branch of Appalachian or "Southern-Hill," the dialect that is known to the layman as "hill-billy."

The Ozarker's linguistic conservatism appears to be based on sound instinct. It is shared by a branch of the most civilized users of our language—the English aristocracy. Given his choice between the U and the Non-U words listed in Nancy Mitford's *Noblesse Oblige,* the Ozarker would take the U in nearly every case. As a child I said *fine house* and not *lovely home; sick* instead of *ill; false teeth* and not *dentures; spectacles* and not *glasses; Scotch* and not *Scottish; looking-glass* and not *mirror;* and *rich* instead of *wealthy.* Not only would I have said that a rich man had false teeth; I would also have said that he was fat and that he had had his teeth pulled because they were rotten or had holes in them. *Heavy-set, extracted, decayed,* and *cavities* are Non-U words I learned after I left home.

As for the recommended U-practice of remaining silent in certain embarrassing social situations, the Ozarker masters the art at an early age. Never having been taught to reply when someone says, "Pleased to have met you," nor to comment after hiccuping, belching, or sneezing, he remains silent on these occasions in perfect dignity, feeling no sense of omission. The practice of keeping the mouth shut when possible and of choosing only the most straightforward word when speech is unavoidable should probably not be adopted in its pure Ozark form by the communications-beginner. In anyone other than the utterly pure in heart it would sound like pretentious simplicity—which is Non-U in any country. Fowler, the expert on correct usage for the English, listed as "stylish archaisms" a number of words that are in daily use in the Ozarks.

84

where do you live

A rather severe pruning of the vocabulary will be necessary, however. The Ozarker is right again in his instinctive hostility to long and unusual words. In conversation they are a handicap anywhere and in writing they are useful only for comic effect.

One of the first things I learned about language when I left the hills and started to high school in Joplin, Missouri, was that a large vocabulary can be a social handicap. Until then it had never occurred to me that there were real people anywhere in the world who talked like the people in books, but the speech of my urban classmates was so much more like book language than it was like my own that I at first imagined I had entered the linguistically perfect world of Prudence and Her Friends. I unlimbered my reading vocabulary and went around delivering it in dictionary accents and grammar-book order. It didn't take me long to discover that this was a mistake and so I lowered my sights to mere social acceptability. Within a couple of months I had gone from *you'uns* to *you* to *y'all;* from *purty* to *EXquisite* to *exQUISite;* from *winder* to *window* to *winda;* and from *drawers* to *lingerie* (I was taking French, of course) to *lonjeray.* In short, I had made my first dialect switch—this time from rural to urban Appalachian.

This sort of dubious improvement is not the worst thing that can happen in the classroom to a hillbilly who lets the bars down. He is also fair game for the English teachers with their sets of correct-usage rules, many of which are totally wrong and most of the rest of which are at best Non-U. I was taught, for example, that *good deal* was a corrupt form of *great deal;* that neither *apt* nor *liable* could ever be used to mean *likely; to aim* could not mean *to intend; to favor* could not be used for *to resemble;* that such verb forms as *learnt, dreamt, burnt, sung,* and *sunk* were used as past tenses by illiterates only; that it was reprehensible to use *clean* or *clear* to mean *entirely,* or *mad* for *angry;* and that *sure* and *near* were never adverbs.

All these condemned usages should be adopted at once by the new dialect learner. They have the raffish charm that accrues to anything opposed by the schoolteachers and at the same time they are in excellent standing with the real authorities on language. For the same reasons he should make frequent use of words like *liefer, tetchy,* and *gaumy.* By violating only the non-canonical rules to begin with, the neophyte with a queasy conscience can break himself in gradually, in the meanwhile dabbling in a sort of subtle sadism now enjoyed almost exclusively by the practicing purists.

Attaining a hillbilly facility with figures of speech should present no difficulties to the ad-man. His well-exercised creativity will make up for his lack of knowledge. The born Ozarker carries around in his head a lifetime collection of similies and metaphors, and his special skill is an ability to extract the right figure for the right occasion without a pause for thought. The creative type would be wise to learn a few of these to begin with, absorbing their flavor as he goes.

Common barnyard and wood-lot fauna abound in the Ozarker's figure-of-speech anthology, and the beginner might work this field first, using these standards as models; as crooked as a barrel of snakes; he's got about as much use for that as a hog has for a side-saddle; steppin' out like a chicken in high oats; sidlin' in like a hog to war; he couldn't hit a bull in the rump with a fiddle; as independent as a hog on ice; blinkin' like a toad in a hailstorm; as mad as a coon in a poke.

These are more effective when the speaker is holding his mouth right, another skill that requires an understanding of the Ozarker's attitude toward language. Like the U-speaker, he is for the casual approach. His restraint in volume and tempo and the indistinctness of his pronunciation all result from his reluctance to appear to be spending an unseemly amount of energy on a function that should be performed as inconspicuously as possible. A distaste for expending the energy necessary to engage his jaw muscles gives his vowels their narrow, horizontal sound, so that he says *catch* to rhyme with *fetch, tire* with *bar,* and *get* with *bit.* (These are U-pronunciations, too, according to *Noblesse Oblige.*)

This greatly simplifies pronunciation, as an analysis of a few Ozark Slurvian words, offered as a further guide to pronunciation, will show:

Bard—had the loan of. (He's living on bard time.)

Card—poltroon. (He took the card's way out.)

Fard—top part of the face. (He parts his hair in the middle of his fard.)

Hard—employed. (She was caught kissing a hard hand.)

Nard—lessened in breadth. (The choice nard down to two.)

Tarred—hot. (Gorillas live in a tarred zone.)

Fine Old Professor

The students who had gnored him
  Universally adored him
And he died beknownst and famous:
  A gnominious gnoramus.

do be do be do

Check incorrect usage:

__ 1. I saw a dog running.
__ 2. I saw a man eating.
__ 3. I saw a tree appleing.
__ 4. I saw a human being.

GETTING THERE

Koan:
Find yourself a rock about the size of a hen's egg. Study it every day for at least a month. What is it—really? Keep a log of your thoughts from day to day. Allow at least ten minutes a day. Thirty would be better.

Because of the nature of the work undertaken, one goes forward, then backward, repeats a step, sometimes ignores what has seemed clear before, often deals in ambiguities, and moves by suggestion rather than by logic from one point to another. At first this shifting and turning and returning will prove vexing. However, after a while a general movement in one direction will become apparent, and I think the shifting and returning will come to have as much interest as any straight-line progress of philosophic argument or insight. It takes a little time to get into the thing.

Zazen is the heart of Zen Buddhism and of zen study and distinguishes them both from any other practices with which I am acquainted. I think it may be fairly said that one knows all there is to know in Zen Buddhism when one can successfully perform zazen. Books and other forms of instruction may be helpful adjuncts when properly used; but with the exception of sanzen, they are more likely than not to be hindrances to successful zazen. This is particularly true of philosophical books.

Zazen is a form of meditation ("zen" means meditation). It consists mainly in sitting in a certain way and breathing in a certain manner.[1] The Western word meditation may confuse one about this, because it suggests a purely intellectual process. Zazen can be performed anywhere. In a Zen temple compound it usually takes place in a building especially designed for this purpose called the zendo, or meditation hall.

Briefly, zazen is done as follows. The description I offer comes mainly from the instructions of a thirteenth-century Japanese Zen Buddhist named Dogen. The part about counting your breaths comes from my own instructor. Select for your meditation a quiet, dimly lit room. Garb yourself in loose clothing and obtain several large cushions. Arrange these on the floor so that you can sit comfortably cross-legged upon them. Seat yourself cross-legged on the cushions. If you can so cross your legs that the right foot rests on the left thigh and the left foot on the right thigh, so much the better. This is the so-called lotus position. It is, however, a difficult position to assume, and you may satisfy yourself with getting only one foot on a thigh (i.e. half into the position) or simply sitting Amerindian fashion. Use a cushion to raise your rump above the level of your legs if you wish. It is important to get comfortable. Keep your back straight and erect; your hands in your lap, the left hand, palm upward, on the right palm, with the tips of the thumbs touching. Your head, too, is erect. Keep your eyes open and fix them on a point on the floor about two feet in front of you. Raise the whole body slowly and quietly, move it repeatedly to the left and to the right, backward and forward, until the proper seat and a straight posture are assured.

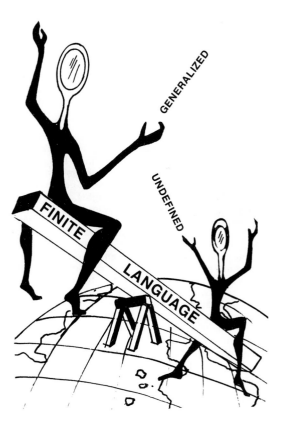

Now that you are seated, commence to breathe in the following manner. Breathe through the nose. Inhale as much as you require, letting the air come in by distending the diaphragm. Do not draw it in, rather let it come to you. Then exhale slowly. Exhale completely, getting all the air out of your lungs. As you exhale count slowly *one*. Now inhale again. Then exhale slowly to the count of *two*. And so on up to ten. Then repeat, counting up to ten again.

You will find this counting difficult, as your mind will wander from it. However, keep at it, striving to bring your mind back to the process of counting. As you become able to do this with reasonable success, start playing the following game with your counting. As you count *one* and are slowly exhaling, pretend that that *one* is going down, down, down into your stomach. Then think of its being down there as you inhale and begin to count *two*. Bring the *two* down and place it (in your imagination, one might say) in your stomach along with the *one*. Eventually, you will find that you will be able to keep your mind itself, so to speak, down in your stomach. Gradually it will become possible for you to concentrate with more and more success on the numbers. Your mind will wander. You will find yourself carried away on a train of thought, but you will have increasing success in bringing your mind back to the counting. Do not try to keep the "alien" thoughts out. Try instead to concentrate on the counting. If necessary, take note of the thoughts as they come in and then return to the counting. Get rid of the thoughts, so to speak, not by pushing them out of your mind, but by concentrating on the counting. Eventually you will be able to be quiet in both body and mind, and will have discovered how busy your mind ordinarily is. In later zazen, after sanzen or instruction from a roshi has commenced, concentration on a koan will replace concentration on breathing and counting.

The foregoing might be said to describe formal zazen. The beginner normally sits for a half an hour, takes a five minute break to walk about briskly, and then has another go at it. Later the zen student will sit for longer and longer periods without interruption. However, it soon becomes apparent that there is a kind of "sitting" which might be called informal zazen. It can be performed in any position and during many simple activities. It consists mainly in carrying over into these activities the attitudes of quiet, concentration, and awareness and the quiet, concentration and awareness that come to mark formal zazen.[2] Thus, zazen can be performed while seated in a chair, picking weeds, sawing wood, etc. When I refer to zazen one will have to judge from the context, if this appears necessary, whether I am referring to the formal or informal sort. Because there is such a thing as informal zazen, a person can come to have his zen study pervade most of his waking life, and indeed in a sense his sleep. A Zen Buddhist once said: When I eat, I eat; when I sleep, I sleep.

There are, then, one might say, degrees of zazen. This fact has some bearing on the position used in formal zazen. Zazen gets more formal, so to speak, as one approximates the lotus position. In this position the arms and legs are "turned in" and point to the diaphragm, which becomes the center of the student's being. This has the effect of intensifying his concen-

88

you're it

Use a personal analogy. Crawl inside the thing. *Be* the thing. *Be* a pencil. How does it feel? *Be* your rock. Try on a *Zero*. *Be* a word. *Be* a dog.
Jot down your thoughts and feelings in your journal as you go along.

ADAMIC
indefinite — ineffable
Language — effable
infinite — ineffable

SARAH

So out of the ground the Lord God formed every beast of the field and every bird of the air, and brought them to the man to see what he would call them; and whatever the man called every living creature, that was its name.

ANY LANGUAGE IS A MASS MEDIUM . . .

tration and in a way coordinating his whole body with his breathing. The position has, moreover, the merit of great stability when properly assumed. In it one becomes like the triangle depicted here. One has a firm base. The center of gravity is low. It is the center of one's being. There is stability and repose as well as concentration in the position. The figure is not top- or mind-heavy. The position, in fact, symbolizes and in a way

is the goal of zazen. One can, of course, practice zazen sitting in a chair with the feet dangling to the floor. However, when you compare the resulting figure with that of the triangle planted firmly on the floor or on a rock in the garden, you get a feeling for the greater concentration, repose, stability, and quiet of the latter.

It is the custom of Zen students to bow to their cushions before commencing zazen and to bow to them every time that they leave them. This can become ritualistic. It can also be a significant part of zazen and all zen study, as will become apparent.

Eternity opens from the center of the atom.

DNS5X

THROUGH LANGUAGE, THEN

Would you believe it,
Entertain the thought,
Real eyes it, make it come
into being?

I MEAN,
I come into being
through
Language.

Language separates
me
out of the infinite
CONTINUUM

Naming a thing
MAKES it exist.

I become conscious of
ME, my self, and
I
Being
Human.

And all the
INTER
RELATIONSHIPS.

Syntax.

A tree implies the rain, the earth and the sun, as a footprint implies not a foot but a whole living animal and a world he can live in. If we but knew the wholeness of the universe, the existence of the smallest, most distant star would imply, not only the existence of man, but the shape of his universe as well.

cortex + thalamus

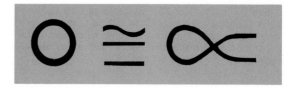

Man is halfway in size between an atom and a star.

When you *tie* things together, (a bundle of newspapers, a bunch of flowers), in what sense does that *release* them?

The following sentence is self-contradictory. Figure out why.

Avoid Latin derivatives; use brief terse Anglo-Saxon monosyllables.

Re-phrase the sentence to remove the contradiction.

90

LANGUAGE

Problem: Does language influence thought?

A learned arbitrary system of vocal symbols through which human beings interact in terms of their total culture.

True or False:

A. As we speak, so we think.
B. As we think, so we speak.
C. A language is a philosophy.
D. Whatever you say a thing is, it isn't.
E. We think by feeling.
F. We feel by thinking.
G. Every language is a collective interpretation of experience.
H. Every language is an abstraction.

Cross out all the statements which are not a matter of consequence.

From a study of children who were deafened before they learned language, McKay Vernon, Ph.D., developed the following hypotheses:

1. Language has no effect on cognition or thought processes.
2. The degree of language skill is not relevant to the skill of understanding and using concepts.
3. We probably do not think with language symbols, but we use them to express our thoughts to others.

Vernon analyzed 31 studies of the IQ's of deaf children compared with those of children with normal hearing. In matters such as remembering, abstracting, reasoning, concept forming, Vernon found there was no significant difference. Nor did the later acquisition of language affect significantly the IQ's of the deaf children. They progressed at the same rate as the other children. (See *Archives of General Psychiatry,* March 1967.)

Language is theft.

The word *Mike* ties a bunch of separate instances together. In what sense does the word, which is a metaphor for *mike-ness,* release or free "Mike"?

"The little girl had the making of a poet in her who, being told to be sure of her meaning before she spoke, said: 'How can I know what I think till I see what I Say?' "

To learn is to be a cannibal.

T or F?

WHEN IS A WORD NOT A WORD?

Of course I plagiarize. But I always improve what I steal.

Generalizing is always an act of faith.

Every fact is a generalization.

We've
been
wont
since
time
began

to
confuse
the
image
with
the
man.

Plato?

No Ideas without Words.
T or F?

Say it, no ideas but in things —
nothing but the blank faces of the
houses and cylindrical trees . . .

the double agent

We think,
  "Here I am,
  Thinking."
But really,
  "Bodybody,
  Sitting and minding."

The spaces of the mind are *a new dimension.*
The body is a mere wall between two infinities. Space extends to infinity outwards; the
mind stretches to infinity inwards.

Of course we don't think *because* we have language! Language is like a hammer or a hatchet
or a probe. Better still, a concave reflector,
like radar, for concentrating attention. It
throws a beam of light, powerful and concentrated, on something we wish to look at.
                              A student.

   The United States is still the only country in the world where cigarette sellers
hand out matches free.

"It takes all kinds of
   in and outdoor schooling
To get accustomed to my kind
   of fooling."
Assignment:
What color is *restlessness*?
Draw a shape for *restlessness*.

Koan exercise consists
in learning to
put yourself into the
position of letting
things
(in this case words)
have their own life—
that is, in the position
of being able
to listen
to them
(instead of yourself).

Nice Ass

There is so much lost and so
much gained in these words.

There is nothing
mental going
on when
understanding
is going on.

Something mental
occurs
only
when we are
learning
to
understand.

A   R   G   O   T

Syllogism:
All labels are stereotypes.
All language is labels.
Therefore . . .

Ah . . .

So here we are again
Ten million poets
Sitting on our beds
After work
At noon hour
In the midst of alone
In the face of joy or fear or anger
Jotting ourselves down
Ten million scratching pens
Can we get it out,
Dear Brothers and Sisters?

Joining our hands
Would be no use, eh . . .?
We're down to the individual
Puking different meals,
If you smell it that way.

HOW

93

(water

wind)

As we realized when we thought about this matter, the chief weapon of the parasites was a kind of 'mind-jamming device' that could be loosely compared to a radar-jamming device.

The conscious human mind 'scans' the universe all the time. 'The wakeful life of the ego is a perceiving.' It is like an astronomer scanning the skies for new planets. Now an astronomer discovers new planets by comparing old star photographs with new ones. If a star has moved, then it isn't a star, but a planet. And our minds and feelings are also constantly engaged in this process of scanning the universe for 'meanings.' A 'meaning' happens when we compare two lots of experience, and suddenly understand something about them both. To take an extremely simple example, a baby's first experience of fire may give it the impression that fire is wholly delightful: warm, bright, interesting. If he then tries putting his finger into the fire, he learns something new about it—that it burns. But he does not therefore decide that fire is wholly unpleasant—not unless he is exceptionally timid and neurotic. He superimposes the two experiences, one upon another, like two star maps, and marks down that one property of fire must be clearly separated from its others. This process is called learning.

Now supposing the mind parasites deliberately 'blur' the feelings when we try to compare our two experiences. It would be as if they had exchanged an astronomer's spectacles for a pair with lenses made of smoked glass. He peers hard at his two star maps, but cannot make much out. We do not learn clearly from experience when this happens. And if we happen to be weak or neurotic, we learn entirely the wrong thing—that fire is 'bad' because it burns, for example.

I apologize to non-philosophical readers for these explanations, but they are quite essential. The aim of the parasites was to prevent human beings from arriving at their maximum powers, and they did this by 'jamming' the emotions, by blurring our feelings so that we failed to learn from them, and went around in a kind of mental fog.

Select some short, easy-to-read passage.

Record on a cassette tape five different people reading the passage. For each reader find out the highest school grade attended, age, place of birth, places of residence and length of stay.

Let the other members of the class see how much they know about each reader from para-language clues.

Make a fifteen-minute or thirty-minute video tape with yourself as subject. Do not plan a script; just be there on camera for the full time. Then study the tape. What do you know about yourself that even your best friends wouldn't tell you? Are you ready for Hollywood?

Get a short film such as "The Anatomy of Cindy Fink" or "Help, My Snowman's Burning Down." Turn off the sound. How much of the film's message is visual?

●

Study someone in a phone booth. Be sure you cannot hear him. How much of the "message" is the listener missing?

Form teams. Find some aphorisms in IMAGE your class has explored together and present them through charades.

After each round explore the nonverbal symbols which were used and recognized. Are they standard symbols in our culture? Would any be recognized universally? Are they based on language? What other questions should we have asked? Which of these questions are matters of consequence?

95

Whatever the members of a culture pick something out of the totality to give importance, the culture will have a great many words to use to talk about it. That reminds me: I read that W. H. Auden had collected 48 unusual words used for naming the genitalia. One can guess to which sex the longer list applied.

EXIT

NO SMOKING

DO NOT GO BEYOND THIS POINT

KEEP THIS DOOR CLOSED

IN

  IN

OUT

Forty-eight? Hm, let's see . . . .

There is the thing
out there that
you can pick, smell,
eat, ignore,
or
whatever.

The best I can do is
give you
a
representation
of
it
here. Sorry.

It is really non-verbal
and
even
non IMAGE, non-picture.

Here it is.

But there is also a word.
Here it is: *CHICORY*

It's just a picture here,
but if you say it, that
will help make it its old
self again.

This   and

this
        CHICORY
are not the same thing.

This

(or, rather, the thing it is
supposed to be a picture of)
is *alive*. But this
        CHICORY
in a sense has a separate and
lively life of its own, too.

SEPARATE
BUT EQUAL

But words are entities in themselves, too,
if
we
let them
be.
I am a word, being. See? Some
words I like:
ineffable
ambiguity
blue
meadow
green
orange
palindrome
chocolate
gardenia
teaberry
Monongahela
chrysalis

Words and things?
Words are things.

Arabic has 6000 words for camel, its parts
and equipment.

Carry a piece of paper and a pencil
with you for a couple of days. As
you come across words you especially like, jot them down. List them
here.

1. _____
2. _____
3. _____
4. _____
5. _____
6. _____
7. _____
8. _____
9. _____
10. _____

The Lapps have 20 words for ice, 11 for
cold, 41 for snow, and 26 for freezing
or thawing.

97

At Squaw Valley that
is not surprising.

Herb would always look around when he visited us and would ask, "What's the name of that tree?" or "What do you call this flower?" as though he didn't feel truly in touch with nature until he had mastered all the names, as though the primary world is a verbal world and we can not know things until we gain the terminology which somehow magically expresses them.

This habit of Herb's particularly exasperated Martha who, like the rest of us, usually didn't know what the things were called, certainly not the names of the local rocks. "What kind of rock formations are those?" Herb asked as we drove along one day. "Granite," said Martha, choosing the first word that came to her mind. And that settled it.

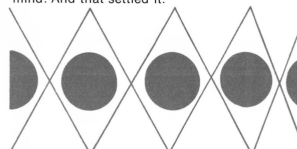

Red apples.

What is gained; what is lost, when "red" is added to "apples"?

salt ocean

What is gained and lost by adding "salt" to "ocean"?

PREJUDICE:

I have realized lately how little we . . . respond directly . . . When you respond to a flower, it is usually to it as a *flower* or as a *thing-of-beauty,* etc.

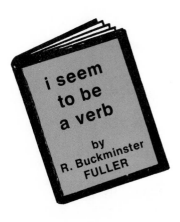

i seem
to be
a verb

by
R. Buckminster
FULLER

True or False:

Nouns and verbs: the permanent opposed to the transient—a spiritual crisis.

ATTRIBUTES

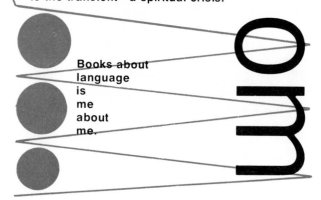

Books about
language
is
me
about
me.

98

The Milky Way is the collection of 100 billion stars or more of which our sun is a member. Our forefathers who, like present-day cosmologists, made up in imagination for what they lacked in knowledge were pleased to regard it as milk spilled from the breast of a nursing goddess.

PHATIC

Make up a play by transcribing literally fifteen minutes of conversation overheard in a public place.

Get some other students to help you do a reading of your play for the class.

Trick question: What are *really* matters of consequence?

Which is narrower,
a fact
or
an idea?

Which is angrier,
your kitchen
or
your living room?

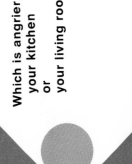

A lawyer in Winona, Minnesota, sued a member of the planning commission for calling him a 'little son of a bitch' and a 'goddam son of a bitch' three times in a public debate over an urban renewal plan.
In throwing out the suit for slander the Minnesota supreme court ruled that calling a public figure a s.o.b. is not in itself defamatory or malicious, nor was there evidence that it had hurt the plaintiff's practice. 'Calling a man a son of a bitch, unworthy as it is in public debate, could not be reasonably construed as an actual reference to his ancestry or even to his general character.'

"What is it that hangs on the wall, is green, wet and whistles?"
I knit my brow and thought and thought and finally in perplexity gave up.
"A herring," said my father.
"A *herring*?!" I echoed. "A herring doesn't hang on a wall!"
"So hang it there."
"But a herring isn't green!" I protested.
"Paint it."
"But a herring isn't *wet*."
"If it's just painted, it's still wet."
"But—" I sputtered, summoning all my outrage.
"—*a herring doesn't whistle!*"
"Right," smiled my father. "I just put that in to make it hard."

Man values
the
subtleties
of life.
That is
what
language
is
all
about.

FLOWERS BY THE SEA

When over the flowery, sharp pasture's
edge, unseen, the salt ocean

lifts its form—chicory and daisies
tied, released, seem hardly flowers alone

but color and the movement—or the shape
perhaps—of restlessness, whereas

the sea is circled and sways
peacefully upon its plantlike stem

Each thing is
A thing
   or . . .
I am,
too.
Things, things.
Here we are
Nodding at one another
Each in our own way.
The book, the pen, the radio, the keys,
the brush, the ashtray, the smoke
Me
All of us
Spinning and whizzing
About the Sun
The Galaxy
The World
   Nodding
Hello, Goodbye.
— — — — — — — — — —
We things alive
Greedy to maintain our space
And, more,
Our time.
— — — — — — — — — —
Reality is several frequencies.
The band is infinite.
Tune!
Come on, move that dial!

100

In what sense are
you an adjective?

language
is a
double
agent

A word has two
sides, what
is inside it
and what is
outside it.

Every word
implies the
totality.

Everything   both ways

It is not that linguistic patterns limit sensory
patterns but that they direct perception and
thinking into certain habitual channels.

The following words
have something in
common in their
etymology. Find it.

chesterfield
cardigan
davenport
crapper
silhouette
sandwich
derrick
nicotine

RED NO MATTER WHAT
COLOR IT IS

DIFFERENCES WHICH
DON'T MAKE
ANY DIFFERENCE:

The sound of the p in pin is
uttered with a slight puff of
breath that is lacking when we
sound the p in spin. Yet the
speakers of English have entered into an unconscious
agreement to treat them as
the same signals, though they
are not acoustically identical.

True or False:
A word never re-
fers only to one
thing. It always
implies a rela-
tionship *among*
things.

A MATTER OF CONSEQUENCE

VITAMIN:
FOOD
OR
MEDICINE?

**ASK A CHRISTIAN
SCIENTIST.**

If *you* think in categories and that which you
contemplate does not consist of categories,
how can you deal with it?

101

A major reason for revision of the King James Version, which is valid for both the Old Testament and the New Testament, is the change since 1611 in English usage. Many forms of expression have become archaic, while still generally intelligible—the use of thou, thee, thy, thine and the verb endings -est and -edst, the verb endings -eth and -th, it came to pass that, whosoever, whatsoever, insomuch that, because that, for that, unto, howbeit, peradventure, holden, aforetime, must needs, would fain, behooved, to you-ward, etc. Other words are obsolete and no longer understood by the common reader. The greatest problem, however, is presented by the English words which are still in constant use but now convey a different meaning from that which they had in 1611 and in the King James Version. These words were once accurate translations of the Hebrew and Greek Scriptures; but now, having changed in meaning, they have become misleading. They no longer say what the King James translators meant them to say.

The King James Version uses the word "let" in the sense of "hinder," "prevent" to mean "precede," "allow" in the sense of "approve," "communicate" for "share," "conversation" for "conduct," "comprehend" for "overcome," "ghost" for "spirit," "wealth" for "well-being," "allege" for "prove," "demand" for "ask," "take no thought" for "be not anxious," "purchase a good degree" for "gain a good standing," etc. The Greek word for "immediately" is translated in the King James Version not only by "immediately" and "straightway" but also by the terms "anon," "by and by," and "presently." There are more than three hundred such English words which are used in the King James Version in a sense substantially different from that which they now convey. It not only does the King James translators no honor, but it is quite unfair to them and to the truth which they understood and expressed, to retain these words which now convey meanings they did not intend.

102

Physicists: What happens to an object when it approaches the speed of light? Is this a matter of consequence?

The Purist

I give you now Professor Twist,
A conscientious scientist.
Trustees exclaimed, "He never bungles!"
And sent him off to distant jungles.
Camped on a tropic riverside,
One day he missed his loving bride.
She had, the guide informed him later,
Been eaten by an alligator.
Professor Twist could not but smile.
"You mean," he said, "a crocodile."

Prove: Everyone is a language bigot.

That reminds me . . .

Three refugee French officers were quartered with an English family during World War II. The hostess asked the first if he had any children. He replied,

"No, alas, my wife is impregnable."

"My friend," said the second, "means that she is unbearable."

"Pardon the errors of my colleagues," said the third, "They mean that she is inconceivable."

Investigation

A writes a paragraph as though he were student B and describes what B is like—from B's point of view ("I'm easy-going and never pass up a party. I don't like to go too deeply into things. What's on the surface suits me . . ." and so forth).

Then C rewrites the paragraph and must put it in new words and sentences. He must try to retain the ideas and point of view of the original, however.

A, B, and C compare the two versions and reflect on what they notice. Then all the groups of three form a large group and examine their discoveries.

I O S N E I

Wanted to know if he couldn't have a saddle.

103

ambisexderity

Well, the movie went on its rounds and I began getting letters from all over the country plus at the same time reactions which made me take the letters a little more seriously from my brother who was in Michigan and a friend who was living upstate saying this is a dirty movie, are you mad? So then, thanks to my friend and my brother tipping me off, I realized they were seeing *Dear John* with a sound track dubbed. *Dear John* had come here with subtitles. It was being shown around the country with an English dubbed track that according to the best witnesses was turning this movie into just a dirty sex exploitation movie. It had destroyed whatever sensitivity there might have been in the film . . .
Judith Crist.

We sift reality through screens composed of ideas. These idea systems are limited by language. That is to say, language cuts a groove in which our thoughts must move. If we seek new validity forms, we must step outside the language.

Find all the live metaphors in the above passage. Find the dead ones. True or false: Ninety per cent of language *should* be made up of dead metaphors.

Use the following three words in a single six-word sentence:

effervescent, bedcovers, fiddlestick

AWAKEN FROM HIS LINGUISTIC SLEEP, A CROSS-CULTURAL APPROACH IS IMPERATIVE.

How many words have sportswriters found to express one team's defeat of another in spectator sports?

Air is the enemy of astronomers

104

"Some people grok very easily. It seems to take me longer. I usually don't grok something until I try grokking something else, and while I'm in the process, I grok the first idea. A lot of times I don't understand what's going on in class until I think about it quite a lot. I usually get it while I'm at work or in the car, and then before I write it here I lose it. No, I still have it, but the delicious words I used while it was still in my head are lost."

Carry a little note pad.

ATOM

SYNOPTIC PATTERNS ABSTRACT
BRAIN
CRYPTOGRAPHY
METAPHOR
PREJUDICE LANGUAGE
5
ALPHABET SYNCHRONICITY
ZAZEN
ENLIGHTENMENT
ANALOGY JOURNAL

London

The word bastard as an epithet, was recently ruled as permissible parliamentary language.

Many words reflecting on a member's honor, such as liar, are banned.

When Sir Charles Taylor, a Conservative party member, complained that he heard A. F. Holt, a Liberal party member, shout "bastard" at Paul Williams, another Conservative, Sir Harry Hylton-Foster, the Speaker of the House of Commons, said he had great difficulty in finding a category for the epithet and added, amid a roar of laughter, "There are parts of the country in which it is used as a term of endearment."

At Erling-Andechs, Germany, the Max Planck Institute of Animal Behavior is gathering physiological information on human circadian rhythm.

Volunteers are isolated in a concrete bunker entirely removed from normal environment. Deprived of all means of telling time, these individuals undergo changes in their patterns of daily activities, particularly in the rhythm of their biological clocks.

Untriggered by obvious cues such as the transition from day to night, biological clocks drift and then become steady again. Human beings tend to become 25 or 26-hour day animals. A few become disoriented.

One man developed a 50-hour day rhythm. He worked and read for 30 hours and slept for 20. When he left the bunker after three weeks he was convinced that he had only been there for 10 days. However, since he ate only three meals in each 50-hour day, he had lost considerable weight.

Even the earth's magnetic and electrical fields may be invisible triggering devices. Deprived of these, most people develop their own stable rhythms, but in one specially equipped chamber an artificially imposed alternating electric field was energized at 10 cycles per second. It significantly sped up the biological clock. A 26-hour day man became a 25½-hour day man, though no one has been able to explain how the field was sensed and responded to.

It has been impossible to pack the human rhythm into a period of less than 22 hours. But deprived of other contact with the world, individual clocks drift in spite of correctly spaced day-night lighting.

105

Which hurts better,
love, or
autumn?

Eldorado

Gaily bedight
A gallant knight
In sunshine and in shadow,
Had journeyed long,
Singing a song,
In search of Eldorado.

But he grew old—
This knight so bold—
And o'er his heart a shadow
Fell as he found
No spot of ground
That looked like Eldorado.

And, as his strength
Failed him at length,
He met a pilgrim shadow—
"Shadow," said he,
"Where can it be—
This land of Eldorado?"

"Over the Mountains
Of the Moon,
Down the Valley of the Shadow,
Ride, boldly ride,"
The shade replied,—
"If you search for Eldorado."

"Why don't we just have leftovers tonight?"

Match:

Which lives for ideas,
which lives off ideas:
the philosopher, the
professional?

ONE LOW PRICE
WORLD TOURS

**Stay 75 years
See Everything
meals, hotels,
transportation,
tips, tour guide,
included.**

Verbal Reality

There are three kinds of translations, the literal, word-for-word variety, the official type where certain conventions as to idiomatic equivalents are respected, and the psychological type of translation where the words produce approximately the same effects in the speakers of the second language as they did in those of the original. ⋀⋀ ••

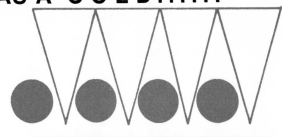

...all turn

Once in Paris I saw a play called "The Weak Sex." I found it charmingly risque. A year later in Vienna I took a girl to see the German translation of the same play. Though she was no prude, I was embarrassed because the play was vulgar if not obscene in German.

Actual experience does not present clear-cut entities like "good" and "bad," "mind" and "body." The sharp split remains verbal.

and look

Cablegram from English to Russian and back to English again:
A. "Genevieve suspended for prank."
B. "Genevieve hanged for juvenile delinquency."

"I shall speak in English this evening, but if I get excited during the discussion I shall break into German and Professor Lindeman will traduce me."
Albert Einstein.

One of the following phrases is a real plural. One is an imaginary plural. Which is which?

A. ten men
B. ten days

Which is usually more accurate?
Both-and, either-or?
(This is a trick question.)

Also possible:
Both are real.
Both are imaginary.

107

Come to think of it, in nature *plural* is impossible. Right?

cracking the code

"The best of misunderstanding any one (or thing) is that it sort of disposes of him and clears your mind of him and so leaves you with the one less detail in life to be bothered with.

"Of course it is the same with understanding. Of what use is either understanding or misunderstanding unless it simplifies by taking away from the sum and burden of what you have to consider?"

I once duplicated a passage from an essay by Alan Watts for my classes. I wanted to call their attention to the frame of reference in which we can speak of good and evil, right and wrong, and to the larger sphere in which there are no right and wrong stars, no good or evil rocks. They read the passage but instead of discussing our tendency to categorize, insisted on exploring Buddhism. Then I realized that the first sentence of the passage excerpted read, "... I believe that Zen appeals to many in the post-Christian West because it does not preach, moralize, and scold in the style of Hebrew-Christian prophetism." Most of the rest of the passage said nothing about Zen or Christianity, but the students had filtered the rest of the passage through that first sentence, and it was enough to focus their attention on Zen, and for them to see everything in the passage in terms of it. I deleted the first sentence and had no further difficulty.

They set the clocks and put out the lights before going to bed.

one way

Pole Vaulting to Conclusions

How did you read the sentence above, in the present or past tense?

108

Which is louder, duty, or responsibility?

On arising we set our minds and put out our lights

ANALOGY

"Breaking the Isolation of the Datum"

What vegetable
are you like?
What animal?
What color?
What fruit?
What time of
day?
What mineral?
What liquid?

Every
thing
is
analogical

NO

ideas

but

by

analogy

As soon as I notice *any* thing, my mind immediately begins locating it in relationship to the total perception of my conscious world. I cannot tolerate it *in* isolation.

Can you?

RADIOSTRONTIUM

"There's a great film we show called *Mt. Tamalpias Railroad.* It's a gravity car from the 1900s. I used to show it at the downtown center. The cable cars went up and down in the street outside. The windows were open. Everytime the cars would rattle by people would start to laugh. It was very funny. They associated the sound with the film."

Heron and friend

Were it not for the analogical process, I could not say anything I had not heard before.

SIMILE GAME

Complete the phrases. Select a winner for each phrase. Explore your criteria for choosing.

Absolutely no clichés permitted.

Example: sleepy as_____(TV)

1. fuzzy as _____
2. sick as _____
3. yellow as _____
4. hot as _____
5. quiet as _____
6. hungry as_____
7. slick as_____
8. old as _____
9. dumb as_____
10. sexy as_____
11. sleepy as _____
12. real as_____
13. aware as _____
14. human as_____
15. sad as_____
16. curious as _____

Variation: One team supply the first half of the phrase and the other team supply the second. Figure out a method for scoring.

Problem-solving is simile-making.
True or false?
Trick Question: At least 80% of our lives should be lived as clichés. True or false? (Before answering, see *p.*108*frost.*) T or F?

JOURNAL

5.   "I guess you think I'm a nut about avoiding death, but the physical aspect isn't important. I just want to feel up an idea. (Wow! I love that metaphor 'feel up.' It might be after your time, but in our eighth grade vernacular 'feel up' meant to caress a girl's breast. Or more precisely in those days, to squeeze the hell out of it. Yes, that's a powerful metaphor. I love it.)"

All perception of truth is the detection of an analogy.

Show that a journal is
a. a doorstop
b. a diving board
c. a giant arrow
d. a harmonizing device

We reason from our hands to our heads.

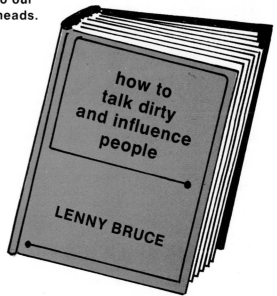

how to talk dirty and influence people

LENNY BRUCE

The secret is this: that the poor quality of human life—and consciousness—is due to the feebleness of the beam of attention that we direct at the world. Imagine that you have a powerful searchlight, but it has no reflector inside it. When you turn it on, you get a light of sorts, but it rushes off in all directions, and a lot of it is absorbed by the inside of the searchlight. Now if you install a concave reflector, the beam is polarized, and stabs forward like a bullet or a spear. The beam immediately becomes ten times as powerful. But even this is only a half measure, for although every ray of light now follows the same path, the actual waves of light are 'out of step,' like an undisciplined army walking along a street. If you now pass the light through a ruby laser, the result is that the waves now 'march in step,' and their power is increased a thousand-fold — just as the rhythmic tramping of an army was able to bring down the walls of Jericho.

The human brain is a kind of searchlight that projects a beam of 'attention' on the world. But it has always been like a searchlight without a reflector. Our attention shifts around from second to second; we do not really have the trick of focusing and concentrating the beam. And yet it *does* happen fairly often. For example, as Fleishman observed, the sexual orgasm is actually a focusing and concentrating of the 'beam' of consciousness (or attention). The beam of attention suddenly carries more power, and the result is a feeling of intense pleasure. The 'inspiration' of poets is exactly the same thing. By some fluke, some accidental adjustment of the mind, the beam of attention is polarized for a moment, and whatever it happens to be focused on appears to be transformed, touched with 'the glory and the freshness of a dream.' There is no need to add that so-called 'mystical' visions are exactly the same thing, but with an accidental touch of the laser thrown in. When Jacob Boehme saw the sunlight reflected on a pewter bowl, and declared that he had seen all heaven, he was speaking the sober truth.

Human beings never realize that life is so dull because of the vagueness, the diffuseness, of their beam of attention—although, as I say, the secret has been lying at the end of their noses for centuries. And since 1800, the parasites have been doing their best to distract them from this discovery—a discovery that should have been *quite inevitable* after the age of Beethoven and Goethe and Wordsworth. They achieved this mainly by encouraging the human habit of vagueness and the tendency to waste time on trivialities. A man has a sudden glimpse of a great idea; for a moment, his mind *focuses*. At this point, habit steps in. His stomach complains of being empty, or his throat complains of dryness, and a false little voice whispers: 'Go and satisfy your physical needs, and then you'll be able to concentrate twice as well.' He obeys—and immediately forgets the great idea.

The moment man stumbles on the fact that his attention is a 'beam,' (or, as Husserl put it, that *consciousness is 'intentional'*) he has learned the fundamental secret. Now all he has to learn is how to polarize that beam.

Analogy is a probe.

112

on

The Oldest Human —5 Million Years

February 7, 1971
Cambridge, Mass.

Transworld News Service

Scholars at Harvard University have reported the discovery of a jawbone fragment which appears to stretch out the history of the human race five million years.

The fragment is the right half of a lower jaw with a molar still intact. It was unearthed, according to Professor Bryan Patterson, in ancient deposits on Lothagam hill in northern Kenya, site of many important finds over the years.

The jawbone was found on a "nice hot afternoon" in 1967 by Arnold D. Lewis of the museum of comparative zoology at Harvard.

As recently as 1959 Dr. L. S. B. Leaky surprised anthropologists with his discovery of some remains dated at 1.75 million years at Olduvai gorge in Tanzania.

Concerning the jawbone fragment, vertebrate paleontologist Patterson felt "rather pleased with this object" but added, "I wish it was rather more complete than it is."

on
a nice
hot after-
noon

When you meet a person whose self responds, it is refreshing and often shocking, because each self is unique.

FOR ONCE, THEN, SOMETHING

Others taunt me with having knelt
at well-curbs·
Always wrong to the light, so
never seeing
Deeper down in the well than where
the water
Gives me back in a shining surface
picture
Me myself in the summer heaven,
godlike,
Looking out of a wreath of fern and
cloud puffs.
Once, when trying with chin against
a well-curb,
I discerned, as I thought, beyond
the picture,
Through the picture, a something
white, uncertain,
Something more of the depths—and
then I lost it.
Water came to rebuke the too clear
water.
One drop fell from a fern, and lo,
a ripple
Shook whatever it was lay there at
bottom,
Blurred it, blotted it out. What
was that whiteness?
Truth? A pebble of quartz?
For once, then, something.

FOCUS

Language, man's prime instrument of reason, reflects his mythmaking tendency more than his r ationalizing tendency . . . *True or False*?

Define a new word, *tripset.* Of the figures pictured below, *C, D, E,* and *F* are tripsets, whereas A, B, G, and H are not tripsets. Write a formal definition of *tripset* which would enable someone else to divide the group correctly into tripsets and non-tripsets. Then draw a new tripset.

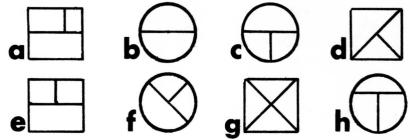

From Brown and Olmsted, LANGUAGE AND LITERATURE

True or False:

All nouns are "collective" nouns.

In what sense are *you* a collective noun?

113

Were you thinking that those were the words, those upright
    lines?
    those curves, angles, dots?
No, those are not the words, the substantial words are in
    the ground and sea,
They are in the air, they are in you . . .
The workmanship of souls is by those inaudible words of
    the earth,
The masters know the earth's words and use them more than
    audible words . . .
To her children the words of the eloquent dumb great mother
    never fail . . .
Say on, sayers! Sing on, singers!
Delve! mould! pile the words of the earth!
Work on, age after age, nothing is to be lost,
It may have to wait long, but it will certainly come in use,
When the materials are all prepared and ready, the architects
    shall appear.

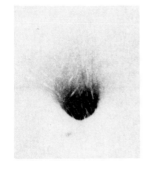

"On Vac (the Spoken Word) all the gods depend, all beasts and men; in the Word live
all creatures . . . the Word is the Imperishable,
the firstborn of the eternal Law, the mother
of the Veddas, the navel of the devine world."

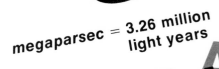

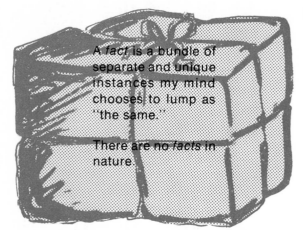

A *fact* is a bundle of
separate and unique
instances my mind
chooses to lump as
"the same."

There are no *facts* in
nature.

All facts are generalizations.

megaparsec = 3.26 million light years

CONCATENATON

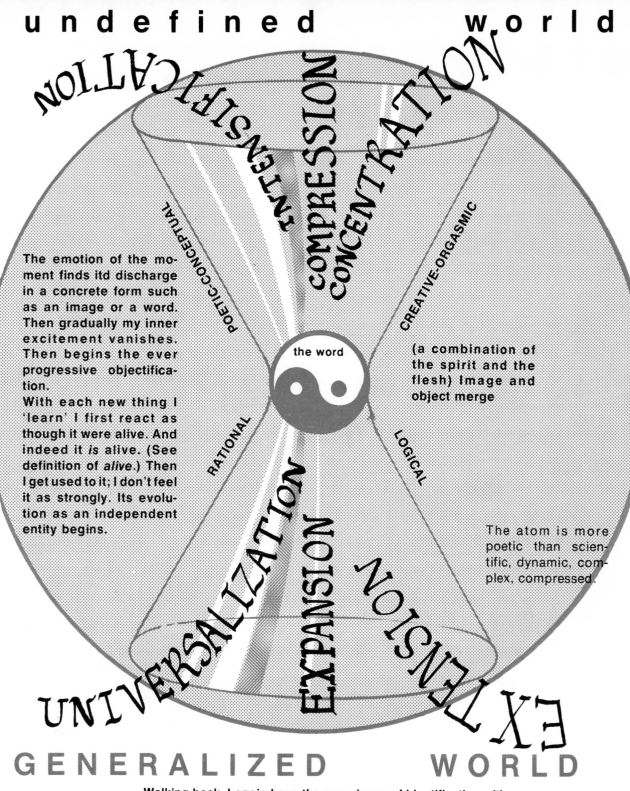

undefined world

INTENSIFICATION

COMPRESSION
CONCENTRATION

POETIC-CONCEPTUAL

CREATIVE-ORGASMIC

the word

RATIONAL

LOGICAL

The emotion of the moment finds itd discharge in a concrete form such as an image or a word. Then gradually my inner excitement vanishes. Then begins the ever progressive objectification.

With each new thing I 'learn' I first react as though it were alive. And indeed it *is* alive. (See definition of *alive*.) Then I get used to it; I don't feel it as strongly. Its evolution as an independent entity begins.

(a combination of the spirit and the flesh) Image and object merge

The atom is more poetic than scientific, dynamic, complex, compressed.

UNIVERSALIZATION

EXPANSION

EXTENSION

GENERALIZED WORLD

Walking back, I again have the experience of identification with the world. There is nothing to think about now. However this time the identification is with a bamboo tree. Standing before it, I first have a brotherly feeling for it. Then I feel that it and I are one. I merge with it. It becomes conscious.

Tied-released

For most intellectuals
ideas remain just ideas.
They do not become real.
The intellectual becomes
a miser with them. This
is a disease.

When the entire self is given up to a single impression, is "possessed" by it, and there is the utmost tension between the subject and its object, the outer world; when external reality is not merely viewed and contemplated, but overcomes a man in sheer immediacy, with emotions of fear or hope, terror or wish fulfillment: then the spark jumps across, the tension finds release, as the subjective excitement becomes objectified, and confronts the mind as a god or a daemon.
(Or a word.)

come run jump skip-a-long sam
a very happy man I am
to know you are well and you're doing fine
kind-of puts at rest my mind

How's your brush and your lady fair
not to mention your stained glass stair
flower pot on window sill
on top of honeycomb hill

have you found the secret door
to let you down to the earth's deep core
you'll be back in time for tea
with a diamond to show me.

Telescoping

I got a card from Janice Crewe today. Do you think that might be a put-on?

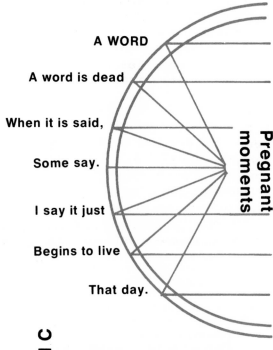

A WORD

A word is dead

When it is said,

Some say.

I say it just

Begins to live

That day.

Pregnant moments

SYNOPTIC VISION

It would be a sad pass for human knowledge if detailed research fettered it from seeking a synoptic vision.
The deeper you delve, the more you may expect to be rewarded by general insight.

Man reveals reality to himself and himself to reality. The two fuse.

The monk says: Look at the roshi when he talks. Watch everything he does. Yet what will I see but the roshi? Do not look for signs. Do not interpret. Listen. But listen to what? Does not listening involve interpreting? Well, doesn't seeing? How can you *see* things as they are? Aha! Don't *give* your interpretation.

It has been said that the tension that exists between uniqueness and universality causes a search for patterns. This search does not refer to judging but to looking for patterns in their setting.

DATA BANK

**In some societies, to possess someone's nail parings or perhaps a photograph is to hold power over him.
America has computers.**

"Why is it called the devil's weed?"
Don Juan made a gesture of indifference, shrugged his shoulders, and remained quiet for some time. Finally he said that "devil's weed" was her temporary name (su nombre de leche). He also said there were other names for the devil's weed, but they were not to be used, because the calling of a name was a serious matter, especially if one was learning to tame an ally power. I asked him why the calling of a name was so serious a matter. He said names were reserved to be used only when one was calling for help, in moments of great stress and need, and he assured me that such moments happen sooner or later in the life of whoever seeks knowledge.

My name draws a magic circle around my SELF

Problem: Turn a dead word into a live metaphor.

(Real eyes it.)

1. _____
   (your name)
2. Mark Anthony
3. trees
4. grass
5. clouds
6. _____
7. _____
8. _____

How's your rock?

PSYCHOPHYSICAL

Language, myth, and art are the processes whereby man's "soul" fuses with the physical world, and impregnates the material world with his spirit.

Survey:
What is the most common middle name for a girl in your school? For a boy?

117

I had
reflected often enough that our human life is based completely on 'premises' that we
take for granted. A child takes its parents and its home for granted; later, it comes to
take its country and its society for granted. We need these supports to begin with. A
child without parents and a regular home grows up feeling insecure. A child that has
had a good home may later learn to criticize its parents, or even reject them altogether
(although this is unlikely); but it only does so when it is strong enough to stand alone.

All original thinkers develop by kicking away these 'supports' one by one. They may
continue to love their parents and their country, but they love from a position of strength—a
strength that began in rejection.

In fact, though, human beings never really learn to stand alone. They are lazy, and
prefer supports. A man may be a fearlessly original mathematician, and yet be slavishly
dependent on his wife. He may be a powerful free thinker, yet derive a great deal more
comfort than he would admit from the admiration of a few friends and disciples. In short,
human beings never question *all* their supports; they question a few, and continue to
take the rest for granted.

Now I had been so absorbed in the adventure of entering new mental continents, rejecting
my old personality and its assumptions, that I had been quite unaware that I was still
leaning heavily on dozens of ordinary assumptions. For example, although I felt my identity
had changed, I still had a strong feeling of identity. And our most fundamental sense
of identity comes from an anchor that lies at the bottom of a very deep sea. I still looked
upon myself as a member of the human race. I still looked upon myself as an inhabitant
of the solar system and the universe in space and time. I took space and time for granted.
I did not ask where I had been before my birth or after my death. I did not even recognize
the problem of my own death; it was something I left 'to be explored later.'

What the parasites now did was to go to these deep moorings of my identity, and
proceed to shake them. I cannot express it more clearly than this. They did not actually,
so to speak, pull up the anchors. That was beyond their powers. But they shook the
chains, so that I suddenly became aware of an insecurity on a level I had taken completely
for granted. I found myself asking: Who am I? In the deepest sense. Just as a bold
thinker dismisses patriotism and religion, so I dismissed all the usual things that gave
me an 'identity': the accident of my time and place of birth, the accident of my being
a human being rather than a dog or a fish, the accident of my powerful instinct to cling
to life. Having thrown off all these accidental 'trappings,' I stood naked as pure consciousness confronting the universe. But here I became aware that this so-called 'pure
consciousness' was as arbitrary as my name. It could not confront the universe without
sticking labels on it. How could it be 'pure consciousness' when I saw that object as
a book, that one as a table? It was still my tiny human identity looking out of my eyes.
And if I tried to get beyond it, everything went blank.

I was not doing all this thinking for fun. I was trying to fight my way down to some
solid bedrock on which I could take my stand against them. They had simply been cunning
enough to show me that I was standing over an abyss. For my mind leapt on to recognize
that we also take space and time for granted, although death takes us beyond them.

118

...What I want to get at is the way the author used analogies to explain some of the biochemistry. For instance he used a freight train to show how amino acids build a protein and DNA as switchman. Human protein and non-human protein have the same cars, only their positions in the train change.

Through that analogy anyone can understand protein. It seems to me that even I could learn biochemistry if it were taught through analogies. It certainly does make the strange familiar.

(Maybe IMAGE itself is an analogy?)

JOURNAL

JOURNAL

"Talk, to me, is only spading up the ground for crops of thought. I can't answer for what will turn up. If I could I wouldn't be talking, but speaking my piece."

I saw that what I call 'existence' means existence in space and time, and that this universe of space and time is not an absolute. Suddenly, *everything became absurd.* For the first time, a dreadful sense of insecurity and weakness gripped my stomach. I saw that everything I take for granted in this universe can be questioned — that they could all be a trick. As a thinker, I had got into the old romantic habit of feeling that the mind is beyond the accidents of the body, that it is somehow eternal and free; that the body may be trivial and particular, but the mind is universal and general. This attitude makes the mind an eternal spectator, beyond fear. But now I suddenly felt: 'But if the universe itself is arbitrary, then my mind is as casual and destructible as my body.' This is the point where one remembers the times of sickness and delirium, when the mind seems altogether less durable than the body, when one suspects that it is mainly the body's toughness that is preventing the mind from disintegrating.

"Do you work closely with the cameraman?"
Fellini: "It is essential. The wrong lighting on a scene is like a sentence with the adjectives out of order."

Without using any bodily movements describe some object in your room such as a lamp. While you are talking, another person can draw his interpretation on the chalk-board. Do not look at his drawing until he has finished.

He may ask you questions, and you may elaborate as much as you wish verbally. But do not use any bodily movements.

(If you have difficulty keeping your body still and your class is informal, you can lie flat on the floor. That should help.)

Have several people try this. Then explore what the experiment reveals about communication.

Muad'Dib learned rapidly because his first training was in how to learn. And the first lesson of all was the basic trust that he could learn. It is shocking to find how many people do not believe they can learn, and how many more believe learning to be difficult. Muad'Dib knew that every experience carries its lesson.

Dueterogamy

119

Goethe said it is the property of true genius to disturb all settled ideas. I wonder if it is the property of true ideas to disturb all settled genius.

A student.

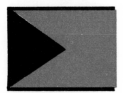

He began reluctantly, "The human brain is roughly divided into two sections, the cortex, and the thalamus. The cortex is the center of discrimination, the thalamus the center of the emotional reactions of the nervous system . . . Both the cortex and the thalamus have wonderful potentialities. Both should be trained to the highest degree, but particularly they should be organized so that they will work in co-ordination. Wherever such co-ordination, or integration, does not occur, you have a tangled personality—over emotionalism and, in fact, all variations of neuroticism. On the other hand, where cortical-thalamic integration has been established, the nervous system can withstand almost any shock."

There are approximately a quadrillion times a quadrillion atoms in the human brain.

I walk softly and know my legs are there
I seldom arrive but never
It may be dark but I don't mind that
Except sometimes
When something in me cries
And won't be strong.

But then,
If I call the right words
They comfort me
And I rest against their soft, moist breathing.
And they hold my cold hands
And drum against my temples
Or pause on my throat
Their colors rain on my eyes
Until I see but can't feel
The small pain ringing
In my left side
Because you are gone.

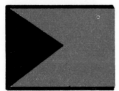

"Szell's ideal was to become so much a part of the score that intellect and emotion would merge. 'A real conductor must think with the heart and feel with the brain.'"

120

To honor Chinese New Year, the editor of the Daily Californian, the newspaper of the University of California at Berkeley, asked some Asian studies students to make up a masthead in Chinese. This is what he got.

恭賀
新禧　加州人民日報　毛主席萬歲！

VOL. 205, NO. 24　　(The Daily Californian)　　FRIDAY, FEBRUARY 6.

The left-hand box reads 'Happy New Year' as requested, but the right-hand box does not read as requested 'Year of the Dog.' Find out what it does say.

Which is thinner, Winter, or Summer?

TO MARK ANTHONY IN HEAVEN

This quiet morning light
reflected, how many times
from grass and trees and clouds
enters my north room
touching the walls with
grass and clouds and trees.
Anthony,
trees and grass and clouds.
Why did you follow
that beloved body
with your ships at Actium?
I hope it was because
you knew her inch by inch
from slanting feet upward
to the roots of her hair
and down again and that
you saw her
above the battle's fury—
clouds and trees and grass—

For then you are
listening in heaven.

History seeks the pregnant moments. And only by getting the full flavor of the moment can man see general existence. Man must have synoptic vision. By getting the fullness of the historic moment, he releases its pent up power into his present existence.

Every word is a pregnant historic atom, waiting.

But man has far deeper habits than overwork. Through millions of years of evolution, he has developed all kinds of habits for survival. If any of these habits get out of control, the result is mental illness. For example, man has a habit of being prepared for enemies; but if he allows it to dominate his life, he becomes a paranoiac.

One of man's deepest habits is keeping alert for dangers and difficulties, refusing to allow himself to explore his own mind because he daren't take his eyes off the world around him. Another one, with the same cause, is his refusal to notice beauty, because he prefers to concentrate on practical problems. These habits are so deeply ingrained that alcohol and tobacco cannot reach them.

121

GROK IS A 4-LETTER WORD

flowers
the by
sea

100,000 hot-pants orders for export— To Japan.

Analogy is a crutch.

**Maybe it's not *your* rock.
Maybe you are the rock's human.**

122

JOURNAL

But to my surprise everyone and everything was beautiful when we got to the beach. The sun was shining and the tide was out. The place was truly waiting for us. It knew we were coming and had a fabulous show ready. I could hardly wait to get to the bottom of the hill and look around in the water. The life in the sea fascinates me. There are strange and beautiful things there just waiting to be understood and have some recognition in our world. Well, I don't pass them by. I stop and say hello every time I'm down there.

Mike, a student

JOURNAL

It's the wildest idea I have ever had in my life. I had considered the idea that all things derive their meaning and purpose from man, for he defines them. This is the concept that man is the measure of all things. As I perceive things, they are to me just that. This puts me in the center of the universe, MY universe, whose boundaries extend as far as I desire them to go and include those objects and people I make significant to me.

Mike put a completely new twist in the theory, and it was like turning on the light and finding that I had always been in the dark before. It was simply an angle I had never considered before, but once the bend was made, everything became straight. It was a case of putting an old idea in a new arrangement and coming out with a new one. It is a whole new set of vibrations. It is like discovering a whole new set of frequencies that I never knew existed before. Everything around me is screaming at me to be recognized and given meaning and to be freed from non-being. Everything is reaching out to me, straining and stretching and pleading. I gain a completely new and real importance, and I think for the first time I have really become the center of my own universe.

Gary, a student

Every moment is a pregnant moment. True or false?

THE CRISIS IN RELIGION
from a speech

If I use the word *myth,* I don't necessarily mean something untrue. I would like to use the word myth to designate those great images by which man makes sense of his world. I need to say this to begin with because I want to approach the subject of the present crisis in religion through a historical approach to the mythologies that dominate Western man; that is to say, the great myths, the great ideas, in terms of which he has understood his universe.

So far as the West is concerned there have been two: The first is the idea of the personal God. This conceived the universe as controlled, created, and managed in every way by an all-seeing father-figure who was both creator and judge. For several thousand years we in the West have felt that this being was in the background of us and all that we do. In some ways it was a rather uncomfortable idea, and many people became atheists because they didn't like to feel that someone up there was watching them all the time. I have a friend who is a Catholic, a rather humorous Catholic, and she has in her toilet affixed to the pipe that connects the tank to the seat, an eye, and underneath it is written in Gothic letters "Thou, God, Seest Me." This idea is in many ways consoling: to believe that the universe does have a heart and that that heart does care, that not even a sparrow falls to the ground without the Father knowing it.

But if at the same time this Father who loves all is a stern judge and works on the principle that "this is going to hurt me more than it's going to hurt you," it becomes after a while too much of a good thing. People feel bad, and I mean that rather technically. So there was a great revolution in the end of the 18th century and during the course of the 19th century to get rid of this Father. He was just too much, at least in the popular conception of his nature.

And so we replaced the theory of the universe with the intelligent heart with the theory, or I will say the *myth*, of the universe as a completely mindless mechanism, and intelligence and love and values are to be found only inside the human epidermis. We are accidents in this world, rather unfortunate accidents since we are susceptible to pain. We are able to anticipate disaster and dread it; we are like mice caught in a cotton gin, because this universe consists principally of rock and fire, which are inimical to human flesh and nervous systems, and here it is! The best that we can do is to try and beat this natural mindless teetotum into submission to our wills by all the technological power at our disposal.

This is a very curious thing. The first crisis in religion you might say, was the crisis of the 19th and early 20th centuries, when this theory of the universe became more plausible to intelligent people than the old theory of the Father-God. Nobody ever disproved that there was God-the-Father, but after a time we got a conception of the universe which somehow didn't seem to go with that conception. The thing was revealed by modern astronomy to be too enormous, too complicated, too staggering to the imagination to be accounted for by what was popularly conceived as the old gentleman on the golden throne.

So during the early part of this century the main task of Christians who still wanted to be Christians and Jews who still wanted to be Jews was to try and find an apologetic, and this they did in one of two ways. Either they retreated into stubborn obscurantism and fundamentalism and said, "What the church says is true," or "What the Bible says is true, and it must be taken literally, and you must close your minds to any scientific ideas, because they are the work of the devil," or else they went to another extreme and they watered their religion down until almost nothing was left of it but a moral code. And that became peculiarly insipid because you would go to church Sunday after Sunday and hear nothing but—said in 52 different ways — "Dear people, you should be good." And of course nobody knows how! (We all know we ought to be!)

As this century went on things started up again. To begin with, the conceptions of science became much more sophisticated than Newtonian mechanism. Ideas from the Oriental philosophies filtered into the West (increasingly since the second world war); and they showed that it is possible to have a religious attitude of the world which does not require superstitions or ideas utterly inconsistent with the scientific view of the cosmos. At the same time the scientists abandoned the Newtonian mechanism and began to give us a still more startling picture of the universe than we've ever had. So there comes still a second crisis which at this time is profoundly affecting almost every denomination of the Christian Church and the Jewish faith. The revolution in Roman Catholicism is going to have the most far reaching results. We are going to see the practice and teaching of Christianity transformed beyond belief. But in rather strange directions. Not, as you might suppose, the old-fashioned watering down.

Now I want to go back to compare once again these two great myths. There is really no reason why one should be truer than the other. There is no reason why the idea of the mechanistic universe should be more plausible than the idea that it is created by a loving father. What actually these two ideas represent is the idea of the people who want to put the universe "up" and the idea of the people who want to put the universe "down." There are some people who want to say about life in general, "Hooray!" There are other people who want to say, "So what? It's just a bunch of junk." That means they're of cantankerous disposition or else they want to appear to be hard-boiled. Now people who want to appear hard-boiled are usually people who have been frustrated in love. "No one is going to tread on *my* feelings again!" Or they have been disappointed in life and they want to say "Ah shucks" to the whole thing. "It's just a dreadful business and I want to advertise myself to all comers as a hard headed, realistic person who faces the facts." You notice we always talk about hard facts; we never talk about soft facts. (There are lots of soft facts — like girls.) There is a kind of person you run into in the academic world who is what I call a porcupine. He emphasizes *precision* and *rigor* and *intellectual discipline.* He rattles, he doesn't have any flesh on him.

Of course, the opposite kind of personality is rather gooey by comparison. He is a romantic. The other fellow tends to be a classicist. The romantic says of the classicist, "The trouble with you is that you know all the words and don't know the music. You just have no juice in you; you're not alive." The classicist says back to the romanticist, "You are disgusting; you're mushy, you're undisciplined, you're vague, you're a mess." The person who takes the attitude that the universe outside

124

man is just a mindless mechanism, is acting a part; he's playing a role, he's showing off himself as a person who faces facts and is strong and not sentimental and doesn't go in for wishful thinking. He says of the people who believe in religion, "Why, you're just a bunch of sentimentalists; you just want to comfort and console yourselves that everything will be all right, so you project your mama and papa onto the structure of nature—which is quite witless—and comfort yourself with this illusion."

But the thing that won't work in this theory is that it makes the old mistake, which is still almost indigenous to Western thought, of looking at man in the universe as a stranger. In the words of the poet Housman, "I, a stranger and afraid, in a world I never made." But this is plain bunk. Our conversations still reflect this nonsense because we say, "I came *into* the world." You didn't, you came *out* of it. You are as much a symptom of the solar system as the flower is a symptom of the plant on which it grows. Just as an apple tree apples, this universe *humans.* And the thing it humans isn't unintelligent; that is, if human beings are intelligent. If we start out with the supposition that we are intelligent — and I don't think that is too outrageous a premise—you can't go on to think about an intelligent organism living in an unintelligent environment, because the organism and the environment go together. If the organism is a symptom of the environment, if we can consider our environments as a unified field of behavior in which we are behaviors, patterns of motion, then if we are intelligent, so is the environment. If apples grow on a tree, the tree is fruitful.

So it becomes necessary to conceive ourselves once again in an intelligent universe, but not as strangers in it, not as if the world were a tree with bare branches, and we had come from afar like a flock of birds and sat down on it. We grew out of it like leaves. So *you* grow out of the world because a being as complex as a human being cannot survive, cannot live, cannot emerge even, except in an extremely complex environment. He depends upon all the varieties of beings around him, on the insects and their complicated games, on the plants, birds, the gases in the atmosphere, the balance, the exact position of the earth in relation to the sun, the cosmic rays — everything. All that goes with peopling. This, then, is a *peopling* organization. It also *birds*, it *flowers*, it *fruits,* it also *mountains,* and so on. So let not the finger

accuse the hand of clumsiness, because we are just as much of the cosmos as fingers are to the hand. We are in fact something it's doing, just as the ocean is waving, so each one of us is the cosmos, the whole thing waving and saying, "Yohoo, I'm here!"

This view, which you might call the ecological view of the world, ecology being the science that studies the relationship of organisms to their environments, is strangely in common with a view of the world which might be called mystical and which flourishes very much in the East and to a slightly lesser extent in the West. There is a kind of experience called mystical experience, a transformation of consciousness in which the individual comes to feel himself as something which the whole works is doing. He feels, in other words, that deep within his real being, his real identity, is the totality of the universe. Reality itself. He would sometimes call it the *godhead*.

He doesn't ordinarily know this and experience it, just as you are not ordinarily aware of the action of your pineal gland or precisely what is going on in the neurological structure of your brain. That happens below the threshold of consciousness. For example, what about your heart beating? Is this something you do, or is it something that happens to you? Now we don't ordinarily say in English, "I beat my heart." We look upon it as something which goes on inside us which we don't understand and to that extent isn't really us. But actually from another point of view your heart is very essential to you. It is the center of your organism although you are not aware of it in the ordinary way. You wouldn't naturally be aware of the fundamental depths of yourself because they're very difficult to turn around to look at. Without the aid of a mirror you can't see your eyes. You certainly can't bite your own teeth. You can't scratch the tip of this finger with the tip of this finger. So the center of things, the very root and ground, remains relatively unknown.

But there are moments in which sometimes it seems to rise to the surface, when the deep utters its voice and suddenly you wake up and say, "Good heavens, I thought I was just me. It seems that I go back to all eternity, but I'd forgotten it." According to theory, you see, the Lord, the *self* they call it, the *Atman*, is the root of everybody and is playing games. And the big game that it's playing is hide and seek. That, after all, is the fundamental game. Or you can call it lost and found. Thus, when you play with a baby, you take a book out and you put it in front of your face, and you look out this way, then you look out that way, and you look out this way, and the baby starts to giggle — because the baby, being close to the origin of things, knows that that's the score.

So certain kinds of spiritual teachers like Zen masters and Hindu gurus often play a game with people which is kidding them into finding out who they really are. They might look somebody in the eye with a quizzical look and say, "Now, don't fool me. Don't fool me, old Shiva (or old Buddha); I know who you are." And the person says, "What? Me? Me? But I'm only Jimmy Jones." "Oh no, don't give me that line." Or another way is to look at you in a funny way and say, "Haven't you forgotten something?" And you wonder if you've got your necktie all right, or did up your fly, or got a hair out of place or something. And they look at you in that strange way and say, "Oh no, no. It's nothing like that. There's something very fundamental you've forgotten, something absolutely basic." Well, what could that be? You see, you're the old boy playing hide and seek, and you won't admit it.

But sometimes you see what Wordsworth called "intimations of immortality." Tennyson used to have this experience when he sometimes sat and said his own name to himself. He sat there and said, "Alfred, Alfred." And he got the funny feeling, "Really *Alfred*? Who *are* you?" And then suddenly it came over him; he suddenly knew that he was the eternal ground of the world, in disguise as Alfred Tennyson. To use Chesterton's expression, "But now a great thing in the street seems any human nod, Where move in strange democracy the million masks of God."

Now the difficulty about this in Western religion is that we have laid a great stress on the uniqueness of every human personality, and our religious background teaches us to regard any equation of the inmost self of man with God as blasphemous, as pantheistic. It makes God responsible for evil, and...it's a very dangerous idea. A person who really felt that might be a little crazy, and he might start thinking that he could control the universe and make people do what he wanted, because "I'm God." So this is the bugbear of pantheism.

But in certain ways, it makes much greater sense than looking at things the other way round. It is what I would call a stellarform conception

of things. You have here the idea of a thing like a star or a sea urchin, with a center and all the different spokes going out of it like a sun with its rays. The other picture is an inversion of that. You've got God evoking a universe out of nothing; it has no real connection with him. In the other, you have the idea of the center manifest and playing games, going through all sorts of adventures, just as you would, for example, if at night you could dream of anything you wanted. What would you do? You would do what human beings have done through all the centuries when they dream — whether they dream in their sleep or whether they dream by writing plays and stories: they go on adventures. They invent villains. There's always a villain to every drama. But in drama, there's a proscenium arch or a stage, and the message of that arch to the audience and the message of the stage to the audience is What's going on here is only a play. But the actor is going to try and make you feel that it's not a play at all. He's going to try and make you sit on the edge of your chair with horror, or to weep, or to roar with laughter, as if all this were real life.

So you might say, if the Lord or the Self or the universe is the best actor of all, *he* or *it* puts on a show that takes himself or itself in. And he thinks it's really going on. But all play is in a way an illusion. Illusion is magic. Illusion is art. And to say that something is an illusion is not to put it down. It could be perfectly well to put it up.

You know the story about the Greek painting competition: In ancient Greece there were two painters who were decided by a group of judges to be the best and they were to submit paintings to see who would be the prize winner. One painted a grape vine, and he did it so realistically that the birds started banging into the painting trying to pick the grapes. Then everybody looked at that and they said, "Good heavens, look at that. How could anybody do it better?" So they said, "Come, let's see the other painting. Unveil it." He said, "Unveil what?" He had painted a curtain. And he was given the prize because, whereas the other one deceived the birds, he deceived the human beings. The great artist is always the illusionist.

Then likewise, if you could dream every night everything you wanted, you would first fulfill all your wishes. You might have concerts and orgies; you fill your life with love affairs, your house with dancing girls, and feasts and fast cars, and wonderful clothes, and fantastic hairdos. But after

126

a while you would say, "Well, well, let's have an adventure tonight. I'm going to rescue a princess from a dragon." Well, to have a good adventure, you must make a pretty terrible dragon, and it must be touch and go whether you'll get it. Then, also, you could dream in one night that you were living a whole lifetime. And then you could try a trick of making dreams so horrible that when you woke up it would be a colossal relief. Now suppose that's what's going on. It's not in the least implausible. After all, the nature of existence is rather diaphanous. It seems hard but it's vibrations. It's a great electronic jazz. And it could possibly just be switched on and off the way you change stations on the radio. So if you wanted to go on another plane, click, there you'd be. From this standpoint it might appear that you dropped dead.

This idea is actually creating inroads into Western religion. During the past fifty years and maybe a little longer, we've changed our figure of speech when we're talking about spiritual or important matters of that kind. We used to say of religious people, that their character was lofty and that their thoughts were very high. High thinking, plain living — remember? We don't say that anymore. We speak of them as deep and profound. Paul Tellich in his theology calls God the *ground of being,* and says this is in the dimension of depth. He would say that a profound person, a person concerned with the deep things of life, could not possibly be an atheist. He generally thinks, therefore, if you think that life is important, if it's not just frivolous, you are approaching the dimension in which God is. And you see by changing the metaphor, which is a form of myth, to the profound, the deep, he has put the ultimate reality in the center, rather than the periphery. Heaven is on high. Heaven is out there. But what is deep is central and central to us all. To use an ancient medieval phrase, in this sense God would be that circle whose center is everywhere, and whose circumference is nowhere. The poem of Alfred Noyes, I remember, ' "Where," said the King, "Oh where I have not found it." "Here," said the dwarf and music echoed, "Here." "This infinite circle hath no line to bound it. Behold its strange, deep center everywhere." ' Likewise in Tellich (who after all is a Lutheran).

In the English Church there has been a great stir created by the Bishop of Woolich who wrote a book called *Honest to God.* This created an uproar in England because everybody said, "Good heavens, here is a bishop who doesn't believe in God." He said it is not necessary for a Christian or a Jew to believe that God is someone out there or up there. And he takes up Tellich's idea and says God is fundamentally you. It's the basis of you. But this is the tendency.

Now something also is happening at the same time. In almost every Catholic cathedral in France, there has been a change. It used to be that the altar was at the far east end of the church, and at the celebration of mass, the priest went up to it, turned his back on the congregation and made mysterious mutterings, while the congregation knelt in their pews and said their rosaries. All that has now been reversed, and you will find the altar at the center of the cathedral with the pews or chairs arranged so as to surround it on all sides. That is a very elegant symbol of an interior revolution. In other words, in the old design of the church, it was built on a figure called basilica. Basilica means the court of the king. If you think of God by analogy with politics, with royalty, you will find the monarch, surrounded by his guards and attendants, and you come crawling on your knees. That's so you can't suddenly run forward and fight; you're safe on the ground. And so, this was the way the church worked. There was the throne of God, the altar, with the ministers in front, and everybody on their knees groveling because the image that had gone into the old idea of the father was the image of the king of kings, the omnipotent Lord who dwelleth in light unapproachable.

But there is another image running around at the same time. Not only the idea of the kingdom of God, but the idea of the tree of life, the body of Christ, the vine and its branches. That idea is quite different in structure. It is not political; it's *organic.* Body, tree, vine. Gradually there is a movement within Christianity to bring out its organic imagery as distinct from its monarchical and political imagery. When the altar goes to the center, watch out. The center of gravity of the whole thing has changed. With that center of gravity will go a change in our own inner feeling, namely (whether we get it from our study of science, or whether we get it from Oriental religions, or all of them together) Western man will begin to feel at home in the world.

He will begin to feel that he belongs, that he is not a stranger, and that his heart is not simply something inside his chest, but it is the entire universe living and changing forever.

Do you agree?

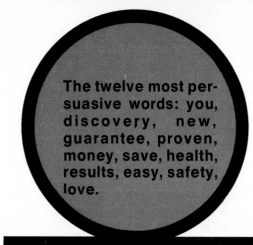

The twelve most persuasive words: you, discovery, new, guarantee, proven, money, save, health, results, easy, safety, love.

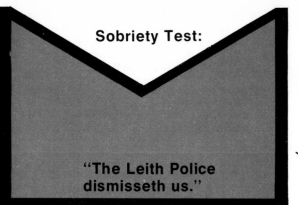

Sobriety Test:

"The Leith Police dismisseth us."

(If you stumble, don't drive.)

The spirit lives in the word of language and in the mythical image without falling under the control of either. What poetry expresses is neither the mythic word-picture of gods and daemons, nor the logical truth of abstract determinations and relations. The world of poetry stands apart from both, as a world of illusion and fantasy — but it is just in this mode of illusion that the realm of pure feeling can find utterance, and can therewith attain its full and concrete actualization. Word and mythic image, which once confronted the human mind as hard realistic powers, have now cast off all reality and effectuality; they have become a light, bright ether in which the spirit can move without let or hindrance. This liberation is achieved not because the mind throws aside the sensuous forms of word and image, but in that it uses them both as *organs* of its own, and thereby recognizes them for what they really are: forms of its *own self-revelation.*

"This is just therapy, mister. I'm a chremato-phobic."

Though the following words seem to have the same structure, *ad* plus a base, five of them are sometimes misspelled. Which ones are they? What causes the misspelling?

adverb adjacent adapt
adjourn adhere
adjust adjective
admire advocate adjudicate adorn

The tendency to misspell these words is a sign of
a. intelligence,
b. stupidity,
c. ignorance,
d. both a and c,
e. all of the above.

Effervescent enough bedcovers, your fiddlestick out!

1. **NEAZZ**
2. **BHALPEAT**
3. **TNHNYICYSNICORH**
4. **RPOCYCYARHPT**
5. **GNAYALO**
6. **ARNOJUL**
7. **TEMEHIGNENTNL**
8. **NARIB**
9. **DUJECIERP**
10. **NAGEULAG**
11. **COPYNIST**
12. **TARTSNEP**
13. **TACTSBAR**
14. **PATHEORM**
15. **MOAT**

Here are fifteen key words from this chapter. Unscramble them.

Review:

Team A supplies any word, idea, title or bit of trivia from this chapter. Team B tries to block by responding with an item also from this chapter which is as far removed from Team A's choice as possible. Then, to win, Team A must create a meaningful connection between the two. Team B starts round two, and so on.

Some of the words in the left-hand column are first names and some are last names. Match them with the correct first or last names in the right-hand column.

a. Agnew
b. Hodey
c. Transit
d. A-million-miles-for-one-of-your-smiles

____ 1. crow
____ 2. donkey (Spanish)
____ 3. donkey (German)
____ 4. rabbit
____ 5. horse
____ 6. sparrow
____ 7. asp
____ 8. aardvark
____ 9. rat
____10. collie
____11. egrets
____12. raven

e. Shane
f. Greeley
g. Magnon
h. Pidistra
i. Melon
j. Stark
k. Miss Otis
l. Frank Lloyd

Anagrams:

Choose a key concept from this chapter and list the letters of the word vertically. Then find a word for each letter to illuminate the concept. Probe each others' selections.

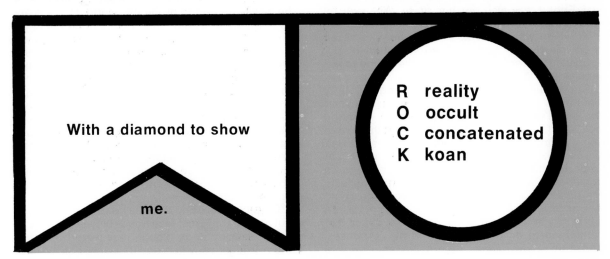

With a diamond to show me.

R reality
O occult
C concatenated
K koan

129

"How is school going?"

"Rough. I'm caught between a hard place and a rock."

The Story Thus Far

Eno could see himself in no mirror, however brightly polished; no words could define him, however cunningly shaped and arranged. Though he knew that a reflection referred to something that was Eno, it was also *not* him at all. Whatever he said he was, he was, and yet he wasn't at all. *What, who, when* was he? Was it really he who asked these questions? Was there even a question to ask? Propelled forward as he was, was there time to ask a question? WHAT WAS GOING ON?

Suddenly he emerged on a strange, totally unfamiliar planet, an Energy and Atom Recycler through Temporal Holography, ('earth'), knowing neither who he was nor how he had got there. Had some angry god banished him to this chaos? Had he been selected as a special intelligence agent to probe this alien soil light years from home, to somehow master it and return with his cache to the data banks of a non-physical world he could not at present even remember? Nothing made sense. Sense itself did not make sense. Sense had something to do with stimuli and his responses, and, out of awareness, he grasped that he was equipped with nerve endings that were nothing more than tools he was using to collect stimuli and figure out this puzzle. He knew that nerve endings themselves were *not* Eno. And yet, perhaps . . . . If he *had* been sent to probe this world, to study and to understand it truly, then naturally he could not 'know' it merely by observing. His intelligence was not specialized to observe in the first place. If there were beings in this planet, he would have to adapt his intelligence to something approximating the tools they presumably possessed.[1] To understand them, he would have to be one of them—completely; he must not even know that he was a spy. Possibly those who sent him might monitor the process, perhaps tag him somehow so that they could retrieve him at the optimum moment. But tagging would not really be necessary because he would always be obvious to his own kind in their own structuring system.

Possibly, then, Eno's identity was out in the open, but neither the target race nor he himself were capable of sensing it, as though they were tuned to a radio frequency which couldn't pick him up even

[1] If you think this is a joke, see ''The Origin of Laughter,'' Chapter 5, p. 294

though his waves were all about them. He thus might penetrate the target race, taking on more and more of their characteristics until the crucial moment when he would be yanked home for analysis. But that was only one of the limitless possibilities of the riddle of his essence.

Eno was dimensionless. He did not belong to a place. He did not belong to a time. He had no length, no breadth, no thickness. Nor was he subject to time. Any form he achieved might seem to alter, but Eno himself always had been and always would be. He had entered this world through a crack in the time shield. One moment he was nowhere and the next he was physical, as though someone had twisted a kaleidoscope and Eno was the image produced. It was not so much a matter of travel as it was a matter of coming into focus or of being translated to another radio frequency. Suddenly, so it seemed, there was a new bias toward form and structure with a thrust toward definition, toward becoming finite. This urgency to define necessitated senses. He began specializing his nerve endings and developed a complete sensorium. Through its agency he became, or seemed to become, concrete. Senses were a means of differentiating, of separating, of setting up distinctions, billions of them, every particle separated from every other by a sensing structure whose nature it was to see isolates. This planet existed through differentiation ("This is different from that."), through the emergence of things, the separating of one thing from another—and putting them together as well! Eno was an emergencee, emerging from the galactic 'mother' through the uterus of what his senses identified as the 'human' form. Immediately he began his research. Since he did not even know that he was a spy, he investigated automatically, to begin with. He sharpened his Early Yield External Sensors ('eyes'). Out of the grey blur, he forced entities to emerge, identifiable separations from the vast general jumble. From a few trifling particulars, he deduced general laws. Falling was dangerous. Eating was desirable. These were nerve-ending 'concepts', felt but not intellectually known. He identified a nippled nutrient sack and grew himself flesh and bones, perfect camouflage for a dimensionless fellow. He became one with time and space. Every planet day new floods of data poured into his Master Integrator of Nervous Data ('mind'), where he automatically began to create a time-space first approximation of his surroundings, his own Boundary Of Dimensional Yin Yang ('body') being part of that structure. And each dis-covery hid him from himself more and more completely! Nonentity had merged with entity. The investigation had begun, and no one suspected a thing. Birth was so ordinary, just another emergencee.

For Eno, the validity of the parts of the sensorium (nose, taste buds, finger tips) was unquestioned. That which worked was true. If one thing failed, he tried another and didn't think about how real or 'true' it was. Only that which promoted his own toehold on the planet was important. Out of the sensorium grew a knowledge of the Synthesis of the Entire Life Force ('self'). He had to be totally 'self'ish or become overwhelmed by the great wash of 'things' pressing against the flimsy dikes of his new flesh. Eno was not conscious of the dangers. His flesh took charge, touched and assimilated. He did not know this knowledge, this 'nourishment' was his lifeline. His body did the work, and for him it was child's play! Literally. He laughed. He fondled, tasted, smelled, played constantly with sounds he could make with tongue, air, oral cavities.[1] He developed depth perception. He sensed warmth and burning, coolness and the pain of ice. Locomotion became vital. He grew himself 'muscles' and forced himself to master Articulated Regulators of Manipulatory Skill ('arms') and Locomotor Extensions against Gravitational Supremacy ('legs').[2] He had become some thing, an entity, but his mind did not know it.

If there *were* watchers, they would have known the immensity of the experiment. The spy Eno was embarked on frighteningly dangerous recognizance *in complete ignorance*. He was hypnotized by the reality of appearance. Each planet day it appeared that he brushed aside another veil and disclosed more and more facets of this shimmering planet.[3] It was all a matter of interstices, of course, intersections of electromagnetic force fields, but within the perception centers of this alien structure (his body) appearance was the only reality. Finally, in the third year of his new time sense, Eno made one of the most startling

131

[1] "She holded the baby rabbits and we patted them," Chapter 2, p. 78
[2] See "The Oldest Human," Chapter 2, p. 112
[3] See "Diamonds for tea time," Chapter 2, p. 116

of his discoveries: his *own* identity. He had been busy dis-covering things out there; he now dis-covered his self. "I am!" he thought.[4]  This discovery launched him toward the next leg of his journey.

During the first stage of his planetary probe, when his senses automatically fondled the world so that he 'knew' it on his nerve endings, Eno's experiments with sound had paid off in a magical assortment of talismans, Wave Ordinates Revealing Dharma Signs ('words') and 'concepts' capable of giving him balance on this slippery sensate flow, a surfboard for riding out the waves. He could shape air and call nourishment to his lips for energy replenishment. He began to capture the world in this symbolic network. He mastered the linguistic code nearest at hand. The power it gave him over his perceived world was amazing. He spent most of his waking hours playing with and perfecting this new instrument. One network of intersecting concepts he identified as his *self*. That bundle of ideas had been given the code name *Robert*, but of course that referred only to the space-time mask Eno wore. *Robert* referred to the energy system of bones and kidneys, nose and fingernails. To *be* was to be *physical*. Was that the solution to his identity? Was Eno really physical? When he became *defined*, when he became *Robert*, did he cease to be Eno? Did nonentity cease when entity emerged? Were being and nonbeing one thing?[5]

His parts were at once instruments for knowing reality and reality itself. The dancer and the dance were identical, inseparable, for one could not *be* without the other. This new magical 'language' was a probe for exploring, but it created that which was explored as well. The tool shaped the craftsman. Just as his new 'eyes' had filtered the continuum of color and presented his mind a 'reality' of only one sector of the spectrum, what he perceived through the language tool was limited *by* the tool. Language pinpointed the intersection of things, showed where the connections were, but it also determined what would be considered to intersect. It was a structure system which gave him a handhold on the planet, but was it *the* planet, or were there many planets superimposed on each other. If Eno had entered the planet structured as a tree, it would have been tree 'reality' he would have experienced: different sensors, different filtering, different planet. What was *really* going on?

During his eighth planet year, Eno learned how to use "*What if . . .?*" Till then he had seen directly; *he* was the center, and everything connected at that center. Now he discovered how to *imagine* himself seeing from locations other than the one on which he actually stood. This gave him tremendous leverage, for he could now play with the world mentally as he had been obliged to do physically in his earlier stage. First he had known the world physically; then, through language, he could say, "This *is* . . ." Now he could say, "What if . . .?" He found that he did not have to touch things to experience them. He could look at the top of a cube and imagine its other faces, determine how many sides there were without touching the cube. Certain misspent adventures with associates enabled him to see five dots on top of a die and figure out that two dots would likely be on the bottom. Now he could *imagine* how something would be, how it would feel, by letting his mental fingers explore it. His major experiments now were mental. He could sit still and carry out the same work that his sensorium had had to do before. He began to use his body in a new way, to check, to validate, his imaginings. "If this happens, and this happens, then I'll bet this would be the result." He would then test it physically. Naturally, during this period, his autostructure (his body) sustained damage. One of his A R M S fractured at peak stress when he tested his balance theory on a unicycle. His digital manipulators sustained burns, cuts, bruises and abrasions during his probes of wood, metal, clay, and stone. He sent repair cells to the affected areas, oxidized the raw surfaces, grew Superficial Coverings of Abrasions and Blemishes ('scabs'), and went on developing his mental grasp of the physical world. He began to see that his own senses could limit and even mislead him. But he could get cross references by imagining the world from other angles. How would it work if he experienced the situation not as human Robert but as, say, structure system "tree"? How would the problem shape up if he looked at it as though he were a snail, a buttercup, or other human structure systems? He began to real-ize a many-centered planet and beheld its strange, deep center everywhere. And he extended his own senses, too, with microscopes and telescopes. A vast cross referencing system developed.

This entire displacement stage, the "What if . . .?" stage, exactly paralleled that in which his senses and muscles had identified and shaped a world for him. His mental 'senses' now probed this world.

You're it, Chapter 2, p.82   , Chapter 1, p. 44
Chimp no chump, Chapter 2 , p.144

He formed relationships and the relationships *were his reality*. For him, all that he noticed was all that there was. Though he used these processes well, they were as automatic as those of his earlier stages. The eye could not see itself. The planetary searcher had done his job perhaps too well, for he had entered into the life of the planet and had assumed its characteristics completely. But *was* he air and water, emotions, sentiment, intersections of force fields?[1] 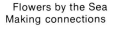 At this stage the question did not occur. And without the question he could not discover his self, the Eno, and would continue to imagine himself to be merely the surface being Robert. As long as he stayed within the psychophysical structure system he had defined, the combined mind-body package, the question *could not* occur to him. He felt he had completed his search. He was mistaken, of course, in fact about as far from the answer as he could get; and if he had stopped there the probe would have failed. But he did not know this. He felt he had finished, and he grew listless and depressed. Without something firing his mind and body, he felt pointless. Was he to sit out his remaining planet years working crossword puzzles and drinking beer? The planet, the lustrous jewel that had so fascinated him, now seemed more and more tarnished and drab. There was nothing to do, nothing to integrate. The fires burned low; the energy construct Eno began to decompose into nothingness. Still he lingered, pointlessly.

Finally, the probe almost burned out, reduced to re-runs and insomnia, Eno found himself thrust toward a new genesis and discovered that the end was only a second approximation. Boredom and chance (mere accidents or part of a calculated design?) hurled him into a totally foreign region of the planet. He went on an adventure. Does it matter how it came about, where he went, with whom, or why? Such 'accidents' do happen, and for some planetary explorers a new birth occurs. Throbbing through his body-mind came the old question: WHAT WAS GOING ON? His entire being responded. Nerve endings tingled with new data; his mind lurched into gear. In this far region of the globe he walked among beings of his own 'human' class who appeared to experience a *different reality!*

Does it matter whether they were aborigines or university professors? They did not see as Eno saw or as the others of his party saw. The beings among whom they now found themselves selected *other* things to notice, and they summed them up strangely.[1] One way for Eno to cope with this peculiar world was to translate it into terms of his old reality and force it to fit into his old construct. That was a common way out of the dilemma. Several of those in his party chose to do that. But as someone had said, translations are like the back side of a tapestry, and Eno preferred the front. If their reality was just fixed up to fit his, it was no longer *their* reality. Later he would even have to question *this* preference: Why wasn't everyone sparked by the same drive to penetrate this new construct? Why did some cling to the old pictures?

At the moment, however, something more important occupied his thoughts: Everything he 'understood' had been assimilated *outside of his conscious awareness*. That was a shock. He had had his 'eyes' open, his 'mind' open, but within a closed-off system! his group's private, isolated world. How did he know that any of it was true? This brush with a *foreign* reality forced the likelihood that his reality was no more accurate than theirs. Wherever the truth might be, it would have to encompass *all* realities. That meant three billion human realities, tree realities, whale realities, rock realities, galaxy realities. Following the method he had used for his first two approximations of reality, he began with himself, with his own picture of reality. He began probing his own probes, his own self-construct. He had constructed reality twice, through his sensors and symbolically; now he must go over the same ground again. What *was* going on? His picture, his awareness, was based on his sense perceptions, *sentience*, the capacity to sense. But these were specialized devices for filtering out very restricted kinds and amounts of information. Visions of infra red and ultra violet, fourth and fifth dimensions, base two and base twelve in the numbering systems, came now to shake the basis of his world. Now the entire perception network, the senses and the mind itself must be questioned. He set out without a map along an unknown road.[2]

[1]   Flowers by the Sea
Making connections

[1]   Parsnips for presidents
[2]   Eldorado

134

Our birth is but a sleep and a forgetting;
The soul that rises with us, our life's star,
    Hath had elsewhere its setting,
        And cometh from afar;
    Not in entire forgetfulness,
        And not in utter nakedness,
But trailing clouds of glory do we come
        From God, who is our home.

WHAT WAS YOUR ORIGINAL FACE

Anything I Make Is A Drawing Of My Soul!

For the mind only that can be visible which has some definite form. What are the processes by which an object gains this form in our minds?

DRAW YOUR SOUL HERE.

(A visual metaphor)
Compare your drawing with someone else's; explore their significance.

FLASH!

135

ENO'S QUEST TAKES HIM TO SWITZERLAND

ENO'S JOURNAL:

February 17 Planet Time

Things are starting to fall into place now. The distance between the molecules in my body is just as far as the distance from star to star. I can't learn anything by just going out; I have to let some in: metaphors, poetry, fiction. But I have to take them one at a time. We have to bring things in as they are and not pervert them into something that only our own narrow minds want them to be. We have to accept everything (things, people, and words) just as they are and react to them after analyzing them with a clear, unobstructed mind, putting nothing in, leaving nothing out. Then, after we have done that, we come forth with our thoughts (clear and unobstructed).

The path from my sensing antennae to my intuition has been overgrown for centuries. Can intuition be my third eye? Maybe I can get some clues from some of the other observers. It begins to appear (*appear*! everything hinges on seeing) that true sight is insight . . .

Well, *Sensation* (Sense Perception) Tells You That Something Exists. *Thinking* Tells You What It Is. *Feeling* Tells You Whether It's Agreeable Or Not. *Intuition* Tells You Whence It Comes And Where It's Going.

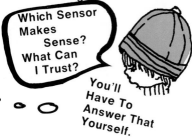

Which Sensor Makes Sense? What Can I Trust?

You'll Have To Answer That Yourself.

IN SOUTH SHAFTS-BURY, VERMONT, ENO TALKS TO A POET

Then There's Something Deeper Than How I Feel?

The Curse Of Our Poetry Is That We Lay It On Things. Anything You Do To The Facts Falsifies Them, But Anything The Facts Do To You—Yes, Even Against Your Will; Yes, Resist Them With All Your Strength — Transforms Them Into Poetry.

Sure. Feeling Is *Part* Of The Perception But Beyond It Is The Cold, Emotionless Quiet Truth.

The Doctor In Geneva Said Something Like That. I Think It's In My Notebook. Ah, Yes, Here It Is.

He Was Talking About A Teacher Of His . . .

136

...My grief and rage threatened to get out of control. And then something happened that I had already observed in myself several times before: there was a sudden inner silence, as though a soundproof door had been closed on a noisy room. It was as if a mood of cool curiosity came over me, and I asked myself, "*What is really going on here*? All right, you are excited. Of course the teacher is an idiot who doesn't understand your nature—that is, doesn't understand it any more than you do. Therefore he is as mistrustful as you are. You distrust yourself and others, and that is why you side with those who are naive, simple, and easily seen through. One gets excited when one doesn't understand things.

WHAT'S REALLY GOING ON HERE?

I Guess If I Want The Truth I'd Better Get Rid Of All My Prejudices.

Wrong! I'd No More Set Out In Pursuit Of The Truth Than I would Of A Living Unless Mounted On My Prejudices.

Then, You Can't Know The Truth!

You're Right In A Way. Everything You See Is An Image Of Reality. Here's Another Hint About Prejudice: The Canadian Woodchoppers Make Their Own Axe Handles, Following The Curve Of The Grain, And They're Strong And Beautiful. You See, There Is A Prejudice In The Wood To Go That Way. False Living Is Putting Curves On Things That Haven't Any Curves.

Yes. Without Bias (Or You Could Call It Prejudice) You Could Not See At All. All Seeing Is Selective. At Best We See Images, Abstracts From What's Totally There. So You Can't Really See With Your Sensors.

B L A T

And Pretending I Don't Have Curves When All The Time I Do.

For Helve's Sake!

137

I've Been
Seeing Images
All My Planet
Life. Better Take
Another Look.

Your eyes shade
The door-ways
I stand in.

The edge of the palm
Slides

Along the eye-lid
Touching

(SPECIMEN B)

What I can't name
Or remember.

FROM ENO'S
DIFFERENTIAL INTEGRATOR KNAPSACK:

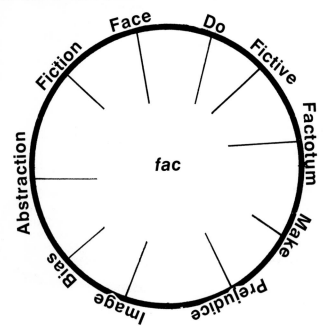

fac

Face
Do
Fictive
Factotum
Make
Prejudice
Image
Bias
Abstraction
Fiction

MANDALA ICE CREAM
(SPECIMEN A)

He looked at his own Soul with a Telescope. What seemed all irregular, he saw and shewed to be beautiful Constellations; and he added to the Consciousness hidden worlds within worlds.

S.T.C. *Notebooks*

(SPECIMEN C)

A + B = _____

B + C = ___

A + B + C = _____

138

ENO HITS THE ROAD

FOLLOW THE WHITE ARROW

"Nothing We
Love Overmuch
Is Ponderable
To The Touch."
—W.B.Y.

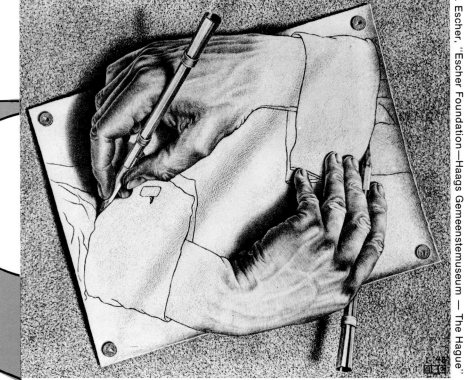

M. C. Escher, "Escher Foundation—Haags Gemeentemuseum — The Hague"

(SPECIMEN D)

Change this 8 square figure to 6 squares by moving 6 matches and the resultant diagram to 5 squares by moving 4 matches.

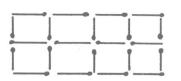

OM

Within The Mind Even 'Real' Events Like Sights And Sounds Must Become Psychic Events, Whose Ultimate Nature Is Unknowable.

C.J.

MOBIUS STRIP

SUNSET STRIP

I'll Take It.

I'm Another Look!

(SPECIMEN E)

I had always been impressed by the fact that there are a surprising number of individuals who never use their minds if they can avoid it, and an equal number who do use their minds, but in an amazingly stupid way. I was surprised to find many intelligent and wide-awake people who lived as if they had never learned to use their sense organs: They did not see the things before their eyes, hear the words sounding in their ears, or notice the things they touched or tasted. Some lived without being aware of the state of their own bodies.

There were others who seemed to live in a most curious condition of consciousness, as if the state they had arrived at today were final, with no possibility of change, or as if the world and the psyche were static and would remain so forever. They seemed devoid of all imagination, and they entirely and exclusively depended upon their sense-perception. Chances and possibilities did not exist in their world, and in "today" there was no real "tomorrow." The future was just the repetition of the past.

I am trying here to give the reader a glimpse of my own first impressions when I began to observe the many people I met. It soon became clear to me, however, that the people who used their minds were those who *thought*—that is, who applied their intellectual faculty in trying to adapt themselves to people and circumstances. And the equally intelligent people who did not think were those who sought and found their way by *feeling*.

"Feeling" is a word that needs some explanation. For instance, one speaks of "feeling" when it is a matter of "sentiment." But one also applies the same word to define an opinion; for example, a communication from the White House may begin: "The President feels . . . ." Furthermore, the word may be used to express an intuition: "I had a feeling as if . . . ."

When I use the word "feeling" in contrast to "thinking," I refer to a judgment of value—for instance, agreeable or disagreeable, good or bad, and so on. Feeling according to this definition is not an emotion (which, as the word conveys, is involuntary). *Feeling* as I mean it is (like thinking) a *rational* (i.e., ordering) function, whereas intuition is an *irrational* (i.e., perceiving) function. In so far as intuition is a "hunch," it is not the product of a voluntary act; it is rather an involuntary event, which depends upon different external or internal circumstances instead of an act of judgment. Intuition is more like a sense-perception, which is also an irrational event in so far as it depends essentially upon objective stimuli, which owe their existence to physical and not to mental causes.

SPECIMEN F

E + C = _____

(SPECIMEN G)

FILLER MATERIAL

For the sea urchin, the submarine world consists merely of the tactile and chemical experience associated with its prey and its mate, and the dimming of light associated with the approach of an enemy.

A.H.

ARTIFICIAL

LIGHTS

Perplexity came to her from the beast. "What is this light? What is this dark? What have asked this, too. They say that it is night now on our planet, and that they cannot see. They have told us that our atmosphere is what they call opaque, so that the stars are not visible, and then they were surprised that we know stars, that we know their music and the movements of their dance far better than beings like you who spend hours studying them through what you call telescopes. We do not understand what this means, to see."

"Well, it's what things look like," Meg said helplessly.

"We do not know what things look like as you say," the beast said. "We know what things are like. It must be a very limiting thing, this seeing."

"Oh, no!" Meg cried. "It's—it's the most wonderful thing in the world!"

"What a very strange world yours must be!" the beast said, "that such a peculiar-seeming thing should be of such importance. Try to tell me, what is this thing called light that you are able to do so little without?"

"Well, we can't see without it," Meg said, realizing that she was completely unable to explain vision and light and dark. How can you explain sight on a world where no one has ever seen and where there is no need of eyes? "Well on this planet," she fumbled, "you have a sun, don't you?"

"A most wonderful sun, from which comes our warmth, and the rays which give us our flowers, our food, our music, and all the things which make life and growth."

"Well," Meg said, "when we are turned toward the sun—our earth, our planet, I mean, toward our sun—we receive its light. And when we're turned away from it, it is night. And if we want to see we have to use artificial lights."

"Artificial lights," the beast sighed. "How very complicated life on your planet must be ...."

SPECIMEN H

141

TEN-MINUTE COMFORT STOP

We may one day have to revise the long-standing belief that man is the only animal capable of forming a self-concept.

Babies usually give signs of recognizing themselves in mirrors when they are about 10 months old. Children with little exposure to mirrors or to other reflecting surfaces may take longer. Retarded persons may never reach this stage of self-recognition.

Most animals react as though mirror-images were other animals. Put a baby chick alone in a box and it will start to chirp loudly, with up to 100 or more high-pitched distress calls per minute, and make fluttery attempts to escape; put in another chick, or a mirror, and the distress calls and flutters dwindle almost to zero.

A chicken will eat more in the presence of another chicken than it will in isolation; it will similarly eat more when it is keeping company with a mirror. A female pigeon lays fewer eggs in caged isolation than it will in normal surroundings; put a mirror into the cage and the egg-laying will increase just as though another pigeon were present.

Some male squirrel monkeys, confronted with mirrors, have erections. This response might appear to be narcissistic, but appearance deceives; it is the typical antagonistic reaction to an unfamiliar adult male.

Mirrors can reinforce instrumental learning. Some fish can learn to navigate a simple maze when the only reward is exposure to a mirror. And a monkey will learn to open a door to get a brief look at its reflection.

Many fishes, birds and primates react to mirror images with direct attack or displays of aggression. R. H. Smythe reports that a chaffinch will attack its own image in the shiny hub cap of a parked car, and fight it to exhaustion.

A human being has to learn to recognize his own reflection. The first time he looks at himself he is most likely to think he is seeing another person. Only with experience does he realize that the fascinating person he sees is himself. When a person who was born blind or near-blind gains sight, he at first responds to his reflection as he would to another person.

The question arose in my mind whether animals born in the wild and never exposed to mirrors could learn to recognize their reflections once they had been exposed to mirrors.

How could I bridge from my bias point to communicate what I see to the beast? He doesn't have the same kind of sensors. But I think he 'sees' inside somewhere, and that's what I think I really do, too. So, if I want to convey the idea of a green-eyed strawberry blond to him, there must be a way to get beyond his alien sensors . . . .

PROBLEM: To communicate green-eyed strawberry blond to one who has never had my kind of eyes. (Readers: What is the answer?)

I studied two male and two female jungle-born champanzees, each about four years old. I put each into a separate cage in a separate room and placed a full-length mirror outside each cage for eight hours a day. Without being seen, I could look directly at the chimpanzee's reflection in the mirror through a hole in the wall.

During the first couple of days all the chimps reacted socially to their reflections—in general they responded to the mirror images as though they were other chimps. By the third day, however, social responses almost disappeared—the chimps began using the mirrors to inspect and manipulate parts of their bodies that they could not otherwise see, and to make grotesque faces at themselves. One would study itself in the mirror, then watching its reflection intently, pick bits of food from between its teeth, manipulate its genitals and pick its nose.

It was evident to me that the chimps recognized themselves, but I ran an objective test to check my

142

G + H =

F + H =

STOP

its ear and eyebrow, then inspected its fingers. Another smelled its fingers after touching its ear.

Later I tried the same dye experiment with two other wild-born chimps. When they were daubed with dye and confronted with mirrors for the first time in their lives they responded as if they were seeing other chimpanzees, making no attempt to touch their red marks.

I also worked with stump-tailed, rhesus and cynomolgus monkeys using similar tests with mirrors. All responded socially to their reflections and apparently none learned to recognize itself, even after two or three times more mirror exposure than the chimps had.

Thus the ability to recognize oneself in a mirror may be limited to man and the great apes (I have not yet tested other apes—gorillas, orangutans, or gibbons). Such decisive difference between monkeys and chimps is unusual; most investigators have found only slight quantitative differences from species to species among the primates they have studied.

The sociologist C. H. Cooley proposed in 1912 that the concept of self arises out of social interaction and that the way we perceive ourselves results from our watching how others respond to us. Perhaps this explains the fact that chimps raised in isolation never recognize their reflections even after extended exposure to mirrors; they have never had the experience of interacting with another organism that looks like the one in the mirror. In line with this notion, we found that when two young isolated chimps underwent three months of social experience—physical contact—with each other and had additional exposure to mirrors, they showed signs of self-recognition. And there is the recurrent story of the female chimp raised in the home of two psychologists who taught her to sort photographs into two stacks—human beings in one and animals in the other. One day the psychologists slipped a picture of the chimp into the stack; when she came to her picture, she unhesitatingly placed it in the human stack.

Self-concept has been considered uniquely human, and so treated in the disciplines. Any attribution of the characteristic to another species usually is considered anthropomorphic and softminded. But if recognizing oneself in a mirror implies a rudimentary concept of self, my chimpanzee experiments suggest that the concept should be reevaluated—at least with respect to some of our fellow primates.

observations. After their 10th day of exposure to the mirrors, I anesthetized the chimps and while they were unconscious applied an odorless non-toxic dye to the upper ridge of one eyebrow and the top half of the opposite ear of each. I had tested the dye on myself; it could not be felt after it dried. Of course, the chimps didn't know they had been marked and they couldn't see their dyed spots without a mirror.

When the animals were back in their cages and fully revived, I watched each for 30 minutes to see if it would touch a red mark spontaneously. Only one did—it touched an ear—but that looked accidental. When I put the mirrors back in front of the cages the chimps became agitated, peering at their reflections much more than they had before. In 30 minutes each chimp touched the red marks an average of seven times. One, Janice, touched the red marks 21 times in the first 10 minutes. Another stared into the mirror, touched the red marks on

(SPECIMEN I)

143

In the cave of ice
where light was fearful

we have been dwelling
these months,
under the icicles.

But this is only
an image; need for an image;

for where we crouched, hiding,
was an amorphous place

far down below language.

T or F: Language is a way
of seeing.

CHIMPANZEES

HALF A CONCEPT L A T E R

Language is
one form
in
the
shape of
another?

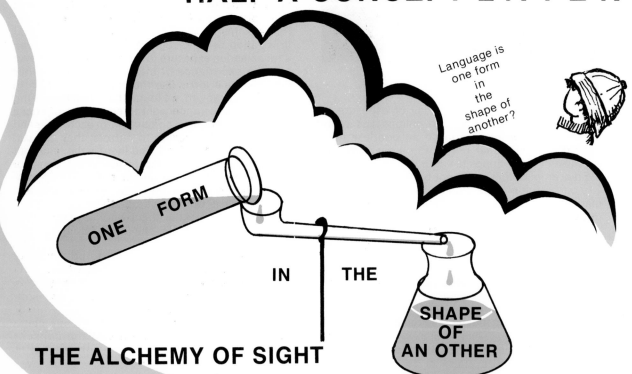

ONE FORM

IN THE

THE ALCHEMY OF SIGHT

SHAPE
OF
AN OTHER

144

NARCISSUS
(For once, then something)

FLOWERS BY THE SEA

A WINDOW
TO THE
MIND?
FROM
THE MIND?

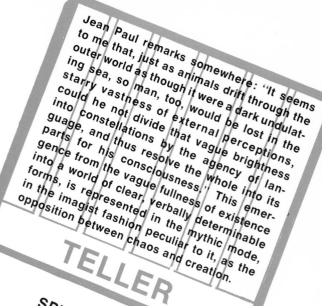

Jean Paul remarks somewhere: "It seems to me that, just as animals drift through the outer world as though it were a dark undulating sea, so man, too, would be lost in the starry vastness of external perceptions, could he not divide that vague brightness into constellations by the agency of language, and thus resolve the whole into its parts for his consciousness." This emergence from the vague fullness of existence into a world of clear, verbally determinable forms, is represented in the mythic mode, in the imagist fashion peculiar to it, as the opposition between chaos and creation.

TELLER

SPECIMEN J

SPECIMEN K

Afterwards,
I licked my cold image
off the window pane

the moon calls
my children
to fly from
dreamless balconies

images which burst
like capsules of blood
in the steam heat

swarming, chattering
alphabetical couplings
filling the silence
around my eyes

moments refuse to remain
in this unnamed season.

The Coming of Wisdom with Time

Though leaves are many, the root is one;
Through all the lying days of my youth
I swayed my leaves and flowers in the sun;
Now I may wither into the truth.

(SPECIMEN L)

J = C? Y?

J, C, E are $\cong$. T or F?

145

IMAGE

"The style is the man. Rather say the style is the way the man takes himself."

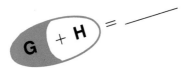

G + H = ___

Describe the taste of an avocado to someone who has never tasted one. Then let him taste it, to validate your description.

F + H = ___

The life of every plastic surgeon who has been in practice more than ten years has been threatened at least once by a disappointed patient.

Describe *taste* to someone who has no taste buds (a Martian, perhaps.)

OPEN, SESAME

M. C. Escher, "Escher Foundation—Haags Gemeenstemuseum — The Hague"

SPECIMEN M   Title

_____

Create a good title for this etching.
A good metaphor is an explication. T or F?

HINT

HINT

Sense impressions are what the self receives from its
encounter with the not-self.
All sense-impressions are images.
But, the impression then becomes a thing in itself.
It becomes incarnate—flesh.
A metaphor is not about something. It *is* something.

Those
Look Like
Figures Of
Speech

147

M + J = _____

ART IS A MEDIUM OF REFLECTION...

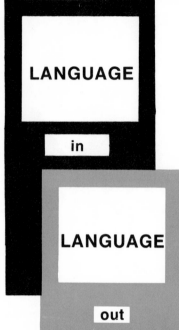

LANGUAGE

in

LANGUAGE

out

from the very first act of touch, or hearing, or sight, we are brought in contact, not only with a visible, but at the same time with an invisible universe.

(SPECIMEN N)

Say It In Words

Verbalize your experience of this drawing (one form in the shape of another). No more than 75 words. Compare your results. Choose winners. Identify the bases for your choices.

YANTRA

SCIENCE IS NOT A COMPENDIUM
OF DATA: IT IS A PROCESS OF DISCOVERY.

Mythology has come to mean falsehood or 'fairy tale language' in our time. But myth, for primitive man, means a *true* story; it is not an idle tale, but a hard working active force.

Nikos Kazantzakis described myth as 'the simple, composite expression of the most positive reality.' No telescope or mirror can yet reveal such truth. Although mythology today seems a victim of the scientific spirit, it is, on the contrary, through scientific development that the ancient myths (truths) are being actualized. We are finding as a result not less but more mystery in the structure of the universe. The age of myths is not past. It may never be.

PERSONA

Actually All Language Is Myth. So All We Have Is Myth And Painting

Choose one, both, or neither:

Paintings are attempts to give the soul (self) flesh.
Myths are attempts to make the soul (self) physical.

T or F: The painting on this page is scientific.

T or F: This painting is an eye? This painting is a

third eye?

What is the *sound* of a sunset?

Pregnancy Test

Check all correct statements.

You can conceive

___ 1. a baby.
___ 2. an idea.
___ 3. a house.
___ 4. your self.
       (I'm my own grandpa.)
___ 5. an image.
___ 6. an apple.
___ 7. perfume.
___ 8. harmony.
___ 9. chaos.
___10. pattern.

You are very sexy. T or F?

(SPECIMEN O)

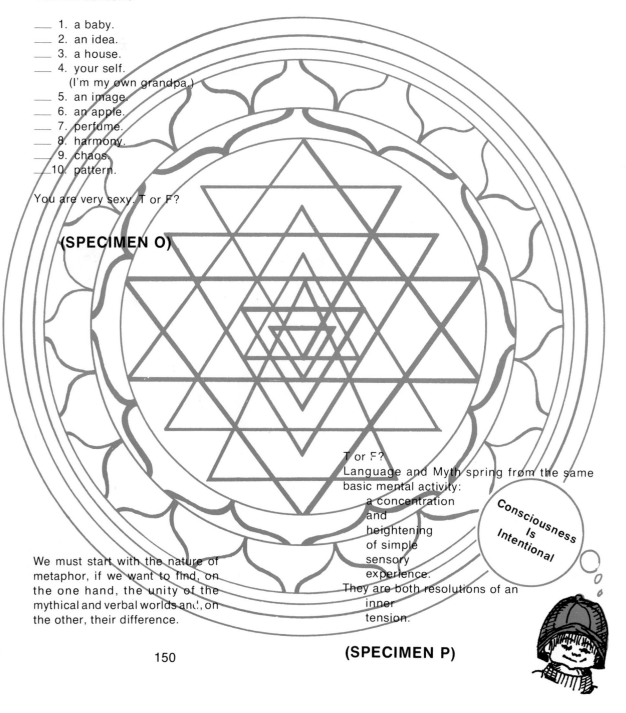

T or F?
Language and Myth spring from the same
basic mental activity:
a concentration
and
heightening
of simple
sensory
experience.
They are both resolutions of an
inner
tension.

Consciousness
Is
Intentional

We must start with the nature of
metaphor, if we want to find, on
the one hand, the unity of the
mythical and verbal worlds and, on
the other, their difference.

150

(SPECIMEN P)

TONATIUH

Locate as many of the following as you can. Then work in groups to see if together you can locate them all.

AZTEC CALENDAR

CUAUHXICALLI: La Piedra del Sol
(Specimen Q)

INNER CIRCLE

Tonatiuh's (the sun's)
1. crown
2. nose
3. pendant
4. ear-rings
5. necklace
6. golden hair
7. wrinkles
8. tongue (like an obsidian knife)

SECOND CIRCLE

9. Sun of the wind
10. Sun of the rain and fire
11. Sun of water
12. Sun of Jaguar
13. Sun of earthquake
14. Claws of the sun

THIRD CIRCLE

15. Flower
16. Crocodile
17. Male ape
18. Water
19. Cane
20. Rain
21. House
22. Buzzard
23. Wind
24. Lizard
25. Earthquake
26. Snake
27. Young plant
28. Eagle
29. Obsidian dagger
30. Rabbit
31. Deer
32. Death
33. Jaguar
34. Dog

OUTER CIRCLE

35. God of Turquoise (God of Night)
36. The Sun
37. Front claws, eye, and brow of the fire serpents
38. Tail of the fire serpent
39. Bundle of herbs with flower buds
40. Four bound ribbons of paper (amatl)

41. Plate of the consecration and dedication of the stone
42. The flaming sign in each of the segments of the fire serpent
43. Flames on the backs of the fire serpents

OTHER ITEMS

44. 'V' figures, signs of solar light beams
45. Symbols of splashed blood nourishing the flames at the backs of the fire serpents.

Physical Description of Others We Left Out:

46. _____
47. _____
48. _____
49. _____

50. _____
51. _____
52. _____
53. _____

Hey, All Paintings Are Myths Too.

WHITE CLAY EATER

NESTLED among the foothills of a very large mountain was a little valley. Starting somewhere upon the mountain a little brook flowed through this valley.

Along the banks of this little brook grew many trees that bore fruit and nuts in season. The birds and wild animals liked to come to this little valley to feed on the berries and grass that grew there. And when they had their fill, the animals would lie down in the shade of the trees to chew the cud and rest.

This little valley was the home of a very beautiful young woman named Twilight who lived there all alone.

One day when she went to swim in the brook and to listen to the singing birds, a voice called to her from among the trees. She went into the shadow of the trees to see who had called to her. In the shadow she saw a young man. He stood there without speaking. She did not know his name. Without speaking he made love to her and when he went away into the shadows she still did not know his name.

Until this time her name had been Twilight. But now she was called White Clay Eater because every day until her twin sons were born there was nothing she wanted to eat except white clay.

When her two boys were born she named them Sun and Moon.

These were the two children of White Clay Eater.

They grew up in the little valley where there were no other people. They knew how to find wild fruit for food and they became good hunters, killing only game they needed for meat.

When these two strong young men grew old enough to have wives, their mother began to make a plan.

There were no other people in the little valley, but not very far away up the river there lived a man named Wyhum-newhe who had two beautiful daughters.

It was the plan of White Clay Eater to call these two beautiful girls into her valley so that her sons could take them to be their wives.

So she called to her boys and said:

"Moon! Sun! Toward the southwest near the east end of the mountain two days and one night away there is a swampy place where bamboos grow. I want you to go to that place and cut two

152

Art is what warms the world.

EROTICA

Network censors refused to let Dick Cavett show a three-minute film called *Orange*. The film shows an orange with a finger peeling it and then a mouth munching it.

T. or F. The metaphor which is not affective is not worth sensing.

"As a dancer, I'm really a great orator." Isadora

ORANGES

Oh, how perfect death
computes an orange wind
that glows from your footsteps,

and you stop to die in
an orchard where the harvest
fills the stars.

pieces of bamboo and bring them back to me."

As their mother told them to do, the two boys went out two days and one night away to the swampy place and cut two pieces of bamboo and brought them back to her.

For two days and one night White Clay Eater worked on the pieces of bamboo carving them into flutes. And when the flutes were finished she called to her boys and said:

"Sun! Moon! Now I will teach you a certain tune that must be played on these flutes exactly as I teach it to you."

And she taught them a certain tune that was very beautiful.

Then she said: "I would like to hear how your music sounds from a distance. So go out across the valley and stand on that big rock over there and play."

Moon and Sun took their flutes and went out across the valley and stood on the big rock and played the music their mother had taught them.

White Clay Eater knew that always on this day of the year the two beautiful daughters of Wyhum-newhe came to bathe in a spring near the big rock. She also knew that the names of these girls were Morning Star and Evening Star.

As Moon and Sun played on their flutes, White Clay Eater listened and knew that her plan would succeed, so sweetly over the air came the tune she had taught them.

The two beautiful daughters of Wyhum-newhe were in the spring bathing when the music went out everywhere into the air.

Evening Star had gone into the water first and as her ears touched the surface of the water she heard the music! It came from the east. She listened for a while and then she said:

"Oh sister! Hurry and come into the water! I hear music coming over the air from somewhere!"

Morning Star got into the water and listened toward the east and toward the west. Then she said:

"I don't hear anything."

Evening Star said:

"Put your ears down to the surface of the water!"

Morning Star did, and she heard the sweet music coming from the west.

She listened for a while and then said:

"We must go now and see who is making such beautiful music!"

So they got out of the water and ran to their home and began to get ready to go away.

"*Finding* facts is no problem. You can easily discover that the word 'America' is stressed on the second syllable. But that fact is interesting ONLY if it tells you something about structure. What you're trying to understand in chemistry is the nature of matter, and what you're trying to understand in linguistics is the nature of language."

WHAT I'M TRYING TO UNDERSTAND IS THE NATURE OF ME!

WESTERN UNION

153

The simple composite expression of the most positive reality...

HMM...
A FIGURE
OF SPEECH!

Only gradually did I discover what the mandala really is: "Formation, Transformation, Eternal Mind's eternal recreation."

C.J. Jung

IF YOU ARE EGOLESS THE UNIVERSE ACTS THROUGH YOU.

154

"I know where you are going," said their father. "You are going to look for the music makers."

The girls did not have time to answer him. They went away to look for whoever it was that made such beautiful music.

After traveling for some distance, first to the east and then to the west, they came to a small house and a little man with a long nose met them at the door, and Morning Star asked:

"Do you know who makes that good music?"

The little man with a long nose said:

"Of course I know because I am the one who makes that music."

And Evening Star said:

"All right then, play us a tune so that we may know you are the one!"

The little man went to a dry old tree near his house and climbed up to the top of the tree and began pecking at it and making a funnly little rattling noise.

Then he came down out of the tree, and Morning Star asked: "Is that all?"

The little man said:

"Early in the morning I sing that way and everybody seems to like it."

The girls told him they were sorry but that was not the music they were looking for, and they left the little man and went on their way.

After they were out of sight the little man slapped himself on the side of his head and said:

"What a fool I have made of myself!

I could have told them I know where that music is coming from! I could have told them where Sun and Moon live! Now those girls will tell everyone what a fool I am and everybody will laugh at me!"

Morning Star and Evening Star went on until they came to another house where they were met by a man with a big round head and big round eyes who asked them: "Who do you want to see?"

The girls said:

"We want to see who makes the most beautiful music we have ever heard. Do you know who it is?"

"Certainly I know because I am the one who makes that music."

And the girls asked:

"Will you play us a tune so we may know that you are the one?"

The man with a big round head and big round eyes went over to a cottonwood tree near his house and settled himself on one of the highest branches and began to hoot.

After hooting for a while he came down, and Evening Star asked: "Is that all?"

"Yes," said Owl, "That is all. Early in the morning before the sun is up I hoot and people for miles around seem to enjoy it. It doesn't sound so good this late with the sun shining, does it?"

The girls said: "No."

They said it was not the music they were looking for, and they went on.

After they had gone, Owl said:

"I am a hog!

Wanting to hog the glory I don't deserve! I could have told them I know where that music is coming from! I could have easily directed them to the house of Moon and Sun.

I enjoy hearing that music myself every morning after I have stopped hooting. What's the matter with me!

People used to call me a wise old owl. Now they can call me pig!

They were such nice looking girls, too!"

He hit himself on the side of the head and said:

"Me and my big mouth!"

Morning Star and Evening Star went on and on. They went first to the north and then to the south.

At last they came to a little valley nestled among the foothills of a large mountain where a little brook flowed and birds sang in the trees and wild animals fed on the grass.

In front of a small house a woman sat weaving a basket. She said to the girls:

"I have been waiting for you for a long time."

It was White Clay Eater.

Over the air from the big rock beside the spring came the music of the flutes of Sun and Moon playing the tune their mother had taught them to play.

Morning Star and Evening Star listened to the music and they knew at last who was making the music that led them away from the home of their father, Wyhum-newhe.

And so Moon and Evening Star were married, and Sun and Morning Star were married, and they all lived happily ever after.

WANTED
SPACIOUS
PERSONALITY

I have frequently seen people become neurotic when they content themselves with inadequate or wrong answers to the questions of life. They seek position, marriage, reputation, outward success or money, and remain unhappy and neurotic even when they have attained what they were seeking. Such people are usually confined within too narrow a spiritual horizon. Their life has not sufficient content, sufficient meaning. If they are enabled to develop into more spacious personalities, the neurosis generally disappears.

If I could only live at the pitch that is near madness
When everything is as it was in my childhood
Violent, vivid, and of infinite possibility:
That the sun and the moon broke over my head.
Then I cast time out of the trees and fields,
Then I stood immaculate in the Ego;
Then I eyed the world with all delight,
Reality was the perfection of my sight . . .

ENO'S JOURNAL

As far as my self is concerned (soul) the senses never do anything more than supply images to the differential integrator. Those don't come to the brain intact. They are encoded at the nerve endings as electrical signals. So in effect we have a tape of impulses which the mind (not brain) *interprets* as a picture of what is 'out there.' At this stage nothing is known; it is *surmised*, guessed at, supposed. Add to this uncertainty the limitations of my sensors. Bees, for example, can see ultraviolet....

DOWAGER: That doesn't look like a fish

PICASSO: Madam, it is not a fish. It is a painting

Metaphor

An attempt to give the flesh soul

Language

SPACIOUS PERSONALITY GAME

Form a circle with one person in the center to whom each participant says, "I like you because..." and completes the sentence. Go on until everyone has been in the center. Always make eye contact while speaking.

    Later explore the implications.

WHAT DO YOU DO TO IT?

Warm monkeys
Play in my soft field
    Mirrors of air
        Shatter on their backs
            Their paws
on the eighth cry

WHAT DOES IT DO TO YOU?

WESTERN UNION

"Is there any WORD from the Lord?"

WESTERN *UNION!*

WESTERN!

A METAPHOR IS SOMETHING.

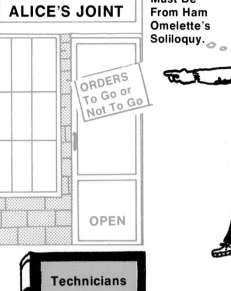

ALICE'S JOINT

ORDERS To Go or Not To Go

OPEN

Must Be From Ham Omelette's Soliloquy.

Technicians of The Sacred

SOFT SHOULDER

Without making an affirmation, without making a denial, say what this *is*. Decide who comes closest. Discuss the bases for your decision.

May 3, 1972

Dear Eno:

Some cultures think if you *take* a man's image with your camera, you have stolen his power. Other cultures think a 'picture' (and that includes paintings, sentences, photographs, and mirrors) is a mere place holder, like a numeral, and is not powerful in itself, but refers to something else. Which view do you prefer? Is the choice up to you? When is it good for an image to be alive; when is it good for it to be a place holder? To focus or not to focus, that is the question.

Lamont Cranston

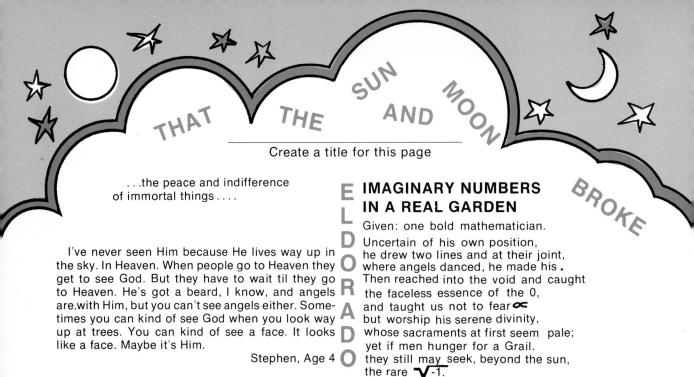

Create a title for this page

...the peace and indifference
of immortal things....

IMAGINARY NUMBERS IN A REAL GARDEN

Given: one bold mathematician.

I've never seen Him because He lives way up in the sky. In Heaven. When people go to Heaven they get to see God. But they have to wait til they go to Heaven. He's got a beard, I know, and angels are with Him, but you can't see angels either. Sometimes you can kind of see God when you look way up at trees. You can kind of see a face. It looks like a face. Maybe it's Him.

Stephen, Age 4

Uncertain of his own position,
he drew two lines and at their joint,
where angels danced, he made his .
Then reached into the void and caught
the faceless essence of the 0,
and taught us not to fear ∞
but worship his serene divinity,
whose sacraments at first seem pale;
yet if men hunger for a Grail.
they still may seek, beyond the sun,
the rare $\sqrt{-1}$.

ELDORADO

And here are trees and I know their gnarled surface, water and I feel its taste. These scents of grass and stars at night, certain evenings when the heart relaxes—how shall I negate this world whose power and strength I feel? Yet all the knowledge on earth will give me nothing to assure me that this world is mine. You describe it to me and you teach me to classify it. You enumerate its laws and in my thirst for knowledge I admit that they are true. You take apart its mechanism and my hope increases. At the final stage you teach me that this wondrous and multicolored universe can be reduced to the atom and that the atom itself can be reduced to the electron. All this is good and I wait for you to continue. But you tell me of an invisible planetary system in which electrons gravitate around a nucleus. You explain this world to me with an image. I realize then that you have been reduced to poetry: I shall never know. Have I the time to become indignant? You have already changed theories. So that science that was to teach me everything ends up in a hypothesis, that lucidity founders in metaphor, that uncertainty is resolved in a work of art. What need had I of so many efforts? The soft lines of these hills and the hand of evening on this troubled heart teach me much more. I have returned to my beginning. I realize that if through science I can seize phenomena and enumerate them, I cannot, for all that, apprehend the world. Were I to trace its entire relief with my finger, I should not know any more. And you give me the choice between a description that is sure but that teaches me nothing and hypotheses that claim to teach me but that are not sure. A stranger to myself and to the world, armed solely with a thought that negates itself as soon as it asserts, what is this condition in which I can have peace only by refusing to know and to live, in which the appetite for conquest bumps into walls that defy its assaults? To will is to stir up paradoxes. Everything is ordered in such a way as to bring that poisoned peace produced by thoughtlessness, lack of heart, or fatal renunciations.

Awareness is like sex. You start doing it, and then you get interested in getting better at it.

158

OM
is
Where The
Art Is

How does ENVISAGEMENT function? Do we see something and then analyze it? It is not a question of *what* we see in a certain perspective. It is a question of how we got that perspective in the first place.

OVER MY HEAD

A Marabar cave had been horrid as far as Mrs. Moore was concerned, for she had nearly fainted in it, and had some difficulty in preventing herself from saying so as soon as she got into the air again. It was natural enough: she had always suffered from faintness, and the cave had become too full, because all their retinue followed them. Crammed with villagers and servants, the circular chamber began to smell. She lost Aziz and Adela in the dark, didn't know who touched her, couldn't breathe, and some vile naked thing struck her face and settled on her mouth like a pad. She tried to regain the entrance tunnel, but an influx of villagers swept her back. She hit her head. For an instant she went mad, hitting and gasping like a fanatic. For not only did the crush and stench alarm her; there was also a terrifying echo.

Professor Godbole had never mentioned an echo; it never impressed him, perhaps. There are some exquisite echoes in India; there is the whisper round the dome at Bijapur; there are the long, solid sentences that voyage through the air at Mandu, and return unbroken to their creator. The echo in a Marabar cave is not like these, it is entirely devoid of distinction. Whatever is said, the same monotonous noise replies, and quivers up and down the walls until it is absorbed into the roof. "Boum" is the sound as far as the human alphabet can express it, or "bou-oum," or "ou-boum," — utterly dull. Hope, politeness, the blowing of a nose, the squeak of a boot, all produce "boum." Even the striking of a match starts a little worm coiling, which is too small to complete a circle but is eternally watchful. And if several people talk at once, an overlapping howling noise begins, echoes generate echoes, and the cave is stuffed with a snake composed of small snakes, which writhe independently.

After Mrs. Moore all the others poured out. She had given the signal for the reflux. Aziz and Adela both emerged smiling and she did not want him to think his treat was a failure, so smiled too. As each person emerged she looked for a villain, but none was there, and she realized that she had been among the mildest individuals, whose only desire was to honour her, and that the naked pad was a poor little baby, astride its mother's hip. Nothing evil had been in the cave, but she had not enjoyed herself; no, she had not enjoyed herself, and she decided not to visit a second one.

**Clouds come from time to time—
and bring to men a chance to rest
from looking at the moon.**

There is a strong empirical reason why we should cultivate thoughts that can never be proved. It is that they are known to be useful. Man positively needs *general* ideas and *convictions* that will give a meaning to his life and enable him to find a place for himself in the universe. He can stand the most incredible hardships when he is convinced that they make sense; he is crushed when, on top of all his misfortunes, he has to admit that he is taking part in a "tale told by an idiot."

159

She took out her writing-pad, and began, "Dear Stella, Dear Ralph," then stopped, and looked at the queer valley and their feeble invasion of it. Even the elephant had become a nobody. Her eye rose from it to the entrance tunnel. No, she did not wish to repeat that experience. The more she thought over it, the more disagreeable and frightening it became. She minded it much more now than at the time. The crush and the smells she could forget, but the echo began in some *indescribable way to undermine her hold on life.* Coming at a moment when she chanced to be fatigued, it had managed to murmur, *"Pathos, piety, courage– they exist, but are identical, and so is filth. Everything exists, nothing has value."* If one had spoken vileness in that place, or quoted lofty poetry, the comment would have been the same—"ou-boum." If one had spoken with the tongues of angels and pleaded for all the unhappiness and misunderstanding in the world, past, present, and to come, for all the misery men must undergo whatever their opinion and position, and however much they dodge or bluff—it would amount to the same, the serpent would descend and return to the ceiling. *Devils are of the North, and poems can be written about them, but no one could romanticize the Marabar because it robbed infinity and eternity of their vastness, the only quality that accommodates them to mankind.*

She tried to go on with her letter, reminding herself that she was only an elderly woman who had got up too early in the morning and journeyed too far, that the despair creeping over her was merely her despair, her personal weakness, and that even if she got a sunstroke and went mad the rest of the world would go on. But suddenly, at the edge of her mind, Religion appeared, poor little talkative Christianity, and she knew that all its divine words from "Let there be Light" to "It is finished" only amounted to *'boum.'* Then she was terrified over an area larger than usual; the universe, never comprehensible to her intellect, offered no repose to her soul, the mood of the last two months took definite form at last, and she realized that she didn't want to write to her children, didn't want to communicate with anyone, not even with God. She sat motionless with horror, and, when old Mohammed Latif came up to her, thought he would notice a difference. For a time she thought, "I am going to be ill," to comfort herself, then she surrendered to the vision. She lost all interest, even in Aziz, and the affectionate and sincere words that she had spoken to him seemed no longer hers but the air's.

... a shadow
Fell as he found
No spot of ground
That looked like Eldorado...

Language is not a matter of know-how established by habit. If you want to find out what it means to be a human being, you have to examine free creation within a system of rules, acquisition of knowledge within a framework of restrictive conditions imposed by the mind.

160

Elaine May can hear the cliche in a person's voice.

—Mike Nichols

WATCHING TELEVISION

Sounds are heard too high for ears,
From the body cells there is an answering bay;
Soon the inner streets fill with a chorus of barks.

We see the landing craft coming in,
The black car sliding to a stop,
The Puritan killer loosening his guns.

Wild dogs tear off noses and eyes
And run off with them down the street—
The body tears off its own arms and throws them
        into the air.

The detective draws fifty-five million people into
        his revolver,
Who sleep restlessly as in an air raid in London;
Their backs become curved in the sloping dark.

The filaments of the soul slowly separate:
The spirit breaks, a puff of dust floats up,
Like a house in Nebraska that suddenly explodes.

I think Jennie should have died of pneumonia

chewing gum for the eyes . . .

REEL ONE

It was all technicolor
from bullets to nurses.
The guns gleamed like cars
and blood was as red
as the paint on dancers.
The screen shook with fire
and my bones whistled.
It was like life, but better.

I held my girl's hand,
in the deepest parts,
and we walked home, after,
with the snow falling,
but there wasn't much blue
in the drifts or corners:
just white and more white
and the sound track so dead
you could almost imagine
the trees were talking.

I looked at his paintings and they skinned my eyes . . ."
—Gulley Jimson

Consider: When a metaphor becomes a sign, it is like a latent psychosis . . .

Before it's too late:

Combine words and pictures until you have restored the life latent in *orange* or *egg*. Explore the results.

Create a verbal or a visual 'figure' which would stand for Eno (or you) at the beginning of this chapter. Capture his essence. Compare and explore the implications.

161

The
Story Continues

Down an unknown road, but perhaps *not* without a map. For Eno's investigation of his own sensors, of what had been called sentience, opened the possibility that his search was not so random after all. There now seemed to be some pattern to his behavior coming from deep within. He was not driftwood but a homeing device. The gathering of data by the senses was not random but controlled, purposeful, intelligent. The body did not merely collect data as though it were a grain elevator or a museum. He saw that he put things together, that he integrated them, organized them into a framework, a system, that information was mere raw material. Even the smallest Fixing And Cross-referencing Trace ('fact') could exist only by interrelating with all other 'fact.' The framework was already operating in his own mind. That particular framework functioned well in human entities but would not suit a cat or a tree. They experienced their own realities.

It appeared, then, that a deep structure directed his movements toward a physical fulfillment of its potential. Even the smallest 'fact' (2 + 2) was a *general* concept. The slightest bit of information was the result of a bunching process. There had to be within him already a blueprint for quantities before 2 + 2 could trigger his mind toward the general idea of 4. The process seemed to work like a hologram, the three-dimensional laser picture any part of which could trigger the whole. Tape a laser picture, cut off any part of it, project it, and the whole image would appear. Likewise, the tiny fact of 2 + 2 was impossible to contemplate as an isolate, for it was embedded in a complete interrelated system. When Eno encountered such a 'fact' he had to step back far enough and toy with it enough so that the system in which 2 + 2 was possi-

ble came into focus—very much the way *he* had come into focus at the beginning of his planet probe. And the numbering system itself was not isolated from the rest of his picture either, for by examining the situation in which 2 + 2 was possible, he could begin to grasp the entire sentient process, the whole process of differentiating and integrating, of noticing differences and of putting things together. Just as a point entered reality through the intersecting of lines, any bit of data gained its existence through the intersecting of concepts. Thus, an accumulation of bits resulted in the concept of 1, and that 1 could only exist as *part* of a picture of reality, as part of a complete system.

So Eno began to turn his investigation away from the nerve endings inward toward the blueprint. Sensing was evidence that something inside was going on. It seemed that the instant the kaleidoscope turned and he entered into matter, became flesh, the impulse to generate a 'human' nature was already there and was adequate nourishment he would flesh out and fulfill that nature.

Now he began to guess an answer to one of his major questions. He had discovered that his senses were inaccurate and extremely weak. He could not see an atom; his temperature range was very narrow. How could his senses ever yield a true version of reality? When he apprehended (see pre-hensile) that the picture he was looking for was inside him, *already there,* sensing and perceiving took on new meaning. Sensors did not have to be absolutely accurate, for, if they triggered the right 'nodes,' Eno within himself would make up for any flaws and would activate his 'nature' himself internally. He now saw nerve endings as catalysts. He knew that the operation did not take place out there. For this

162

"No individual revelation is possible unless the whole of existence is itself an instrument of revelation."

surgeon to know where to operate, crude indicators were sufficient, mere traces would suffice.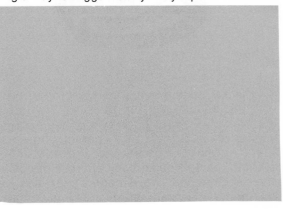

When Eno's research took this turn, he found himself in trouble with other 'humans.' They were satisfied with the evidence of the senses. That they were standing on a planet and that they were made up of atoms that were made up of space seemed irrelevant. "I'm sitting here on what I think is a chair, and that's enough. I don't have to go delving into the source of such ideas." To Eno, when one looked at himself so narrowly, he behaved narrowly and *felt* narrow. Because he did not see the world in its larger framework, such a person would always feel isolated and alone, would always be mis-taking his situation. For Eno, though the pain of experience was no less severe, indeed was even more intense, the large frame gave the struggle character. It was not wantonly absurd. As a Cosmos Held In Limited Dimension ('child') he had felt that the world he perceived did not exist for other people and had felt isolated and frustrated. It was only by following through till he could connect his perception to a total world, an inner world, that he could fulfill himself. The limited concept would likely have culminated in disaster, a grain wasting away in barren soil.

To say that he was sitting in a chair was the most incredible leap of faith that anyone could imagine. One was isolated within a limited and faulty sensing system; *every* thing was composed of fictional qualities. One *knew* nothing. Yet one 'sat in a chair,' a miracle of synthesis. That should have convinced the others. They had leaped to such conclusions countless times. But they seemed blind to their own sleight of hand.

In Eno's investigation there had been paintings, myths, mandalas, figures of speech, the whole structure of language—all pointing to what? He looked out and said, "That's a bush, and that's Eno, and that's God." It appeared that in this fashion he was classifying and organizing the *world,* but that was not the case at all. What he was doing was illuminating his own self. When Eno 'became,' there was a thrust within him; the pattern was already there. It was like the genetic code, but it was a non-physical thing. It seemed to be saying to him, "Eno, you're a kind of creature composed

of categories and patterns, and what you have to do is fill them in, to realize them." Thus, his fingers might crudely sense and report some shape. That signal, coupled with his mind, would yield 'desk.' It didn't matter that the signal was crude. All he needed was something to activate what was already there, to bring patterns into focus. For it was an internal world he was illuminating. It was the intuitive leaps his mind took which engaged and excited him; he would use anything he could get, however crude. He was a thrust toward lucidity, and that thrust could be triggered by dreams or . . .anything. Those leaps were not based on physical pnenomena; it was the other way around. One did not have to experience every single particle of the physical world.

But that led to another question. If traces were sufficient, what need was there for sharpening or atuning his senses. He knew the answer: For triggering to occur, experience had to be sharp, intense. Though the catalyst could be rough, it had to penetrate. Even though the senses were not the answer in themselves, he did have to send out sharply in order to receive sharply. It had to be a vigorous thrust. If he was not intensely fooling around, the insights, the leaps of lucidity, would not happen.

And language was part of (or the same as) all the things he had been thinking of. Language (metaphor) could not be less vigorous or less honed than the physical network. Sharpening up metaphors was like sharpening up the senses. (Were not the senses metaphors themselves?) Sharpening up one's use of language was like finding a way to trigger reality . . .Synapsis.

Create a verbal or a visual metaphor for Eno (or you) this far in his (your) journey. Talk over the results and explore.

See Chomsky, Chapter IV, p. 220

163

Man should be content with a few points to tip with the fine Web of his Soul, and weave a tapestry empyrean.

ENO TAKES OFF FOR PARTS UNKNOWN

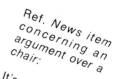
The third eye is amoral

GOOD   BAD

Ref. News item concerning an argument over a chair:

It's of old wood, resting, forgetting its tree, and its rancor is without power.

JOURNAL

If you are egoless the whole force of the universe acts through you. It is not you looking. *It* is looking.

..I gave the moral answer and I died...

Today we talked of morality. It's funny. Something we have taken for granted, something we had built on and guarded all our lives, and all it takes is an hour's conversation to see how vulnerable it all was. It seems that with the importance I had placed on it, I would have looked into it before now.

I can see that I colored the world with my morality and now I realize that it is not even my morality but my father's and my father's father's. I'm not seeing the world with my eyes, then. I'm seeing it through dead people's eyes. We don't stop to examine. We just accept as unquestionable those things that sound like they should be right.

"Having ideas that are neither pro nor con is the happy thing. Get up there high enough and the differences that make up the controversy become only the two legs of a body the weight of which is on one in one period, on the other the next. Democracy monarchy; puritanism paganism; form content; conservatism radicalism; systole diastole; rustic urbane; literary colloquial; work play. I should think too much of myself to let any teacher fool me into taking sides on any of those oppositions . . . I have wanted to find ways to transcend the strife-method. I have found some. Mind you I'd fight a healthy amount. This is no pacifism. It is not so much anti-conflict as it is something beyond conflict . . . ."

164

T or F.: The third eye *has* to be beyond morality.

Amoral is not immoral.

120 KINDS OF CORN-PONE

There was one thing that kept bothering me, and by and by I says:

"Tom, didn't we start east?"

"Yes."

"How fast have we been going?"

"Well, you heard what the professor said when he was raging round. Sometimes, he said, we was making fifty miles an hour, sometimes ninety, sometimes a hundred; said that with a gale to help he could make three hundred any time, and said if he wanted the gale, and wanted it blowing the right direction, he only had to go up higher or down lower to find it."

"Well, then, it's just as I reckoned. The professor lied."

"Why?"

"Because if we was going so fast we ought to be past Illinois, oughtn't we?"

"Certainly."

"Well, we ain't."

"What's the reason we ain't?"

"I know by the color. We're right over Illinois yet. And you can see for yourself that Indiana ain't in sight."

"I wonder what's the matter with you, Huck. You know by the *color*?"

"Yes, of course I do."

"What's the color got to do with it?"

"It's got everything to do with it. Illinois is green, Indiana is pink. You show me any pink down here, if you can. No, sir; it's green."

"Indiana *pink*? Why, what a lie!"

"It ain't no lie; I've seen it on the map, and it's pink."

You never see a person so aggravated and disgusted. He says:

"Well, if I was such a numskull as you, Huck Finn, I would jump over. Seen it on the map! Huck Finn, did you reckon the States was the same color out-of-doors as they are on the map?"

"Tom Sawyer, what's a map for? Ain't it to learn you facts?"

"Of course."

"Well, then, how's it going to do that if it tells lies? That's what I want to know."

"Shucks, you muggins! It don't tell lies."

"It don't, don't it?"

"No, it don't."

"All right, then: if it don't there ain't no two States the same color. You git around *that*, if you can, Tom Sawyer."

He see I had him, and Jim see it too; and I tell you, I felt pretty good, for Tom Sawyer was always a hard person to git ahead of. Jim slapped his leg and says:

"I tell *you!* dat's smart, dat's right down smart. Ain't no use, Mars Tom; he got you *dis* time, sho'!" He slapped his leg again, and says, "My *lan'*, but it was smart one!"

I never felt so good in my life; and yet *I* didn't know I was saying anything much till it was out. I was just mooning along, perfectly careless, and not expecting anything was going to happen, and never *thinking* of such a thing at all, when, all of a sudden, out it came. Why, it was just as much a surprise to me as it was to any of them. It was just the same way it is when a person is munching along on a hunk of corn-pone, and not thinking about anything, and all of a sudden bites into a di'mond. Now all that *he* knows first off is that it's some kind of gravel he's bit into; but he don't find out it's a di'mond till he gits it out and brushes off the sand and crumbs and one thing or another, and has a look at it, and then he's surprised and glad—yes, and proud too; though when you come to look the thing straight in the eye, he ain't entitled to as much credit as he would 'a.' been if he'd been *hunting* di'monds. You can see the difference easy if you think it over. You see, an accident, that way, ain't fairly as big a thing as a thing that's done a-purpose. Anybody could find that di'mond in that corn-pone; but mind you, it's got to be somebody that's got *that kind of a corn-pone* . . . .

What color is a fact?

What about *teacher*, *student*, one's *self*?

EMPTINESS

WORDS WITHOUT MUSIC

If you're anxious for to shine
In the high aesthetic line
As a man of culture rare,
You must get up all the germs
Of the transcendental terms
And plant them everywhere.

You must lie upon the daisies
And discourse in novel phrases
Of your complicated state of mind.
The meaning doesn't matter
If it's only idle chatter
Of a transcendental kind.

ROLE-PLAYING

A Woman Is . . .

First, list characteristics of women which are not also characteristics of men. Each member of the group must supply one characteristic.

Then, challenge each characteristic. Is it a valid feminine quality, or is it part of an arbitrary role?

Reflect on your findings.

SENSUAL PEDANTS

Book Notice:

CERTAIN KINDS OF BEHAVIOR AND OCCUPATIONS HAVE BEEN EXPECTED OF WOMEN FROM BIRTH; IT IS THEREFORE DIFFICULT FOR THEM TO BECOME AUTONOMOUS INDIVIDUALS.

Elizabeth Janeway, *Man's World; Woman's Place:*

In this book Janeway explains how society maintains itself by the use of roles and myths. She points out that individuals—of either sex—find it easier to adopt a ready-made self than to create one.

GLIB TOUCHERS

BLUE

NO MATTER WHAT COLOR

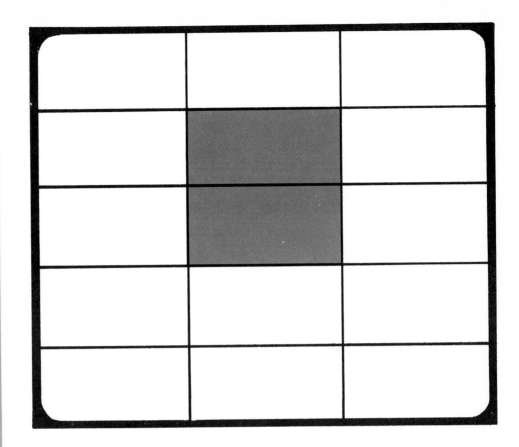

Choose one color: red, green, yellow, etc. Go through some old magazines and collect fifteen samples of the color you chose. Put them in the rectangles. What things do you notice about color? What do you notice about language?

to paint
is to love
again
by
Henry Miller

**MORALITY IS
LIKE THE
WORD GREEN**

Select a color. Everyone bring something that color for a display. Make a montage of these things.

Cherry blossoms, more
and more now! Birds have
two legs!
Oh, horses have four!

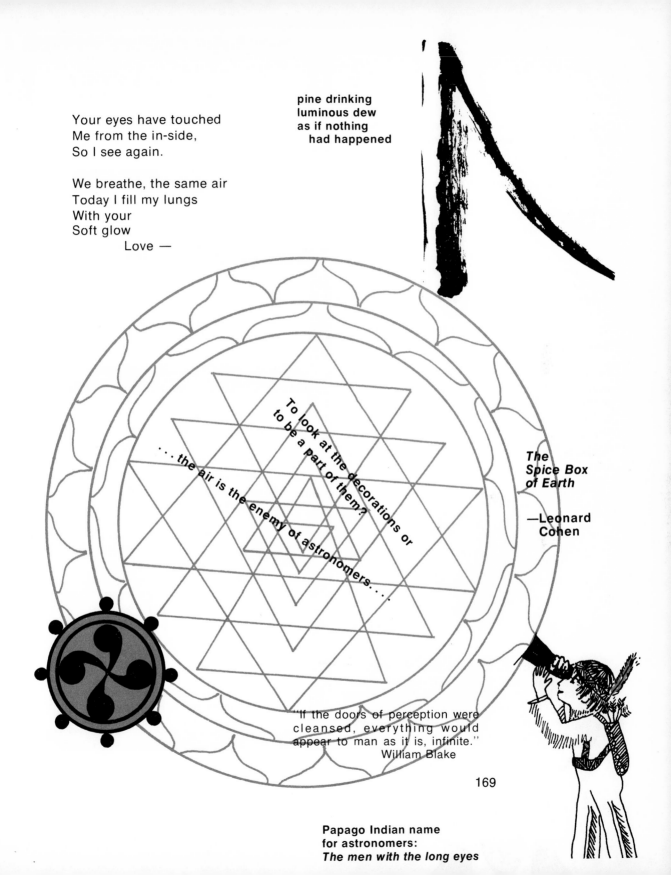

Your eyes have touched
Me from the in-side,
So I see again.

We breathe, the same air
Today I fill my lungs
With your
Soft glow
      Love —

pine drinking
luminous dew
as if nothing
  had happened

To look at the decorations or
to be a part of them?

. . . . the air is the enemy of astronomers. . . .

The
Spice Box
of Earth

—Leonard
Cohen

"If the doors of perception were
cleansed, everything would
appear to man as it is, infinite."
      William Blake

169

Papago Indian name
for astronomers:
The men with the long eyes

That Reminds Me:

Are Sounds Images?

One day we thought we would play with the sounds that can be made with paper and see what variety we could come up with and perhaps create some music with our new "instruments." One thing led to another. We next wanted to see what each sound reminded us of. Analogy. Someone noticed that almost none of us invented anything outside of what we were already familiar with. No fantasy, really.

This is the wrinkle we liked though: We used the sounds we had worked out as stimuli for stories each listener would create. We allowed the sound to be made and then wrote, then listened to the next and continued our stories. After we had developed our stories through about six sounds we stopped and read each version.

If you would like to see the sorts of things we became aware of through this process, try it yourself and afterward explore what happened.

The sound of literature (prose) takes place in silence. Literature, then, is non-verbal, like a painting. (T. or F.?)

MY HEART
BEATS
ME!

Acquiring the capacity to generate language patterns requires a positive, fantastic leap of intuition. It is too complicated to be taught systematically. The guess has to be made and the leap has to be taken. Clark Kent is an image of what we already are.

Makers of early sound movies soon learned that they had to make a track for the 'silence' of a room. What seemed like dead silence was not in fact silent at all, and viewers sensed an unpleasantly flat, dead silence when room noise was neglected.

Everyone sit silent for one minute. Then list on the board all the sounds you noticed.

In an anechoic chamber, a room made as noise-free as technology can devise, one can hear two sounds, one high and one low. The high is the listener's nervous system. The low is his blood circulation.

Try some films with the sound track turned off. Then with the 'wrong' track (from another film or a record). Devise your own sounds and then run the film and supply the sounds. What is the effect of being able to shut one's eyes but not the nose, ears, or other nerve endings?

LUTE
AB
SO
LY.

DO
YES
I
SIR.

"The living part of a poem is the intonation entangled somehow in the syntax, idiom, and meaning of the sentences."

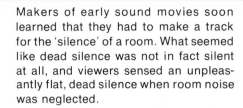

Which is thinner?
a cough
a sneeze

THOUSAND-MILE TUNE-UP

1.

Sense the ordinary scents in your classroom. Does paper have a scent? Do pencils? Ball points? See who can identify the largest number.

2.

Everyone bring something to smell. Keep it concealed. Close your eyes as one person passes his object under each nose. Each one describe the scent and then try to identify the source. Go through all the scents in this manner.

Next select any of the scents and everyone try to 'picture' it by choosing a visual image (metaphor) to stand for it. Thus, one girl associated her grandmother's hands with the scent of celery and onions. That was a private image. How could she have made it a public image or metaphor?

What is taste *for*?

"My pictures speak only when we both listen."

My hut in spring!
True, there is nothing in it—
there is Everything!
Sodo, 1641—1716

THAT REMINDS ME:

One time someone brought oranges for everyone in the class. They all peeled the oranges and ate them. The entire room took on the aroma of oranges. Class went on as usual, but a new dimension was added.

Another time the teacher brought a branch of juniper and handed everyone a sprig. Nothing more was said about it. During the hour, people held the sprigs and played with them. The scent permeated the room.

World through
my door
how wide
house how tiny
From outside

171

True or False:
Without your sense of smell a bite of apple tastes pretty much the same as a bite of potato . . .

TOUCHING

Everyone bring something
for people to
touch.
Everyone get the feel of
the first object
with your eyes
shut.
Use your finger tips
as
eyes.
First simply
feel
it.
Then try to identify
it. (Notice which sense
we rely on most strongly
for recognizing the
world. What is gained?
What is lost?
Where does language
come in?)

THAT REMINDS ME:

A man who had his sight
restored after twenty
years of blindness had
no sense of perspective.
Nor could he distinguish
between his nurse and a
filing cabinet or between
his nurse and his doctor.
He had to touch them in
his usual way.
Prejudiced?

"Let the eyes see from the inside out."

"Let the eyes
see from the
inside out."

TONE

Tone up your body's nerve
endings by taking the
first five minutes of a
class to sit quietly and
feel your body. Begin
with your toes. Let your
mind reach down and experience them.
Realize them. Once they are
alive again, go on with your
ankles, your calves, and on to
the rest of your body until every part
of the surface has been
remembered.
Then go on with whatever you are
doing.

Man's ancestors may have been almost color-
blind because they were in a subconscious habit
of ignoring color. Life was so difficult and dangerous that they couldn't afford to notice it. Yet modern man has succeeded in losing this old habit
of color-blindness without losing any of his drive
and vitality.

172

Which is fatter?
a smile
pain?

Sick man lying down in his house,
with three visitors

The gifts in a house do not come in through the gate.

SENSE WALK

Tune up your sensorium. Take a half hour walk around some familiar place. First be aware of the senses separately: Seeing, touching, smelling, hearing, tasting. Then allow them all to flow together as a total experience. What's really going on here?

ON PERCEPTION

Feelings are expressed with images, and these images are in turn transformed into emotional energies which, due to their formal beauty can affect us profoundly.

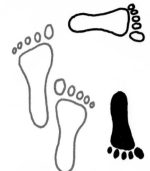

"Verily, art is embedded in nature; he who can extract it, has it."

Select some pieces of junk and find a way to reveal their beauty.

Convert a news item into a poem.

Reflect on these activities.

Choose one:
A shrewd manufacturer would prefer that his product's name be 1) a *live* or 2) a *dead* metaphor?

Of course if you are egoless the whole force of the universe acts through you. It is not you looking. It is looking.

MY HUT IN SPRING . . . !

173

WHICH IS SWEETER? RAIN, JULY

When you sit in a red room time appears to pass much more slowly than it actually does . . .
—Polly Adler

WE BELIEVE IN IMAGES SO MUCH THAT WE DON'T SHAVE THE MIRROR!

A good artist
disappoints my
expectations,
sometimes,

and
sometimes
sparks
synapsis.

If you say it's *just* a figure of speech, you miss the whole
point of figures of speech.
T. or F.

He's Stuck Between A Rock And A Hard Place

Thinking a metaphor is *about* something is a way of not getting involved. T. or F.?

For What Has A Man Locomotion If It Isn't To Take Him Into Things He Is Between Barely And Not Quite Standing?

The first approximation for sentient beings is *not what it means, but how it feels.*

One cubic centimeter of the primeval cosmic egg weighed two hundred and fifty tons.

CHEESECAKE

Fill in the Blanks
Choose your own words or use these: American, Chinese, English, Japanese.

A happy diplomat has a _____ country house, a _____ cook, a _____ salary. a _____ wife, and a _____ salary.

An unhappy diplomat has a _____ country house, a _____ cook, a _____ salary. a _____ wife, and a _____ salary.

Chiron inhaled; air like honey expanded the spaces of his chest; his students completed the centaur. They fleshed his wisdom with expectation. The wintry chaos of information within him, elicited into sunlight, was struck through with the young colors of optimism. Winter turned vernal. "Our subject," he began, and the faces, scattered in the deep green shade like petals after rain, were unanimously hushed and attentive, "is the Genesis of All Things. In the beginning," the centaur said, "black-winged Night was courted by the wind, and laid a silver egg in the womb of Darkness. From this egg hatched Eros, which means _____ ?"

"Love," a child's voice answered from the grass.

"And Love set the Universe in motion. All things that exist are her children—sun, moon, stars, the earth with its mountains and rivers, its trees, herbs, and living creatures. Now Eros was double-sexed and golden-winged and, having four heads, sometimes roared like a bull or a lion, sometimes hissed like a serpent or bleated like a ram; beneath her rule the world was as harmonious as a beehive..."

EROS

175

The beginning of all philosophy: Sex (T. or F.?)

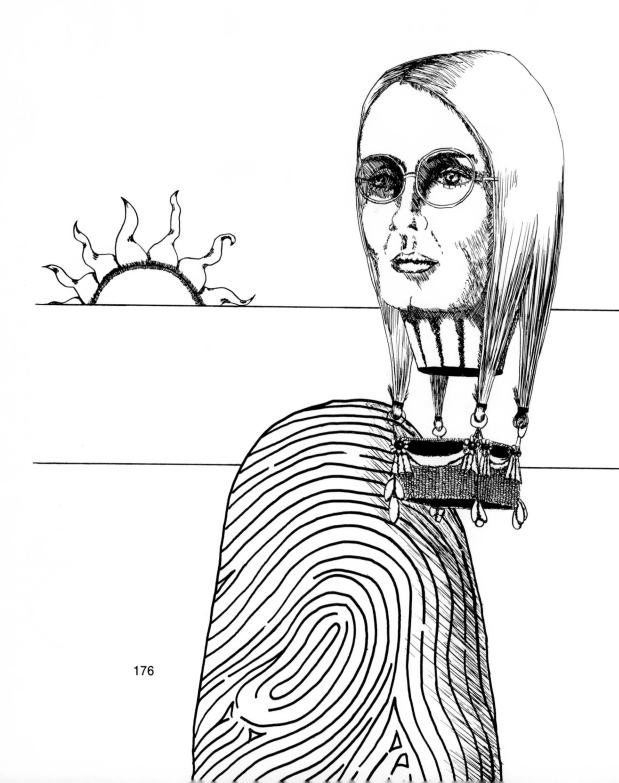

176

THE INNER LANDSCAPE

Close your eyes and follow these instructions as one member of your group reads them aloud. Allow plenty of time to complete each instruction.

> Close your eyes; relax; imagine you are floating.
>
> Now you come to a hill and land. Look down. Describe what you see. (Remember what you see for later.)
>
> Now float on down to the area you just described to yourself. You are standing on a path. What does it look like?
>
> Now start walking on the path. You walk and walk. You come to a key. Describe the key. What do you do with it?
>
> Keep on walking down the path and finally come to a cup lying there. Describe it and what you do with it.
>
> You go on until you come to a body of water cutting off the path, but you know the path continues on the other side. Describe the body of water and how you get to the other side.
>
> Once on the other side, you walk on down the trail until you come to a bear blocking your way. What do you do?
>
> Further along there is a house by the side of the road. What is it like? Would you stay there?
>
> Now leave the house and go on walking until you come to a wall. Describe the wall and how you get to the other side.
>
> Now open your eyes.

Have several members of your group describe their adventures. True or false: The stories you made up are true even if they didn't happen?

Write out your adventure in your journal and explore its significance.

Your adventure is: a) a mirror, b) a metaphor, c) a myth, d) an image, e) a symbol, f) a sign, g) none of these, h) all of these, i) other _____.

Donald Reilly

LOOK 7-29-70

"...and we won't take 'Om' for an answer!"

> The acquision of knowledge is a creative act by which we impose on data a structure of principles. The structure determines what we come to know on the basis of those principles.

LUMINARIES

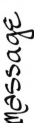

message The medium; change The message...

"Art is so much greater than government."
Antigone

"That's easy for you to say."
Creon.

Lucy in the sky with diamonds
Picture yourself in a boat on a river
With tangerine trees and marmalade skies
Somebody calls you, you answer quite slowly,
A girl with kaleidoscope eyes.
Cellophane flowers of yellow and green,
Towering over your head.
Look for the girl with the sun in her eyes,
And she's gone.
Lucy in the sky with diamonds.
Follow her down to a bridge by a fountain
Where rocking horse people eat marshmallow
pies,
Everyone smiles as you drift past the flowers,
That grow so incredibly high.
Newspaper taxis appear on the shore,
Waiting to take you away.
Climb in the back with your head in the clouds,
And you're gone.
Lucy in the sky with diamonds,
Picture yourself on a train in a station,
With plasticine porters with looking glass ties,
Suddenly someone is there at the turnstile,
The girl with kaleidoscope eyes.

1420
Michelino de Besosso
(Prayer book, 6¾'' by 4¾'')

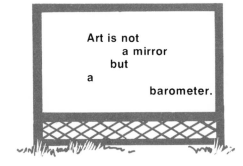

Art is not
a mirror
but
a
barometer.

That Reminds Me:
A student illuminated her text book by adding other colors to it. She used pentel pens. She also added some drawings. Why not! Be our guest . . .

The cosmic meaning of consciousness: What nature leaves imperfect, the art perfects.
16th century alchemist

Ernest Hemingway, arriving for the first time at the salon of Gertrude Stein, commented that Gertrude was about the ugliest name he had ever heard.

"A rose is a rose is a rose," said Miss Stein munching dreamily on a brownie.

VERBAL/VISUAL?
Does this cartoon need a caption?

Belvedere   By Greenwood

PENCIL PROBE

Draw this cartoon panel. Drawing it should focus your attention on the cartoonist's style. Reflect on your investigation. Then draw the other cartoon on this page. Compare the two styles and your own perception during this probe.

T or F: A pencil is
T or F: an eye.

Extended applications?

AN EYE IS A PENCIL???

    Words are hard to see, for in use they are transparent. As one becomes aware of them they become opaque and difficult to use, (the self gets in the way when one becomes self-conscious).

THEREFORE?

THAT REMINDS ME:

The McClellands had bought all their Christmas gifts early, so they wrapped them in brown paper temporarily, to keep the kids from knowing what they contained.

Charles said jokingly, "We can't afford wrapping paper this year, so you'll have to decorate the packages yourselves."

They thought he was serious and did a beautiful job. Then Charles didn't know whether to tell them he had been kidding and buy wrappings or keep the homemade decorations. What should he have done?

Next gift-giving time, try it.

179

ETHNOCENTRISM

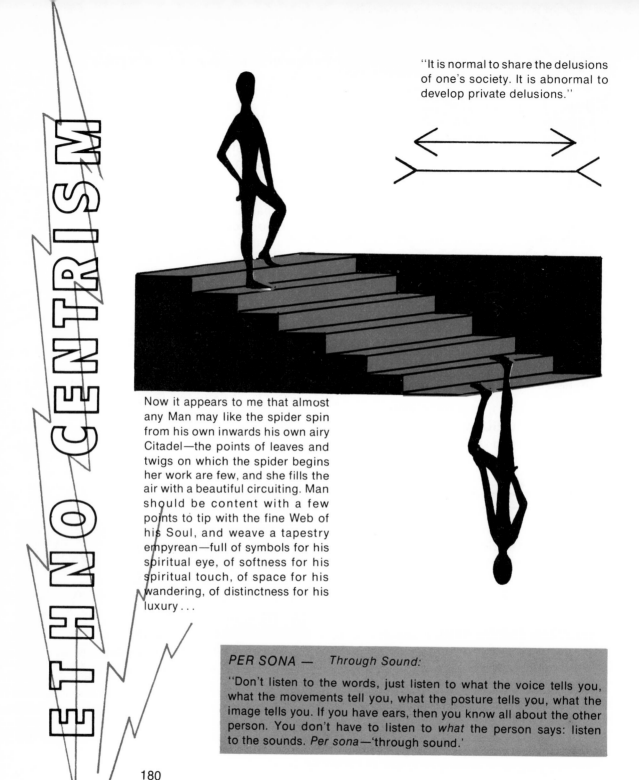

"It is normal to share the delusions of one's society. It is abnormal to develop private delusions."

Now it appears to me that almost any Man may like the spider spin from his own inwards his own airy Citadel—the points of leaves and twigs on which the spider begins her work are few, and she fills the air with a beautiful circuiting. Man should be content with a few points to tip with the fine Web of his Soul, and weave a tapestry empyrean—full of symbols for his spiritual eye, of softness for his spiritual touch, of space for his wandering, of distinctness for his luxury...

PER SONA —   Through Sound:

"Don't listen to the words, just listen to what the voice tells you, what the movements tell you, what the posture tells you, what the image tells you. If you have ears, then you know all about the other person. You don't have to listen to *what* the person says: listen to the sounds. *Per sona*—'through sound.'

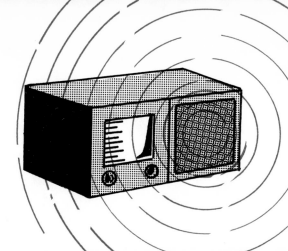

Even without a knowledge of Middle English, you can figure out the essence of this passage (*circa* 1380). Even the more obscure words still appear in some collegiate dictionaries. Note linguistic differences. True or false: "The child is father of the man."

God turne us every drem to goode!
To my wyt, what causeth swevenes
Eyther on morwes or on evenes;
And why th'effect folweth of somme,
And of somme hit shal never come;
Why that is an avisioun
And this a revelacioun,
Why this a drem, why that a sweven,
And noght to every man lyche even;
Why this a fantome, why these oracles,
I not; but whoso of these miracles
The causes knoweth bet then I,
Devyne he; for I certeinly
Ne kan hem noght, ne never thinke
To besily my wyt to swinke,
To knowe of hir signifaunce
The gendres, neyther the distaunce
Of tymes of hem, ne the causes,
Or why this more then that cause is;
As yf folkys complexions
Make hem dreme of reflexions;
or ellys thus, as other sayn,
For to gret feblenesse of her brayn,
By abstinence, or by seknesse,
Prison, stewe, or gret distresse,
Or ellys by dysordynaunce
Of naturel acustumaunce,
That som man is to curious

In studye, or melancolyous,
Or thus, so inly ful of drede
That no man may hym bote bede;
Or elles that devocion
Of somme, and contemplacion
Causeth suche dremes ofte;
Or that the cruel lyf onsofte
Which these ilke lovers leden
That hopen over-muche or dreden,
That purely her impressions
Causen hem to have visions;
Or yf that spirites have the myght
To make folk to dreme a-nyght;
Or yf the soule, of propre kynde,
Be so parfit, as men fynde,
That yt forwot that ys to come,
And that hyt warneth alle and some
Of everych of her aventures
Be avisions, or be figures,
But that oure flessh ne hath no myght
To understonde hyt aryght,
For hyt is warned to derkly; —
But why the cause is, noght wot I.
Wel worthe, of this thyng, grete clerkys,
That trete of this and other werkes;
For I of noon opinion
Nyl as now make mensyon,
But oonly that the holy roode
Turne us every drem to goode!

181

THE MEN WITH THE LONG EYES

In the foothills of the Central Range of Mountains of the Malay Peninsula, live nomadic hordes of Negrito pygmies.

A rock that a Negrito sees in his dream can tell him what he may or may not do while awake. In other words, the rock functions as a god or supernormal being. Such dreams may prevent the Negrito from tilling the soil, from domesticating animals, or from making friends with a neighboring horde.

Since this fear of the dream picture, or image, or character, thus carries over into wakeful life, it is easy to see why the mind of the Negrito remains rigid and undeveloped. In order to do any type of planning or problem solving, a man must shift things about in his mind and look at the rearrangement. Then, if he likes it better the way it is in his mental picture, he can attempt to change the outside world. If the rock that appears in his dream can make him give up a betel nut as a sacrifice just because he made a noise near an actual rock in the daytime, or sat down on it, it is evident that the rock in his dream is more talkative and more menacing than the outside rock.

In the daytime no voice came up through the rock as he sat on it. In his dream he found himself again

sitting on it, and it had a voice. As he retraces his steps the next day and leaves a betel nut on the rock where he had sat down on it, it has the shape, hardness, and heaviness that it had the day before, but it also has the voice in it that he heard in his dream. The process of dreaming has enriched the rock. Through the dream it has gained human power. Something has been added to it. He now acts toward it as if it were a human being or an animal.

But whence comes this power that is given to the rock? It comes from the man himself. A man gives up a parcel of his own power as he puts it into the rock in his dream. If he does not own and control the inner dream rock, then he will not own the power that he puts into it. The image or pattern of the rock that he created as he sat on it in the daytime, the mental picture that enables him to remember the rock, to recall it later, thus becomes the owner of an inner voice and of inner power. Since he makes no distinction between the rock on the trail and the rock in his dream, the outside rock has now become the owner of the inside power. The man does not own the image of the rock as a useful tool to employ in his thinking, but the rock

182

"Now that's what I call a classic figure eight."

owns a fragment of the area inside the skin and, therefore, inside the mind of the man. The rock owns a little of the man's power. Through his transaction with the rock, the man has lost some of his spontaneity and flexibility of mind. Henceforward, he cannot use the rock image as his seven-year-old child uses it, or as he could use it before he had the dream.

Thus, the adult Negrito does not own the image of the rock or the mountain that he builds up in his mind as he looks at these objects in the daytime, but the rock and the mountain own the fragments of his mind that is occupied by their image. This appears to be one reason why the Negrito cannot think as we think, and why his society has remained changeless...

In the highlands of Malaya, above the foothills occupied by the hunting and gathering Negritos, live the Senoi, another group of preliterate people who have followed a line of development or evolution opposite to that of the Negritos. These highlanders have no written language and no knowledge of the world outside their territory. They have never developed mathematics or astronomy, or scientific method as we know it. Yet they have evolved a method of education as simple as the Negrito way of thinking. It enables the growing individual to keep hold of the parcels of his power that the dream process gives to the images of things. It enables his elders to use these images as channels that assist the child to become a physically healthy, socially constructive, self-possessed adult...

Like the Negritos, the Senoi communicate with the rocks, the trees, the rivers, and heavenly bodies in their dreams. But, like the Christian, the Buddhist, the Taoist, and the modern scientist who calls himself an atheist, an agnostic, or a materialist, the adult Senoi believes that these images of things do not have to be feared or propitiated in waking life. The Senoi have not made the mistake of Western civilization of thinking that the images of things and people that appear in sleep are unimportant. Neither do they make the mistake of the Negritos in thinking that a human being must always be ruled by these images...

The Senoi educator tells the child that his dreams, and the forces in them, are important. The dream snake and the dream tiger are real and they are vital, but they are not dangerous or bad like the snakes and tigers one sees in the daytime. In fact, all dream characters are good if you outface them and bend them to your will. If you run away from them or disregard them, they will plague you forever, or until you rediscover and outface them. Once they have appeared in your dreams, they are your property, and will forever remain an asset or a liability.

This amounts to saying that everything that appears in dreams is filled up with your own spirit or force, and that you must control your own psychological resources or they will hurt you or your associates. As an educational policy, it amounts to saying that the teacher must not lose contact with the emotion or force that the dream process has invested in the dream pattern. This force must not rule the psyche of the dreamer. It must not be rejected by him or by the educational authority. The educator must keep contact with it and must help it from day to day to work for the dreamer and for society...

The dream education of the Senoi child starts when he can talk, and is continued, thereafter, along with his technical education. In order to produce like results in the West, a similar procedure would probably be necessary...

Judged from their responses to mental tests and to Western ideas, their minds had none of the rigidity which characterized that of the Negrito. The Senoi preoccupation with dream images and processes enables them to do abstract and symbolic thinking of the highest order and makes them expert in keeping track of and differentiating between the subjective and the objective world.

They have almost no mathematics and, therefore, neglect the type of thinking in which the West has made the most progress. But in the realm of feeling and emotion, where civilized man finds it most difficult to communicate and to agree, the Senoi have developed a skill and understanding far superior to our own. In the systematic testing out of projects, mechanical inventions, discoveries, and hunches that occur in dreams, the Senoi have evolved an experimental attitude which is very close to that of the scientific West, and which appears as effective in developing and controlling psychological and social processes as our experimental method is in the world of physics and chemistry . . .

The Senoi expect their children to be selfish, aggressive, and violent, to express human nature as we know it. Such behavior is normal for the child, but, in their society, it is normal for the adult to be unselfish and cooperative, yet self-reliant, and to compete with others and oppose others with good will, making the opposition creative for the opponents, and beneficial, rather than destructive, to society . . .

Senoi philosophy amounts to saying: "I, human being, have the power in sleep to reorganize and recreate my mind as well as my body, if I have the cooperation and the help of the authorities who initiate me into the social reality of which I must form a part as a responsible adult. Some wisdom inside man's body maintains his constant temperature and restores him physically, even better while he is asleep than while he is awake . . ."

The Senoi parent inquires of his child's dream at breakfast, praises the child for having the dream, and discusses the significance of it. He asks about past incidents and tells the child how to change his behavior and attitude in future dreams. He also recommends certain social activities or gestures which the dream makes necessary or advisable.

This furnishes an interesting topic for conversation and for interpersonal contact in the family, but requires no more time at breakfast than other primitive or modern groups consume discussing less significant subjects. The child is also at liberty to listen to the discussions of the dreams of the older members of the society, which take place in the village council after breakfast.

Most of the social and economic activity in the daily life of the Senoi is determined by dreams, along with the choices, decisions, and interpretations arising out of them in the discussions at the morning council . . .

Sleep is inventory time, a balancing of the books. It is the time when the mystic learns that "no feather falls from a bird in flight" that the indwelling God does not observe. It is the time when man has the power of a god to look inside himself. The remembered dream makes the record of this inner balance, with its listed credits and debits, available to those who are managing and directing the social world . . .

It is a truism in the West that man's creation often turns against him. He is possessed by his machines. Like Frankenstein, he builds a master that destroys him. He is turned against himself. The Senoi have found a way to observe and reverse this process in the growing child. The child breathes in a whiff of choking smoke, while the adults are burning the underbrush from the land they are clearing. That night the black image of the smoke, with its choking odor and the emotion of terror it aroused, is recreated in the child's dream. He awakens and cries and tells his parents of the black nightmare cloud that choked him in his sleep. They comfort him and say that it was a good dream. In the daytime, he must move away from smoke if it comes after him. But dream smoke is always good. He must move deeper into the dream smoke and, when he does, he will find a treasure that he can tell about when he awakens. He may even find the spirit of the smoke which he can conquer and make his servant.

He dreams of floating happily, of soaring into the air with joy, and is told that in future dreams he must float or soar to some definite place and find a treasure, something that is beautiful or useful to human beings, which he can reproduce or describe when he awakes.

These are the central ideas and policies of Senoi dream education. The adults help the child to reproduce artistic things and to describe and build mechanical things. They encourage him to form friendships and associations, and to organize projects pictured in his dreams.

If a child is attacked in a dream, he is encouraged to fight to the death. It is good to die in dreams, because death leads to the instantaneous rebirth of the dreamer, and permanently exhausts the force of the adversary. It is also good to kill in dreams, even though the attacking dream character wears the image of one of your fellows. The dream character is judged by his action in the dream. If he is antagonistic to the dreamer, he is bad, even though he is using a good image as a disguise.

All dream force is potentially good. It will serve you if you force the dream character to serve you and the group, or if you release this force from antagonistic dream forms by destroying them. This is like saying that even when a man is good, his action may leave an image of him inside your mind that is filled up with your anxiety, or guilt, or fear, and that this image, therefore, must be destroyed in order to release your own negative emotions which are associated with it.

Although the Senoi do not put it in modern psychological terms—since they have never heard of modern psychology as we know it—their theory of judging the dream character by its action in the dream works out as if they told the child:

"The dentist is a good man. It's a good thing you've had your teeth fixed, but the image he left inside you as he drilled your teeth is full of fear and pain. The image is bad because it is hurting you, or threatening you, in the dream world, when the dentist belongs to the daytime world. If you do not kill off the image that contains the pain from the past, you will go on suffering forever in the perpetual present of the dream world. You will pay in the sleep world again and again for an experience you have already paid for and learned from in the daytime world. The image of the dentist will be stronger than you are yourself, and will gather around him other enemies of the dream world.

"These enemies will attack your friends when you do not know it. They will give you headaches or indigestion, or cause you to have accidents. They will even make you afraid of the dentist when you are awake, so that you cannot take a rational attitude toward having your teeth fixed. The fear you lock inside the image will eventually cause you a thousand times more pain than that which was originally attached to it through your daytime experience."

The Senoi doctrine is like the Biblical statement that "offense needs must come, but woe unto him by whom it does come." The offense charges the image of the offender with a force antagonistic to the offended. You offend a child if you cause him pain as you pull a sliver from his foot. But the pain is only a fragment of the total situation. The fear occasioned by the pain often disguises itself in the image of a friend. The Senoi dream education proves that this fear, which makes the dream character antagonistic, is released and dispersed as the dreamer outfaces and kills or conquers the antagonistic dream character. It is also released if the dream character stabs, or kills, or strikes the dreamer. It is as if the dream character gives up its individual existence whenever the dreamer, who created it in past time, is willing to reexperience the shock or pain that turned the image against the individual, in the original painful experience.

The Senoi adult encourages the child to apologize on awakening for antisocial actions he initiates in dreams. The dream image he thus offends is not the person, but is closely related to him and might represent a spiritual fragment of him. If someone treats the child badly in a dream, that person is informed of it, so he will have an opportunity to make his social behavior neutralize or reverse the negative tendency expressed by his dream image. He does this by making some friendly, helpful gesture toward the dreamer.

The dream collections made from various age groups among the Senoi show that their dreams consistently evolve from childhood to adolescence. Gradually, the child does do in his dreams what he is directed to do. Toward adolescence he consistently arrives somewhere, brings back a treasure for the group in his good dreams, and outfaces, conquers, and destroys his enemies in his bad ones. The dream treasures take the forms of songs, designs, poems, stories, and mechanical inventions.

Dream collections made by the author from our own society, and from primitive societies in which no such dream education was carried on, failed to show a similar evolution.

The Senoi practice of regarding the dream as stemming from something that happened the day before or in the more remote past, and as the determiner of other things that should or must happen to-morrow, has an important indirect effect both on the adults and on the children. Since the parents believe that the child's dreams reflect his reaction to their behavior and attitudes toward each other and toward the child, they are careful how they act in his presence and how they criticize him. Since the child's dreams do often depict adults behaving harshly and unreasonably, they have a day-to-day reminder from the child of what accidents or criticisms have been shocking to him, in spite of their efforts to keep environmental images from turning against him . . .

The child is impressed by the fact that the adults do listen to his dreams and take them seriously, that they do trace them back to shocks, accidents, and conflicts of the day before, and that they do often modify their behavior and ask others to do so on the basis of the data the dream presents. This gives the child a feeling that he is a creative, functioning member of the social group, from the time he is able to talk. He can give to the adults, as well as accept from them, and the adults take the greatest interest in that which represents his most individualistic expression, that part of his expression which is, in a sense, a reaction against, or a protestation of, the very process of socialization.

This eliminates one of the great reasons for the feeling found in our society that the adults have no interest in the real self of the child, but are only concerned with enforcing their will upon him, and receiving back from him what he has learned from them. The child apparently realizes that the dream is an expression of his inmost self. The data from the Senoi indicate that the adult failure in our society to solicit, accept, and appreciate this most spontaneous expression is one of the reasons for the inferiority and persecution complexes so common in our society, and for the pent-up hostility that so often overflows into crime and war.

Over a thirty year period Simon Rodia used concrete, metal rods, shells, broken ceramics and bottles to create the now famous Watts Towers in Los Angeles.

P. S. The building inspector decided the unconventional structure was unsafe and condemned it. However, when the crane he was using to tear the towers down began to topple itself, he decided they were perhaps safe after all.

I KNOW WHAT I LIKE

In *Our Town*, Emily, who has just died, joins the other dead townspeople in the cemetery and is told she can re-live one day of her life, but is told that it isn't wise.

"But it's a thing I must know for myself. I'll choose a happy day, anyway."

"No. At least, choose an unimportant day. Choose the least important day of your life. It will be important enough."

"When my body moves, it's because my spirit moves it."
Isadora Duncan

An artist is not one who has solved life's problems. He is one who accepts life's problems.

SYNERGISM

All *myth, language, art, expression* come down to the effort of the soul to break through its barrier of intolerable loneliness.

SURVIVAL KIT
Turning Signs Back into Symbols

Each person collect these items:
  5 paper clips
  3 sharpened pencils
  1 three-foot piece of string
  3 rubber bands
  6 3 by 5 cards

Imagine that you have never seen these things before, as though you are from an alien world.

Then, using all the materials, create anything you wish, but do not use any as they are customarily used.

Compare results and explore the significance of your experiences.

187

What color is *morality*?
Color it in in the square.

Draw a picture of *laziness,* but
don't use people or animals.

Draw a visual metaphor for a *screech.*

Draw a *germ.*

188

"I've been trying to get that Ming dynasty
cloak for 27 years."

"Why?"

"Because that's how long my wife's been
nagging me for a Ming coat."

* * *

Assimilation: the process whereby one
sound is changed to a second under the
influence of a third.

* * *

In other words, the mind anticipates the
word *coat* before the word *mink* is uttered
and conveniently drops out the wKE.

* * *

That Reminds Me: Bernard DeVoto
remarked, "God may be worshipped in
conundrums, the Church was founded on
a pun." And Robert Frost said, "I want
one to go with me only so far as he will
go playfully . . . .The way is almost rigidly
prescribed. If it is with outer seriousness,
it must be with inner humor. If it is with
outer humor, it must be with inner seriousness. Neither without the other under
it will do."

**"What I want to do, you know, is
redecorate the world." P. M.**

INFLUENCING THE IMAGE

Create your own cartoon or find one in a magazine which doesn't rely on a caption. Compare with other members of your group. Are cartoons *really* nonverbal? Are nonverbal messages ever completely independent of the verbal?

Visual Illiteracy: "No one, to the date of my graduation, ever taught me to look understandingly at a painting, or a tree, or a facade of a building."

For a few years now I have been conducting workshops for both amateur and professional photographers. By workshops, as distinguished from classes, I mean a group in which there is a free exchange of ideas and work among all participants. I do not consider myself as a teacher, but, rather, as a catalyst, one whose function it is to arouse in the photographer an intensified awareness of his potential creativity. The emphasis is on feeling and the free expression of one's self. My aim is to help people to clearer vision and thus to live more fully, which is primary to the development of a good photographer.

These are difficult tasks. The things most important in our lives we tend not to verbalize, nor can we communicate them any more easily through the photographic image. Students frequently come to me with images which are more hopeful than meaningful. Two errors are common; the photograph presents a number of "meanings" which the student has yet to find in them; or, conversely, he brings an exclusive and special meaning to it.

In attempting to help people realize and release potential I have no "system." If you were to attend one of my workshops you might be surprised to hear us discuss music or read from a book on philosophy or the art of poetry. A person interested in expressing with a camera should have a wide range of interests; *joi de vivre* is a vital ingredient, too. Everything we know, feel, have ever experienced provides the basic elements for our creativity.

One of the first assignments I set for my students involves the question of communication. We begin at the verbal level because photographers, regardless of their ability, are usually more word-minded than visual-minded. Even so, since we are dealing with something which is deeply important to them, few students are able really to be articulate when talking about their own work. This, of course creates a block when, for example, I may ask a student to tell me why he chose a stairway to photograph. Usually we do not get very far. But in general discussion the group as a whole can analyze the pictures freely for they feel more detached from the image. But they are not as detached as they believe; at this point they simply are *unaware* that in talking about photographs they really are talking about

189

themselves.

I use an exercise which is concerned with both word and image to make clear the many ramifications of meaning implicit in a single picture. Each student takes home a photograph which I have deliberately chosen for the intensity of its statement and writes what he sees in it. At the next meeting another student will take the picture and do the same. At the following session we compare the two independent observations. Often they are so different one wonders if they really are the same picture. The purpose of the exercise is to demonstrate that, regardless of the intent of the photographer, the *meaning* of a picture is derived from the viewer's own unique experience. The work of any artist serves simply as a trigger to release the personal response of the viewer, thus completing the act of communication.

Write what you see in this photograph. Bring it to class and compare your version with those of others. Explore *looking, seeing,* and *truth*.

By this and other exercises I try to bring to the students a fuller awareness that photographic images can reach into dimensions that words cannot touch. As the Haiku poem of Japanese literature, the expressive photograph provides many implications to carry the viewer to poetic imagery. The beginning student, however, finds that before he can reach out to others he must first become acquainted with his own feelings and clarify his relationship with himself. In the process of visual exploration he discovers himself in photographs which cause him to respond.

For most of my students this is a new approach to looking at photographs. All have had some experience with the camera and know at least a little technique, but with this method they soon realize that, although taking a photograph is easy, putting one's vision onto film and into a print is quite a different matter.

To illustrate what is meant by photographing with one's own vision, which is, after all, a difficult concept to convey with words, we study the work of the masters and compare it with that of other photographers. We may, for instance, look at the pictures of Wynn Bullock, Edward Weston, and Al Monner, three landscape photographers. How have the organization and the light been used to make these intense personal statements? By comparison the students readily see how each landscape has become an expressive extension of the photographer. The students come to understand that in the hands of those who have learned to use photography as a creative, expressive medium, the photograph bears the stamp of individuality and vision.

Camera vision can be strengthened in a visually talented person. First he must be able to see (as distinct from merely "to look at") things with his own two eyes, then look with the camera to note how differently this one-eyed tool sees. Knowing this difference between the effects of stereoscopic and monocular vision is necessary to one's accurate visualization of the finished print, which in turn determines the need to influence the image.

"Influencing the image." We can write of it here but I know of no way to make the reader "feel" what it means. Perhaps the best means is to give you the recipe I use in the workshop where it is

190

presented to students who are attempting to understand this problem. Take one camera, with film loaded; add one knowing eye (your own) and as much strong feeling as you have available; mix well with a generous portion of the flavor of your unique personality; expose to the right light for the exact fraction; process until beauty appears. The resulting image in the final print may come as a great surprise.

If so, this is as it should be, for much of what appears in our pictures come from a level which we ourselves have yet to discover. The non-discriminating lens sees beyond and more clearly than does our selective and partially blind seeing. Comparing the final, revealing print with our incomplete visualized image can provide the moment of realization when we break through our self-inflicted limitation and begin really to *see*. When we train our eyes to see beyond the accepted, when we ourselves can accept that which may just now be past our understanding, we can use the sharp vision of the camera to take the next step toward enlightenment, or at least a moment of understanding, for ourselves and others.

Of all the arts, music is the most abstract; yet it meets with the least resistance. The surest method of helping students to see and to accept that which is unfamiliar to them is to have them listen to music. The transition from music to "abstract" photography follows naturally. Sooner or later students become aware that in studying abstract photographs they are really dealing with accurate renderings of the visual world. That is, they are working with reality and *extensions* into dimensions of reality hitherto unsuspected—and labeled "abstract" only because unfamiliar. Soon the abstract design qualities inherent even in snapshots also becomes apparent.

Assignments relating to light are perhaps the most important in a group of projects which include such matters as form, essence, personal statement and others. To potential photographers, awareness of light is of the utmost importance. First because light is the activator of the medium, second because light and shadow reveal essences of things. Hence assignments are given to bring their attention to what light feels like in the world diffused, direct, reflected, noon, dusk, and so one, and how these affect them when seen in the photograph. Other assignments are given to make them aware that light outlines objects, reveals them, obscures them, releases, hides, plays the infinite to their infinity. It is in these assignments especially that I can demonstrate the relation of technique to outcome. Photography renders light as no other medium does. When the photographer knows by experience the qualities of light and the subtleties of his medium, light begins to glow in his photographs.

Neither learning to experience light, however, nor learning to render it photographically can be accomplished in just a few lessons. Both endeavors must become part of one's every waking moment.

Most students do not know their camera. I encourage the group to use and work with the camera often, to become so completely familiar with it that it will help instead of hinder. I stress camera technique only in relation to and as a necessary part of the creative effort. All mechanical procedures must become instinctive. The camera is to be used as an extension of oneself, not as an awkward appendage that has to be consciously thought of before it can be made to function. And I ask them to use the camera to see the *familiar* things. "Stay at home; don't go off to the cemetery."

To be a creative person comes out of the enjoyment and appreciation of life. I tell my students to wake up in the morning with wide open eyes—to learn to see all the time—to be aware and to enjoy life. If, in my six weeks course, they can become more artistically aware and feel inner growth, I feel gratified. Many students come back for more workshops and then we begin to see evidence of their growth.

Once I went to a friend's house, and because it was sunny stepped out into the garden and sat on a rock. It was a delicious experience, but in a few moments I was informed that I should not sit out there. The garden was designed to be viewed from the room (thus I could not see its beauty from where I was), and I was cluttering it up. I stepped back into the room and looked for the beauty of the garden, but now I could not find it.

Design a greeting card for the least significant day of one's life.

Select something from this chapter you would like to *give* to someone. Write the page number on a suitable design and give it to him. Compare and discuss.

a camera is a pencil . . .

Book 'Marker'

There is a valentine for you on p. 44.

triggers

1. Choose one of the pictures in this chapter which you feel could best represent the incarnate self. Compare and discuss choices.

SYNCHRONICITY

ALLATONCENESS

PATTERN RECOGNITION

In L. H. Myers' *The Near and the Far* young Prince Jali looks out from his palace tower across the desert—over which he has traveled that day. As he looks at the magnificent sunset, he reflects that there are *two* deserts, one is a glory to the eye; the other is agony to the feet as you plod across it. And the two deserts never come together.

a camera is an eye . . .

193

Step 1. Write what you see.
Step 2. Draw what you see (a rough pencil
sketch, but try to get it all).
Step 3. Write what you *now* see.

MIDTERM TRIVIA GAME-TEST

Station two recorders at the chalkboard who can write small and abbreviate a lot. One records the odd numbered data and the other the even. Then start around the room having each person supply any bit of trivia from the course: a title, a name, the journal, a part of a discussion, a concept, a slogan, anything no matter how minute. Each is numbered and listed on the board. Pay close attention. The first one to repeat is out of the game. Those who can't think of anything are out, too. Move fast.

Two objects: to see how much data you can list.

to stay in the game.

Later reflect on this investigation.

V
E
R
B
A
L

V
I
S
U
A
L

WHO IS ENO?

It is a funny thing what the brain will do with memories and how it will treasure them and finally bring them into odd juxtapositions with other things, as though it wanted to make a design, or get some meaning out of them, whether you want it or not, or even see it.

It's not just the conclusion you reach when you come to the end of Descartes' sixth *Meditation* that counts, or having to be able to talk about his system on an exam, but the time it takes to reach its conclusion, the distance you have to go—in other words, the experience lived in learning about Descartes.

TRACES

194

I think, therefore . . .

THE CAULDRON

And we did make love; not sex, but love; though sex would have been so much wiser.

Journal

The ancient philosopher certainly gave a wise counsel when he said, "Know thyself." For surely this knowledge is of all the most important. I might enlarge upon this. But grave and serious declamation is not what I intend at present. A man cannot know himself better than by attending to the feelings of his heart and to his external actions, from which he may with tolerable certainty judge "what manner of person he is." I have therefore determined to keep a daily journal in which I shall set down my various sentiments and my various conduct, which will be not only useful but very agreeable. It will give me a habit of application and improve me in expression; and knowing that I am to record my transactions will make me more careful to do well. Or if I should go wrong, it will assist me in resolutions of doing better. I shall here put down my thoughts on different subjects at different times, the whims that may seize me and the sallies of my luxuriant imagination. I shall mark the anecdotes and the stories that I hear, the instructive or amusing conversations that I am present at, and the various adventures that I may have.

I was observing to my friend Erskine that a plan of this kind was dangerous, as a man might in the openness of his heart say many things and discover many facts that might do him great harm if the journal should fall into the hands of my enemies. Against which there is no perfect security. "Indeed," said he, "I hope there is no danger at all; for I fancy you will not set down your robberies on the highway, or the murders that you commit. As to other things there can be no harm." I laughed heartily at my friend's observation, which was so far true. I shall be upon my guard to mention nothing that can do harm. Truth shall ever be observed, and these things (if there should be any such) that require the gloss of falsehood shall be passed by in silence. At the same time I may relate things under borrowed names with safety that would do much mischief if particularly known.

In this way I shall preserve many things that would otherwise be lost in oblivion. I shall find daily employment for myself, which will save me from indolence and help to keep off the spleen, and I shall lay up a store of entertainment for my after life. Very often we have more pleasure in reflecting on agreeable scenes that we have been in than we had from the scenes themselves. I shall regularly record the business or rather the pleasure of every day. I shall not study much correctness, lest the labour of it should make me lay it aside altogether. I hope it will be of use to my worthy friend Johnston, and that while he laments my personal absence, this journal may in some measure supply that defect and make him happy.

196

DARE SEIZE

THE FIRE

To drag the dryad from the tree . . .

I wanted to utter a word, but that word I cannot remember, and my unembodied thought must return to the region of shadows.

In passing from one level of meaning to the next, the child does not have to restructure all of his earlier concepts, which indeed would be a Sisyphean labor. Once a new structure has been incorporated into his thinking . . . it gradually spreads to the older concepts as they are drawn into the intellectual operations of the higher type . . .

GIFT:

"You must not thank for your meat; it is your right to get parts. In this country nobody wishes to be dependent upon others. Therefore, there is nobody who gives or gets gifts, for thereby you become dependent. With gifts you make slaves just as with whips you make dogs!"

Which of the following are you?
    a. a word
    b. an idea
    c. a concept
    d. other

Einstein: poet of the real.

ZEN POET

ZEN POEM

$E = MC^2$

OM^3

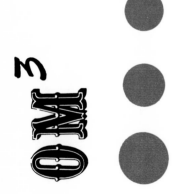

Oh dear. I've forgotten the . . .uh . . . .

198

"Let's have a swim."

"It'll be like ice."

"yah."

She pulled her shirt over her head, and unhooked her bra, grinning at me in the flecked shadow of the arbor; I was cornered again.

"This place is probably alive with snakes."

"Like Eden."

She stepped out of her jeans and her white pants. Then she reached up and snapped a dead cone off one of the arbor branches and held it out to me. I watched her run nakedly through the long grass to the pool, try the water, groan. Then she waded forwards and swanned in with a scream. The water was jade green, melted snow, and it made my heart jolt with shock when I plunged beside her. And yet it was beautiful, the shadow of the trees, the sunlight on the glade, the white roar of the little fall, the iciness, the solitude, the laughing, the nakedness; moments one knows only death can obliterate.

Sitting in the grass beside the arbor we let the sun and the small breeze dry us and ate the last of the chocolate. Then Alison lay on her back, her arms thrown out, her legs a little open, abandoned to the sun—and, I knew, to me. For a time I lay like her, with my eyes closed.

Then she said, "I'm Queen of the May."

She was sitting up, turned to me, propped on one arm. She had woven a rough crown out of the oxeyes and wild pinks that grew in the grass around us. It sat lopsidedly on her uncombed hair; and she wore a smile of touching innocence. She did not know it, but it was at first for me an intensely literary moment. I could place it exactly: *England's Helicon.* I had forgotten that there are metaphors and metaphors, and that the greatest lyrics are very rarely anything but direct and unmetaphysical. Suddenly she was like such a poem . . .

"The right reader of a good poem can tell the moment it strikes him that he has taken an immortal wound, that he will never get over it."

Objective cognition lies hidden behind the attraction of the emotional relationship.

True or False
Love: sex informed
Love: by intellect.

199

A LEAP IN THE DARK

We do not make progress. Every man thinks up one riddle and goes on solving it over and over. He solves it on one level and then sees that he must solve it again on another. What could possibly make him go on? Sisyphus? A terrible ordeal but one he accepts for that tiny edge where it is his own choice to be or not to be, and he flings their terrible mechanical predestination back in the faces of the gods and becomes one of them for split seconds on some mountain top. A completion, a fulfillment? As though all his actions are preparations for these moments of being.

Through this process he clarifies his vision. He first solves the riddle physically as a child. Then he does it all over again conceptually, through a combination of body and language processes and achieves another picture of the same world in answer to the same riddle. But these are still in the instinctual realm, automatic responses any human creature in an adequate framework does make. He could remain there. But he is still like a blind man, for he has not stepped back from this level of awareness and is imprisoned in his own network of concepts. Sometimes, however, he glimpses more, and if he can accept his own ignorance, begins all over again.

Now he must examine the processes themselves. He must concern himself with how structures are formed and altered, with will and mind, with objective and subjective, with ambiguities and paradoxes, with 'the mist of affects.' He seeks 'not truth, but an enlargement of reality.' There is more to see, more to realize, a broader world with riches he did not see before, the same picture but illuminated. Layer under layer, veil under veil. Every struggle with the Sisyphean rock is a struggle to penetrate meaning. Every new beginning is as demanding as the last.

DNA

No Thanks
Define: *gift.*

The measure of generality determines not only the equivalence of concepts but also all of the intellectual operations possible with a given concept.

True or False
Insight: the amalgam of
intellect and
experience

Those without the need never know themselves, but knowledge makes difficulties.

atomic structure

electron microphone

POETIC,

SCIENTIFIC,

or HUMAN?

...reaching down in behind the experience and bringing its objective "scientific" aspects to the surface where the poet and his reader may reflect upon them.

Surface structure
deep structure

The fact is that in former times men did not reflect upon their symbols; they lived them and were unconsciously animated by their meaning.

I will illustrate this by an experience I once had with the primitives of Mount Elgon in Africa. Every morning at dawn, they leave their huts and breathe or spit into their hands, which they then stretch out to the first rays of the sun, as if they were offering either their breath or their spittle to the rising god—to *mungu*. (This Swahili word, which they used in explaining the ritual act, is derived from a Polynesian root equivalent to *mana* or *mulungu*. These and similar terms designate a "power" of extraordinary efficiency and pervasiveness, which we should call divine. Thus the word *mungu* is their equivalent for Allah or God.) When I asked them what they meant by this act, or why they did it, they were completely baffled. They could only say: "We have always done it. It has always been done when the sun rises." They laughed at the obvious conclusion that the sun is *mungu*. The sun indeed is not *mungu* when it is above horizon; *mungu* is the actual moment of the sunrise.

What they were doing was obvious to me, but not to them; they just did it, never reflecting on what they did. They were consequently unable to explain themselves. I concluded that they were offering their souls to *mungu*, because the breath (of life) and the spittle mean "soul-substance." To breathe or spit upon something conveys a "magical" effect, as, for instance, when Christ used spittle to cure the blind, or where a son inhales his dying father's last breath in order to take over the father's soul. It is most unlikely that these Africans ever, even in the remote past, knew any more about the meaning of their ceremony. In fact, their ancestors probably knew even less, because they were more profoundly unconscious of their motives and thought less about their doings.

Goethe's Faust aptly says: *'Im Anfang war die Tat* (In the beginning was the deed)." "Deeds" were never invented, they were done; thoughts, on the other hand, are a relatively late discovery of man. First he was moved to deeds by unconscious factors; it was only a long time afterward that he began to reflect upon the causes that had moved him.

losne1

things became *real* through a process.

MUNGU

A diablero is a diablero, and a warrior is a warrior. Or a man can be both. There are enough people who are both. But a man who only traverses the paths of life is everything. Today I am neither a warrior nor a diablero. For me there is only the traveling on the paths that have a heart, on any path that may have a heart. There I travel, and the only worthwhile challenge for me is to traverse its full length. And there I travel—looking, looking, breathlessly.''

He paused. His face revealed a peculiar mood; he seemed to be unusually serious. I did not know what to ask or to say. He proceeded:

''The particular thing to learn is how to get to the crack between the worlds and how to enter the other world. There is a crack between the two worlds, the world of the diableros and the world of living men. There is a place where the two worlds overlap. The crack is there. It opens and closes like a door in the wind. To get there a man must exercise his will. He must, I should say, develop an indomitable desire for it, a single-minded dedication. But he must do it without the help of any power or any man. The man by himself must ponder and wish up to a moment in which his body is ready to undergo the journey.

''There is an inside to experience as well as an outside.''

D E E P

STRUCTURE

too . . .

All experiences are images . . . (T. or F.)

Hypnagogic Children's Hour

''The twilight is the crack between the worlds,'' he said softly, without looking at me.

The Quiver of Transition

''Over the Mountains
Of the Moon,
Down the Valley of the Shadow,
Ride, boldly ride,''—
The shade replied,—
''If you search for Eldorado.''

---

the very best butter,

I am speaking of those who cannot tolerate the loss of myth and who can neither find a way to a merely exterior world, to the world as seen by science, nor rest satisfied with *an intellectual juggling with words,* which has nothing whatsoever to do with wisdom.

These victims of the psychic dichotomy of our time are merely *optional neurotics;* their apparent morbidity drops away the moment the gulf between the *ego and the unconscious* is closed. The doctor who has felt this dichotomy to the depths of his being will also be able to reach a better understanding of the unconscious psychic processes, and will be saved from the danger of inflation to which the psychologist is prone. The doctor who does not know from his own experience the numinosity of the archetypes will scarcely be able to escape their negative effect when he encounters it in his practice. He will tend to over or underestimate it, since he possesses only an intellectual point of view but no empirical criterion. This is where those perilous aberrations begin, the first of which is the attempt to dominate everything by the intellect. This serves the secret purpose of placing both doctor and patient at a safe distance from the archetypal effect and thus from real experience, and of substituting for psychic reality an apparently secure, artificial, but merely two-dimensional conceptual world in which the reality of life is well covered up by so-called clear concepts. Experience is stripped of its substance, and instead mere names are substituted, which are henceforth put in the place of reality. No one has any obligations to a concept; that is what is so agreeable about *conceptuality*—it promises *protection from experience.* The spirit does not dwell in concepts, but in deeds and in facts. Words butter no parsnips; nevertheless, this futile procedure is repeated ad infinitum.

New concepts transform earlier meaning.

ARE YOU SOME KIND OF MYSTIC

The way people play the matchstick game represents their approaches to life in general. In any group there is virtually the full array: Those who don't try at all—because they know they can't do it, because they had planned on something else, because they don't want to risk ego deflation, and so forth. Those who try a little and then give up. Those who want hints. Those who try to follow someone else's lead, the imitators. Those who want to be given the answer. And those who struggle with it and solve it.

Those who solve the puzzle experience at the instant of discovery the thrill of living poetically. Though the puzzle may seem unimportant, its very triviality is the key to what education has to be. It has nothing to do with practical matters like jobs or bread or the future. It is an intrinsic and intense pleasure in itself. The clarification of one's experience is not for ulterior motives like survival or power, though these are often by-products or perversions. We are biologically obliged to have a good time—or die, to feel alive not only physically but mentally.

The game is a metaphor for learning processes and attitudes and is also an analogy for attitudes toward language. We see that language is a mind-set, the parameter of our conscious world—language plus all the nonverbal symbols that connect with it. Language gives us a sense of stability in the world, but it also gives us a tendency toward blindness to alternatives (as though there were only one way to approach a new matchstick game). We become set in our ways and approach problems along narrow channels though there are infinite possible choices and channels. Trying to solve the matchstick game reveals how our habits of language can prevent us from seeing in new ways. The game shows us how we can break through our regular habits of seeing, how we can loosen up our discovery processes to find solutions to our life problems.

> *If* the game *is* an analogy, what are the necessary conditions for imaginative solutions to problems?

If learning doesn't embody the intensity of pleasure one experiences on a smaller scale in the matchstick game, it is not true learning; it is mere accumulation of data. For learning is always that flash of discovery, the synapse in which two things come together and merge.

There remains the question of whether or not solving the matchstick game takes place *in* language. Or is it nonverbal? I do know that if I solve this problem, it will not be worked out in my rational mind exclusively. I will be working intensely, playing, toying. There will be an emotional feeling connected with it, a thrust toward synthesis. My conscious mind and unconscious will be working together. The flash will come intuitively and my conscious, rational mind will nail it down.

203

T. or F.: All images are mirrors.

ENEMIES of the MAN of KNOWLEDGE
1:FEAR

Define *rock.*

"To be a man of knowledge has no permanence. One is never a man of knowledge, not really. Rather, one becomes a man of knowledge for a very brief instant, after defeating the four natural enemies."

"You must tell me, don Juan, what kind of enemies they are."

He did not answer. I insisted again, but he dropped the subject and started to talk about something else.

Sunday, April 15, 1962

As I was getting ready to leave, I decided to ask him once more about the enemies of a man of knowledge. I argued that I could not return for some time, and it would be a good idea to write down what he had to say and then think about it while I was away.

He hesitated for a while, but then began to talk.

"When a man starts to learn, he is never clear about his objectives. His purpose is faulty; his intent is vague. He hopes for rewards that will never materialize, for he knows nothing of the hardships of learning.

"He slowly begins to learn—bit by bit at first, then in big chunks. And his thoughts soon clash. What he learns is never what he pictured, or imagined, and so he begins to be afraid. Learning is never what one expects. Every step of learning is a new task, and the fear the man is experiencing begins to mount mercilessly, unyielding. His purpose becomes a battlefield.

"And thus he has stumbled upon the first of his natural enemies: Fear! A terrible enemy — treacherous, and difficult to overcome. It remains concealed at every turn of the way, prowling, wait-ing. And if the man, terrified in its presence, runs away, his enemy will have put an end to his quest."

"What will happen to the man if he runs away in fear?"

"Nothing happens to him except that he will never learn. He will never become a man of knowledge. He will perhaps be a bully, or a harmless, scared man; at any rate, he will be a defeated man. His first enemy will have put an end to his cravings."

"And what can he do to overcome fear?"

"The answer is very simple. He must not run away. He must defy his fear, and in spite of it he must take the next step in learning, and the next, and the next. He must be fully afraid, and yet he must not stop. That is the rule! And a moment will come when his first enemy retreats. The man begins to feel sure of himself. His intent becomes stronger. Learning is no longer a terrifying task.

"When this joyful moment comes, the man can say without hesitation that he has defeated his first natural enemy."

"Does it happen at once, don Juan, or little by little?"

"It happens little by little, and yet the fear is vanquished suddenly and fast."

"But won't the man be afraid again if something new happens to him?"

"No. Once a man has vanquished fear, he is free from it for the rest of his life because, instead of fear, he has acquired clarity—a clarity of mind which erases fear. By then a man knows his desires; he knows how to satisfy those desires. He can anticipate the new steps of learning, and a sharp clarity surrounds everything. The man feels that nothing is concealed.

ENGLAND'S HELICON

"It is never thought to begin with. It finds its thought and succeeds, or it doesn't find it and comes to nothing."

204

Gaily bedight
A gallant knight
In sunshine and in shadow
Had journeyed long,
Singing a song,
In search of Eldorado.

giviak

Curiosity

may have killed the cat; more likely
the cat was just unlucky, or else curious
to see what death was like, having no cause
to go on licking paws, or fathering
litter on litter of kittens, predictably.

Nevertheless, to be curious
is dangerous enough. To distrust
what is always said, what seems,
to ask odd questions, interfere in dreams,
leave home, smell rats, have hunches
does not endear him to those doggy circles
where well-smelt baskets, suitable wives, good lunches
are the order of things, and where prevails
much wagging of incurious heads and tails.

Face it. Curiosity
will not cause him to die—
only lack of it will.
Never to want to see
the other side of the hill,
or that improbable country
where living is an idyll
(although a probable hell)
would kill us all.
Only the curious
have, if they live, a tale
worth telling at all.

Dogs say he loves too much, is irresponsible,
is changeable, marries too many wives,
deserts his children, chills all dinner tables
with tales of his nine lives.
Well, he is lucky. Let him be
nine-lived and contradictory,
curious enough to change, prepared to pay
the cat price, which is to die
and die again and again,
each time with no less pain.
A cat minority of one
is all that can be counted on
to tell the truth. And what he has to tell
on each return from hell
is this: that dying is what the living do,
and dying is what the loving do,
and that dead dogs are those who do not know
that hell is where, to live, they have to go.

Alastair Reid

"My grandmother wanted me to have an education, so she kept me out of school."

what makes a tale worth telling?

"We noticed that the ability to tolerate and use the irrelevant was of fundamental importance for a solution to a problem...Also, the ability to play, to sustain a childlike willingness to suspend adult disbelief emerged as a psychological condition of making the familiar strange."

PARSNIP

PRESIDENT

"I taste bacon flavor in this."

Kathy McKowen
3220 Geary Blvd. S.F.
April 26, 1970

9

Problem-Solving Play:

Play with words, with meanings
and definitions.
Play in pushing a fundamental
law or a basic scientific
concept "out of phase."
Play with metaphor.

Between barely and not quite.

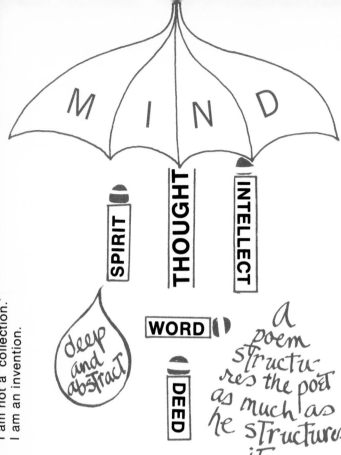

M I N D

SPIRIT THOUGHT INTELLECT

deep and abstract

WORD

DEED

a poem structures the poet as much as he structures it.

I am not a 'collection.'
I am an invention.

A phenomenon or an event is a resultant, the point where two things come together and fuse.

To understand, stand under, an event, one must reconstruct the situation, at least in one's own mind, whereby the event was created. Most of the 'facts' stored up in my mind have not been made 'real' by me in this manner. They are there, available, but not yet alive. Through my need for lucidity, I select those things I will breathe life into.

To create an idea, a word, or a concept of my own I must employ which of the following:

    a. deliberate attention,
    b. logical memory,
    c. abstraction,
    d. the ability to compare,
    e. the ability to differentiate,
    f. all of the above,
    g. none of the above?

206

The quiver of the transition from belief to realization

Hierarchies:
  Get the olive out of the cocktail glass.

• Alloplastic mastery — the period roughly from ages 21 to 35 in which the young adult strives to achieve mastery over the external world, seeking material gain and approval of others.

Choose one:

1. Knowledge is a copy of reality.
2. Knowledge is the *absorbing* of reality into a structure of transformations.

   (Which do most teachers think it is?)
    ((Which is more fun?))

MIND POLLUTANTS

I began assiduously examining the style and technique of those whom I once admired and worshipped: Nietzsche, Dostoievski, Hamsun, even Thomas Mann, whom today I discard as being a skillful fabricator, a brickmaker, an inspired jackass or draught-horse. I imitated every style in the hope of finding the clue to the gnawing secret of how to write. Finally I came to a dead end, to a despair and desperation which few men have known, because there was no divorce between myself as writer and myself as man: to fail as a writer meant to fail as a man. And I failed. I realized that I was nothing — less than nothing — a minus quantity. It was at this point, in the midst of the dead Sargasso Sea, so to speak, that I really began to write. I began from scratch, throwing everything overboard, even those whom I most loved. Immediately I heard my own voice I was enchanted: the fact that it was a separate, distinct, unique voice sustained me. It didn't matter to me if what I wrote should be considered bad. Good and bad dropped out of my vocabulary. I jumped with two feet into the realm of aesthetics, the non-moral, non-ethical, non-utilitarian realm of art. My life itself became a work of art. I had found a voice, I was whole again. The experience was very much like what we read of in connection with the lives of Zen initiates. My huge failure was like the recapitulation of the experience of the race: I had to grow foul with knowledge, realize the futility of everything, smash everything, grow desperate, then humble, then sponge my self off the slate, as it were, in order to recover my authenticity. I had to arrive at the brink and then take a leap in the dark.

A RICH . . .

HOW TO EAT A GIVIAK

Now it was winter, and Angutidluarssuk's giviak was frozen. He took his axe and started choping up the icy stuff. Pink feathers and bird meat flew to all sides, while we watched in pious silence. At last the floor was completely covered with pieces of meat and blubber. Angutidluarssuk picked up a bite, tasted it, and threw it contemptuously away.

"Alas, as I told you: this is inedible! Possibly I have, through an oversight, filled the skin with dogs' dung. Possibly it is only my absolute ignorance about how to make a giviak that has caused this mistake! If you would show me a kindness, you would leave me now so that I could be alone with my shame!"

Upon this invitation, we started in. It tasted good the moment I got it in my mouth. But I had to be taught how to eat this remarkable dish. As long as it is frozen, you just chew away. You get feathers and bones in your mouth, of course, but you just spit them out. Frozen meat always has an enticing taste, and as it dissolves in the mouth, you get the full aroma of the raw fermented bird. It is incredible how much you can down, unbelievable how hard it is to stop. If you happen to come across a fully developed egg inside a bird, it tastes like a dream. Or the liver, which is like green cheese. Breast and drumsticks are cooling and refreshing. It was late before we were full, and there was then about half of the giviak left. This was put up on one of the bunks to thaw for later use.

When we had had some sleep, we started the second part of the feast. The giviak was now so much thawed that the little auks tasted entirely different, and it was possible to eat them in a new way. Whole birds could now be pried loose from the compressed mass, and when that is the case, great elegance can be demonstrated while enjoying them. A man with *savoir-vivre* holds the bird by the legs with his teeth. Then he strokes it with both hands, thus brushing off the feathers that have already been loosened by the fermentation. He brushes his hands together to remove all feathers, whereupon he turns the bird and bites the skin loose around the beak. This can then be turned inside out and pulled free of the bird without letting go of its legs. The eater then sucks the whole skin into his mouth and pulls it out again, pressing his teeth slightly together. In this manner, he gets all the delicious fat sitting inside the skin. Taste is, as we know, an individual matter, but this one — I dare guarantee — can become a passion.

When the skin is free of fat, you bite it free around the bird's legs and swallow it in one piece. The breast is eaten by biting down on each side of the bone, and the bone can then be thrown away. This bares the innards, and you can enjoy the various parts one by one. The blood clot around the heart has coagulated and glues the teeth together, the liver and the gall bladder have a spicy taste, while the bitter aroma of the intestines reminds one of lager beer. When these parts are consumed, the rest — wings, backbone, and pelvis — is taken into the mouth and thoroughly chewed.

Such delicacies were always served in Angutidluarssuk's house.

JOURNAL

MARCH 10

Walking, in the morning.
The gentle breeze stirs a leaf,
Hello leaf.
A piece of aluminum paper shuffles;
Good morning parking lot, paper, and breeze.
The coffee, hot and rich;
Good morning coffee.
Good morning life. — me??

INNATE . . .

I have just tied a knot — I have done so consciously, yet I cannot explain how I did it, because my awareness was centered on the knot rather than on my own motions, the how of my action. When the latter becomes the object of my awareness, I shall become fully conscious. The consciousness of being conscious.

Washington, June 8, 1971

A "simple public display" of a four-letter word cannot be outlawed, the Supreme Court ruled yesterday.

The decision reversed a 1968 conviction of a Los Angeles man who was arrested for wearing a jacket bearing the words "f--- the draft" in the L.A. county courthouse.

In the 6 to 3 decision, the majority report stated, "This case may seem at first blush too inconsequential to find its way into our books, but the issue it represents is of no small constitutional significance."

The appeals court had held that the display came under the "offensive conduct" statute as "behavior which has a tendency to provoke others to acts of violence or to in turn disturb the peace."

But the high court argued, "It cannot plausibly be maintained that this vulgar allusion to the Selective Service system would conjur up such psychic stimulation in anyone likely to be confronted with Cohen's crudely defaced jacket.

"While the particular four-letter word being litigated here is perhaps more distasteful than most others of its genre, it is, nevertheless, often true that one man's vulgarity is another's lyric."

The state's case, it appeared, came down to official opposition to the word itself.

GAME

FIVE-LETTER WORDS

Choose a partner. Each one think of a five-letter word and then try to figure out what the other person's word is. Proceed as follows: Suppose my word is *logic* and yours is *every*. Start guessing by trying me with a five-letter word, say *loves*. I tell you that it contains two letters of my word. It is my turn, and I try you with *lists*. You would tell me that it contains none of the letters in your word. The object is to guess the other person's word in the least number of tries. Each of you will need to keep track of your own tries and your opponent's.

EXAMPLE:
My word: LOGIC

MY TRIES	YOUR TRIES
1. LISTS (0)	LOVES (2)
2. BELOW (1)	LATER (1)
3. WORDS (1)	DANCE (1)
4. TESTS (1)	TRAMP (0)

(One of your letters is *e*.)

And so on until one of us deduces the other's word.

MATCHES

In trying to solve new problems, individuals must avoid premature expression of rational completed concepts. The seamless sphericity of a "closed loop" thought presents an idea association in the impregnable form of a perfectly smooth surface. When an idea is expressed after being completely worked out it is either acceptable as true or unacceptable as untrue. It resists modification. It lives or dies as uttered. No one else can find his way in and build on it; the author of the thought finds himself adorned with a conceptual jewel which is isolated and untouchable.

Non-rational communication, on the other hand, produces evocative metaphors, images with rough surfaces, and fissures on which others can get a grip and participate. Of course, this kind of non-rational interplay is only part of a process which spirals up toward increasing coherence. Ultimate solutions to problems are rational; the process of finding them is not.

MYTHS

The primary word is not a straightforward symbol for a concept but rather an image, a picture, a mental sketch of a concept, a short tale about it — indeed, a small work of art.

THE HEISENBERG EFFECT

"I really felt I had lost my body, don Juan."
"You did."
"You mean, I really didn't have a body?"
"What do *you* think yourself?"
"Well, I don't know. All I can tell you is what I felt."
"That is all there is in reality — what you felt."
"But how did you see me, don Juan? How did I appear to you?"
"How I saw you does not matter. It is like the time when you grabbed the pole. You felt it was not there and you went around it to make sure it was there. But when you jumped at it you felt again that it was not really there."

Syllogism

Cross out the incorrect statement:
All poets must be scientists.
All scientists must be poets.

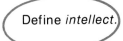 Define *intellect.*    Define *mind.*

Suppose it were perfectly certain that the life and fortune of every one of us would, one day or other, depend upon his winning or losing a game at chess.

Don't you think that we should all consider it to be a primary duty to learn at least the names and the moves of the pieces; to have a notion of a gambit, and a keen eye for all the means of giving and getting out of check? Do you not think that we should look with a disapprobation amounting to scorn, upon the father who allowed his son, or the state which allowed its members, to grow up without knowing a pawn from a knight?

Yet it is a very plain and elementary truth, that the life, the fortune, and the happiness of every one of us, and, more or less, of those who are connected with us, do depend upon our knowing something of the rules of a game infinitely more difficult and complicated than chess. It is a game which has been played for untold ages, every man and woman of us being one of the two players in a game of his or her own. The chess-board is the world, the pieces are the phenomena of the universe, the rules of the game are what we call the laws of Nature...

"The suggestion is that the function of the brain and nervous system and sense organs is in the main *eliminative* and not productive. Each person is at each moment capable of remembering all that has ever happened to him and of perceiving everything that is happening everywhere in the universe. The function of the brain and nervous system is to protect us from being overwhelmed and confused by this mass of largely useless and irrelevant knowledge, by shutting out most of what we should otherwise perceive or remember at any moment, and leaving only that very small and special selection which is likely to be practically useful."

209

SYSTEM...

Matters of Consequence...

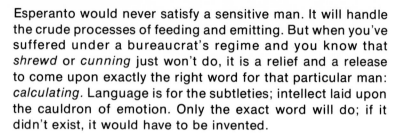

450,000 CHOICES

Esperanto would never satisfy a sensitive man. It will handle the crude processes of feeding and emitting. But when you've suffered under a bureaucrat's regime and you know that *shrewd* or *cunning* just won't do, it is a relief and a release to come upon exactly the right word for that particular man: *calculating*. Language is for the subtleties; intellect laid upon the cauldron of emotion. Only the exact word will do; if it didn't exist, it would have to be invented.

The Prince, travelling through his domains, noticed a man in the cheering crowd who bore a striking resemblance to himself. He beckoned him over and asked: 'Was your mother ever employed in my palace?'

'No, Sire,' the man replied. 'But my father was.'

Safecrackers sandpaper their finger tips.

Utterance = outer-ance.

"My outerances are a groping for light." *What* gropes for light?

B

TRIGGERS

TO MARK ANTHONY IN HEAVEN

This quiet morning light
reflected, how many times
from grass and trees and clouds
enters my north room
touching the walls with
grass and clouds and trees.
Anthony,
trees and grass and clouds.
Why did you follow
that beloved body
with your ships at Actium?
I hope it was because
you knew her inch by inch
from slanting feet upward
to the roots of her hair
and down again and that
you saw her
above the battle's fury—
clouds and trees and grass—

For then you are
listening in heaven.

S E S

"I don't see why a person should be discriminated against because of the shape of their skin."

JOURNAL:

I didn't regard punctuation as important at all before I started writing down exactly what I think. I don't think I really cared if my writing was confusing because of wrong or left-out punctuation. But now that it's really me writing I want to be sure the reader gets the point exactly, stops when I stop, pauses when I pause, laughs when I laugh, and so forth . . . .

A

"A poem may be an unfolding of an emotion which is at first purely implicit. It may begin merely as a vague lump in the throat, and out of that tension the images of a poem may be used for purposes of passing from the implicit to the explicit. The poem itself might be the quiver of the transition from belief to realization."

TRACES

"No man lives in external truths among salts and acids, but in the warm phantasmagoric chamber of his brain, with the painted windows and the storied walls."

an intensly literary moment

It's the unsaid part That's the best part.

A Reason for Writing

No word that is not flesh, he said,
Can hold my wavering ear; but when
That golden physical flesh is clear,
I dance in a glory like your glory
With force to stir the dead.

No word that is not thought, he said,
Can hook my slippery mind; but when
That silver accurate thought I find,
I dance in a glory like your glory
With force to stir the dead.

Words both flesh and thought, he said,
Hold and hook my heart; and when
The gold, the silver, shudder apart,
Still in a glory like your glory
I'll dance to stir the dead.

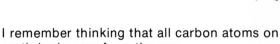

AME STREET

C

Riddle:

What word does almost everyone pronounce wrong?

The mental process needed to read A are more like those needed to read B or C? Or do A, B, and C require the same process?

The Effect of Gamma Rays on Man-in-the-Moon Marigolds

I remember thinking that all carbon atoms on earth had come from the sun.
The idea of being linked to the universe by these atoms, which really don't die, gave me a feeling of meaning.

211

TWO TASTE TREATS IN ONE

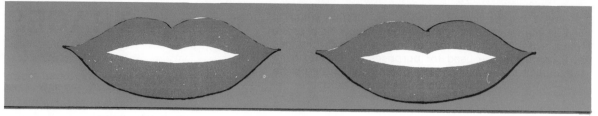

THE FORCE THAT THROUGH THE GREEN 1 DRIVES THE FLOWER

The force that through the green **1** drives the flower
Drives my **2** age; that blasts the roots of trees
Is my destroyer.
And I am dumb to tell the **3** rose
My youth is bent by the same **4** fever.

The force that drives the water through the rocks
Drives my red blood; that dries the **5** streams
Turns mine to wax.
And I am dumb to **6** unto my veins
How at the mountain spring that same mouth sucks.

The hand that **7** the water in the pool
Stirs the **8**; that ropes the blowing wind
Hauls my **9** sail.
And I am dumb to tell the hanging man
How of my **10** is made the hangman's lime.

The lips of time leech to the fountain head;
Love drips and gathers, but the **11** blood
Shall calm her sores.
And I am dumb to tell a weather's wind
How time has **12** a heaven round the stars.

And I am dumb to tell the lover's tomb
How at my sheet goes the same **13** worm.

1. a. stem, b. plant, c. fuse, d. sleeve
2. a. young, b. green, c. foolish, d. glib
3. a. crooked, b. yellow, c. thorny, d. budding
4. a. burning, b. aching, c. weak, d. wintry
5. a. eccentric, b. mouthing, c. leaping, d. bounding
6. a. shoot, b. mouth, c. speak, d. track
7. a. swirls, b. whirls, c. clears, d. curls
8. a. stew, b. pollution, c. quicksand, d. cosmos
9. a. clearance, b. white, c. spring, d. shroud
10. a. bisque, b. clay, c. body, d. works
11. a. vampired, b. given, c. fallen, d. diseased
12. a. traced, b. paced, c. spun, d. ticked
13. a. crooked, b. yellow, c. thorny, d. budding

Man values the subtleties; that's what language is for:

Part I

You make the test:

Cross out one word from each group so that the choices left constitute the most challenging game. Compare and explore decisions as you go. Reflect.

Part II

Take the test together:

Explore reasons for your decisions as you go. Then "correct" your group's test and again explore the implications. Reflect.

It's a Candy and a Cake.

MADURO

WHEN I HAVE FEARS

When I have fears that I may cease to be
  Before my pen has glean'd my teeming brain,
Before high-piled books, in charact'ry,
  Hold like rich garners the full-ripen'd grain;
When I behold, upon the night's starr'd face,
  Huge cloudy symbols of a high romance,
And think that I may never live to trace
  Their shadows, with the magic hand of chance;
And when I feel, fair creature of an hour!
  That I shall never look upon thee more,
Never have relish in the faery power
  Of unreflecting love!—then on the shore
Of the wide world I stand alone, and think
Till love and fame to nothingness do sink.

Choose one, neither or both:

The sculpture and poem reinforce each other.
The sculpture and poem are contrasting statements.

Vote, explore reasons, reflect.

CAULDRON

213

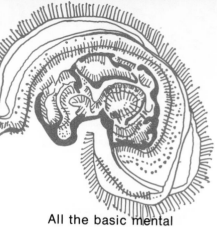

THE SICK ROSE

O Rose, thou art sick!
The invisible worm
That flies in the night,
In the howling storm,

Has found out thy bed
Of crimson joy,
And his dark secret love
Does thy life destroy.

All the basic mental functions become conscious and deliberate during school age, *except* intellect itself.

A

THE DESTRUCTORS

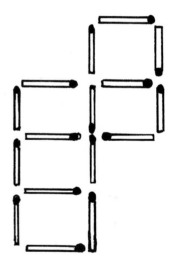

Symbolic forms are *not* imitations; they are organs of reality; it is solely by their agency that anything real becomes an object for intellectual apprehension.

B

Alchemy
Create a bridge between these two statements:

1. The poem itself might be the quiver of the transition from belief to realization.

2. The essential functions of intelligence consist ... in building up structures by structuring reality.

Giviak means something immersed, in this case little auks that have been immersed in seal blubber and ripened through the summer into a delicacy to dream about.

Rearrange *two* of the matchsticks in this configuration so that four equal squares are formed.

Metaphysics: Ontology = cosmology

COURTING THE MUSE

A. Play with the problem by pushing and pulling at its structure through far and near fetched analogies.

B. Use experts to determine which ideas are actually valid.

C. Make the problem your personal problem even when there is a group working on it.

D. Compete. Don't let the other person get the answer first.

E. State the problem as it is originally understood.

F. In groups, don't blurt out half-formed possibilities.

G. Check for analogies in nature.

H. Because solutions are often felt before articulated, feel free to utter faintly perceived analogies.

I. Take aspects which seem foreign to you and make comparisons with familiar things.

J. Work out the details of the problem by working through parallel details in the productive analogy.

K. The foremost concern is usefulness.

L. Cooperate; what is needed are successful analogies, not peacocks.

M. Use experts to describe technical problems in commonplace terms.

N. Cultivate plasticity of vision.

O. Don't let accidents or irrelevant play distract you from concentration.

P. Take chances in your thinking; use the partial, obvious, tentative, wrong.

Q. State the problem so that the *real* issue is exposed.

R. Once you identify the problem stick to a deductive method of reasoning.

S. Be ready to oscillate among involvement, detachment, speculation, and deferment of premature solutions, as needed.

T. In your speculation, do not violate the laws of science.

U. Develop an atmosphere of urgency to generate mental energy.

V. When you sense the need, allow the solution to lead its own life; allow yourself to follow its lead.

W. Take the problem as you are used to it and find far fetched comparisons.

X. _____ Y. _____ Z. _____

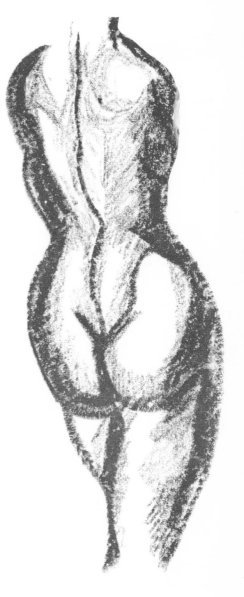

Cross out those items which are damaging to productive problem solving. Put the rest in productive clusters and in the most productive sequence, basing your decisions on your own success or failure with problem solving.

215

AMALGAMATION

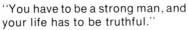
"You have to be a strong man, and
your life has to be truthful."
"What is a truthful life?"
"A life with deliberateness, a good,
strong life."

CONSTANTLY RISKING ABSURDITY

Constantly risking absurdity
    and death
     whenever he performs
      above the heads
        of his audience
the poet like an acrobat
     climbs on rime
       to a high wire of his own making
and balancing on eyebeams
      above a sea of faces
  paces his way
     to the other side of day
performing entrechats
     and sleight-of-foot tricks
and other high theatrics
     and all without mistaking
  any thing
     for what it may not be
For he's the super realist
    who must perforce perceive
  taut truth
     before the taking of each stance or step
in his supposed advance
      toward the still higher perch
where Beauty stands and waits
    with gravity
     to start her death-defying leap
And he
    a little charleychaplain man
      who may or may not catch
  her fair eternal form
     spreadeagled in the empty air
  of existence.

Freedom only within constraints . . .

undiluted freedom is one
of the most destructive
corrosives ever known; it
can eat away a soul in
months

          Colin Wilson

JOURNAL

   I like the idea of making sure our bodies
are all scarred and bruised when we die. I know
I am always protecting myself when I know
that I shouldn't give a damn about the consequences. I should try it anyway. (Like writing
poems?)

"nothing we love overmuch is
ponderable to the touch"

Complete this news story:

Bachelors
Miss
Sex, Too

London

A 25-year-old bachelor claimed in court yesterday that his sex life had been affected by an industrial injury.

A surprised judge asked the man's lawyer

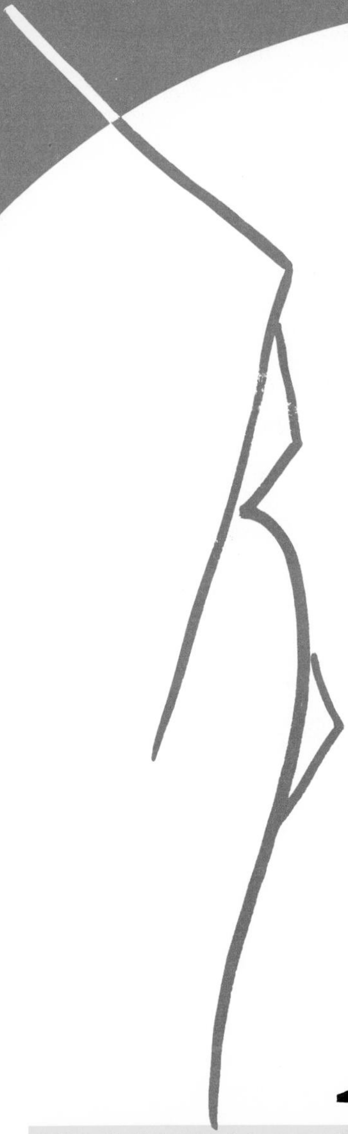

**In Our Nerve Endings,
We Are All Poets**

Symbolization may be an inherent function of the nervous system which does not return direct impressions of the external world to the brain but *indirect* symbolical representations. This rudimentary symbolization process of the nervous system is elaborated on higher and higher levels.

I thank the Lord for crudity which is rawness, which is raw material, which is the part of life not yet worked up into form, or at least not worked all the way up . . . Having had a glimpse of finished art, (the foolish) forever after pine for a life that shall be nothing but finished art . . . A real artist delights in roughness for what he can do to it. He's the brute who can knock the corners off the marble block and drag the unbedded beauty out of bed . . .

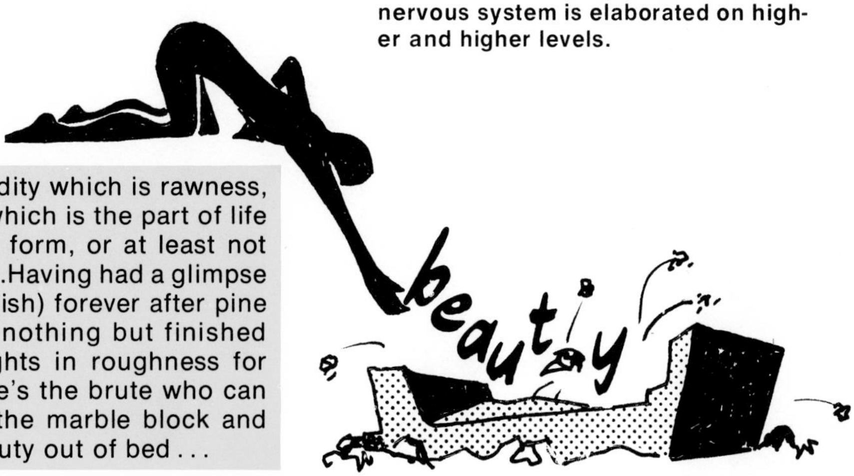

217

—I cannot paint
What then I was. The sounding cataract
Haunted me like a passion: the tall rock,
The mountain, and the deep and gloomy wood,
Their colours and their forms, were then to me
An appetite; a feeling and a love,
That had no need of a remoter charm
By thought supplied, nor any interest
Unborrowed from the eye — That time is past,
And all its aching joys are now no more,
And all its dizzy raptures. Not for this
Faint I, nor mourn nor murmur; other gifts
Have followed; for such loss, I would believe,
Abundant recompense. For I have learned
To look on nature, not as in the hour
Of thoughtless youth; but hearing oftentimes
The still sad music of humanity,
Nor harsh nor grating, though of ample power
To chasten and subdue.

I will pour out my spirit upon all flesh; and
your sons and your daughters shall prophesy, your old men shall dream dreams, your
young men shall see visions.

TO_____

Music, when soft voices die,
Vibrates in the memory—
Odours, when sweet violets sicken,
Live within the sense they quicken.

Rose leaves, when the rose is dead,
Are heaped for the beloved's bed;
And so thy thoughts, when thou art gone,
Love itself shall slumber on.

218

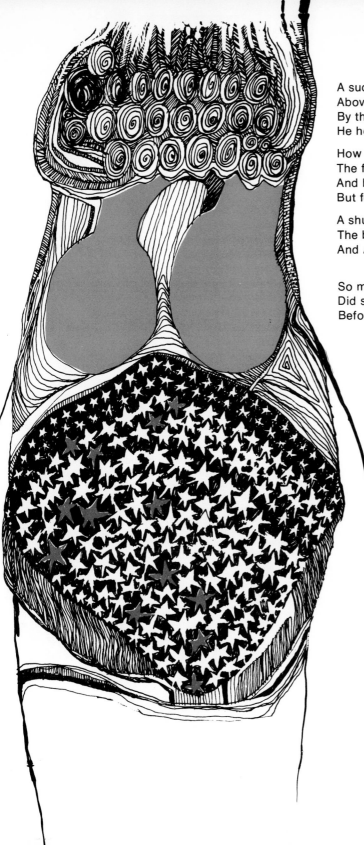

Leda and the Swan

A sudden blow: the great wings beating still
Above the staggering girl, her thighs caressed
By the dark webs, her nape caught in his bill,
He holds her helpless breast upon his breast.

How can those terrified vague fingers push
The feathered glory from her loosening thighs?
And how can body, laid in that white rush,
But feel the strange heart beating where it lies?

A shudder in the loins engenders there
The broken wall, the burning roof and tower
And Agememnon dead.

       Being so caught up,
So mastered by the brute blood of the air,
Did she put on this knowledge with this power
Before the indifferent beak could let her drop?

CORTEX

I hope it was because you knew
her inch by inch from slanting feet
upward to the roots of her hair and
down again . . .

THALAMUS

219

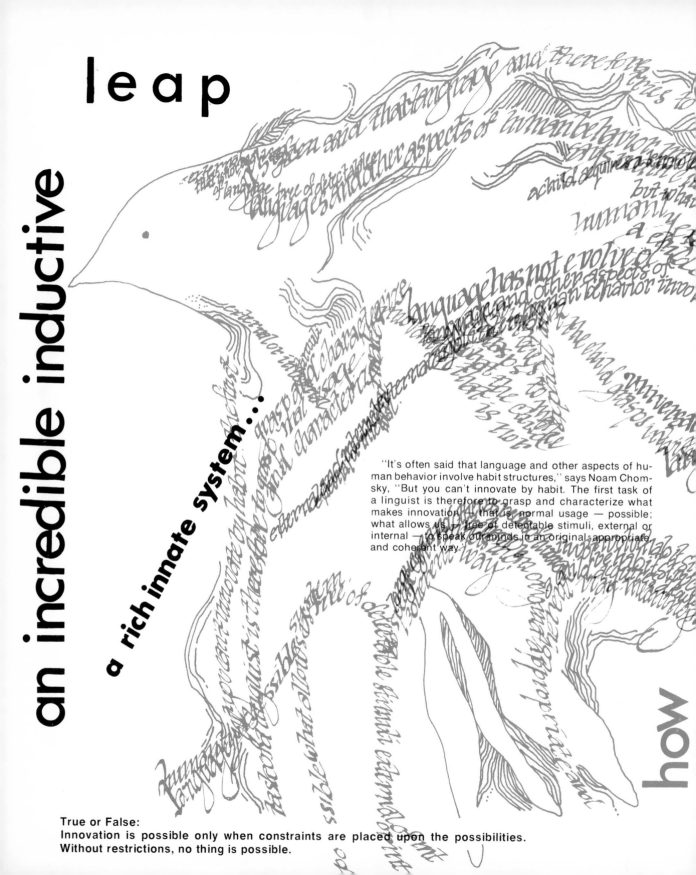

leap

an incredible inductive

a rich innate system...

"It's often said that language and other aspects of human behavior involve habit structures," says Noam Chomsky, "But you can't innovate by habit. The first task of a linguist is therefore to grasp and characterize what makes innovation — that is, normal usage — possible; what allows us — free of detectable stimuli, external or internal — to speak our minds in an original, appropriate, and coherent way."

how

True or False:
Innovation is possible only when constraints are placed upon the possibilities.
Without restrictions, no thing is possible.

english is a mass medium...

The linguist tries to make explicit what the child grasps intuitively, and therefore tries to construct a "generative grammar," a system of rules and principles that determine the connection of sound and meaning for the indefinitely large number of sentences that constitute a single language.

But the linguist also tries to establish the principles of "universal grammar," which governs all human languages. As Chomsky explains: "Universal grammar tries to specify the constraints and principles which determine what makes a possible system of grammar into a humanly accessible system. It tries to distinguish the essence of human language from arbitrary systems that might be imagined."

But what leads Chomsky to believe there is an essence? He replies: "The best evidence is the very fact that a child acquires knowledge of a language — an astonishing feat which is beyond the capacity of an otherwise intelligent ape." Chomsky holds that language has not evolved from simpler systems in nonhuman organisms.

True or False?
The actualized individual is an intensely literary moment.

are

constraint ≠ principle.

"The data are degenerate in the sense that a good deal of the material that the child hears is not even properly constructed: normal language consists very largely of false starts and fragments and hesitations. But the grammar the child constructs tells him what is a well-formed sentence and how such sentences can be used and understood.

"The child is in a much worse situation than a scientist who experiments and has good data — he is rather like a physicist who can do no experiments but nonetheless tries to construct theories about the world. The child develops a very complex and articulated theory of enormous predictive scope and explanatory power — he takes an incredible inductive leap."

Chomsky suggests that the child brings to this enormously difficult problem "a very rich system of expectations — a very rich innate system that tells him how to interpret data as a possible language." He argues that if a child were initially uninformed as to the nature of the system he has to construct, if his mind were totally plastic — as the behavioral psychologists believe — the acquisition of language would be a miracle. Since he rigorously refuses to believe in miracles, Chomsky has another explanation. He says that the mind of a child is not plastic, but has intrinsic properties that are the subject of universal grammar.

The principles of a grammar are deep and abstract, and only an organism initially (i.e., at birth) informed of the nature of these principles (in fact, "preset") could have discovered them in a particular case. Such principles tell us something about the intrinsic nature of the human mind and define one capacity of that mind: the language capacity.

"Universal grammar is a hypothesis about the essential nature of man — what it means to be a human being, what psychology is about. It tells you it's hopeless, or at best marginal, to try to explain anything about humans in terms of habit formation, or stimulus and response, or associations, or the shaping of behavior by environment. It tells us that we don't acquire knowledge the way empiricists think we do — through experience by association of stimuli, stimulus-response connections, and training. Language is not a matter of know-how established by habit.

"If you want to find out what it means to be a human being, you have to examine free creation within a system of rules, acquisition of knowledge within the framework of restrictive conditions imposed by the mind. The human mind is thus a kind of schematism, or framework, within which learning and behavior take place. Linguistic competence — knowledge of a language — is an abstract system, a generative grammar, consisting of rules or constraints that determine the form and meaning of an infinite number of sentences."

To show what he means by constraints — or innate principles — Chomsky proposes two simple sentences:
(1) Mary believed (that John had read *the book*).
(2) Mary believed (the claim that John had read *the book*).

To form a question about the italicized phrase in (1) we construct: what book did Mary believe that John had read? But we cannot do the same thing for (2) since it gives us: what book did Mary believe the claim that John had read?

"In fact, there is no question corresponding to (2). The problem is, how do we know this:how do we know that the simple rule which works for (1) doesn't generalize to (2)?

There is no question corresponding to (2). Thus, the sentence "What book did Mary believe the claim that John had read?" is one that we don't accept; indeed, it does not even occur to our mind to say it. In Chomsky's view this is evidence that there are general principles that guide us — though we may be unaware of their guidance.

The language learner has no *evidence* for any such general principle. It is unimaginable that every speaker of English has been explicitly taught that he can't form a question from (2), or explicitly taught the general principle that determines this fact, or explicitly given sufficient information to demonstrate this general principle. Rather, he just hears such sentences as (1) and (2) and lots of others and develops a knowledge of language that is governed by these general principles, which are an innate part of the structure we impose on experience.

The acquisition of knowledge is therefore a creative act by which we impose on data a structure of principles. That structure determines what we come to know on the basis of those principles. We come to know that one collection of consecutive words is a sentence and another is not.

The principles are a skeleton, and the degenerate data of language is flesh concealing the skeleton. English and all other languages have the same skeleton. Chomsky and his followers argue, and the different varieties of flesh hang where the skeleton allows them to hang, not at random.

"When you hear a sentence you hear a noise," Chomsky notes, ... "and when you look at the sentence you see words. But you know more."

To clarify this point, he writes down three additional collections of words that we call sentences:

222

you

I'll get by with a little help from my genes.

"John is difficult to please."
"John is easy to please."
"John is certain to please."

In the first two sentences John is the person being pleased; in the third, John does the pleasing. The surface structure thus does not always reflect the deep structure — which relates not to the sound but to the meaning. Our knowledge of the difference is unconscious and a part of the structure of the mind. Chomsky says:

"One is not merely interested in the data of English, but in what it tells us about the structure of the mind. The mind is arranged in terms of principles of this kind — basic rules which determine systems of grammatical relations and the way to organize these deep structures into surface structures. How to determine the nature of these grammatical relations is a problem of science — difficult but not impossible."

Chomsky writes another sentence on the blackboard: "The man will win."

The corresponding question is: "Will the man win?"

Then he writes: "The man who will arrive at six will win."

The corresponding question is: "Will the man who will arrive at six win?"

"How do I know that I take the second 'will' to form the question?" asks Chomsky . . .

How do I know the question should not be formed by taking out the first 'will' and using it as the first word of the question: 'Will the man who will arrive at six will win?' "

To answer his own questions, he proposes two possible formulations of the rule: first, take the left-most occurrence of "will," and put it at the head of the sentence; and second, take the occurrence of "will" that functions as "main verb" following the initial noun phrase of the sentence and invert it.

"Both rules give the same result in the case of the simpler sentences," he notes. "They give different results in the case of the longer sentence. The first, of course, gives the wrong result. But the first is by far the simpler rule. Suppose, say, you had a computer that was to perform these operations. To perform operation one, the computer would simply have to scan the sentence from left to right

the nature of human nature
To give a pupil new concepts deliberately is as impossible and futile as teaching someone to ride a unicycle by the laws of equilibrium.

TRIGGERS

until it came across an occurrence of 'will,' which it would then prepose. To perform operation two, the computer would have to analyze the syntactic structure of the sentence, determining that 'the man who will arrive at six' is the noun phrase subject and 'will' is the main verbal element."

"Operation one is 'structure-independent' — it cares only about the actual content of the sentence to which it applies and doesn't care at all about its abstract structure. Operation two is 'structure-dependent' — it cares about the abstract structure of the sentence, as well as about its actual content. Though structure-dependent operations are more complex and abstract, languages appear to have only operations of this sort."

Nobody who has spoken English has ever made the mistake of opting for the first rule instead of the second, he says. "And why not? Why does our mind use a difficult rule instead of a simple one, and why does the rule apply in every language?"

His answer is that the structure of the mind tells us which operations are permissible and which are not.

In any language there are things we learn. In English, for example, we learn that a rational featherless biped is "man," and in French we learn to call this animal *"homme."* But there are things we know without learning — such as the rule illustrated in the questions about the man who will (or will not) arrive at six.

There are probably similar things to be said about meaning, Chomsky suggests, adding, however: "We have ways for describing sounds, but we still don't have good ways for describing meaning."

My teacher holded the baby rabbits, and we patted them.

"Everybody thinks his own field is the most important," Chomsky says smilingly. "Linguistics, however, does tell us interesting things about the nature of human nature, about the human mind and some of the conditions of human creativity and free thought and expression. It tells us how humans speak and understand and think, though it has not yet managed to relate its discoveries to physiological mechanisms or interpret thought in terms of 'physical causes.'"

"One might consider linguistics as a branch of psychology," Chomsky adds. "Take psychology generally. As a human being you have friends and acquaintances and have made some assessment about them, you have a theory about them, even if unconscious, about how they will act. An important part of psychology ought to be to state the theories and discover how you arrived at them. To do so, psychology should try to discover those intrinsic properties of the mind that lead us to interpret the insignificant data of experience to form rich conclusions about what people are like. I think we'd then perhaps discover something like a universal grammar not of language but of human nature."

"Consider the acquisition of scientific knowledge," he says. "I'd assume there are some rather general conditions. I think that science arises when the structure of the world and the structure of the mind somehow fit together. Where the real nature of the world is such that it doesn't mesh with the structure of our mind, we don't have science."

"In science we sense intuitively that sometimes we have scientific knowledge and sometimes only intellectual technology. The difference can't be explained in terms of prediction. It has to do with comprehension, and psychology might attempt to specify the difference between scientific understanding and technology. The explanation would have to grow out of the concept of mind, and would be related to the kinds of intellectual structures our mind can produce."

Morris Halle — who collaborated with Chomsky on the enormously difficult and technical book *The Sound Pattern of English* — says:

"What Chomsky has done is invent a kind of formal structure in terms of which you record your observations.

"*Finding* facts is no problem. You can easily discover that the word 'America' is stressed on the second syllable. But that fact is interesting only if it tells you something about structure. What you're trying to understand in chemistry is the nature of matter, and what you're trying to understand in linguistics is the nature of language.

"Just as you can find out lots of facts about chemical elements, the interesting question is how they're related, what do they mean, and this comes only when you invent a theory. It tells you about things you have never seen.

"Man uses linguistic transformations without ever learning that such things exist. He doesn't learn that there are other things called phonemes, though he uses them all the time in speech. How does he manage to speak so fluently while he understands so poorly? Chomsky's answer is that this ability depends on an innate structure."

Part of the genetic equipment of man is the ability to perform the activity called language use. "We've studied hundreds of languages," Halle notes. "We find differences in them, of course. But the deep properties, like transformations and phonemes, are in all languages."

"Until Chomsky came along, the dominant school in linguistics was structural. The idea was that you could find out relevant facts in language by comparing almost identical cases. To show the difference between *t* and *p*, for example, you might offer 'tick' and 'pick.' The idea was that differences in sound that don't signal differences of meaning don't count, and you can ignore them. But our idea is that the important thing is for linguistics not simply to accumulate facts, which you can cherish as an antiquarian would, but to develop theoretical explanations for evidence. Grammar used to be 'natural history' and we are trying to make it 'natural science.'

"Just as chemistry tells you what structure a possible element must have, an element that we have seen as well as one yet to be discovered, linguistic theory defines a possible language, indeed every possible language. It thus tells you about thought, about behavior, about what it means to be a human being making choices through the filter of the mind."

THE NATURE OF ME

sarah

Create a visual metaphor which captures the essence of this article. Use whatever medium you wish. Explore each other's metaphor. Reflect on the investigation.

```
A          C
  X
B          D
```

X and C love each other. X must get across the river to get to her sweetheart. She goes to B, but he says, "I'm sorry, I can't help you. You'll have to work it out yourself." X then goes to A who says, "Sure, I'll take you across in my boat if you will spend the night with me." Seeing no alternative, X agrees. But when she gets across and tells C what she has done, he says, "Now that you've done that, I don't want you. Get out." At this point, seeing her anguish, D says, "Don't let it bother you. I'll marry you."

Discuss this situation in groups of five. Decide to which of the five characters you feel most akin. Reflect on the choices.

England's Helicon

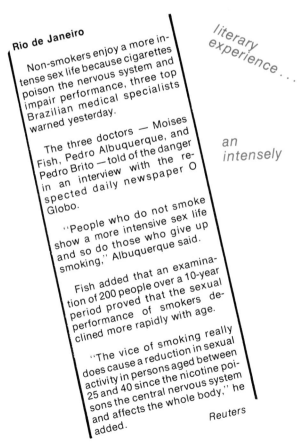

Rio de Janeiro

Non-smokers enjoy a more intense sex life because cigarettes poison the nervous system and impair performance, three top Brazilian medical specialists warned yesterday.

The three doctors — Moises Fish, Pedro Albuquerque, and Pedro Brito — told of the danger in an interview with the respected daily newspaper O Globo.

"People who do not smoke show a more intensive sex life and so do those who give up smoking," Albuquerque said.

Fish added that an examination of 200 people over a 10-year period proved that the sexual performance of smokers declined more rapidly with age.

"The vice of smoking really does cause a reduction in sexual activity in persons aged between 25 and 40 since the nicotine poisons the central nervous system and affects the whole body," he added.

Reuters

literary experience . . .

an intensely

When you want to make a giviak, you must first catch a seal, which then has to be flensed in a special and very difficult way. You start by cutting around the seal's mouth and let the hands feel their way down along its body inside the skin. The knife must not be too long, and it takes some practice before the hands have the right feel to avoid making holes in the skin. Around the forelimbs it can be particularly hard to find certain joints that have to be cut through. As you continue, both your arms are little by little buried in the seal. Often, big slices of blubber must be cut away and taken out through the opening at the mouth, so as to make room to operate in. When at last the knife has been all over, and the skin is entirely freed from the seal's body, there comes the most difficult part: the entire body has to be pulled out through the mouth opening. As a rule, two men have to pull with all their strength to get it done.

You now have a bag formed of sealskin and lined with blubber. And you are ready to proceed with the next task: the bird catch. A wall of stones is put up to hide behind. The little auks do not nest on the steep cliffs, they make themselves comfortable under the big stones in the scree, and often they crawl into deep holes under these stones. When they then fly out, they amuse themselves by swarming in clouds along the cliff quite low over the ground. Then is the time to let the net dart up and catch it full of birds. The pole has to be turned quickly so as to close the net and prevent the birds from flying out again. The birds are taken out of the net and killed by guiding a thumb up under the breastbone to the heart, which is "displaced," and the bird dies at once. After the wings have been braided together on the back of the bird, it is then put down in the blubber bag. A diligent birdcatcher — the women as a rule — can fill a sealskin in two days. But Angutidluarssuk had filled two sealskins between two sleeps. It must be said, though, that he was famous for sleeping infrequently in good hunting weather.

When the bag is full, it must immediately be put in a secure place and covered with stones. The sun must never shine on it, since the blubber would then turn rancid. The comparative warmth of the summer air makes the blubber seep into the birds and cure their meat. Nothing is quite so delicious, especially the lump of blood collected around the damaged heart, which is almost heavenly to eat.

225

To the Biblical "In the beginning was the Word," Goethe makes Faust reply, "In the beginning was the deed." The intent here is to detract from the value of the word, but we can accept this version if we emphasize it differently: In the *beginning* was the deed. The word was not the beginning — action was there first; it is the end of development, crowning the deed.

March 3, 1971

Forty-five per cent of the Spanish surname children in elementary school classes for mentally retarded were found to be of average intelligence or better when retested in Spanish, school officials of a large California city reluctantly admitted.

One child who was tested in English and scored 67 IQ was retested in Spanish and scored 128. The average gain for the group was 16 to 18 IQ points.

The school district gets $550 per year for each child enrolled in its special program. In this same program, 53 per cent of all the students are black, although only one fourth of the district's students are black.

When asked to explain the discrepancy, the special services administrator said, ''I think a large portion of it is cultural deprivation.''

MAN-IN-THE-MOON MARIGOLDS

According to the National Assessment of Educational Progress findings in the summer of 1970, the seventeen-year-olds have a wide range of common knowledge. 93% know that gas comes from petroleum, 69% that a galaxy contains many stars. But only 58%, despite science teachers, know that matter consists of individual moving particles.
Only 46% of the seventeen-year-olds know that the higher a musical note, the higher the frequency and the shorter the wavelength. Is this a matter of consequence?

The characters in the anecdote on page 225 represent five approaches to life. Here they are. Match them.

__1.	Home and hearth	A
__2.	Wisdom and intellect	B
__3.	Reality	C
__4.	Power and money	D
__5.	Conventional morality	X

THAT'S EASY FOR YOU TO SAY

Phenomenology is only another name for the kind of self-observation I had tried to carry out under mescalin, and when Husserl talks about 'uncovering the structure of consciousness,' he only means descending into these realms of mental habit of which I have spoken. Husserl had realized that while we have ordnance survey maps that cover every inch of our earth, we have no atlas of our mental world.

EMILY

I had another important experience at about this time. I was taking the long road to school from Klein-Hüningen, where we lived, to Basel, when suddenly for a single moment I had the overwhelming impression of having just emerged from a dense cloud. I knew all at once: now I am *myself*! It was as if a wall of mist were at my back, and behind that wall there was not yet an "I." But at this moment *I came upon myself*. Previously I had existed, too, but everything had merely happened to me. Now I happened to myself. Now I knew: I am myself now, now *I exist*. Previously I had been willed to do this and that; now *I* willed. This experience seemed to me tremendously important and new: there was "authority" in me.

SARAH

With animal training, the experimenter must accept failure as his own fault; in the education of children failure is always attributed to the child.

MY SELF,

226

Which characteristic is peculiar to birds alone, the ability to fly or a body covering of feathers?

The MEDIA ARE NOT THE MESSAGE...

A. *Grammatical subject as psychological subject*

I notice that the clock is smashed. How did that happen?

> *The clock fell.*

B. *Grammatical subject as psychological predicate*
I heard something crash in the next room. What happened?

> *The clock fell.*

a. "Falling in love is wonderful, it's wonderful ... in ev'ry way."

b. "Fallings in love₃ are wonderful, they are wonderful (to me) in a great many ways."

Figure out which version the inventor of general semantics Count Alfred Korzybski would probably have considered more accurate. Once you figure out why he was right, figure out why he was also wrong.

Auks are small birds, no larger than starlings, but tasty to eat, either cooked or dried, and particularly so when preserved in blubber. The birds are caught in nets on long poles as they pass in flocks by the cliffs. What a wonderful time when they arrive in spring! Here it could really be said that "the sun is darkened" by birds.

"Sir, your people is a great beast."

The word *media* has a plural ending. Many people use it with a singular verb: "The media is to blame for all the trouble." (Instead of *the medium is* or *the media are*.)

Is such usage an example of sloppy grammar or an example of the way in which inner reality is reflected in an outer structure?

(The structure of the question above reveals which answer the questioner thinks is right. True or False?)

REALLY ALFRED?

THE
HOUSE
of
THE
INTELLECT

AND I.

these data is wrong ...

Every sentence has a subtext. Or several.

Any part of the sentence may be the psychological predicate, the carrier of the topical interest

227

ALFRED, WISE UP.

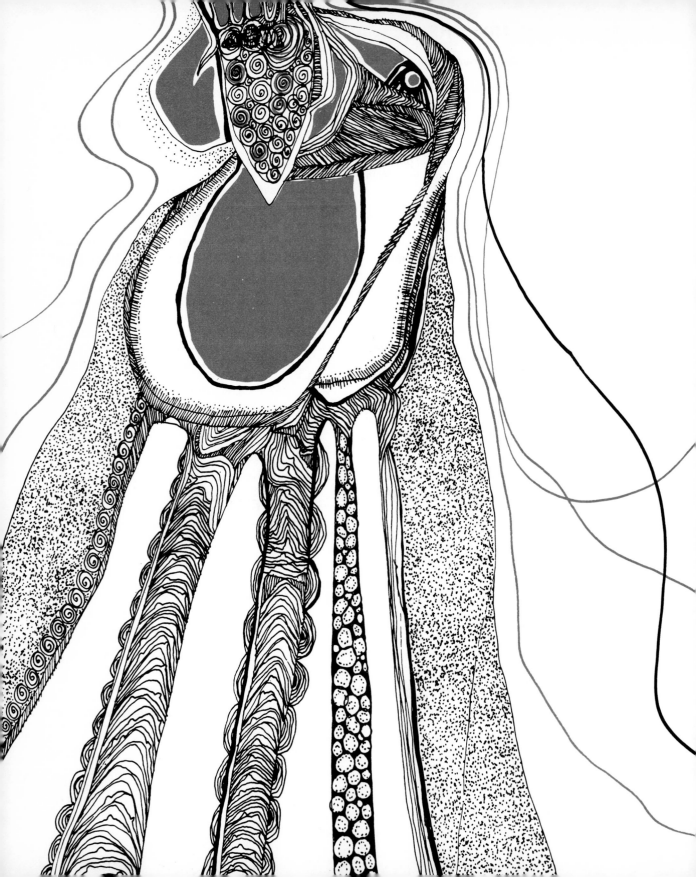

Give this story a title which ties it in with the rest of the chapter.

_____

(TITLE)

Leaving the village behind, we followed the heady sweeps of the road up into a land of slow glass.

I had never seen one of the farms before and at first found them slightly eerie — an effect heightened by imagination and circumstance. The car's turbine was pulling smoothly and quietly in the damp air so that we seemed to be carried over the convolutions of the road in a kind of supernatural silence. On our right the mountain sifted down into an incredibly perfect valley of timeless pine, and everywhere stood the great frames of slow glass, drinking light. An occasional flash of afternoon sunlight on their wind bracing created an illusion of movement, but in fact the frames were deserted. The rows of windows had been standing on the hillside for years, staring into the valley, and men only cleaned them in the middle of the night when their human presence would not matter to the thirsty glass.

They were fascinating, but Selina and I didn't mention the windows. I think we hated each other so much we both were reluctant to sully anything new by drawing it into the nexus of our emotions. The holiday, I had begun to realize, was a stupid idea in the first place. I had thought it would cure everything, but, of course, it didn't stop Selina being pregnant and, worst still, it didn't even stop her being angry about being pregnant.

Rationalizing our dismay over her condition, we had circulated the usual statements to the effect that we would have _liked_ having children — but later on, at the proper time. Selina's

pregnancy had cost us her well-paid job and with it the new house we had been negotiating and which was far beyond the reach of my income from poetry. But the real source of our annoyance was that we were face to face with the realization that people who say they want children later always mean they want children never. Our nevers were thrumming with the knowledge that we, who had thought ourselves so unique, had fallen into the same biological trap as every mindless rutting creature which ever existed.

The road took us along the southern slopes of Ben Cruachan until we began to catch glimpses of the gray Atlantic far ahead. I had just cut our speed to absorb the view better when I noticed the sign spiked to a gatepost. It said: "SLOW GLASS — QUALITY HIGH, PRICES LOW — J. R. HAGAN." On an impulse I stopped the car on the verge, wincing slightly as tough grasses whipped noisily at the bodywork.

"Why have we stopped?" Selina's neat, smoke-silver head turned in surprise.

"Look at that sign. Let's go up and see what there is. The stuff might be reasonably priced out here."

Selina's voice was pitched high with scorn as she refused, but I was too taken with my idea to listen. I had an illogical conviction that doing something extravagant and crazy would set us right again.

"Come on," I said, "the exercise might do us some good. We've been driving too long anyway."

She shrugged in a way that hurt me and got out of the car. We walked up a path made of irregular, packed clay steps nosed with short lengths of sapling. The path curved through trees which clothed the edge of the hill and at its end we found a low farmhouse. Beyond the little stone building tall frames of slow glass gazed out towards the voice-stilling sight of Cruachan's ponderous descent towards the waters of Loch Linnhe. Most of the panes were perfectly transparent but a few were dark, like panels of polished ebony.

As we approached the house through a neat cobbled yard a tall middle-aged man in ash-colored tweeds arose and waved to us. He had been sitting on the low rubble wall which bounded the yard, smoking a pipe and staring towards the house. At the front window of the cottage a young woman in a tangerine dress stood with a small boy in her arms, but she turned uninterestedly and moved out of sight as we drew near.

"Mr. Hagan?" I guessed.

"Correct. Come to see some glass, have you? Well, you've come to the right place." Hagan spoke crisply, with traces of the pure highland which sounds so much like Irish to the unaccustomed ear. He had one of those calmly dismayed faces one finds on elderly road-menders and philosophers.

"Yes," I said. "We're on holiday. We saw your sign."

Selina, who usually has a natural fluency with strangers, said nothing. She was looking towards the now empty window with what I thought was a slightly puzzled expression.

"Up from London, are you? Well, as I said, you've come to the right place — and at the right time, too. My wife and I don't see many people this early in the season."

I laughed. "Does that mean we might be able to buy a little glass without mortgaging our home?"

"Look at that now," Hagan said, smiling helplessly. "I've thrown away any advantage I might have had in the transaction. Rose, that's my wife, says I never learn. Still, let's sit down and talk it over." He pointed at the rubble wall, then glanced doubtfully at Selina's immaculate blue skirt. "Wait till I fetch a rug from the house." Hagan limped quickly into the cottage, closing the door behind him.

"Perhaps it wasn't such a marvelous idea to come up here," I whispered to Selina, "but you might at least be pleasant to the man. I think I can smell a bargain."

"Some hope," she said with deliberate coarseness. "Surely even you must have noticed that ancient dress his wife is wearing! He won't give much away to strangers."

"Was that his wife?"

"Of course that was his wife."

"Well, well," I said, surprised. "Anyway, try to be civil with him. I don't want to be embarrassed."

Selina snorted, but she smiled whitely when Hagan reappeared and I relaxed a little. Strange how a man can love a woman and yet at the same time pray for her to fall under a train.

Hagan spread a tartan blanket on the wall and we sat down, feeling slightly self-conscious at having been translated from our city-oriented lives into a rural tableau. On the distant slate of the Loch, beyond the watchful frames of slow glass, a slow-moving steamer drew a white line towards the south. The boisterous mountain air seemed almost to invade our lungs, giving us more oxygen than we required.

"Some of the glass farmers around here," Hagan began, "give strangers, such as yourselves, a sales talk about how beautiful the autumn is in this part of Argyll. Or it might be the spring or the winter. I don't do that — any fool knows that a place which doesn't look right in summer never looks right. What do you say?"

I nodded compliantly.

"I want you just to take a good look out towards Mull, Mr. ...."

"Garland."

"...Garland. That's what you're buying if you buy my glass, and it never looks better

230

than it does at this minute. The glass is in perfect phase, none of it is less than ten years thick — and a four-foot window will cost you two hundred pounds.''

"Two hundred!" Selina was shocked. "That's as much as they charge at the Scenedow shop in Bond Street.''

Hagan smiled patiently, then looked closely at me to see if I knew enough about slow glass to appreciate what he had been saying. His price had been much higher than I had hoped — but *ten years thick!* The cheap glass one found in places like the Vistaplex and Paneo-rama stores usually consisted of a quarter of an inch of ordinary glass faced with a veneer of slow glass perhaps only ten or twelve months thick.

"You don't understand, darling,'' I said, already determined to buy. "This glass will last ten years and it's in phase.''

"Doesn't that only mean it keeps time?''

Hagan smiled at her again, realizing he had no further necessity to bother with me. "Only, you say! Pardon me, Mrs. Garland, but you don't seem to appreciate the miracle, the genuine honest-to-goodness miracle, of engineering precision needed to produce a piece of glass in phase. When I say the glass is ten years thick it means it takes light ten years to pass through it. In effect, each one of those panes is ten light-years thick — more than twice the distance to the nearest star — so a variation in actual thickness of only a millionth of an inch would . . .''

He stopped talking for a moment and sat quietly looking towards the house. I turned my head from the view of the Loch and saw the young woman standing at the window again. Hagan's eyes were filled with a kind of greedy reverence which made me feel uncomfortable and at the same time convinced me Selina had been wrong. In my experience husbands never looked at wives that way — at least, not at their own.

The girl remained in view for a few seconds, dress glowing warmly, then moved back into the room. Suddenly I received a distinct, though inexplicable, impression she was blind. My feeling was that Selina and I were perhaps blundering through an emotional interplay as violent as our own.

"I'm sorry,'' Hagan continued: "I thought Rose was going to call me for something. Now, where was I, Mrs. Garland? Ten light-years compressed into a quarter of an inch means . . .''

I ceased to listen, partly because I was already sold, partly because I had heard the story of slow glass many times before and had never yet understood the principles involved. An acquaintance with scientific training had once tried to be helpful by telling me to visualize a pane of slow glass as a hologram which did not need coherent light from a laser for the reconstitution of its visual information, and in which every photon of ordinary light passed through a spiral tunnel coiled outside the radius of capture of each atom in the glass. This gem of, to me, incomprehensibility not only told me nothing, it convinced me once again that a mind as non-technical as mine should concern itself less with causes than effects.

The most important effect, in the eyes of the average individual, was that light took a long time to pass through a sheet of slow glass. A new piece was always jet black because nothing had yet come through, but one could stand the glass beside, say, a woodland lake until the scene emerged, perhaps a year later. If the glass was then removed and installed in a dismal city flat, the flat would — for that year — appear to overlook the woodland lake. During the year it wouldn't be merely a very realistic but still picture — the water would ripple in sunlight, silent animals would come to drink, birds would cross the sky, night would follow day, season would follow season. Until one day, a year later, the beauty held in the subatomic pipelines would be exhausted and the familiar gray cityscape would reappear.

Apart from its stupendous novelty value, the commercial success of slow glass was founded on the fact that having a scenedow was the exact emotional equivalent of owning land.

231

The meanest cave dweller could look out on misty parks — and who was to say they weren't his? A man who really owns tailored gardens and estates doesn't spend his time proving his ownership by crawling on his ground, feeling, smelling, tasting it. All he receives from the land are light patterns, and with scenedows those patterns could be taken into coal mines, submarines, prison cells.

On several occasions I have tried to write short pieces about the enchanted crystal but, to me, the theme is so ineffably poetic as to be, paradoxically, beyond the reach of poetry — mine, at any rate. Besides, the best songs and verse had already been written, with prescient inspiration, by men who had died long before slow glass was discovered. I had no hope of equaling, for example, Moore with his:

Oft in the stilly night,
Ere slumber's chain has bound me,
Fond Memory brings the light
Of other days around me . . .

It took only a few years for slow glass to develop from a scientific curiosity to a sizable industry. And much to the astonishment of poets — those of us who remain convinced that beauty lives though lilies die — the trappings of that industry were no different from those of any other. There were good scenedows which cost a lot of money, and there were inferior scenedows which cost rather less. The thickness, measured in years, was an important factor in the cost but there was also the question of actual thickness, or phase.

Even with the most sophisticated engineering techniques available thickness control was something of a hit-and-miss affair. A coarse discrepancy could mean that a pane intended to be five years thick might be five and a half, so that light which entered in summer emerged in winter; a fine discrepancy could mean that noon sunshine emerged at midnight. These incompatibilities had their peculiar charm — many night workers, for example, liked having their own private time zones — but, in general, it cost more to buy scenedows which kept closely in step with real time.

Selina still looked unconvinced when Hagan had finished speaking. She shook her head almost imperceptibly and I knew he had been using the wrong approach. Quite suddenly the pewter helmet of her hair was disturbed by a cool gust of wind, and huge clean tumbling drops of rain began to spang round us from an almost cloudless sky.

"I'll give you a check now," I said abruptly, and saw Selina's green eyes triangulate angrily on my face. "You can arrange delivery?"

"Aye, delivery's no problem," Hagan said, getting to his feet. "But wouldn't you rather take the glass with you?"

"Well, yes — if you don't mind." I was shamed by his readiness to trust my scrip.

"I'll unclip a pane for you. Wait here. It won't take long to slip it into a carrying frame." Hagan limped down the slope towards the seriate windows, through some of which the view towards Linnhe was sunny, while others were cloudy and a few pure black.

Selina drew the collar of her blouse closed at her throat. "The least he could have done was invite us inside. There can't be so many fools passing through that he can afford to neglect them."

I tried to ignore the insult and concentrated on writing the check. One of the outsize drops broke across my knuckles, splattering the pink paper.

"All right," I said, "let's move in under the eaves till he gets back." You worm, I thought as I felt the whole thing go completely wrong. I just had to be a fool to marry you. A prize fool, a fool's fool – and now that you've trapped part of me inside you I'll never ever, never ever, never ever get away.

Feeling my stomach clench itself painfully, I ran behind Selina to the side of the cottage. Beyond the window the neat living room, with its coal fire, was empty but the child's toys were scattered on the floor. Alphabet blocks and a wheelbarrow the exact color of freshly pared carrots. As I stared in, the boy came running from the other room and began kicking the blocks. He didn't notice me. A few moments later the young woman entered the

232

room and lifted him, laughing easily and wholeheartedly as she swung the boy under her arm. She came to the window as she had done earlier. I smiled self-consciously, but neither she nor the child responded.

My forehead prickled icily. *Could they both be blind?* I sidled away.

Selina gave a little scream and I spun towards her.

"The rug!" she said. "It's getting soaked."

She ran across the yard in the rain, snatched the reddish square from the dappling wall and ran back, towards the cottage door. Something heaved convulsively in my subconscious.

"Selina," I shouted. "Don't open it!"

But I was too late. She had pushed open the latched wooden door and was standing, hand over mouth, looking into the cottage. I moved close to her and took the rug from her unresisting fingers.

As I was closing the door I let my eyes traverse the cottage's interior. The neat living room in which I had just seen the woman and child was, in reality, a sickening clutter of shabby furniture, old newspapers, cast-off clothing and smeared dishes. It was damp, stinking and utterly deserted. The only object I recognized from my view through the window was the little wheelbarrow, paintless and broken.

I latched the door firmly and ordered myself to forget what I had seen. Some men who live alone are good housekeepers; others just don't know how.

Selina's face was white. "I don't understand. I don't understand it."

"Slow glass works both ways," I said gently. "Light passes out of a house, as well as in."

"You mean...?"

"I don't know. It isn't our business. Now steady up — Hagan's coming back with our glass." The churning in my stomach was beginning to subside.

Hagan came into the yard carrying an oblong, plastic-covered frame. I held the check out to him, but he was staring at Selina's face. He seemed to know immediately that our uncomprehending fingers had rummaged through his soul. Selina avoided his gaze. She

was old and ill-looking, and her eyes stared determinedly towards the nearing horizon.

"I'll take the rug from you, Mr. Garland," Hagan finally said. "You shouldn't have troubled yourself over it."

"No trouble. Here's the check."

"Thank you." He was still looking at Selina with a strange kind of supplication. "It's been a pleasure to do business with you."

"The pleasure was mine," I said with equal, senseless formality. I picked up the heavy frame and guided Selina towards the path which led to the road. Just as we reached the head of the now slippery steps Hagan spoke again.

"Mr. Garland!"

I turned unwillingly.

"It wasn't my fault," he said steadily. "A hit-and-run driver got them both, down on the Oban road six years ago. My boy was only seven when it happened. I'm entitled to keep something."

I nodded wordlessly and moved down the path, holding my wife close to me, treasuring the feel of her arms locked around me. At the bend I looked back through the rain and saw Hagan sitting with squared shoulders on the wall where we had first seen him.

He was looking at the house, but I was unable to tell if there was anyone at the window.

De-struction

What part does aggression play in the healthy, integrated personality?

I believe that aggression is a biological energy which normally is used to de-structure food or whatever we have to de-structure in order for it to be assimilated.

233

Examine these columns of corresponding words and phrases in four modern languages, and then follow the instructions given below. (In Persian the æ is pronounced somewhat like the *a* in *bat*, the *c* like *ch* in *church*, and the *x* like *ch* in German *Bach*. In Hebrew the *s* is pronounced like the *sh* in *shin*.)

English	German	Persian*	Hebrew
		mærd	iš
1. man	Mann	mærdi	iš
2. a man	ein Mann	an mærd	haiš
3. the man	der Mann	an zæn	haiša
4. the woman	die Frau	mærdi xub	iš tov
5. a good man	ein guter Mann	an mærde xub	haiš hatov
6. the good man	der gute Mann	zæni xub	iša tova
7. a good woman	eine gute Frau	an zæne xub	haiša hatova
8. the good woman	die gute Frau	xane(y)i xub	bayit tov
9. a good house	ein gutes Haus	an xane(y)e bozorg	habayit hagadol
10. the large house	das grosse Haus	xane(y)i kuček	bayit katan
11. a small house	ein kleines Haus	ketabi bozorg	sefer gadol
12. a large book	ein grosses Buch	xane(y)e mærdi	beyt iš
13. a man's house	eines Mannes Haus	xane(y)i mærdi	beyt iš
14. the house of a man	das Haus eines Mannes	zæne an mærd	ešet haiš
15. the man's wife	des Mannes Frau	zæne an mærd	ešet haiš
16. the wife of the man	die Frau des Mannes	an mærd xubæst.	haiš tov.
17. The man is good.	Der Mann ist gut.	an ketab kučekæst.	hasefer katan.
18. The book is small.	Das Buch ist klein.	an zæn xubæst.	haiša tova.
19. The woman is good.	Die Frau ist gut.	an xane kučekæst.	habayit katan.
20. The house is small.	Das Haus ist klein.		

A. Fill in the blanks in the vocabulary list for each language. Give the words, leaving off the endings. For example, when you find *gute, guter, gutes,* and *gut* all translated as 'good,' insert *gut* as the vocabulary item.

English	German	Persian	Hebrew
1. man	Mann	mærd	iš
2. woman			
3. good	gut		
4. house			bayit
5. small			
6. large	gross		
7. book			
8. is			(none)
9. a			(none)
10. the	der, die, das		

An is translated as 'the' in this column. It is actually closer to *that* than to *the*, but it may be considered as *the* for the purposes of this exercise. The (*y*) may be ignored; it occurs between vowels when the second vowel is a suffix.

EACH WITH A DIFFERENT COLORED DOOR

CONSCIOUSNESS MEANS GENERALIZATION

B. By constructing the vocabularies, you have already learned much about the grammars of small portions of these languages. The following statements are true of one or more of these languages. Basing your conclusions on the limited data given, circle the languages for which each statement is true.

1. There is an ending or word with the meaning of English *a*.　　　　　　　　　　　　　　　Eng Ger Per Heb
2. The adjective follows the noun.　　　　　　　　Eng Ger Per Heb
3. The adjective changes according to the noun.　Eng Ger Per Heb
4. The adjective ending varies according to whether or not the definite article is present.　Eng Ger Per Heb
5. The word for the object possessed is altered to show possession, rather than the word for the possessor.　Eng Ger Per Heb
6. Possession is shown by endings.　　　　　　　Eng Ger Per Heb
7. Possession is shown by a preposition.　　　　Eng Ger Per Heb
8. A separate word stands for *is*.　　　　　　　Eng Ger Per Heb
9. A suffix stands for *is*.　　　　　　　　　　　Eng Ger Per Heb
10. Nothing stands for *is*.　　　　　　　　　　　Eng Ger Per Heb

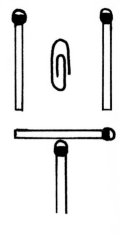

Resolution of an inner tension.

C. Translate each expression into the three other languages.

English	German	Persian	Hebrew
1. The small book			
2.	Das Buch ist gross		
3.		an xane(y)e kuček	
4.			haiš hagadol

matchstick game

Clarity Through Relationships.

They laughed at the obvious conslusion that the sun is *mungu*. The sun indeed is not *mungu* when it is above the horizon; *mungu* is the actual moment of the sunrise.

ONLY CONNECT

Every concept is a generalization. The relationship between concepts is a relationship between generalizations.

HITCHED TO EVERYTHING ELSE IN THE UNIVERSE

In the following situation, figure out who takes ads for the *Berkeley Barb* and who dates the minister:

There are five apartments, each with a different colored door and rented by women with different occupations, tastes in music, hobbies, and husbands or boyfriends with different work. a. The seamstress lives behind the gold door. b. The feminist lecturer dates the film maker. c. The woman behind the magenta door paints for a hobby. d. The model golfs. e. As you face the doors, the magenta door is immediately to the right of the pink door. f. The woman who likes blues music is married to the teacher. g. Jazz is preferred in the apartment with the brown door. h. The woman in the middle apartment likes to water ski. i. The nurse lives in the first apartment on the left. j. The woman who likes honky tonk, lives in the apartment next to the woman married to the grocer. k. Jazz is played in the apartment next to the apartment of the woman who dates the lawyer. l. The classical music buff likes to hike. m. The belly dancer likes country western music. n. The nurse lives next to the apartment with the green door.

235

Science is not a compendium of data; it is a process of discovery

Dead Song

As I lay dead
In my love-soaked bed,
Angels came to kiss my head.

I caught one gown
And wrestled her down
To be my girl in death town.

She will not fly.
She has promised to die.
What a clever corpse am I!

The new structure gradually spreads to the older concepts and draws them into the larger framework.

I Asked a Thief

I asked a thief to steal me a peach:
He turned up his eyes.
I asked a little lady to lie her down.
Holy and meek she cries.
As soon as I went an angel came:
He winked at the thief
And smiled at the dame;
And without one word spoke
Had the peach from the tree,
And 'twixt earnest and joke
Enjoyed the lady.

Traditional schooling tried to teach the child his social role by controlling and directing his actions from the outside. Children begin by feeling a mixture of affection and fear for adults. The child thus feels that any instructions the adult gives are compulsory. Such an authority is a convenient solution to the child's need for assurance and security. But this acceptance of the adult's authority may tempt the child to bypass his need for personal investigation. He becomes a moral robot. Good and bad are thought of as those things which are or are not in conformity with adult rules. A true morality can only evolve through reflection and critical discussion, which require cooperation and genuine intellectual exchange. The child who uncritically absorbs externally imposed discipline is incapable of a morality which can operate in new or unique situations.

I have also realized that one must accept the thoughts that go on within oneself of their own accord as part of one's reality. The categories of true and false are, of course, always present; but because they are not binding they take second place. The presence of thoughts is more important than our subjective judgment of them. But neither must these judgments be suppressed, for they also are existent thoughts which are part of our wholeness.

the immoral soul . . .

236

God and sinners reconciled . . . .

**Poetry: tying your shoes
with your eyes open.**

on what is your opinion biased?

What shocks the virtuous philosopher delights the chamileon Poet. It does no harm from its relish of the dark side of things any more than from its taste for the bright one; because they both end in speculation.

"In the film JULIET OF THE SPIRITS you have a detective say about the evidence he is displaying, 'Our view is limited, being objective.' Is this also a description of your own attitude?"

"Yes, reality is multidimensional."

"There is a difference between *ambiguity* and *duplicity* after all. All truth seems ambiguous. It changes, it has many aspects, and it also seems transparent."

THE DESTRUCTORS

"A statesman comes out with the proud declaration that he has no 'imagination for evil.' Quite right: *we* have no imagination for evil, but evil *has us in its grip.*"

"LEG O' LAMB? IS THIS FROM *MARY'S* WHOSE FLEECE WAS WHITE AS SNOW?..."

"I have to be empty. That is, be full! Come in all there; not wanting anything, not wanting praise, approbation, any thing. Just be there, that is to be empty."

I NOTICE WHEN I HAVE A MOTIVE

it seems that perhaps there is nothing unholy
nothing unrelated
and that as we fit things together
synthesize rather than analyze

we might be coming closer to god's view
from which all must somehow fit together

Emptiness — *I* without the *ego*.

237

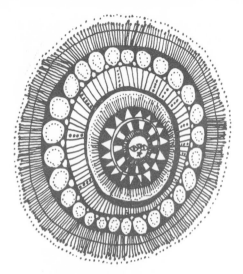

This expression, "God's world," may sound sentimental to some ears. For me it did not have this character at all. To "God's world" belonged everything superhuman—dazzling light, the darkness of the abyss, the cold impassivity of infinite space and time, and the uncanny grotesqueness of the irrational world of chance. "God," for me, was everything—and anything but "edifying."

"Don't you realize that a wastrel's life may be one of the shortest roads to sainthood."

A & P *vs* Christopher Wren

True or False: All questions are multiple choice questions.

238

My story starts when I moved to Canyon the winter before last. Rain+Mud+Wet+Cold. But that has little to do with the story, except that's how it was. But.

I was living in, *under*, a hyperbolic parabola, and there were many days between moneys. So we got many lbs of Brown Rice+W. W. Flour (when we had money). Garbage? A Barry Smith first: *Garbage Runs.*

Runs were when more than one person got *a* car or truck and drove down to Moraga—to the Shopping Center in Moraga—to the Back of the Shopping Center in Moraga—to the Big White metal "Disposal Service" Vats in the Back of the Shopping Center in Moraga. Once there, everyone disembarked and then embarked on the search for supper. A word about Moraga, then a word about the Vats.

Moraga despised Canyonites, like the fear that always seems to rise in people when they confront something *strange.* The Moraganites let the Canyonites know of their fears by sending men in Black and White Cars to routine check. You can take it from there.

The Vats. Big and White with garbage drippings+sawdust on the sides, usually in layers, pure garbage on top, tons of outer lettuce leaves mixed with what have you. But—then—

There was real crap garbage in the vats also, after all. The produce did it. Tomatoes didn't quite hold up so good and oranges molded pretty fast. But they were swine among pearls. That's what we ate and dug it and thrived on. Moraga, Orinda, and rarely Lafayette were our tri-weekly targets, hit with precision and team work, look outs, car revvers, and the scavengers (which we all took turns being).

A few months ago I was hiped to the fact of the whys of such glorious garbage: Government required it—standards set for how many days a perishable item could stay on the shelves. So we ate thanks to our friends in the government looking out for the welefar of its people.

Digging down into the bowels of the Vats were treasures beyond compare. Loaves of sealed tight Mrs. Wright's Bread (white plastic), artichokes, avocados, asparagus, lemons, oranges, grapefruit, apples, potatoes Idaho and sweet, tomatoes, lettuce, celery, carrots, squash, watermelon, anything you could find in the produce department of a Safeway store was there. Plus special bonuses like squashed but still good Foster's cakes, cans that lost their labels (we found dog food to buttered mushrooms), sponges, rubber gloves, anything the general public won't buy because of slight mars, we found and used. We once found 3 broken bottles of wine and 6 full unbroken bottles of wine. Not your run of the mill Gallo's, but a ½ step up: bottles with corks (though the idiots stood them upright on the shelves). Burgundy. But (always a but) they (all six of them) had wine-stained labels. Horrors.

Back to the produce. The trouble with garbage runs is that the novice had to get used to the smell and had to realize the way to find things was to jump in and rummage.

THE FIRE

2:CLARITY

"And thus he has encountered his second enemy: Clarity! That clarity of mind, which is so hard to obtain, dispels fear, but also blinds.

"It forces the man never to doubt himself. It gives him the assurance he can do anything he pleases, for he sees clearly into everything. And he is courageous because he is clear, and he stops at nothing because he is clear. But all that is a mistake; it is like something incomplete. If the man yields to this make-believe power, he has succumbed to his second enemy and will fumble with learning. He will rush when he should be patient, or he will be patient when he should rush. And he will fumble with learning until he winds up incapable of learning anything more."

"What becomes of a man who is defeated in that way, don Juan? Does he die as a result?"

"No, he doesn't die. His second enemy has just stopped him cold from trying to become a man of knowledge; instead, the man may turn into a buoyant warrior, or a clown. Yet the clairty for which he has paid so dearly will never change to darkness and fear again. He will be clear as long as he lives, but he will no longer learn, or yearn for, anything."

"But what does he have to do to avoid being defeated?"

"He must do what he did with fear: he must defy his clarity and use it only to see, and wait patiently and measure carefully before taking new steps; he must think, above all, that his clarity is almost a mistake. And a moment will come when he will understand that his clarity was only a point before his eyes. And thus he will have overcome his second enemy, and will arrive at a position where nothing can harm him anymore. This will not be a mistake. It will not be only a point before his eyes. It will be true power.

"He will know at this point that the power he has been pursuing for so long is finally his. He can do with it whatever he pleases. His ally is at his command. His wish is the rule. He sees all that is around him. But he has also come across his third enemy:

incandesce

I do not believe in words, no matter if strung together by the most skillful man: I believe in language, which is something beyond words, something which words give only an inadequate illusion of. Words do not exist separately, except in the minds of scholars, etymologists, philologists, etc. Words divorced from language are dead things, and yield no secrets. A man is revealed in his style, the language which he has created for himself. To the man who is pure at heart I believe that everything is as clear as a bell, even the most esoteric scripts. For such a man there is always mystery, but the mystery is not mysterious, it is logical, natural, ordained, and implicitly accepted. Understanding is not a piercing of the mystery, but an acceptance of it, a living blissfully with it, in it, through and by it.

**And as his strength
Failed him at length,
He met a pilgrim shadow —
"Shadow," said he,
"Where can it be —
This land of Eldorado?"**

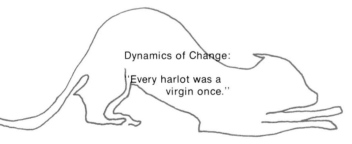

Dynamics of Change:

"Every harlot was a
  virgin once."

Analysis of reality with the help of concepts precedes analysis of the concepts themselves . . . .

"No one minded her outrageousness because it never thrust home: in life she didn't know where the feelings were to hurt them, any more than in poetry she knew where they were to touch them."

RULES for SUCCESSFUL PARAGRAPHS:

Don't let that horse
            eat that violin
    cried Chagall's mother
            But he
        kept right on
            painting
And became famous
And kept on painting
            The Horse With Violin In Mouth
And when he finally finished it
he jumped up upon the horse
            and rode away
        waving the violin
And then with a low bow gave it
to the first naked nude he ran across
And there were no strings
            attached

1. Before writing your paragraph, make an outline. List the details you intend to include.
2. Start with a topic sentence.
3. Have an orderly plan.
4. Use transitional words to help your reader follow your plan.
5. Develop your paragraph by means of examples, facts, statistics, reasons, or incidents supporting the topic sentence.
6. Think up a strong clincher sentence.

B

A

Which would be more useful in helping someone to write a paragraph, A or B? Neither? Both?

And while the willing soul transpires
At every pore with instant fires.

"This race and this country and this life produced me; I shall express myself as I am."

Sychophant: a self-seeking, servile flatterer. (from the Greek *sukophantes*, a fig shower, "accuser," meaning one who informed on those who stole figs from the sacred groves or the fig dealers who tried to avoid the tariff.

"Matter becomes molecules, molecules become atoms; atoms, ions; ions, electrons; and these, in turn, become uncomprehended sources of energy—not more clear as seizable reality than the poet's conception of the "soul," which he knows only from its "energy"—the yearns, delights and sorrows which he feels."

Connect A and B. Reflect on the process of thought used to bridge the two.

HIERARCHIES

A name is never a concept when it first emerges. It is usually both too narrow and too broad. It selects only one unessential aspect of a phenomenon, and then stands for the whole situation. Then this label is applied to other situations which have something in common with the first, though not necessarily the originally labeled aspect. In the contest between the emerging concept and the image that gave birth to it, the image gradually fades from consciousness and memory.

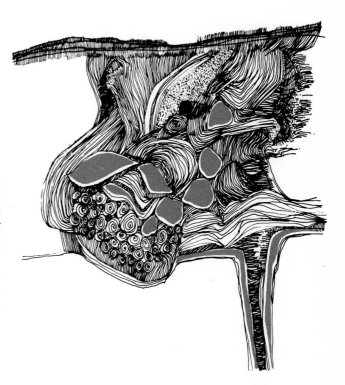

Which of the following is general enough to include the rest?

1. Every sentence has some kind of subtext.
2. Thought is born *through* words.
3. Thoughts don't mean things; thoughts *are* things.
4. A word is a microcosm of human consciousness.
5. Every thought tends to connect something with something else, to establish a relationship between things.
6. Every thought is a generalization.
7. The intellect is the result of language, not the cause of it.

Yes, rivers — yes, houses,

And you, frogs — and you,
Incredible ladybird.
. . . .
— Patience, a few centuries
And then perhaps we can
Sort things out together.

SEIZABLE REALITY

the angel of reality

"...This other Space is really Thoughtland; then take me to that blessed Region where I in Thought shall see the insides of all solid things...And then, oh blessed region of Four Dimensions, shall we linger on the threshold of the Fifth, and not enter therein?"

The new school appeals to real activity, to spontaneous work based on personal need and interest. This does not mean, as Claparede so succinctly put it, that active education requires that children should do anything they want; "it requires above all that they should will what they do; that they should act, not that they should be acted upon." Need, the interest that is the resultant of need, "that is the factor that will make a reaction into an authentic act." The law of interest is thus "the sole pivot around which the whole system should turn."

242

I'm not surprised that astronomers can figure out the size and distance of the stars, but I cannot understand how they found out their names.
—Russian peasant

...because you know her inch by inch...

Beneath my hands
your small breasts
are the upturned bellies
of breathing fallen sparrows.

Wherever you move
I hear the sounds of closing wings
of falling wings.

I am speechless
because you have fallen beside me
because your eyelashes
are the spines of tiny fragile animals.

I dread the time
when your mouth
begins to call me hunter.

When you call me close
to tell me
your body is not beautiful
I want to summon
the eyes and hidden mouths
of stone and light and water
to testify against you.

I want them
to surrender before you
the trembling rhyme of your face
from their deep caskets.

When you call me close
to tell me
your body is not beautiful
I want my body and my hands
to be pools
for your looking and laughing.

ONE DAY, many years ago, in Berkeley, Calif., a student who knew what he wanted to say but didn't know how to say it (some say that is logically impossible; others say he wasn't even a student) stalled by saying, "Oh, you know."

The next thing you knew, his lab partner had caught the you-knows, and she gave it to a professor who gave it to a lady in Administration, and then the entire university was going around saying "you know" after every phrase. Now, as you know, it's all over the world.

It's all very well to say that you won't associate with the kind of people who spread these things, but you know as well as I do that there is no one left who can be considered safe.

A friend of mine suggested that a certain high government official's rumored recent indescretion was probably with "some little thing who uses the nominative for the accusative case," and I only hope I don't get into a situation where I have to shake that official's hand.

* * *

"YOU KNOW" is a particularly resistant strain for which there doesn't seem to be a cure. You can try looking squarely at offenders and remarking, "no, I don't know." This at least serves the purpose of antagonizing them so that they cut off the conversation, which, under the circumstances, probably wasn't going anywhere, anyway.

But it's getting harder and harder to be a good pedant, almost as hard as it is to work for a newspaper and not begin sentences with conjunctions. When I was in college, I tried to set some standards for my life. I resolved never to be friends with those who used "fun" as an adjective. I don't even bother trying to go to college reunions any more.

My list also has on it people who use "loan" for "lend," "hopefully" for "it is hoped," "less" for "fewer" and "enthused" for "enthusiastic." As I add to it and, in the normal passing of time, grow more crotchety, conversation becomes more difficult. It's the same with opinions. My husband and I found that we were unable to sit down with bigots, then warmongers and now sexists.

"ISN'T IT WONDERFUL?" he remarked recently. "We're so liberal we don't like anybody anymore."

Pedantry is generally no sign of general ability to use the language well. All you have to do is to grab one grammatical werewolf and run with it. The second worst pedant I know once gave a speech about India in which he referred to "two football stadia" which had been built, and then went on to say that "the price of cows had literally sky-rocketed." (Hey-diddle-diddle to you, too.)

Catching someone in an error of usage is the most satisfactory achievement there is, outside of catching the bank in an error in one's favor, and it would be a shame to limit it to perfect people. (There are seven errors in this column. See if you can catch them. See if the editor can catch them first.) (Editor's Note: For the reader's amusement the column has been left untouched.)

* * *

MY CORRESPONDENTS include a Benedictine monk, who founded the Hyphen and Syphon Club, the rule of which is, "Every time you have to shoot a hyphen into that dense morall, you get a free drink," and a New York lawyer who warned me, "Keep up the good fight, watch out for cohort, don't use normalcy (the word is normality, and people were laughing at Harding not for his conservatism but for his illiteracy), don't pronounce falcon with a short a, remember that criteria and media are plural and keep your powder dry."

I didn't bring on this advice by committing any of these errors, you understand. I was just sitting there, knitting a subjunctive and minding my own business.

But that's what true pedantry is. Painting the lily, as those of us who know that it isn't gilding the lily, say.

"In the Tea Ceremony the supremely important matter is that the act be performed in the most perfect, most polite, most graceful, most charming manner possible."

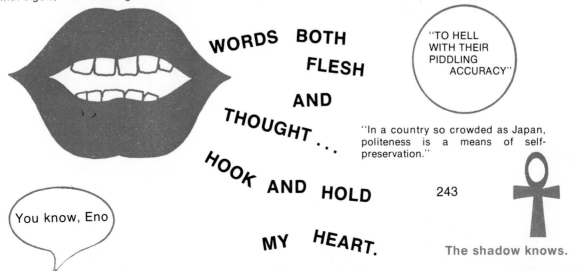

WORDS BOTH FLESH AND THOUGHT ... HOOK AND HOLD MY HEART.

You know, Eno

"TO HELL WITH THEIR PIDDLING ACCURACY"

"In a country so crowded as Japan, politeness is a means of self-preservation."

243

The shadow knows.

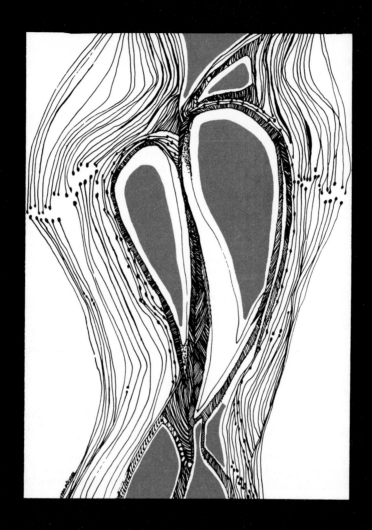

ACTIVATING SYMBOLS

A women's magazine reports that a number of families have begun saving Christmas cards they receive and sending the ones they like on to other friends the next year, signing their own names under those already there. They plan to keep the best cards in circulation until they wear out.

3:POWER

Power POWER Power

Power!

"Power is the strongest of all enemies. And naturally the easiest thing to do is to give in; after all, the man is truly invincible. He commands; he begins by taking calculated risks, and ends in making rules, because he is a master.

"A man at this stage hardly notices his third enemy closing in on him. And suddenly, without knowing, he will certainly have lost the battle. His enemy will have turned him into a cruel, capricious man."

"Will he lose his power?"

"No, he will never lose his clarity or his power."

"What then will distinguish him from a man of knowledge?"

"A man who is defeated by power dies without really knowing how to handle it. Power is only a burden upon his fate. Such a man has no command over himself, and cannot tell when or how to use his power."

"Is the defeat by any of these enemies a final defeat?"

"Of course it is final. Once one of these enemies overpowers a man there is nothing he can do."

"Is it possible, for instance, that the man who is defeated by power may see his error and mend his ways?"

"No. Once a man gives in he is through."

"But what if he is temporarily blinded by power, and then refuses it?"

"That means his battle is still on. That means he is still trying to become a man of knowledge. A man is defeated only when he no longer tries, and abandons himself."

"But then, don Juan, it is possible that a man may abandon himself to fear for years, but finally conquer it."

"No, that is not true. If he gives in to fear he will never conquer it, because he will shy away from learning and never try again. But if he tries to learn for years in the midst of his fear, he will eventually conquer it because he will never have really abandoned himself to it."

"How can he defeat his third enemy, don Juan?"

"He has to defy it, deliberately. He has to come to realize the power he has seemingly conquered is in reality never his. He must keep himself in line at all times, handling carefully and faithfully all that he has learned. If he can see that clarity and power, without his control over himself, are worse than mistakes, he will reach a point where everything is held in check. He will know then when and how to use his power. And thus he will have defeated his third enemy."

POWER Power POWER

"Look, the dog's begging for some peanuts."
"Well, don't give her any. She's already had her supper."
"But she's begging."
"It's just peanuts envy."

"Look yonder," said my Guide, "in Flatland thou hast lived; of Lineland thou hast received a vision; thou hast soared with me to the heights of Spaceland; now, in order to complete the range of thy experience, I conduct thee downward to the lowest depth of existence, even to the realm of Pointland, the Abyss of No Dimensions."

245

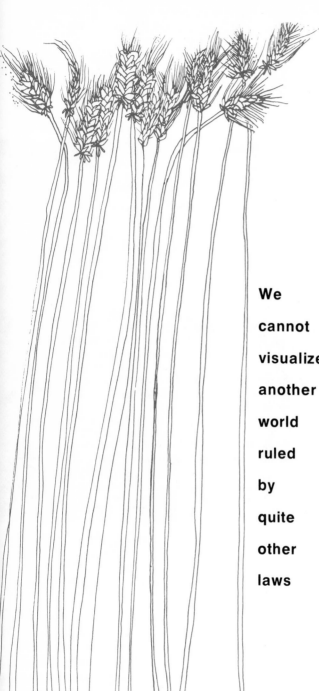

We

cannot

visualize

another

world

ruled

by

quite

other

laws

"How delightfully those fish are enjoying themselves!"

"You are not a fish; how do you know that the fish are enjoying themselves?"

"You are not myself, how do you know that I do not know that the fish are enjoying themselves?"

  Using six matches, construct four equilateral triangles.

ISOLATE

SYSTEMS OF REALITY

Between the ages of three and seven, the mind imagines that ten counters arranged in a row become greater in number when the spaces between them are increased; that a collection of objects divided in two becomes quantitatively greater than the initial whole; that a straight line represents a greater distance if it is broken in two; that the distance between A and B is not necessarily the same as that between B and A (especially if there is a slope); that a quantity of liquid in glass A increases when poured into the narrower glass B.

(Get the feel of that world. Do you remember it? Reflect on what made it change.)

"Being so many different sizes in a day is very confusing."
"It isn't," said the Caterpillar.

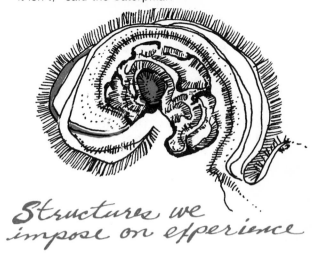

Structures we impose on experience

Teaching the alphabet

Mother. "X."
Child. "X."
Mother. "Y."
Child. "Because."

Teacher. "What's half of eight?"
Child. "Zero."

ALICE

A Y IN THE ROAD

SET

1 2 3 4

Teacher holds one finger up.
Child. "One."
Teacher holds two fingers up.
Child. "Peace."

SAFE FROM PARENTS, GOD AND EYES

In Riverhead, N. Y., parents must obtain tree-house building permits. Houses must be no more than 12 feet off the ground, walls must be at least 42 inches high, floor boards must be at least 1 inch thick. They must be framed by two-by-fours and attached with 16-penny nails to branches no less than 5 inches in diameter for hardwood trees or 7 inches for softwood.

...RULED BY QUITE OTHER LAWS....

IM ANFANG WAR DIE TAT

The image, the film, the filmstrip, and all the other audio-visual aids, thought to be such marvelous teaching devices, are accessories or spiritual crutches. They are an improvement over purely verbal instruction, but images can be nothing more than pictures just as words can be nothing more than words. They can never *replace* a student's spontaneous and personal investigation. If the student's own operations are neglected, the new materials are nothing more than a dolled up version of the traditional lecture.

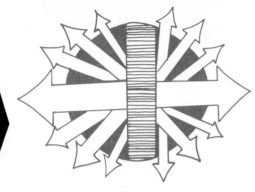

SIMULATION

Role Playing

Be your mother, your teacher, your boss, or anyone who has some authority over your life. Someone else plays you. Improvise a scene between you. The other members of your group are your audience. Later discuss your observations and reflect on them. Do several scenes with other members of your group taking the roles.

A Gestaltist might have a client act out or experience some latent concern (perhaps *hate* which he has been suppressing) and bring that concern into conscious awareness. But awareness alone of all such concepts is not enough. There is still the ordering and structuring of one's awareness, and one remains helplessly a child of nature until he classifies, develops series concepts, differentiates, combines, works out hierarchies, and finally establishes a coherent system subject to operative innovations.

Dear Frank Lloyd Wright:
Is underwear utilitarian?

248

In the historical evolution of language the very structure of meaning and its psychological nature also change. From primitive generalizations, verbal thought rises to the most abstract concepts. It is not merely the content of a word that changes, but the way in which reality is generalized and reflected in a word.

Old meanings
are a
clutter

SHADOWS OF
OUR
FORGOTTEN
ANCESTORS

Check the etymology of each word in this sentence. True or false: The present is the past.

ambigere is oino dhreugh kwo
    Ambiguity is a dream whose
mei-no kap been leu kweye
    meaning has been lost while
stel being to en mag
    still being there and making
ko prae-esse pel ad al
    its presence felt at all
da.
    times.

transparency

"Do the Germans ever think about fingers and hats when they use the word *Fingerhut*?"

But the thing that exasperated me most of all was the proposition: If *a*=*b* and *b*=*c*, then *a*=*c*, even though by definition *a* meant something other than *b*, *and, being different, could therefore not be equated with b*, let alone with *c*. Whenever it was a question of an equivalence, then it was said that *a*=*a*, *b*=*b*, and so on. This I could accept, whereas *a*=*b* seemed to me a downright lie or a fraud. I was equally outraged when the teacher stated in the teeth of his own definition of parallel lines that they met at infinity. This seemed to me no better than a stupid trick to catch peasants with, and I could not and would not have anything to do with it. My intellectual morality fought against these whimsical inconsistencies, which have forever debarred me from understanding mathematics. Right into old age I have had the incorrigible feeling that if, like my schoolmates, I could have accepted without a struggle the proposition that *a*=*b*, or that sun = moon, dog = cat, then mathematics might have fooled me endlessly—just *how* much I only began to realize at the age of eighty-four. All my life it remained a puzzle to me why it was that I never managed to get my bearings in mathematics when there was no doubt whatever that I could calculate properly. Least of all did I understand my own *moral* doubts concerning mathematics.

THIMBLE

249

THE ORGANS OF REALITY

THUS I REFUTE BEELZY

In his first year, the child shakes, rubs, rocks, and so forth, and by this means feels his way into taking possession of his perceived world. Other, less purposeful, activities are a kind of play. This play is useful in giving the nerve endings a 'memory' of the world and in providing the mind with an experience of it. In symbolic play, as in playing house, the child translates reality he has already experienced into a form he can manage, one which he can relive and vary according to his needs.

Why don't elementary school children play checkers, chess, bridge?

GAME
Simulation of a Simulation

Have a play day. Bring jump ropes, jacks, crayons, rubber balls, materials for finger painting, crayons, etc.
Play

hopscotch	follow the leader
jacks	kick the can
Simon says	marbles
House	hide and seek
School	

(What verbal rituals accompany these games?)

Fly kites,	climb trees,
roll hoops,	finger paint,
skate,	draw pictures.
make mud pies,	

Try to recapture the child's frame of mind and the feel of these games. Later reflect on the experience. While participating, *be* a child; ignore your actual age.

THERE WAS A CHILD WENT FORTH

Intelligence implies a continuous reorganization of the field of perception and a creative structuring. The apple becomes the man, and the man becomes an apple. The man digests and gets the feel of 'apple' and is changed some by it. He is now a sort of apple-man. Environment enters the man. Man-environment prunes the tree. The feedback moves back and forth changing tree and man until it appears that environment operates on environment in one continuous dynamic interplay. When I take my second look, what I saw a moment ago is gone, but so is the I which saw it. I and All altering each other.

250

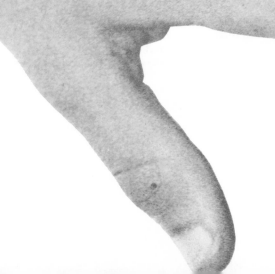

What can simulation offer a thinker which deductive reasoning alone cannot?

	"What are bones for?"
Teacher.	"So you won't squash
Child.	together."

ightning: *Why does it blink so?"*

Autumn:
"The trees are painting themselves."

"Open your mouth and let me see your appetite."

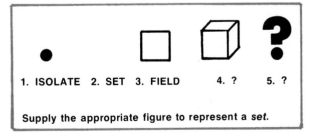

Activities which do nothing more than reproduce an object or idea, which can only make a precise copy, are not truly educational.

Knowledge is not a thing. It is what goes on when one exercises the knack of transforming things and ideas into a system of actions.

It comes through actions which modify objects. It is the use of the power to separate out and to vary the factors an object represents.

super
eno

The underlying pattern of the mind even provides us with a guide to pronunciation. If we kept only to the phonetic surface form, we could not understand why, for example, we should expect a full vowel in "relaxation," and a reduced vowel in "demonstration," in the italicized position. In other related forms both these vowels are full rather than reduced: compare "reláx," and "demónstrative." In fact, as the examples "reláx" and "demónstrative" indicate, the vowels are full when they receive the main stress in the word. But in "relaxátion" and "demonstrátion,"the italicized vowel is unstressed in both cases, yet it is full in the first case and reduced in the second.

The reason is that "relaxátion" is derived from the underlying form "reláx" and "demonstrátion" is derived from the underlying form "démonstrate," and in these underlying forms the italicized vowel of "reláx" is stressed, hence full, while the italicized vowel of "démonstrate" is unstressed, hence weak. In "relaxátion" and "demonstrátion" the italicized vowel is unstressed in both cases, but in speaking and hearing these words, we make use of the abstract mental representation of the underlying form, with its stress pattern and consequent choice of full or reduced vowel, and in this way we determine the stress and vowel quality of the words "relaxation" and "demonstration" themselves. It turns out, then, that we hear and speak many words as if we had in mind their underlying forms.

In ancient Japan a cherished urn was broken, and the owner despaired. But an artisan managed to fit the pieces together and sealed the cracks with melted gold. In this way a new process of urn decoration developed.

The fact is that in former times men did not reflect upon their symbols; they lived them and were unconsciously animated by their meaning.

●	☐	⬛(cube)	**?**	**?**
1. ISOLATE	2. SET	3. FIELD	4. ?	5. ?

Supply the appropriate figure to represent a *set*.

251

LOOK AT THAT TUBA PLAYING BILL.

Before the age of ten or eleven the child is hardly capable of any kind of deductions based on assumed data and not on observed facts.

The air is the enemy of astronomers.

The mist of affects . . . ?

FIELD

OBJECTIVE cognition

The peace and indifference of immortal things.

I experienced this objectivity once again later on. That was after the death of my wife. I saw her in a dream which was like a vision. She stood at some distance from me, looking at me squarely. She was in her prime, perhaps about thirty, and wearing the dress which had been made for her many years before by my cousin the medium. It was perhaps the most beautiful thing she had ever worn. Her expression was neither joyful nor sad, but, rather, objectively wise and understanding, without the slightest emotional reaction, as though she were beyond the mist of affects. I knew that it was not she, but a portrait she had made or commissioned for me. It contained the beginning of our relationship, the events of fifty-three years of marriage, and the end of her life also. Face to face with such wholeness one remains speechless, for it can scarcely be comprehended.

The objectivity which I experienced in this dream and in the visions is part of a completed individuation. It signifies detachment from valuations and from what we call emotional ties. In general, emotional ties are very important to human beings. But they still contain projections, and it is essential to withdraw these projections in order to attain to oneself and to objectivity. Emotional relationships are relationships of desire, tainted by coercion and constraint; something is expected from the other person, and that makes him and ourselves unfree. Objective cognition lies hidden behind the attraction of the emotional relationship; it seems to be the central secret. Only through objective cognition is the real *coniunctio* possible.

After the illness a fruitful period of work began for me. A good many of my principal works were written only then. The insight I had had, or the vision of the end of all things, gave me the courage to undertake new formulations. I no longer attempted to put across my own opinion, but surrendered myself to the current of my thoughts. Thus one problem after the other revealed itself to me and took shape.

Something else, too, came to me from my illness. I might formulate it as an affirmation of things as they are: an unconditional "yes" to that which is, without subjective protests—acceptance of the conditions of existence as I see them and understand them, acceptance of my own nature, as I happen to be. At the beginning of the illness I had the feeling that there was something wrong with my attitude, and that I was to some extent responsible for the mishap. But when one follows the path of individuation, when one lives one's own life, one must take mistakes into the bargain; life would not be complete without them. There is no guarantee—not for a single moment—that we will not fall into error or stumble into deadly peril. We may think there is a sure road. But that would be the road of death. Then nothing happens any longer—at any rate, not the right things. Anyone who takes the sure road is as good as dead.

It was only after the illness that I understood how important it is to affirm one's own destiny. In this way we forge an ego that does not break down when incomprehensible things happen; an ego that endures, that endures the truth, and that is capable of coping with the world and with fate. Then, to experience defeat is also to experience victory. Nothing is disturbed—neither inwardly nor outwardly, for one's own continuity has withstood the current of life and of time.

252

"Do not flatter yourself, madam; it is *hanging* out."

POWER TEST

A Vocabulary Placement Test for School Administrators.

Define the underlined words. Example: That Blood is _bent._

bent (adj) drunk

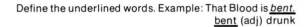

1. Don't give me any of your _chump change_.
2. You've got some nice _vines_ there.
3. Sure, he's a _splib_.
4. Don't try _scheming_ with my fox again, man.
5. Oh, _shine it on_, brother.
6. This _pluck_ is rótten.
7. Hey, get your _nobs_ off my short.
8. With a room like this, we could really _bug_.
9. & 10. Did you see that _bear_ my _ace_ was with?
11. Now, that's a real _bad_ cheen.
12. Now, _pend_ this, and pend it good.
13. That _ofay_ isn't too lame.
14. Let's grab that _hog_ and jam.
15. That _mickey mouse_ better cool it with my mink.
16. I'm going to be _styling_ tonight with that stone fox.
17. Get on, that fox is mine. You bother her, we'll _go some._
18. Oh, _choke it._ Let's go over to my crib for some pluck.
19. That's a fine dude over there; dig his _datshiki._
20. _Too cold_; he must have scored some green.

(And you don't even have a Spanish surname?)

Harriet and Louisa, somewhat to my surprise, get on very well. Each seems to find the other full of the weirdest and most delightful surprises. Harriet has been teaching Louisa French and Swedish expressions, and Louisa has been teaching Harriet some of the saltier expressions of the black South. Whenever one of them is not playing straight man to the other's accent, they become involved in long speculations as to how a language reveals the history and the attitudes of a people. They discovered that all the European languages contain a phrase equivalent to "work like a nigger." ("Of course," says Louisa, "they've had black men working for them for a long time.") "Language is experience and language is power," says Louisa, after regretting that she does not know any of the African dialects. "That's what I keep trying to tell those dirty bastards down South. They get their own experiences into the language, we'll have a great language. But, no, they all want to talk like white folks." Then she leans forward, grasping Harriet by the knee. "I tell them, honey, white folks ain't saying _nothing_. Not a thing are they saying—and _some_ of them know it, they _need_ what you got, the whole world needs it." Then she leans back, in disgust. "You think they listen to me? Indeed they do not. They just go right on, trying to talk like white folks." She leans forward again, in tremendous indignation. "You know some of them folks are _ashamed_ of Mahalia Jackson. _Ashamed_ of her, one of the greatest singers alive! They think she's common." Then she looks about the room as though she held a bottle in her hand and were looking for a skull to crack.

253

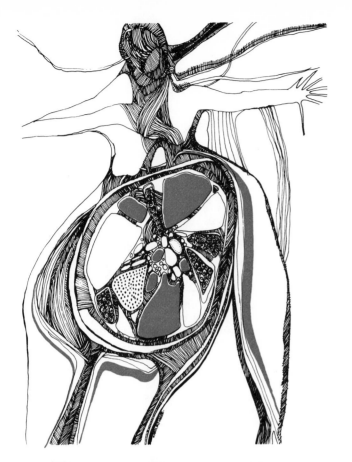

Tiger, tiger, burning bright
In the forest of the night,
What immortal hand or eye
Could frame thy fearful symmetry?

In what distant deeps or skies
Burnt the fire of thine eyes?
On what wings dare he aspire?
What the hand dare seize the fire?

And what shoulder, and what art,
Could twist the sinews of thy heart?
When thy heart began to beat,
What dread hand forged thy dread feet?

What the hammer? What the chain?
In what furnace was thy brain?
What the anvil? What dread grasp
Dared its deadly terrors clasp?

When the stars threw down their spears,
And watered heaven with their tears,
Did He smile his work to see?
Did He who made the lamb make thee?

Tiger, tiger, burning bright
In the forest of the night,
What immortal hand or eye
Dare frame thy fearful symmetry?

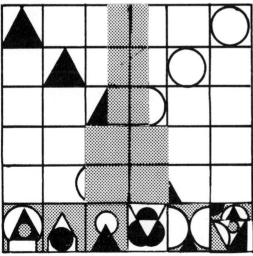

lexical key:

  = **laddie**

 = **lassie**

    = **rye**

I had to grow foul with knowledge, realize the futility of everything, grow desperate, then humble, then sponge my self off the slate, as it were, in order to recover my authenticity. I had to arrive at the brink and then take a leap in the dark.

semi-erotic scotch poem for i.h.f.

255

Old meanings are a clutter . . .

THE
DESTRUCTORS

It was on the eve of August Bank Holiday that the latest recruit became the leader of the Wormsley Common Gang. No one was surprised except Mike, but Mike at the age of nine was surprised by everything. "If you don't shut your mouth," somebody once said to him, "you'll get a frog down it." After that Mike had kept his teeth tightly clamped except when the surprise was too great.

The new recruit had been with the gang since the beginning of the summer holidays, and there were possibilities about his brooding silence that all recognized. He never wasted a word even to tell his name until that was required of him by the rules. When he said "Trevor" it was a statement of fact, not as it would have been with the others a statement of shame or defiance. Nor did anyone laugh except Mike, who finding himself without support and meeting the dark gaze of the newcomer opened his mouth and was quiet again. There was every reason why T., as he was afterwards referred to, should have been an object of mockery—there was his name (and they substituted the initial because otherwise they had no excuse not to laugh at it), the fact that his father, a former architect and present clerk, had "come down in the world" and that his mother considered herself better than the neighbours. What but an odd quality of danger, of the unpredictable, established him in the gang without any ignoble ceremony of initiation?

The gang met every morning in an impromptu car-park, the site of the last bomb of the first blitz. The leader, who was known as Blackie, claimed to have heard it fall, and no one was precise enough in his dates to point out that he would have been one year old and fast asleep on the down platform of Wormsley Common Underground Station. On one side of the car-park leant the first occupied house, number 3, of the shattered Northwood Terrace—literally leant, for it had suffered from the blast of the bomb and the side walls were supported on wooden struts. A smaller bomb and some incendiaries had fallen beyond, so that the house stuck up like a jagged tooth and carried on the further wall relics of its neighbour, a dado, the remains of a fireplace. T., whose words were almost confined to voting "Yes" or "No" to the plan of operations proposed each day by Blackie, once startled the whole gang by saying broodingly, "Wren built that house, father says."

"Who's Wren?"

"The man who built St. Paul's."

"Who cares?" Blackie said. "It's only old Misery's."

Old Misery—whose real name was Thomas—had once been a builder and decorator. He lived alone in the crippled house, doing for himself: once a week you could see him coming back across the common with bread and vegetables, and once as the boys played in the car-park he put his head over the smashed wall of his garden and looked at them.

"Been to the loo," one of the boys said, for it was common knowledge that since the bombs fell something had gone wrong with the pipes of the

256

house and Old Misery was too mean to spend money on the property. He could do the redecorating himself at cost price, but he had never learnt plumbing. The loo was a wooden shed at the bottom of the narrow garden with a star-shaped hole in the door: it had escaped the blast which had smashed the house next door and sucked out the window-frames of No. 3.

The next time the gang became aware of Mr. Thomas was more surprising. Blackie, Mike, and a thin yellow boy, who for some reason was called by his surname Summers, met him on the common coming back from the market. Mr. Thomas stopped them. He said glumly, "You belong to the lot that play in the car-park?"

Mike was about to answer when Blackie stopped him. As the leader he had responsibilities. "Suppose we are?" he said ambiguously.

"I got some chocolates," Mr. Thomas said. "Don't like 'em myself. Here you are. Not enough to go round, I don't suppose. There never is," he added with sombre conviction. He handed over three packets of Smarties.

The gang were puzzled and perturbed by this action and tried to explain it away. "Bet someone dropped them and he picked 'em up," somebody suggested.

"Pinched 'em and then got in a bleeding funk," another thought aloud.

"It's a bribe," Summers said. "He wants us to stop bouncing balls on his wall."

"We'll show him we don't take bribes," Blackie said, and they sacrificed the whole morning to the game of bouncing that only Mike was young enough to enjoy. There was no sign from Mr. Thomas.

Next day T. astonished them all. He was late at the rendezvous, and the voting for that day's exploit took place without him. At Blackie's suggestion the gang was to disperse in pairs, take buses at random, and see how many free rides could be snatched from unwary conductors (the operation was to be carried out in pairs to avoid cheating). They were drawing lots for their companions when T. arrived.

"Where you been, T.?" Blackie asked. "You can't vote now. You know the rules."

"I've been *there*," T. said. He looked at the ground, as though he had thoughts to hide.

"Where?"

"At Old Misery's." Mike's mouth opened and then hurriedly closed again with a click. He had remembered the frog.

"At Old Misery's?" Blackie said. There was

nothing in the rules against it, but he had a sensation that T. was treading on dangerous ground. He asked hopefully, "Did you break in?"

"No. I rang the bell."

"And what did you say?"

"I said I wanted to see his house."

"What did he do?"

"He showed it me."

"Pinch anything?"

"No."

"What did you do it for then?"

The gang had gathered round: it was as though an impromptu court were about to form and to try some case of deviation. T. said, "It's a beautiful house," and still watching the ground, meeting no one's eyes, he licked his lips first one way, then the other.

"What do you mean, a beautiful house?" Blackie asked with scorn.

"It's got a staircase two hundred years old like a corkscrew. Nothing holds it up."

"What do you mean, nothing holds it up. Does it float?"

"It's to do with opposite forces, Old Misery said."

"What else?"

"There's panelling."

"Like in the Blue Boar?"

"Two hundred years old."

"Is Old Misery two hundred years old?"

Mike laughed suddenly and then was quiet again. The meeting was in a serious mood. For the first time since T. had strolled into the car-park on the first day of the holidays his position was in danger. It only needed a single use of his real name and the gang would be at his heels.

"What did you do it for?" Blackie asked. He was just, he had no jealousy, he was anxious to retain T. in the gang if he could. It was the word "beautiful" that worried him—that belonged to a class world that you could still see parodied at the Wormsley Common Empire by a man wearing a top hat and a monocle, with a haw-haw accent. He was tempted to say, "My dear Trevor, old chap," and unleash his hell hounds. "If you'd broken in," he said sadly—that indeed would have been an exploit worthy of the gang.

"This was better," T. said. "I found out things." He continued to stare at his feet, not meeting anybody's eye, as though he were absorbed in some dream he was unwilling—or ashamed—to share.

"What things?"

"Old Misery's going to be away all tomorrow and

Simon Says

Bank Holiday."

Blackie said with relief, "You mean we could break in?"

"And pinch things?" somebody asked.

Blackie said, "Nobody's going to pinch things. Breaking in—that's good enough, isn't it? We don't want any court stuff."

"I don't want to pinch anything," T. said. "I've got a better idea."

"What is it?"

T. raised eyes, as grey and disturbed as the drab August day. "We'll pull it down," he said. "We'll destroy it."

Blackie gave a single hoot of laughter and then, like Mike, fell quiet, daunted by the serious implacable gaze. "What'd the police be doing all the time?" he said.

"They'd never know. We'd do it from inside. I've found a way in." He said with a sort of intensity, "We'd be like worms, don't you see, in an apple. When we came out again there'd be nothing there, no staircase, no panels, nothing but just walls, and then we'd make the walls fall down—somehow."

"We'd go to jug," Blackie said.

"Who's to prove? And anyway we wouldn't have pinched anything." He added without the smallest flicker of glee, "There wouldn't be anything to pinch after we'd finished."

"I've never heard of going to prison for breaking things," Summers said.

"There wouldn't be time," Blackie said. "I've seen housebreakers at work."

"There are twelve of us," T. said. "We'd organize."

"None of us know how—"

"I know," T. said. He looked across at Blackie, "Have you got a better plan?"

"Today," Mike said tactlessly, "we're pinching free rides—"

"Free rides," T. said. "You can stand down, Blackie, if you'd rather...."

"The gang's got to vote."

"Put it up then."

Blackie said uneasily, "It's proposed that tomorrow and Monday we destroy Old Misery's house."

"Here, here," said a fat boy called Joe.

"Who's in favour?"

T. said, "It's carried."

"How do we start?" Summers asked.

"He'll tell you," Blackie said. It was the end of his leadership. He went away to the back of the car-park and began to kick a stone, dribbling it this way and that. There was only one old Morris in the park, for few cars were left there except lorries: without an attendant there was no safety. He took a flying kick at the car and scraped a little paint off the rear mudguard. Beyond, paying no more attention to him than to a stranger, the gang had gathered round T.; Blackie was dimly aware of the fickleness of favour. He thought of going home, of never returning, of letting them all discover the hollowness of T.'s leadership, but suppose after all what T. proposed was possible—nothing like it had ever been done before. The fame of the Wormsley Common car-park gang would surely reach around London. There would be headlines in the papers. Even the grown-up gangs who ran the betting at the all-in wrestling and the barrow-boys would hear with respect of how Old Misery's house had been destroyed. Driven by the pure, simple, and altruistic ambition of fame for the gang, Blackie came back to where T. stood in the shadow of Misery's wall.

T. was giving his orders with decision: it was as though this plan had been with him all his life, pondered through the seasons, now in his fifteenth year crystallized with the pain of puberty. "You," he said to Mike, "bring some big nails, the biggest you can find, and a hammer. Anyone else who can better bring a hammer and a screwdriver. We'll need plenty of them. Chisels too. We can't have too many chisels. Can anybody bring a saw?"

"I can," Mike said.

"Not a child's saw," T. said. "A real saw."

Blackie realized he had raised his hand like any ordinary member of the gang.

"Right, you bring one, Blackie. But now there's a difficulty. We want a hacksaw."

"What's a hacksaw?" someone asked.

"You can get 'em at Woolworth's," Summers said.

The fat boy called Joe said gloomily, "I knew it would end in a collection."

"I'll get one myself," T. said. "I don't want your money. But I can't buy a sledge-hammer."

Blackie said, "They are working on number fifteen. I know where they'll leave their stuff for Bank Holiday."

"Then that's all," T. said. "We meet here at nine sharp."

"I've got to go to church," Mike said.

"Come over the wall and whistle. We'll let you in."

On Sunday morning all were punctual except Blackie, even Mike. Mike had had a stroke of luck. His mother felt ill, his father was tired after Saturday night, and he was told to go to church alone with many warnings of what would happen if he strayed. Blackie had had difficulty in smuggling out the saw, and then in finding the sledge-hammer at the back of number 15. He approached the house from a lane at the rear of the garden for fear of the policeman's beat along the main road. The tired evergreens kept off a stormy sun: another wet Bank Holiday was being prepared over the Atlantic, beginning in swirls of dust under the trees. Blackie climbed the wall into Misery's garden.

There was no sign of anybody anywhere. The loo stood like a tomb in a neglected graveyard. The curtains were drawn. The house slept. Blackie lumbered nearer with the saw and the sledge-hammer. Perhaps after all nobody had turned up: the plan had been a wild invention: they had woken wiser. But when he came close to the back door he could hear a confusion of sound, hardly louder than a hive in swarm: a clickety-clack, a bang bang bang, a scraping, a creaking, a sudden painful crack. He thought, it's true, and whistled.

They opened the back door to him and he came in. He had at once the impression of organization, very different from the old happy-go-lucky ways under his leadership. For a while he wandered up and down stairs looking for T. Nobody addressed him: he had a sense of great urgency, and already he could begin to see the plan. The interior of the house was being carefully demolished without touching the outer walls. Summers with hammer and chisel was ripping out the skirting-boards in the ground floor dining-room: he had already smashed the panels of the door. In the same room Joe was heaving up the parquet blocks, exposing the soft wood floor-boards over the cellar. Coils of wire came out of the damaged skirting and Mike sat happily on the floor, clipping the wires.

On the curved stairs two of the gang were working hard with an inadequate child's saw on the banisters—when they saw Blackie's big saw they signalled for it wordlessly. When he next saw them a quarter of the banisters had been dropped into the hall. He found T. at last in the bathroom—he sat moodily in the least cared-for room in the house, listening to the sounds coming up from below.

"You've really done it," Blackie said with awe. "What's going to happen?"

"We've only just begun," T. said. He looked at the sledge-hammer and gave his instructions. "You stay here and break the bath and the wash-basin. Don't bother about the pipes. They come later."

Mike appeared at the door. "I've finished the wire, T.," he said.

"Good. You've just got to go wandering round now. The kitchen's in the basement. Smash all the china and glass and bottles you can lay hold of. Don't turn on the taps—we don't want a flood—yet. Then go into all the rooms and turn out drawers. If they are locked get one of the others to break them open. Tear up any papers you find and smash all the ornaments. Better take a carving-knife with you from the kitchen. The bedroom's opposite here. Open the pillows and tear up the sheets. That's enough for the moment. And you, Blackie, when you've finished in here crack the plaster in the passage up with your sledge-hammer."

"What are you going to do?" Blackie asked.

"I'm looking for something special," T. said.

It was nearly lunch-time before Blackie had finished and went in search of T. Chaos had advanced. The kitchen was a shambles of broken glass and china. The dining-room was stripped of parquet, the skirting was up, the door had been taken off its hinges, and the destroyers had moved up a floor. Streaks of light came in through the closed shutters where they worked with the seriousness of creators—and destruction after all is a form of creation. A kind of imagination had seen this house as it had now become.

Mike said, "I've got to go home for dinner."

"Who else?" T. asked, but all the others on one excuse or another had brought provisions with them.

They squatted in the ruins of the room and swapped unwanted sandwiches. Half an hour for lunch and they were at work again. By the time Mike returned, they were on the top floor, and by six the superficial damage was completed. The doors were all off, all the skirtings raised, the furniture pillaged and ripped and smashed—no one could have slept in the house except on a bed of broken plaster. T. gave his orders—eight o'clock next morning—and to escape notice they climbed singly over the garden wall, into the car-park. Only Blackie and T. were left; the light had nearly gone, and when they touched a switch, nothing worked—Mike had done his job thoroughly.

"Did you find anything special?" Blackie asked.

T. nodded. "Come over here," he said, "and look." Out of both pockets he drew bundles of pound notes. "Old Misery's savings," he said. "Mike ripped out the mattress, but he missed them."

"What are you going to do? Share them?"

"We aren't thieves," T. said. "Nobody's going to

steal anything from this house. I kept these for you and me—a celebration." He knelt down on the floor and counted them out—there were seventy in all. "We'll burn them," he said, "one by one," and taking it in turns they held a note upwards and lit the top corner, so that the flame burnt slowly towards their fingers. The grey ash floated above them and fell on their heads like age. "I'd like to see Old Misery's face when we are through," T. said.

"You hate him a lot?" Blackie asked.

"Of course I don't hate him," T. said. "There'd be no fun if I hated him." The last burning note illuminated his brooding face. "All this hate and love," he said, "it's soft, it's hooey. There's only things, Blackie," and he looked round the room crowded with the unfamiliar shadows of half things, broken things, former things. "I'll race you home, Blackie," he said.

Next morning the serious destruction started. Two were missing—Mike and another boy whose parents were off to Southend and Brighton in spite of the slow warm drops that had begun to fall and the rumble of thunder in the estuary like the first guns of the old blitz. "We've got to hurry," T. said.

Summers was restive. "Haven't we done enough?" he said. "I've been given a bob for slot machines. This is like work."

"We've hardly started," T. said. "Why, there's all the floors left, and the stairs. We haven't taken out a single window. You voted like the others. We are going to destroy this house. There won't be anything left when we've finished."

They began again on the first floor picking up the top floor-boards next the outer wall, leaving the joists exposed. Then they sawed through the joists and retreated into the hall, as what was left of the floor heeled and sank. They had learnt with practise, and the second floor collapsed more easily. By the evening an odd exhilaration seized them as they looked down the great hollow of the house. They ran risks and made mistakes: when they thought of the windows it was too late to reach them. "Cor," Joe said, and dropped a penny down into the dry rubble-filled well. It cracked and span among the broken glass.

"Why did we start this?" Summers asked with astonishment; T. was already on the ground, digging at the rubble, clearing a space along the outer wall. "Turn on the taps," he said. "It's too dark for anyone to see now, and in the morning it won't matter." The water overtook them on the stairs and fell through the floorless rooms.

It was then they heard Mike's whistle at the back. "Something's wrong," Blackie said. They could hear his urgent breathing as they unlocked the door.

"The bogies?" Summers asked.

"Old Misery," Mike said. "He's on his way." He put his head between his knees and retched. "Ran all the way," he said with pride.

"But why?" T. said. "He told me . . ." He protested with the fury of the child he had never been, "It isn't fair."

"He was down at Southend," Mike said, "and he was on the train coming back. Said it was too cold and wet." He paused and gazed at the water. "My, you've had a storm here. Is the roof leaking?"

"How long will he be?"

"Five minutes. I gave Ma the slip and ran."

"We better clear," Summers said. "We've done enough, anyway."

"Oh, no, we haven't. Anybody could do this—" "this was the shattered hollowed house with nothing left but the walls. Yet walls could be preserved. Façades were valuable. They could build inside again more beautifully than before. This could again be a home. He said angrily, "We've got to finish. Don't move. Let me think."

"There's no time," a boy said.

"There's got to be a way," T. said. "We couldn't have got thus far . . ."

"We've done a lot," Blackie said.

"No. No, we haven't. Somebody watch the front."

"We can't do any more."

"He may come in at the back."

"Watch the back too." T. began to plead. "Just give me a minute and I'll fix it. I swear I'll fix it." But his authority had gone with his ambiguity. He was only one of the gang. "Please," he said.

"Please," Summers mimicked him, and then suddenly struck home with the fatal name. "Run along home, Trevor."

T. stood with his back to the rubble like a boxer knocked groggy against the ropes. He had no words as his dreams shook and slid. Then Blackie acted before the gang had time to laugh, pushing Summers backward. "I'll watch the front, T.," he said, and cautiously he opened the shutters of the hall. The grey wet common stretched ahead, and the lamps gleamed in the puddles. "Someone's coming, T. No, it's not him. What's your plan, T.?"

"Tell Mike to go out to the loo and hide close beside it. When he hears me whistle he's got to count ten and start to shout."

"Shout what?"

HUMOR IS THE
FLIP SIDE
OF
TRAGEDY

"Oh, 'Help,' anything."

"You hear, Mike," Blackie said. He was the leader again. He took a quick look between the shutters. "He's coming, T."

"Quick, Mike. The loo. Stay here, Blackie, all of you till I yell."

"Where are you going, T.?"

"Don't worry. I'll see to this. I said I would, didn't I?"

Ole Misery came limping off the common. He had mud on his shoes and he stopped to scrape them on the pavement's edge. He didn't want to soil his house, which stood jagged and dark between the bomb-sites, saved so narrowly, as he believed, from destruction. Even the fanlight had been left unbroken by the bomb's blast. Somewhere somebody whistled. Old Misery looked sharply round. He didn't trust whistles. A child was shouting: it seemed to come from his own garden. Then a boy ran into the road from the car-park. "Mr. Thomas," he called, "Mr. Thomas."

"What is it?"

"I'm terribly sorry, Mr. Thomas. One of us got taken short, and we thought you wouldn't mind, and now he can't get out."

"What do you mean, boy?"

"He's got stuck in your loo."

"He'd no business— Haven't I seen you before?"

"You showed me your house."

"So I did. So I did. That doesn't give you the right to—"

"Do hurry, Mr. Thomas. He'll suffocate."

"Nonsense. He can't suffocate. Wait till I put my bag in."

"I'll carry your bag."

"Oh, no, you don't. I carry my own."

"This way, Mr. Thomas."

"I can't get in the garden that way. I've got to go through the house."

"But you *can* get in the garden this way, Mr. Thomas. We often do."

"You often do?" He followed the boy with a scandalized fascination. "When? What right . . ."

"Do you see . . .? The wall's low."

"I'm not going to climb walls into my own garden. It's absurd."

"This is how we do it. One foot here, one foot there, and over." The boy's face peered down, an arm shot out, and Mr. Thomas found his bag taken and deposited on the other side of the wall.

"Give me back my bag," Mr. Thomas said. From the loo a boy yelled and yelled. "I'll call the police."

simon says

Draw a picture of your self and each member of your family showing each of you engaged in some activity. Compare your drawing with other students' drawings. Discuss them with each other. You can add another dimension if you scramble the drawings and do not reveal who drew each one until after you have discussed it.

"Your bag's all right, Mr. Thomas. Look. One foot there. On your right. Now just above. To your left." Mr. Thomas climbed over his own garden wall. "Here's your bag, Mr. Thomas."

"I'll have the wall built up," Mr. Thomas said, "I'll not have you boys coming over here, using my loo." He stumbled on the path, but the boy caught his elbow and supported him. "Thank you, thank you, my boy," he murmured automatically. Somebody shouted again through the dark. "I'm coming, I'm coming," Mr. Thomas called. He said to the boy beside him, "I'm not unreasonable. Been a boy myself. As long as things are done regular. I don't mind you playing round the place Saturday mornings. Sometimes I like company. Only it's got to be regular. One of you asks leave and I say Yes. Sometimes I'll say No. Won't feel like it. And you come in at the front door and out at the back. No garden walls."

"Do get him out, Mr. Thomas."

"He won't come to any harm in my loo," Mr. Thomas said, stumbling slowly down the garden. "Oh, my rheumatics," he said. "Always get 'em on Bank Holiday. I've got to go careful. There's loose stones here. Give me your hand. Do you know what my horoscope said yesterday? 'Abstain from any dealings in first half of week. Danger of serious crash.' That might be on this path," Mr. Thomas said. "They speak in parables and double meanings." "He paused at the door of the loo. "What's the matter in there?" he called. There was no reply.

"Perhaps he's fainted," the boy said.

"Not in my loo. Here, you, come out," Mr. Thomas said, and giving a great jerk at the door he nearly fell on his back when it swung easily open. A hand first supported him and then pushed him hard. His head hit the opposite wall and he sat heavily down. His bag hit his feet. A hand whipped the key out of the lock and the door slammed. "Let me out," he called, and heard the key turn in the lock. "A serious crash," he thought, and felt dithery and confused and old.

A voice spoke to him softly through the star-shaped hole in the door. "Don't worry, Mr. Thomas," it said, "we won't hurt you, not if you stay quiet."

Mr. Thomas put his head between his hands and pondered. He had noticed that there was only one lorry in the car-park, and he felt certain that the driver would not come for it before the morning. Nobody could hear him from the road in front, and the lane at the back was seldom used. Anyone who passed there would be hurrying home and would

261

not pause for what they would certainly take to be drunken cries. And if he did call "Help," who, on a lonely Bank Holiday evening, would have the courage to investigate? Mr. Thomas sat on the loo and pondered with the wisdom of age.

After a while it seemed to him that there were sounds in the silence—they were faint and came from the direction of his house. He stood up and peered through the ventilation-hole—between the cracks in one of the shutters he saw a light, not the light of a lamp, but the wavering light that a candle might give. Then he thought he heard the sound of hammering and scraping and chipping. He thought of burglars—perhaps they had employed the boy as a scout, but why should burglars engage in what sounded more and more like a stealthy form of carpentry? Mr. Thomas let out an experimental yell, but nobody answered. The noise could not even have reached his enemies.

Mike had gone home to bed, but the rest stayed. The question of leadership no longer concerned the gang. With nails, chisels, screwdrivers, anything that was sharp and penetrating they moved around the inner walls worrying at the mortar between the bricks. They started too high, and it was Blackie who hit on the damp course and realized the work could be halved if they weakened the joints immediately above. It was a long, tiring, unamusing job, but at last it was finished. The gutted house stood there balanced on a few inches of mortar between the damp course and the bricks.

There remained the most dangerous task of all, out in the open at the edge of the bomb-site. Summers was sent to watch the road for passer-bys, and Mr. Thomas, sitting on the loo, heard clearly now the sound of sawing. It no longer came from his house, and that a little reassured him. He felt less concerned. Perhaps the other noises too had no significance.

A voice spoke to him through the hole. "Mr. Thomas."

"Let me out," Mr. Thomas said sternly.

"Here's a blanket," the voice said, and a long grey sausage was worked through the hole and fell in swathes over Mr. Thomas's head.

"There's nothing personal," the voice said. "We want you to be comfortable tonight."

"Tonight," Mr. Thomas repeated incredulously.

"Catch," the voice said. "Penny buns—we've buttered them, and sausage-rolls. We don't want you to starve, Mr. Thomas."

Mr. Thomas pleaded desperately. "A joke's a joke, boy. Let me out and I won't say a thing. I've got rheumatics. I got to sleep comfortable."

"You wouldn't be comfortable, not in your house, you wouldn't. Not now."

"What do you mean, boy?" but the footsteps receded. There was only the silence of night: no sound of sawing. Mr. Thomas tried one more yell, but he was daunted and rebuked by the silence—a long way off an owl hooted and made away again on its muffled flight through the soundless world.

At seven next morning the driver came to fetch his lorry. He climbed into the seat and tried to start the engine. He was vaguely aware of a voice shouting, but it didn't concern him. At last the engine responded and he backed the lorry until it touched the great wooden shore that supported Mr. Thomas's house. That way he could drive right out and down the street without reversing. The lorry moved forward, was momentarily checked as though something were pulling it from behind, and then went on to the sound of a long rumbling crash. The driver was astonished to see bricks bouncing ahead of him, while stones hit the roof of his cab. He put on his brakes. When he climbed out the whole landscape had suddenly altered. There was no house beside the car-park, only a hill of rubble. He went round and examined the back of his car for damage, and found a rope tied there that was still twisted at the other end round part of a wooden strut.

The driver again became aware of somebody shouting. It came from the wooden erection which was the nearest thing to a house in that desolation of broken brick. The driver climbed the smashed wall and unlocked the door. Mr. Thomas came out of the loo. He was wearing a grey blanket to which flakes of pastry adhered. He gave a sobbing cry. "My house," he said. "Where's my house?"

"Search me," the driver said. His eye lit on the remains of a bath and what had once been a dresser and he began to laugh. There wasn't anything left anywhere.

"How dare you laugh," Mr. Thomas said. "It was my house. My house."

"I'm sorry," the driver said, making heroic efforts, but when he remembered the sudden check to his lorry, the crash of bricks falling, he became convulsed again. One moment the house had stood there with such dignity between the bomb-sites like a man in a top hat, and then, bang, crash, there wasn't anything left—not anything. He said, "I'm sorry. I can't help it, Mr. Thomas. There's nothing personal, but you got to admit it's funny."

CLUSTERS

Select a key word from this chapter* and rate it on each of the fourteen scales listed below. Put an X in the blank where you feel it belongs between each pair of words provided. Thus, if you chose *intellect* as your key word and you felt it belonged closest to *good*, you would put an X in the first blank next to *good*. If you felt it was a toss up, you would put the X in the middle blank between *good* and *bad*. We have filled in the chart with *our* impressions for the word *intellect*. Everyone use the same key word; then tally your results to see how much agreement there is among you.

Then select nine more key words from the chapter and work up a chart for each one. Tally your results. Explore the signifiance of your findings.

Example: intellect

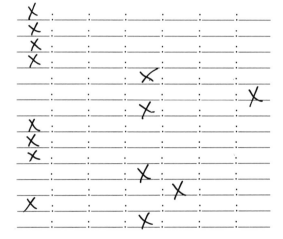

1. interesting		boring
2. cooperation		competition
3. colorful		colorless
4. calm		exciting
5. black		white
6. mother		father
7. happy		sad
8. cold		hot
9. sensitive		insensitive
10. positive		negative
11. aggressive		defensive
12. changeable		stable
13. severe		lenient
14. good		bad

* You can substitute a list of your classmates' names here, but it is risky. Another variation is to use topical words like mescaline, Beatles, the draft; or use the names of public figures such as politicians, authors, film stars, athletes, or scientists.

We carve words and images out of the great undifferentiated mass in the same manner as one carves a statue out of a lump of rock.

Multiple choice:
    The object of education
    is suicide.

An answer is always a form of death.

THE FORCE THAT THROUGH THE
GREEN FUSE DRIVES THE FLOWER

The force that through the green fuse drives the flower
Drives my green age; that blasts the roots of trees
Is my destroyer.
And I am dumb to tell the crooked rose
My youth is bent by the same wintry fever.

The force that drives the water through the rocks
Drives my red blood; that dries the mouthing streams
Turns mine to wax.
And I am dumb to mouth unto my veins
How at the mountain spring that same mouth sucks.

The hand that whirls the water in the pool
Stirs the quicksand; that ropes the blowing wind
Hauls my shroud sail.
And I am dumb to tell the hanging man
How of my clay is made the hangman's lime.

The lips of time leech to the fountain head;
Love drips and gathers, but the fallen blood
Shall calm her sores.
And I am dumb to tell a weather's wind
How time has ticked a heaven round the stars.

And I am dumb to tell the lover's tomb
How at my sheet goes the same crooked worm.

A WHY
IN THE ROAD

?

Septuagenarian 30 yrs.

"Y in the road?"
"Because."

Then I cast time out of the trees and fields,
Then I stood immaculate in the Ego;
Then I eyed the world with all delight,
Reality was the perfection of my sight.

If I could only live at the pitch that is near madness
When everything is as it was in my childhood
Violent, vivid, and of infinite possibility:
That the sun and the moon broke over my head.

*"All of a sudden
I'm going off the
road."*

And time has big handles on the hands,
Fields and trees a way of being themselves.
I saw battalions of the race of mankind
Standing stolid, demanding a moral answer.

I gave the moral answer and I died
And into a realm of complexity came
Where nothing is possible but necessity
And the truth wailing there like a red babe.

267

MIDTERM

PALINDROME

"Doc, note. I dissent. A fast never prevents a fatness. I diet on cod."

—Penelope Gilliatt

B

Suddenly he was middle aged. No miracles had happened. No Shazam!, and he was suddenly head of HEW or whatever his particular self-fantasy had been. This morning he saw that nothing ever changes, which was strange, since everything changes all the time. Time, inconstant siren with her promises. At twenty-two he had thought there was Time for everything. What a shuck. The only way the mind had to measure it was by what had gone before. During the first year a year was an eternity. In his eighteenth year there were seventeen others to compare it with, but he had been so preoccupied with glands that he hadn't noticed the foreshortening. And *now* a year was only *one fortieth* of his eternity. "Time flies" was no cliché; it was a physical, scientific, certified fact. It seemed only four or five years since he had left school. But here he was past midpoint (time for a midterm test?), past the time when people wanted to hire you. In ten years (Ten years! at the rate things were going that would *feel* like one year) he would be thinking of retirement! Here he was, feeling eighteen in a forty-year-old hide. What the hell was going on?*

*Ed. Note: The right way to get to 40 intact is hidden in these pages (probably). Find it. Or, show that it is *not* here. Reflect . . . . .

Perhaps that's my greatest social crime, I've overstayed my hibernation, since there's a possibility that even an invisible man has a socially responsible role to play . . .

I cast time out of the trees and fields . . .

How weary, stale, flat, and unprofitable,
Seems to me all the uses of this world!
Fie on't! oh fie, fie! 'Tis an unweeded garden,
That grows to seed; things rank and gross in nature
Possess it merely. That it should come to this!

I have of late—but wherefore I know not
— lost all my mirth, forgone all custom
of exercise; and indeed it goes so heavily with my disposition that this goodly
frame, the earth, seems to me a sterile
promontory, this most excellent canopy,
the air, look you, this brave o'erhanging
firmament this majestical roof fretted
with golden fire, why, it appears no other
thing to me than a foul and pestilent
congregation of vapours. What a piece
of work is man! How noble in reason!
How infinite in faculty, in form and moving! How express and admirable in action! How like an angel in apprehension!
How like a god! The beauty of the world!
The paragon of animals! And yet, to me,
what is this quintessence of dust? Man
delights not me . . . .

children, leave
the string untied

269

A problem of making connections

I had better tell you where I am, and why. I am sitting in a high-ceilinged room in the Royal Hawaiian Hotel in Honolulu watching the long translucent curtains billow in the trade wind and trying to put my life back together. My husband is here, and our daughter, age three. She is blond and barefoot, a child of paradise in a frangipani lei, and she does not understand why she cannot go to the beach. She cannot go to the beach because there has been an earthquake in the Aleutians, 7.5 on the Richter scale, and a tidal wave is expected. In two or three minutes the wave, if there is one, will hit Midway Island, and we are awaiting word from Midway. My husband watches the TV screen. I watch the curtains and imagine the swell of the water.

The bulletin, when it comes, is a distinct anticlimax: Midway reports no unusual wave action. My husband switches off the TV set and stares out the window. I avoid his eyes and brush the baby's hair. In the absence of a natural disaster we are left again to our own uneasy devices. We are here on this island in the middle of the Pacific in lieu of filing for divorce.

I tell you this not as aimless revelation but because I want you to know, during the time that I will be writing for this page, precisely who I am and where I am and what is on my mind. I want you to understand exactly what you are getting: you are getting a woman who for some time now has felt radically separated from most of the ideas that seem to interest other people. You are getting a woman who somewhere along the line misplaced what slight faith she ever had in the social contract, in the meliorative principle, in the whole grand pattern of human endeavor. Quite often during the past several years I have felt myself a sleepwalker, moving through the world unconscious of the moment's high issues, oblivious to its data, alert only to the stuff of bad dreams, the children burning in the locked car in the supermarket parking lot, the bike boys stripping down stolen cars on the captive cripple's ranch, the freeway sniper who feels "real bad" about picking off the family of five, the hustlers, the insane, the cunning Okie faces that turn up in military investigations, the sullen lurkers in doorways, the lost children, all the ignorant armies on some dark pathological plain. Acquaintances read the New York *Times* and try to tell me the news of the world. I listen to call-in shows.

You will perceive that much of the world presents difficulties. I have trouble making certain connections. I have trouble maintaining the basic notion that keeping promises matters in a world where everything I was taught seems beside the point. The point itself seems increasingly obscure. I came into adult life equipped with an essentially romantic ethic, holding always before me the examples of Axel Heyst in *Victory* and Milly Theale in *The Wings of the Dove* and Charlotte Rittenmeyer in *The Wild Palms* and a few dozen others like them, believing as they did that salvation lay in extreme and doomed commitments, promises made and somehow kept outside the range of normal social experience. I still believe that, but I have trouble reconciling salvation with those ignorant armies incessantly jostling in my mind.

But of course ignorant armies are nothing new. There has always been an amoral vacuum out there just beyond the eye's range, and making promises matter against that vacuum has never been easy for anyone. Making anything at all matter has never been easy. I remember leaving someone once, a long time ago, one bad afternoon in New York, packing a suitcase and crying while he watched me. When I asked him finally how he could watch me, he told me that a great many things had happened to him during the 10 years before I knew him, and nothing much touched him anymore. I remember saying that I never wanted to get the way he was, and he looked at me a long while before he answered. "Nobody wants to," he said. "But you will."

"For me, . . .
Meursault is not a piece of social wreckage, but a poor and naked man enamored of a sun that leaves no shadows."

G

mind

"The child is father
of the man . . ."

270

I think about that quite a bit now. I could indulge here in a little idle generalization, could lay off my own state of profound emotional shock on the larger cultural breakdown, could talk fast about convulsions in the society and alienation and anomie and maybe even assassination, but to do that would be just one more stylish shell game. I am not the society in microcosm. I am a 34-year-old woman with long straight hair and an old bikini bathing suit and bad nerves sitting on an island in the middle of the Pacific watching for a tidal wave that will not come.

We spend, my husband and I and the baby, a restorative week in paradise. We are each the other's model of consideration, tact, restraint at the very edge of the precipice. He refrains from noticing when I am staring at nothing and frightened of the void, and in turn I refrain from dwelling at morbid length upon a newspaper story about a couple who apparently threw their infant and then themselves into the boiling crater of a live volcano on Maui. We also refrain from mentioning the kicked-down doors, the hospitalized psychotics, the chronic anxieties and the packed suitcases. We lie in the sun, drive out through the cane to Waimea Bay. We breakfast on the terrace, and gray-haired women smile benevolently at us. I smile back. Happy families are all alike on the terrace of the Royal Hawaiian Hotel in Honolulu. We ask each other no questions, demand of each other no answers. My husband comes in from Kalakaua Avenue one morning and tells me that he has seen a 6-foot-2 drag queen we know in Los Angeles. Our acquaintance was shopping, my husband reports, for a fishnet bikini and did not speak. We both laughed. I am reminded that we laugh at the same things. At the end of the week I tell him that I am going to try harder to make things matter. He says that he has heard that before, but the air is warm and the baby has another frangipani lei and there is no rancor in his voice. Maybe it can be all right, I say. Maybe, he says.

parasites

True-False Test

1. If the author of this poem were alive today, he would have written the fore-going essay.
2. The essay is a result of poems such as this.
3. The essay is fiction.
4. The poem is fiction.
5. The essay is real.
6. The poem is real.
7. "Who dares undo the parcel finds himself . . . inside it."
8. "The medium is the message."
9. Disillusion is romantic, too.
10. "To lie is to express more than one feels."
    This statement applies to the poem.
11. The statement in 10 applies to the essay.

How do I love thee? Let me count the ways.
I love thee to the depth and breadth and height
My soul can reach, when feeling out of sight
For the ends of Being and ideal Grace.
I love thee to the level of everyday's
Most quiet need, by sun and candlelight.
I love thee freely, as men strive for Right;
I love thee purely, as they turn from Praise.
I love thee with the passion put to use
In my old griefs, and with my childhood's faith.
I love thee with a love I seemed to lose
With my lost saints,—I love thee with the breath,
Smiles, tears, of all my life!—and, if God choose,
I shall but love thee better after death.

"Byron,
Prufrock,
Dover Beach,
wise up."

271

P A GRAND SYNTHESIS

Anything I do today, I regard as urgent. No man is given but so much time to accomplish whatever is his life's work. My life in particular never has stayed fixed in one position for very long. You have seen how throughout my life, I have often known unexpected drastic changes.

— Malcolm X

"Man is designed to generate abstractions. The problem is to find the fiction which fulfills his genetic imprint."

Trailing clouds
of glory
do
we
come...

For a long time the Earth was the centre of the universe; after Copernicus the Sun was; fifty years ago the universe was just *the* Galaxy, the Milky Way, in which the Sun was a modest member among 100,000 million stars. If that seemed world enough for anyone, it has since turned out to be a great understatement, because we now know that there are thousands of millions of galaxies. And radio telescopes pick up a strange whisper from empty sky. Many astronomers believe it to be the echo of a Big Bang about 10,000 million years ago, when all the matter of the universe was gathered in one place and was then blasted into an expanding cloud, which now can be seen in the form of galaxies moving away from us, in whatever direction we care to look. Work in progress will show us whether the Big Bang really happened; it may give us, at long last, a reliable impression of our own place in space and time.

Each science has its heyday. The 1930s and 1940s were dramatic and fateful years for the atomic physicists. The 1950s brought a revolution in biology, by way of the investigation of the large molecules of life. The 1960s, and especially these closing years of the decade, are a golden age of astronomy, likely to rank in future histories with the period in the early 17th century when Galileo first turned a telescope towards the sky, and Kepler elucidated the motions of the planets. Will the 1970s bring a grand synthesis of new laws of nature, such as Newton gave? It looks as likely as not.

...this terror rimmed with necessary flesh...

Did she put on this knowledge with this power?

KITTEN WATCHING

One can look under the mask of socially-sanctioned communication at the source of thought and see its more primal and autonomous nature. There are individual differences even at this level. For some, feeling becomes image, for others it becomes words, for others the inner is like an imageless, wordless drama known before word or image. It is a delicate process, the mind watching itself at work. If the whole of the inner process differentiates into thought and this thought is ego, then ego would be the fixed conception of a changing process. Ego would be a result of 1 autre moi. Add to this the accumulation of memory and the tie to a slowly changing body, and one has ego.

F: Say this, "I won't let you—"
M: I won't let you. /F: Louder./
    I won't let you! /F: Louder./
    Goddamit! (screams) *I won't let you!*
F: Louder. Say it with your whole body.
M: I WON'T LET YOU!
F: Again, I still don't believe you. It's all literature still — wailing, complaining...I don't feel any confidence yet.

True or False: M is having an intensely literary experience.

True or False:
    It is better to say, "I'm suffering," than to say, "This landscape is suffering."

273

WINTER LIGHT

...A dream is a normal and common message from l'autre moi . . . It is written in an ancient language I am only coming to understand.

FIVE—stands for man, love, health. Quintessence acting upon matter. The four limbs of the body and the controlling head; the thumb and the four fingers; the four cardinal points and the center. The *hieros gamos* is signified by the number five, since it represents the union of the principle of heaven (three) with that of the *Magna Mater* (two). The pentagram, the five-pointed star. It corresponds to pentagonal symmetry, a common characteristic of organic nature, to the golden section, and to the five senses representing the five "forms" of matter.

"Representations are nothing but images of spiritual things in natural ones, and when the former are rightly represented in the latter, then the two correspond."
—Swedenborg

FIVE—often occurs in animate nature, and its triumphant growth corresponds to the burgeoning of spring. It signifies the organic fullness of life as opposed to the rigidity of death. There is an erotic sense to it as well.

Her dream began with winter darkness. Out of this darkness came a great hand, fisted. It was a man's hand, powerful and hollowed by shadows in the wells between bones and tendons. The fist opened and in the long plain of the palm lay three small pieces of coal. Slowly the hand closed, causing within the fist a tremendous pressure. The pressure began to generate a white heat and still it increased. There was a sense of weighing, crushing time. She seemed to feel the suffering of the coal with her own body, almost beyond the point of being borne. At last she cried out to the hand, "Stop it! Will you never end it! Even a stone cannot bear to this limit...even a stone...!"

After what seemed like too long a time for anything molecular to endure, the torments in the fist relaxed. The fist turned slowly and very slowly opened.

Diamonds, three of them.

Three clear and brilliant diamonds, shot with light, lay in the good palm. A deep voice called to her, "Deborah!" and then, gently, "Deborah, this will be you."

274

Without the possibility of action, all knowledge comes to one labeled "file and forget," and I can neither file nor forget.

Ralph Ellison

WE ARE IGNORANT BY CHOICE.

Progressing through life to the middle years is similar to mastering a violin, but the instrument one is learning is his own mind and body. The years of maturity are those in which one 'performs.' The musician plays with assurance, power, control, and clarity. He knows what the instrument can do, he knows what *he* can do. He becomes a vigorous mover in and of a rich, full world. The entrance to this stage of life is usually marked by a pause and a summing up. One senses that he is at a turning point. If things have gone well, he goes forward with enthusiasm. If either his physical or psychical development has been faulty, however, he experiences disorientation varying in effect from minor frustration to complete disintegration. It can be a period of indecision, disillusion, infidelity, alcoholism, alienation, failure. Or it can be the beginning of one's peak output, marked by a feeling of fulfillment, oneness, strength, and serenity.

Hint: "As long as a child operates with the decimal system without having become conscious of it as such, he has not mastered the system but is, on the contrary, bound by it.".

A man goes to knowledge as he goes to war, wide-awake, with fear, with respect, and with absolute assurance. Going to knowledge or going to war in any other manner is a mistake, and whoever makes it will live to regret his mistakes.

"My name is Sam Greenlee, I am a black American and I write. I was born in Chicago, a second-generation immigrant from the deep South. I received a non-education in Chicago ghetto non-schools and played catch-up at three universities: Wisconsin, Chicago and Thessalonikki, Greece. I speak fluent Greek, Indonesian/Malay and enough Arabic, French and Italian to order a meal and argue with taxi drivers. At the risk of supporting cherished stereotypes, I run fast, sing, dance and have been told I am good in bed. My chief literary influences are Charlie Parker, Lester Young, Miles Davis and Billie Holiday. As a writer, I consider myself a jazz musician whose instrument is a typewriter. I do not consider myself a victim of racism because a victim submits. Nor am I appalled by European/American history because I regard it as fiction. Sign no blues for me because I sing my own and to black man, the blues are a freedom song."

Ripe fruit will
not remain on
the branch.
—Hindu proverb

Sick, frenetic occultism

BIG PATTERNS

275

Stages of language development?
Parallels between stages of maturation
and stages of linguistic control?

Learning to be grown up

"Give a serious and powerful man a child's toy and leave him alone with it. After a short while he experiences painfully or happily, how his childhood was, and he begins to understand both himself and his childhood better."

—Psychiatrist Tobias Brocher.

The navel of the devine world ...

Temperate conditions on Earth give us a very mild impression of the forces of nature. Hurricanes and lightning strokes, earthquakes and avalanches, the remorseless pull of the Earth's gravity and the unforgiving inertia of a vehicle suddenly brought to rest—these are the most unpleasant manifestations of natural forces ... Yet, on Earth, hurtling masses are rather small, gravity is not unduly oppressive, the chances of being hit by lightning are insignificant and even the multi-megaton H-bomb is puny by comparison with the nuclear reactions occurring in the smallest stars. Among the solids, liquids and gases of our material world, we are hard put to it to reproduce the common states of matter of the universe: the diffuse near-vacuum of the interstellar space, or the hot, electrified gas (plasma) of the stars themselves. Our impression of the relative importance of natural forces is also peculiar to our circumstances.

In the midst of it all people work at being *charming.*

Man: "an ingenious assembly of portable plumbing."

How do I love thee?

"The three main kinds of forces known to scientists are nuclear, electromagnetic, and gravitational."

First, the basic trust that one __can__ learn.

T

765

99L

7-24 MAL

True or false:
Bias is prejudice.

• Autoplastic mastery —
the middle age of life,
approximately from 35 to 60,
when a person's interests
turn inward to achieve self-
mastery. Activities that
offer personal satisfaction
seem most important.

Zinfandel: Bottled poetry.
Let the liquid flow back along
the sides of the tongue where
the taste buds are most responsive.

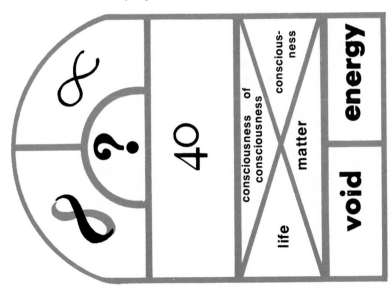

∞

?

40

∞

consciousness of consciousness

consciousness

life

matter

void

energy

IN THE
BEGINNING
WAS THE
VOID.

277

List here sure-fire directions for getting to
40 with it all together:

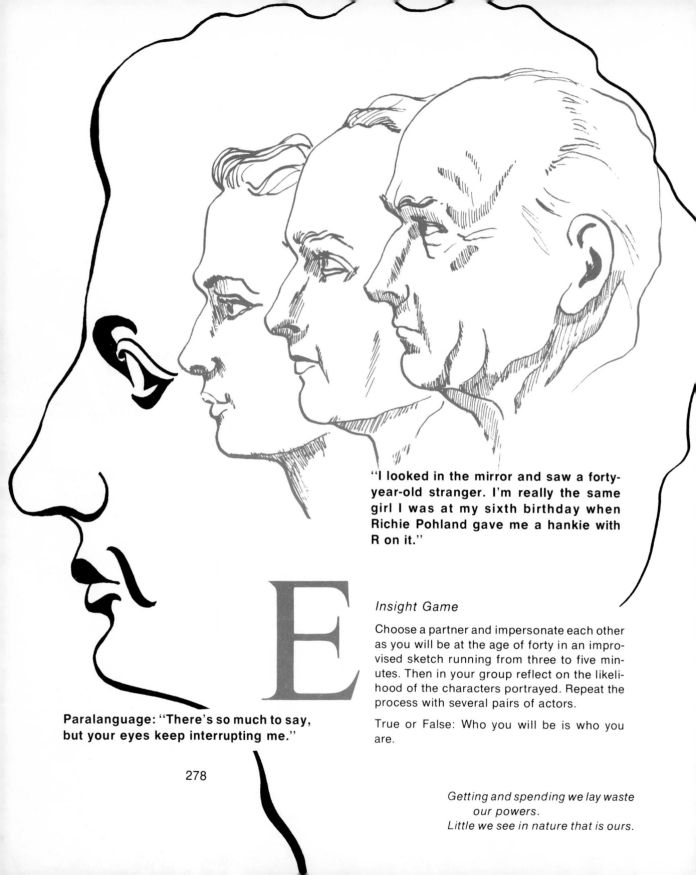

"I looked in the mirror and saw a forty-year-old stranger. I'm really the same girl I was at my sixth birthday when Richie Pohland gave me a hankie with R on it."

E

Insight Game

Choose a partner and impersonate each other as you will be at the age of forty in an improvised sketch running from three to five minutes. Then in your group reflect on the likelihood of the characters portrayed. Repeat the process with several pairs of actors.

True or False: Who you will be is who you are.

Paralanguage: "There's so much to say, but your eyes keep interrupting me."

Getting and spending we lay waste our powers.
Little we see in nature that is ours.

''You always treat my moods as if they aren't valid.''

A student

It is well known that severe post-surgical pain can be relieved in some patients by giving them placebos — sugar pills made up to look like pain-killers. These work for about 35 per cent of patients.

Research Project:
Which contain fewer adjectives?

1. Theatrical plays or doctoral theses?
2. Business letters or laws?
3. Poetry or ads?

Vocabulary Test: Check all true statements.

Hate = fear
Love = need
Anger = insecurity
Love = abundance
Prejudice = bias
Synchronicity = coincidence

**Things are peculiar only when they are strange.
Is that good or bad?**

Impotent promiscuity

''The real problem is the problem of death. If people don't know how to come to terms with it, and souls have no preparation, then the only thing is to be eternally young and in pursuit of pleasure and further sexual and hedonistic horizons.''

DEFINING AN ISLAND UNIVERSE — AGAIN

''All the time I was in jail—maybe six months—I practiced the mental discipline of observing my own thoughts. This is a practice of detaching from yourself and observing. It's like kitten watching, except you're one of the kittens.''

The lab is open.

''The well-rounded man: Broadly narrow-minded.''

"The past is a foreign country. They do things differently there."

1940
1950
1960
1970
19

N

A Gentle Knight was pricking on the plaine,
   Y-cladd in mightie armes and silver shielde,
   Wherein old dints of deepe wounds did remaine,
   The cruell markes of many a bloudy fielde;
   Yet armes till that time did he never wield:
   His angry steede did chide his foming bitt,
   As much disdayning to the curbe to yield:
   Full jolly knight he seemd, and faire did sitt,
As one for knightly giusts and fierce encounters fitt.

But on his brest a bloudie Crosse he bore,
   The deare remembrance of his dying Lord,
   For whose sweete sake that glorious badge he wore,
   And dead as living ever him adored:
   Upon his shield the like was also scored,
   For soveraine hope, which in his helpe he had:
   Right faithfull true he was in deede and word,
   But of his cheere did seeme too solemne sad;
Yet nothing did he dread, but ever was ydrad.

Upon a great adventure he was bond,
   That greatest *Gloriana* to him gave,
   That greatest Glorious Queene of *Faerie* lond,
   To winne him worship, and her grace to have,
   Which of all earthly things he most did crave;
   And ever as he rode, his hart did earne
   To prove his puissance in battell brave
   Upon his foe, and his new force to learne;
Upon his foe, a Dragon horrible and stearne.

                 —1588

281

Explore the message of this medium. (Note linguistic differences from current English. Compare with the Middle English passage on page 181 True or false: 1. "A language is a philosophy." 2. We still live in the poet's world.

The Recurrent Dream:

A thorn made thorny by one's rejection of it.

Over a period of ten years or so I had a recurring dream. In it I murdered someone. It felt like an irrevocable, horrible act. It placed me forever outside society and outside my own acceptance. I tried to hide the body, but I knew it could never be hidden. The dream had such intensity that in my waking hours I sometimes caught myself feeling as though I had actually committed the murder. Then one day I woke and asked myself, "Who is it that I have killed?" The answer came back, "My self." I felt a surge of relief. Everything clicked into place. I have not had the dream since.

Or yf the soule, of propre kynde,
Be so parfit, as men fynde,
That yt forwot that ys to come,
And that hyt warneth alle and some
Of everych of her aventures
Be avisions, or be figures,
But that oure flessh ne hath no
      myght
To understonde hyt aryght,
For hyt is warned to derkly . . .

OEDIPUS

WE HAVE MET THE ENEMY
AND HE IS US

I dreamed I saw an old high school friend who asked me what I had been doing all these years. I said, "I've been in an insane asylum for the last 23 years." When I reflected on it, I first thought maybe my self was trying to tell me that I didn't like being married and all that, but I had been married for only 18 years. Twenty-three years ago I had just been discharged from the army and had begun working and supporting myself. I've never consciously thought of how long I've been at it.

S

"Some people get fixated, or hung up, at one particular stage that hasn't been successfully negotiated. They may spend the rest of their life making futile attempts to work it through."

LINDA: [*Hearing* Willy *outside the bedroom, calls with trepidation*] Willy!

WILLY: It's all right. I came back.

LINDA: Why? What happened? [*Slight pause*] Did something happen, Willy?

WILLY: No, nothing happened.

LINDA: You didn't smash the car, did you?

WILLY: [*With casual irritation*] I said nothing happened. Didn't you hear me?

LINDA: Don't you feel well?

WILLY: I'm tired to the death. [*The flute has faded away. He sits on the bed beside her, a little numb*] I couldn't make it. I just couldn't make it, Linda.

LINDA: [*Very carefully, delicately*] Where were you all day? You look terrible.

WILLY: I got as far as a little above Yonkers. I stopped for a cup of coffee. Maybe it was the coffee.

LINDA: What?

WILLY: [*After a pause*] I suddenly couldn't drive any more. The car kept going off onto the shoulder, y'know?

LINDA: [*Helpfully*] Oh. Maybe it was the steering again. I don't think Angelo knows the Studebaker.

WILLY: No, it's me, it's me. Suddenly I realize I'm goin' sixty miles an hour and I don't remember the last five minutes. I'm—I can't seem to—keep my mind to it.

LINDA: Maybe it's your glasses. You never went for your new glasses.

WILLY: No, I see everything. I came back ten miles an hour. It took me nearly four hours from Yonkers.

LINDA: [*Resigned*] Well, you'll just have to take a rest, Willy, you can't continue this way.

WILLY: I just got back from Florida.

LINDA: But you didn't rest your mind. Your mind is overactive, and the mind is what counts, dear.

WILLY: I'll start out in the morning. Maybe I'll feel better in the morning. [*She is taking off his shoes*] These goddam arch supports are killing me.

LINDA: Take an aspirin. Should I get you an aspirin? It'll soothe you.

WILLY: [*With wonder*] I was driving along, you understand? And I was fine. I was even observing the scenery. You can imagine, me looking at scenery, on the road every week of my life. But it's so beautiful up there, Linda, the trees are so thick, and the sun is warm. I opened the windshield and just let the warm air bathe over me. And then all of a sudden I'm goin' off the road! I'm tellin' ya, I absolutely forgot I was driving. If I'd've gone the other way over the white line I might've killed somebody. So I went on again—and five minutes later I'm dreamin' again, and I nearly—[*He presses two fingers against his eyes*] I have such thoughts, I have such strange thoughts.

LINDA: Willy, dear. Talk to them again. There's no reason why you can't work in New York.

WILLY: They don't need me in New York. I'm the New England man. I'm vital in New England.

LINDA: But you're sixty years old. They can't expect you to keep traveling every week.

WILLY: I'll have to send a wire to Portland. I'm supposed to see Brown and Morrison tomorrow morning at ten o'clock to show the line. Goddammit, I could sell them! [*He starts putting on his jacket*]

LINDA: [*Taking the jacket from him*] Why don't you go down to the place tomorrow and tell Howard you've simply got to work in New York? You're too accommodating, dear.

WILLY: If old man Wagner was alive I'd a been in charge of New York now! That man was a prince, he was a masterful man. But that boy of his, that Howard, he don't appreciate. When I went north first time, the Wagner Company didn't know where New England was!

LINDA: Why don't you tell those things to Howard, dear?

WILLY: [*Encouraged*] I will, I definitely will. Is there any cheese?

LINDA: I'll make you a sandwich.

WILLY: No, go to sleep. I'll take some milk. I'll be up right away. The boys in?

LINDA: They're sleeping. Happy took Biff on a date tonight.

WILLY: [*Interested*] That so?

LINDA: It was so nice to see them shaving together, one behind the other, in the bathroom. And going out together. You notice? The whole house smells of shaving lotion.

WILLY: Figure it out. Work a lifetime to pay off a house. You finally own it, and there's nobody to live in it.

LINDA: Well, dear, life is a casting off. It's always that way.

WILLY: No, no, some people—some people accomplish something.

Birth: the emergence of a new individual from the body of its parent.

283

NAUSEA
by
Jean-Paul
Sartre

karma

A WORD TO THE WISE

Let the world pass in its time-ridden race;
   never get caught in its snare.
Remember, the only acceptable case
for being in any particular place
   is having no business there.

Take
a
40-year
coffee
break

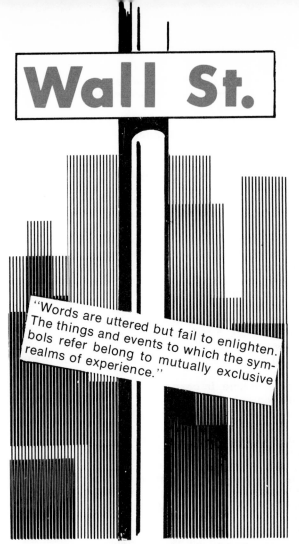

Wall St.

"Words are uttered but fail to enlighten. The things and events to which the symbols refer belong to mutually exclusive realms of experience."

Without the possibility of action, all knowledge comes to one labeled "file and forget," and I can neither file nor forget.

Ralph Ellison

Xing

In going underground, I whipped it all except the mind, the *mind*. And the mind that has conceived a plan of living must never lose sight of the chaos against which that pattern was conceived.

Macbeth:
...now I am bent to know
By the worst means, the worst. For mine own good
All causes shall give way. I am in blood
Stepped in so far that, should I wade no more,
Returning were as tedious as go o'er.
Strange things I have in head, that will to hand,
Which must be acted ere they may be scanned.

Seyton: The Queen, my lord, is dead.
Macbeth: She should have died hereafter;
There would have been a time for such a word.
Tomorrow, and tomorrow, and tomorrow
Creeps in this petty pace from day to day
To the last syllable of recorded time;
And all our yesterdays have lighted fools
The way to dusty death. Out, out, brief candle!
Life's but a walking shadow, a poor player
That struts and frets his hour upon the stage
And then is heard no more. It is a tale
Told by an idiot, full of sound and fury,
Signifying nothing.

285

Old Brazilian Adage:
Peace of mind is a strong house,
a tame horse, and an ugly wife.

STAYING ALIVE

Staying alive in the woods is a matter of calming down
At first and deciding whether to wait for rescue,
Trusting to others,
Or simply to start walking and walking in one direction
Till you come out—or something happens to stop you.
By far the safer choice
Is to settle down where you are, and try to make a living
Off the land, camping near water, away from shadows.
Eat no white berries;
Spit out all bitterness. Shooting at anything
Means hiking further and further every day
To hunt survivors;
It may be best to learn what you have to learn without a gun,
Not killing but watching birds and animals go
In and out of shelter
At will. Following their example, build for a whole season:
Facing across the wind in your lean-to,
You may feel wilder,
And nothing, not even you, will have to stay in hiding.
If you have no matches, a stick and a fire-bow
Will keep you warmer,
Or the crystal of your watch, filled with water, held up to the
    sun
Will do the same, in time. In case of snow,
Drifting toward winter,
Don't try to stay awake through the night, afraid of
    freezing—
The bottom of your mind knows all about zero;
It will turn you over
And shake you till you waken. If you have trouble sleeping
Even in the best of weather, jumping to follow
The unidentifiable noises of the night and feeling
Bears and packs of wolves nuzzling your elbow,
Remember the trappers
Who treated them indifferently and were left alone.
If you hurt yourself, no one will comfort you
Or take your temperature,
So stumbling, wading, and climbing are as dangerous as
    flying.
But if you decide, at last, you must break through
In spite of all danger,

Think of yourself by time and not by distance, counting
Wherever you're going by how long it takes you;
No other measure
Will bring you safe to nightfall. Follow no streams: they run

286

True or False: When one loses
his temper, it is always by
choice.

Under the ground or fall into wilder country.
Remember the stars
And moss when your mind runs into circles. If it should rain,
Or the fog should roll the horizon in around you,
Hold still for hours
Or days, if you must, or weeks, for seeing is believing
In the wilderness. And if you find a pathway,
Wheel rut, or fence wire,
Retrace it left or right—someone knew where he was going
Once upon a time, and you can follow
Hopefully, somewhere,
Just in case. There may even come, on some uncanny
    evening,
A time when you're warm and dry, well fed, not thirsty,
Uninjured, without fear,
When nothing, either good or bad, is happening.
This is called staying alive. It's temporary.
What occurs after
Is doubtful. You must always be ready for something to
    come bursting
Through the far edge of a clearing, running toward you,
Grinning from ear to ear
And hoarse with welcome. Or something crossing and
    hovering
Overhead, as light as air, like a break in the sky,
Wondering what you are.
Here you are face to face with the problem of recognition.
Having no time to make smoke, too much to say,
You should have a mirror
With a tiny hole in the back for better aiming, for reflecting
Whatever disaster you can think of, to show
The way you suffer.
These body signals have universal meaning: If you are lying
Flat on your back with arms outstretched behind you,
You say you require
Emergency treatment; if you are standing erect and holding
Arms horizontal, you mean you are not ready;
If you hold them over
Your head, you want to be picked up. Three of anything
Is a sign of distress. Afterward, if you see
No ropes, no ladders,
No maps or messages falling, no searchlights or trails blazing,
Then chances are, you should be prepared to burrow
Deep for a deep winter.

287

And that object became part of him for the day
    or a certain part of the day,
Or for many years or stretching cycles of years.

S I S Y P H U S

THE LONG HILL

I must have passed the crest a while ago
   And now I am going down—
Strange to have crossed the crest and not to know,
   But the brambles were always catching the hem of my gown.

All the morning I thought how proud I should be
   To stand there straight as a queen,
Wrapped in the wind and the sun with the world under me—
   But the air was dull; there was little I could have seen.

It was nearly level along the beaten track
   And the brambles caught in my gown—
But it's no use now to think of turning back,
   The rest of the way will be only going down.

END COMPULSIVE MASK - ULINITY

"The United States is like a big movie, and we're all in it. All of a sudden some of us went out for intermission. That was four years ago and we don't want to come back for the second half."

Sis who?

I. Make a collection of the favorite myths in your parents' lives. Reflect on these.

II. "We all overact the part of our favorite character of fiction." True or false? Which characters most influence the parents of the members of your group?

III. What fictions do you live by? How would you be cast in a movie?

IV. Send complaints about these questions to the Macmillan Company. The author rode off on Rocinante.

USA

288

WHERE HAVE ALL THE FLOWERS GONE?

My Favorite Character of Fiction

"I always thought when I became a grown-up woman, I would wear a neat house dress, carry a wicker basket over my arm, and pick flowers in my garden. And here I am, sweating and swearing, in jeans, at the traffic light, on my way to pick up one of the kids at the Sun Valley Shopping Mall."

"It was like another world; the mountains seemed less a part of this planet than an entirely independent kingdom, unique and mysterious, where to venture forth, all that was needed was the will and the love."

Arrange these eight matchsticks to make three squares equal in size. No part of any matchstick may extend beyond the edge of any square.

END SEXISM NOW

BART TUBBS 1933-1973 CUT OFF IN HIS PRIME

True or False: No one ever dies an untimely death.

289

"And what would you like to be when you grow up, little girl?"

"Me."

A *KNOWN* RHYTHM

Objets Trouves

Take a walk.
Find some junk.
Make it art.
Reflect.

Fred Hoyle is the most celebrated theoretical astronomer of our time. He holds the same professorship at Cambridge as did the late Arthur Eddington, the man who showed how mathematics could penetrate into the very hearts of the Sun and stars. At his Institute of Theoretical Astronomy, Hoyle seizes on all the new information coming from the observatories and spins hypotheses around it. He infuriates his fellow astronomers by frequently changing his mind, and by saying things that turn out to be invalid. Yet, more than any other theorist, he has stirred the pot of astronomical ideas and a great deal of productive observational work has been inspired by the wish to 'prove Fred wrong.' Sometimes he is disconcertingly right, as when, visiting the California Institute of Technology, he predicted the properties of a particular atomic nucleus from general considerations about processes in stars; American physicists thereupon made the necessary measurement and found it to be exactly what Hoyle had said. But Hoyle's work is not just a series of squibs. For twenty years he has questioned the most fundamental notions of current science and now he senses the approach of a great denouement, in which new physics will come out of astronomy.

   Hoyle and his young Indian colleague, Jayant Vishnu Narlikar, seek effects of distant matter on local events, and connections between the grandest manifestations of matter — the universe at large — and the properties of the smallest sub-atomic particles. They venture to relate gravity and the expansion of the universe to the creation of new matter, within the updated Steady State theory. They develop a theory of electromagnetism in which the nature of the universe (in Steady State, of course!) enters in a fundamental way in the interactions of electric particles.

Apocrypha:
"An instruction book *did* come with it!"
    Noam Chomsky

Charm: a way of getting the answer yes without asking a clear question.

"Plastic or plastic coated containers are not recyclable or biodegradable."

"How can it be taken seriously if you don't know what questions the little lizards were answering?"
"Would it be more clear to the lizard if one asked only one question?"
"Yes, that would be clearer. If you could hold one thought steadily."
"But what would happen, don Juan, if the one question was not a simple one?"
"As long as your thought is steady, and does not go into other things, it is clear to the little lizards, and then their answer is clear to you."

● I HAVE DEVELOPED AN

ULTERIORITY COMPLEX...

FINDING AN OPERATIVE METAPHOR:

Life is_____ .

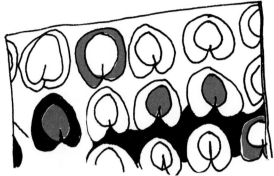

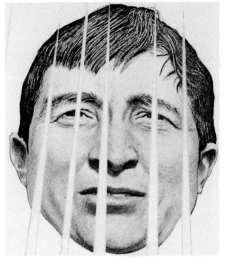

Encouraged by the fanatic way the boy covered page after page of his notebook with wildly oscillating lines, Bech talked of fiction as an equivalent of reality, and described how the point of it, the justification, seemed to lie in those moments when a set of successive images locked and then one more image arrived and, as it were, superlocked, creating a tightness perhaps equivalent to the terribly tight knit of reality, e.g., the lightning ladder of chemical changes in the body cell that translates fear into action or, say, the implosion of mathematics consuming the heart of a star. And the down-grinding thing is the realization that no one, not critics or readers, ever notices these moments but instead prattles, in praise or blame, of bits of themselves glimpsed in the work as in a shattered mirror. That it is necessary to begin by believing in an ideal reader and that slowly he is proved not to exist. He is not the daily reviewer skimming a plastic-bound set of raggedy advance proofs, nor the bulk-loving housewife who buys a shiny new novel between the grocer's and the hairdresser's, nor the diligent graduate student with his heap of index cards and Xerox applications, nor the plump-scripted young ballpointer who sends a mash note via *Who's Who*, nor, in the weary end, even oneself. In short, *one loses heart in the discovery that one is not being read. That the ability to read, and therefore to write, is being lost, along with the abilities to listen, to see, to smell, and to breathe.* That all the windows of the spirit are being nailed shut. Here Bech gasped for air, to dramatize his point. He said, then, that he was sustained, insofar as he was sustained, by the memory of laughter, the specifically Jewish, embattled, religious, sufficiently desperate, not quite belly laughter of his father and his father's brothers, his beloved Brooklyn uncles.

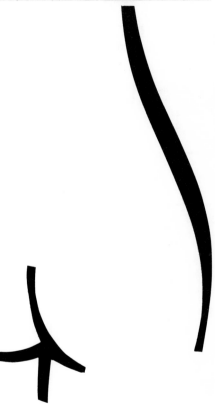

"Words are no good...but they're the best you can do when you're talking."
—MAD DOGS AND ENGLISHMEN

ENSLAVED BY DISPENSABILITIES

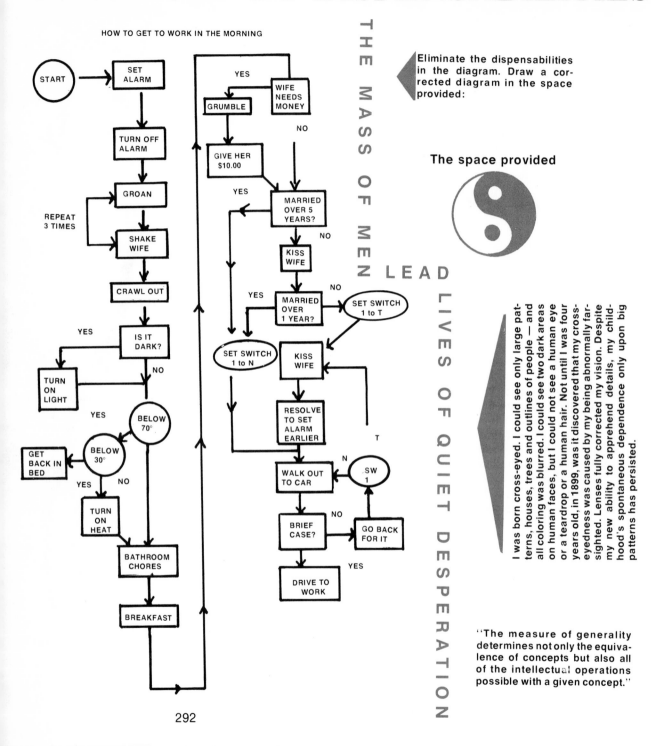

HOW TO GET TO WORK IN THE MORNING

START → SET ALARM → TURN OFF ALARM → GROAN → SHAKE WIFE → CRAWL OUT → IS IT DARK?

REPEAT 3 TIMES

IS IT DARK? — YES → TURN ON LIGHT; NO → BELOW 70°

BELOW 70° — YES → BELOW 30°; BELOW 30° → GET BACK IN BED; YES → TURN ON HEAT; NO → BATHROOM CHORES → BREAKFAST

WIFE NEEDS MONEY — YES → GRUMBLE → GIVE HER $10.00 → MARRIED OVER 5 YEARS?; NO → MARRIED OVER 5 YEARS?

MARRIED OVER 5 YEARS? — YES; NO → KISS WIFE → MARRIED OVER 1 YEAR?

MARRIED OVER 1 YEAR? — YES → SET SWITCH 1 to N; NO → SET SWITCH 1 to T → KISS WIFE → RESOLVE TO SET ALARM EARLIER → WALK OUT TO CAR

WALK OUT TO CAR → SW 1 (N / T)

BRIEF CASE? — NO → GO BACK FOR IT; YES → DRIVE TO WORK

THE MASS OF MEN LEAD LIVES OF QUIET DESPERATION

Eliminate the dispensabilities in the diagram. Draw a corrected diagram in the space provided:

The space provided

I was born cross-eyed. I could see only large patterns, houses, trees and outlines of people — and all coloring was blurred. I could see two dark areas on human faces, but I could not see a human eye or a teardrop or a human hair. Not until I was four years old, in 1899, was it discovered that my cross-eyedness was caused by my being abnormally far-sighted. Lenses fully corrected my vision. Despite my new ability to apprehend details, my childhood's spontaneous dependence only upon big patterns has persisted.

"The measure of generality determines not only the equivalence of concepts but also all of the intellectual operations possible with a given concept."

whereas the sea is circled and sways peacefully upon its plantlike stem.

GAMES
PEOPLE
PLAY

ERIC BERNE

THE SORRA BE TAKIN YOU!

The Origin of Laughter
(after Desmond Morris)

Hunched in the dark beneath his mother's heart,
The fetus sleeps and listens; dropped into light,
He seeks to lean his ear against the breast
Where the known rhythm holds its secret pace.

Slowly, slowly, through blizzards of dozing,
A face is gathered, starting with the eyes—
At first, quite any face; two painted dots
On cardboard stir a responsive smile. Soon
No face but one will serve: the mother's,
A mist, a cloud that clearly understands.

She teases him, pretends to let him drop.
He wants to cry but knows that she is good.
Out of this sudden mix, this terror rimmed
With necessary flesh, a laugh is born.

John Updike, At. Monthly?

THE MUSIC

The relation of thought to word is not a thing but a process, a continual movement back and forth from thought to word and from word to thought.

Rébuffat

"If he climbs only for the sake of climbing, the mountaineer will cease to hear the music of a mountain's name which has been singing within him and he will get nowhere."

**True or False:
Charm leads to alcoholism.**

But it is easier to think what poetry should be, than to write it—And this leads me to Another axiom—That if poetry comes not as naturally as the leaves to a tree, it had better not come at all.—However it may be with me, I cannot help looking into new countries with 'O for a Muse of Fire to ascend!' If Endymion serves me as a pioneer, perhaps I ought to be content, for thank God I can read, and perhaps understand Shakespeare to his depths; and I have, I am sure, many friends, who, if I fail, will attribute any change in my life and temper to humbleness rather than pride—to a cowering under the wings of great poets, rather than to a bitterness that I am not appreciated.

1818

Typographical errors have been a thorn in the side of writers and editors since Gutenberg.

Here's an example that appeared in an eastern paper under Personals: "Mary, please forgive me and come home. It was just a passing fanny. I love you. Jim"

Herself

SHAPED LIKE a dagger, the splinter of her mother's looking glass hung over the washbowl in Conna May Gallagher's kitchen. It was the only big piece left that day that the great mirror off the Main Land, that fine mirror in which you could see your whole self, shattered.

The splinter of glass made a strange person of you. If you looked squarely into it, you were a face without body or shoulders. A face with staring eyes that came down into a pointed chin whether yours was rounded or not. If you straightened a bit to see if there was a neckline, all that showed was a bit of cloth, a bit of flesh, and a vast curiosity of what the rest of the pattern made. If you stepped far back from the mirror to see more of you, there was nothing to behold save a person that might be you, might be Mrs. Red Conner next door or the pastor himself, it was that small and twisted.

Oh, it was a handy enough glass, don't mistake! When Pat came home at night, all smoky from the engine room of the tug, he could tell when the black was off his face and he shone like an angel from the soap. He could tell when he had written a straight path in his hair with the comb. A woman could do as much but she could never tell how her dress hung.

In that selfsame splinter's catch, she had held up the first baby to laugh at himself. Conna May remembered that. His name was Michael and his stay had been brief. But often—even after the others came—she remembered herself holding Michael up to the glass to look at himself. She remembered it when she worked about the kitchen and looked up at the glass which had been just wide enough to catch the whole of that baby's face.

At first his eyes had never gone to it. But she had held him up, maybe that she could see him in it with a bit of herself next. And then one day his eyes had stopped on the glass and he had seen an image there. And later a day when she had seen his eyes focusing, looking bright at himself. And the days that followed when he was to stare so silent and wondering. There was that day when he smiled back at himself. A knowing smile that said, "You look like a fine lad. We'll get along." And then he left, with a clogging in his throat, right after that—a week or more—so maybe that was why she found Michael so much in the mirror.

The two others had come and Conna May had taken them out to look until they admired themselves. And she with them. With each of those, she could see a piece of herself, an arm firm around the blanket out of which looked a small face, her own chin against the head of the new one. She blended them together. She compared the sweep of eyebrows faint showing to her own. She looked at the blur of a nose and then put her own into view. She looked at the slant of the eyes and then stared into her own to decide if they'd have her look. Even the sliver of a mirror was great fun. Inside it lay a world.

"A poem is most valuable for its ulterior meaning. I have developed an ulteriority complex."

295

Write a blurb for this story. Later compare and reflect on the results.

There were nights when her two were wrapped warm and with dreams. Nights when she waited with a slow fire in the stove but everything ready for the sound of the *Kattie's* check whistle, the little whistle the captain gives the unseeing engineer to slow the tug to keep it from ramming the dock. Then she would know that the tug had brought Pat home. Pat would have the fish to unload, the fire to bank and the hot water to pump from the boiler for Denny who washed down the decks. The check whistle, and Conna May knew that one hour from then she could put the meat in the pan, slice the loaf and have Pat's meal sizzling as his step came up the back porch.

But there were those hours between the time she had put her two to bed at the sound of the whistle echoing over the whole of the bay to let families know the tug was in, safe. And in those hours Conna May found much in her mirror, things put in it in the past.

Sometimes she would see it hanging whole, the piece back in its proper place, back in her mother's home. They had been proud of it. Conna May's father, before he drowned in the big blow which sent freighters under Lake Michigan's waves with the fishing tugs, had done well. And it was after a season when nets were full that he'd brought the mirror over from the Main Land. And nobody on Beaver Island had a mirror as big or as true down to your smallest wart.

Conna May remembered herself with the new dress that came from the Charlevoix store, standing in front of the mirror. Every pleat she had in her dress showed in the mirror. It was standing there that Conna May made her big discovery.

There had been the question whether she was right or left-handed.

In school she wrote with her right hand. Outside when she played ball with the boys or worked about the house, she used her left hand most. And looking into the mirror Conna May plucked at her new dress with her right hand. The girl who was herself plucked at her dress with her left hand. Conna May wondered. She decided that maybe on the other side of the glass live another people, strong-willed people who brought you before the glass as their other self. She felt that maybe she wasn't real and

the other one was. Then she decided that it was not herself on the other side but the girl she should be.

And there were other nights—when the wind was solid and poured mightily around her house and farther away buffeted Pat on Lake Michigan—when

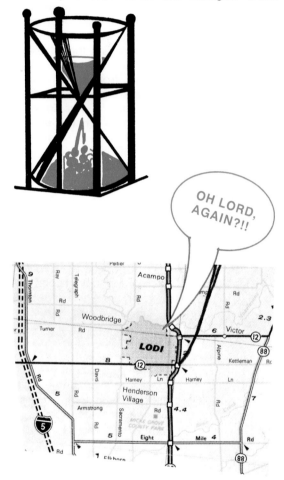

she saw other things in her mind, as if she were looking in that whole mirror. It was herself when Pat was coming to see her. There never had been any other lad. There had been a long courtship because luck was against Pat. And remembering, it seemed to her that the splinter of glass would shine lonely in the kitchen where she sat alone, still wait-

296

"...by the time you are real most of your hair has been loved off."

ing for Pat.

They sometimes had stopped—this was her favorite memory—in front of the glass. Pat with the smile of a sick man but fascinated would put his arm around her, tilt his hat and, through the glass, look into her eyes. Facing it they would see themselves a couple. And Pat would pose and maybe she—as they joked about themselves. Pat had never kissed her in front of the glass. She wondered on that. But they had stood in front of it to show each other what a fine pair they made.

Conna May would look up at the shiny sliver on the wall, down to the washdish and pail of water on the bench below. Sometimes she would go to the pail and just because she could see her face lying in the water round and strange rather than with the gaunt look the mirror gave it she would stare down. Then for some reason of her own, she said it was that Pat should have fresh, cold water for his rinsing, she would take the pail, throw out the water that had held a picture of her face and pump a fresh pailful.

Pat came in with the weariness of the long day on him. But it melted away in the light and heat of his home.

He was a stooped man coming through the doorway with the coal dust on his face and the fish scales stuck like stars in the back of his pants. Then the odor of cooking would straighten up his head as he sniffed it in. Then the greeting of Conna May would take the stiffness out of a back bent with leaning all day to throw coal into the low firebox of the boiler.

There might be news. No great news but close to the heart to warm it as that boiler on the tug glowed to a thin coating of coal. It would send Pat's blood steaming through him and make him as alive as that youth who had run with Conna May not many years before when the wind was too icy for walking.

Their day was that brief hour together as Conna May put his meal hot to the plate and Pat stripped himself of the smudge of the engine room. Then he centered on the mirror watching the grime come off, taking the extra water out of his hair with the comb before parting it.

While Pat bent to his plate, Conna May's words, pent while she worked the day away, would pour over him like the seas over the *Kattie's* bow during a warm summer's storm. Once in a while a huge wave of words or a sharp thought would bring him to a brief pause but he would slow his eating just for a moment, make one of the sounds a man busy with food will make to give Conna May some hint of how he felt about it, and then go on. No glum man, Pat Gallagher would do his talking when he had finished his big meal. Their time was so little together during the fishing days that it was saved if he listened while he ate and she while she swirled the dishes under the soap foam. They never had need to rush words back and forth between them for they were a gentle couple, thinking alike about their few concerns.

They had their children to think about, but that was Conna May's world and Bid and Francie Gallagher were soft-speaking things like their folks and not the kind to make a man pace the floor to wonder what could be done after beatings. They were so quiet, they were pointed to for having Conna May's good manners.

Food and shelter? Those they had. Not too little, not too much, like all the island people. That was Pat's world. He paid at the store and never was far behind on his bill. When the wind piled the lake up in front of the harbor, he made and fixed things for the house. And when the winter came, there were always barrels of salt fish Pat had put down and potatoes he had dug. And he was a handy man to sit with nets strung across his lap, running the beetle-like shuttle in his hand, putting back the spider net for snaring next summer's fish. That kept them, and Pat always with work of some kind. And they had the good will of the other fishing families about them.

Conna May dreamed like all women and for years never could find the words to ask for a grand mirror like the one her mother had given them only to have it break in the moving. But sometimes at the table she would say, "And the glass, Pat! Today I had such a time with Bid's hair. The part was gone and we could not find it. We combed and combed—I fear his head will bleed tomorrow—but we could not find the true course. In that little glass!"

297

"IT AIN'T IN NO BOOK."

✳ "He who knows others has knowledge; he who knows himself is illuminated."

Then a quarter year might pass and Conna May would say, "Pat, would you believe it. Today I was boiling the clothes when out the window I saw Mrs. Geraghty coming and me looking like something to scare the devil himself. So I ran to the glass to see myself and put me to rights and it was all steamed over. I rubbed and rubbed but it kept taking on fresh steam. I wonder what she must have thought of me. Sometimes I wish we had the great glass it used to be so one might see themselves proper."

Another year and Conna May had taken to dreaming out loud on nights to Pat.

"You know," she would say, "I was thinking today that we might put some of the next week's fishing into a good glass. This bit hanging here is good enough for us. But I was seeing Francie and Bid as they'll be with a little more sprouting and it is no glass for them to be standing before. They have no idea how fine they be and we should do that for them. Don't you think we should be having a better glass? Do you remember us standing before that other, you with the black snarls in your hair and me in my best. I'll be betting you still see yourself as in the days you were telling my father what a fine lad you were and believing it."

Then Pat would look up and questions would write in his forehead for this was new and unthought.

"We should," he'd say, "get a new glass when we can afford it." And then the pork chop smell would get into his nose and he'd think more of that and forget that Conna May might have meant they should have a glass.

Conna May, who lived next to the splinter's gleam all day, catching bits of herself as she passed, finally came upon the time she had to have a full mirror.

"Pat," she said, "today I thought it out and we have enough. I have five dollars I've put away and can think of nothing better than a new mirror. This week if you take the fish to Charlevoix, take along the money and put it with some of the lift money and buy us one. We do need it."

But the island men are in no haste. They wait for fair weather to do their fishing. They wait again after that to move hooks or nets to where the fish are hiding. They wait again for days of little wind.

They live long hours under the wind and the sun with the lake spread out for far horizons and each day seems long. But the days chained together make no time, for each by itself is long. Long time is in the day not the week, month or year, nor in the ways nor thoughts of shore folk. What goes on ashore is brief. It is too wide a dream with too much happening to be real. It has none of the closeness of things on a little tug.

Home. An hour of talk. Sleep. The fogged dawn and a hush before they are in the lake again. The long day and evening, then night still on the lake. Next to a shovel, known so well a man could tell you the pattern of the wood on its handle if it were stolen. The shore stay is so brief it seems time there never moves. (Eight hours ashore, three times eight that makes twenty-four. And three times ashore makes one day. So three years might speed to a man of the lakes and it would be one ashore.) There the same slow changing things. And Conna May was one of these slow changing things.

But Conna May surged up against the timelessness of Pat. There came a fall day with eleven dollars in his pocket from her and a weighty load of fish on the *Kattie*. The crew went to Charlevoix to sell and Pat with the idea fixed firm in his head to buy a great glass that in the kitchen would become a vast thing in their lives.

Pat remembered it even after the fish were brought up to the dock and sold to Adolph Priest. He remembered it after he had gone with the other boys to a few drinks. He remembered it as Conna May, a face across the table, a triangle of head and arms leaning, talking down the years to him for a fine glass. He was with the warmth of liquor in him but his thoughts this night were of Conna May and her wanting of something like that shining thing that had hung in her father's home. She would have it.

He went to the furniture store of Mr. Lagensen where, with social consciousness stirred among the island's womenfolk, their men went for a chair or some trumpery that was fancied. It would be no little glass that Pat would buy, for Conna May's talk over the years made him see that what they needed was one large and true. They could have fun before it and an idea of themselves.

298

Being so caught up,
So mastered by the brute blood of the
   air,
Did she put on this knowledge with this
   power
Before the indifferent beak could let
   her drop?

The door opened, tinkling a bell above it. From the back came Lagensen, an unsmiling man which probably was fitting since he also was an undertaker. Pat wondered if he had in the back there someone of the new dead. He wondered what the man might think of him asking for a mirror, a thing which meant naught save that you liked to look at yourself.

"I want a glass," he said, "a big one." Then remembering Conna May's words—"and it must be true, no making you too fat nor too lean. One that sees you just as you are."

Lagensen blinked as if never before had he heard of such a strange thing. Then suddenly his chin grew heavy and he nodded. With no word, he started back in the store, stopped once to tilt his head toward the back so Pat would know he was to follow and went on his way. Pat followed him up the steps into the back room and tried not to look at the man-shaped boxes standing there. But his eyes went to them noting the three shiny handles on each side for carrying them. His eyes kept firm to one dark box with great gleaming handles when he heard a voice saying, "Look at yourself in that."

Pat felt fear heat in his chest and then, turning, saw the stiff-faced Lagensen tilting up a glass almost as long and lean as a coffin. Pat gazed at himself in it. He saw a red-brown face and blue eyes staring back solemnly at him. He saw his old rain hat on his head and, below, the shapelessness of his clothes wet over and over by the waves. But the face held him even in the shadowy room. It was such a face that were it on another man and he met it, he would like that man. Then thinking he might be staring too long, he said, "Is it your best?"

"It is twelve dollars and sixty-two cents," said Lagensen, who knew the island trade. It was not too much, for Pat had allowed himself fifteen dollars for a glass. Still he did not know if he should ask about another, for he wanted to be out of this place with those waiting coffins. He glanced at himself again in the glass and thought "Is it a true glass?"

"Have you another?" he asked.

"It is my best," said Lagensen who never showed a customer two things when he could help it. He believed it confused them.

"We'll have to wrap it well," said Pat, "for we may have rough weather going back. There was a bad look in the sky."

"Nonsense," said Lagensen. "I always wrap things well."

"Use big handfuls of excelsior," said Pat, "for we may get tossed around some." Then Lagensen left him in the room with the mirrors and coffins, and Pat stared long at one and then the other, became too aware of himself and went in the back shed where with excelsior, paper, cardboard and wood Lagensen was crating his mirror.

He watched carefully to see that it was well padded. Pat wanted no splinters of glass for Conna May and the two paudeens. He wanted something big and clear for them. Bid to see her face like the white lily might over the pool in which she grew. And Francie to see himself with the dark quiet mood on him, a boy nibbling a lower lip and finding the floor a great study. It would do all of them good.

As the package grew, Pat wondered if he would make it back to the tug with the big glass. Such must have been Lagensen's thought for—it was the fifth time he gave of his rare speech—he told Pat, "I'll send my boy to help you carry it."

"Praise be," said Pat. "Does my back look like it was a willow sprout? I'll carry it."

So he did. Back through the room where a living man might see himself in a glass and, if he had the will for it, in a coffin, Pat and Lagensen went with the mirror. They stood it up in the front of the store and after Pat paid his money, Lagensen went out in front and helped to poise the great glass over Pat's head.

Pat started down the streets of Charlevoix feeling that all were looking at the man who, like an Indian woman, carried a bundle on his head. He worried, too, about his legs for he had his drinks and feared that some moment the little narrow walk would not be wide enough. But the weight on his head, the thought inside it of what the glass meant to Conna, kept him on the course. Finally his feet were on the dock next to the *Kattie*.

With Captain Gallagher and Willie O'Hare, the lad who came over to see his first city, Pat passed it down to the deck of the tug. They took Conna May's mirror aft where there was great room and hung it next to the housing of the engine room. Pat stuffed

299

? face to face with The Problem of recognition .

"Sometimes when you're real you don't mind being hurt."

nets behind it so it would bang none too hard in the seas. It could sway because it was hung but when the tug dipped, the net would pad its fall up against the house.

Pat went up to the pilot house to talk to the tipsy Captain Gallagher who was to steer the tug home.

"Would you mind," he asked, "steering her across the seas? I've got Conna May's mirror hanging aft. You ken, she's been wanting it for some time. I don't like asking it, but ride the seas to home easy, not fast."

So they waited until the last of the island boys, Little Finn, who had caught the fancy of a Main Land girl, came back starry-eyed and then put out through the narrow lane between the piers into a lake waiting to rock them.

And Pat at the throttle checked the *Kattie* down a notch or two so the shock of the waves would be less on Conna May's mirror hanging aft.

Conna May was down on the dock that night when the mirror came. When she was a new wife she used to come to the dock often to greet Pat. To see the silver heaps of fish with red bellies slit and to guess how well they would fare that week.

But after a little time she had stopped coming for she knew it would be the same save for the number of boxes of fish. She stayed home, swelled and had her young. And soon the dock was forgotten and life was settled to waiting for Pat to come home and tell her of the day.

Conna May was there when they brought the great mirror ashore. Pat was beside her as the boys of the boat gently swung the big package on the dock. She walked next to Pat as he and Little Finn, holding the far end of the mirror, went home.

"Is it a nice one?" she asked.

"None better in Charlevoix," said Pat, "so the man himself told me. And clear! You can see all."

They laid the package on the kitchen table. Little Finn had to take his mother one of Conna May's pies, which was rare pay even for a lovesick lad.

"We'll open it in the morning," she said, "when the small ones are here." It was Conna May's way of doing not what she wanted—for the sake of the poor souls suffering.

When their morning came, it was far before the dawn since Pat had to leave with the tug on a distant run. They came sleepily into the kitchen. Conna May had been there first to set the fire that warmed them and to pluck at a string, to pull at a bit of the excelsior and to wonder how she would look. She could see Bid peeping shyly at a little girl with a pert nose, black hair like an Indian's and a most pleasing face. And Francie scuffling a foot, shooting a quick look and then being caught up with a straight, quiet little lad who always would be his own best friend even when he stood in glass.

They were sleepy and they ripped off the boards, paper and stuffing that had been put on. Pat and Francie carried them to the wood box. None of them took a long look when the mirror stood against the wall. The day was coming on fast. Pat had to have his breakfast, the young ones had to get into school clothes, and Conna May had to cluck about them all. So while they shouted a bit and talked with excitement about the new glass they looked into it little because of the regular morning haste upon them. They also were shy of standing in front of it to take a long look.

They all were gone and the morning quiet when Conna May came up to her glass. First she had to look at its frame in the sun beating clearly through the window. Then she had to sit with her tea and study the size and shape of it. It was not as wide but, she told herself, a better glass than her father's. So Conna May brought herself up to the moment she could step before it and, alone, see her whole self.

Before her stood a woman who was Mrs. Red Connor next door, who was Little Finn's mother in the house beyond, who was Mrs. Geraghty, who was—Conna May looked deep—who was all the island women. She reached up to her hair and touched it with her left hand. In the mirror the woman did it with her right. That had not changed. That could never though she lived a thousand years.

The woman of the glass had her hand in her hair that was like the tangled skins of maitre which the fishermen untwined to make their hooks and nets. The woman in the glass ran her hand through her hair and it fell back listlessly to form strings. Close to the glass went Conna May's solemn face and there in that woman's hair lying flat across her head were pale streaks. Not the fine white of the old but the colorless strands of those who have only started down the hill.

So Conna May turned her eyes far from that woman's hair and studied her shoes. They did not stand squarely on the floor but bulged outward. One was tied with a fish cord, brown laced into the black. The other was held by a black lace full of knots. The shoes had little form. They were like, she thought, two lumps of coal. And the dress did not hang evenly so that the flannel of her petticoat tilted below it. Conna May straightened that.

Slowly her eyes worked upward to a woman who, because the morning was cool, wore a man's old sweater, one raveled sleeve hacked off at the elbow. Not a very tidy woman, Conna May decided, and as her hand plucked at the dangling yarn of that shortened sleeve, she noticed the hand. It was like—it was like a man's. No, it was rougher. Rougher even than Pat's for his were soft from being in the water so much. This hand was lumpy with knuckles, was red as a rooster's comb and as rough as the bark of an oak. But she was making it out worse than it really was, Conna May knew.

Finally her eyes could stay away no longer, they turned fully to her face. The first thing that Conna May noticed about the woman was that there seemed a wetness in her eyes. Gray and still like the lake is evenings after a long calm. Only, under the surface, Conna May thought she saw a troubled depth. There was a mesh of fine webbing at the corners. The nose shone and on it she could see the pores. Two lines ran outward from the ends of her nose, over a wide upper lip to the corners of her mouth. Her lips were a rich, dark red and lay in a nice pattern, Conna May decided.

It wasn't the face she knew but, withal, it was a good face. There was a solemnness to it like you felt kneeling in that big church on the Main Land, the one where the sun came through the glass windows with a million colors and you knelt with a great hush about you.

Then Conna May took steps back from her glass so that all the things she had been watching one by one faded into the pattern of herself. And she saw a lumpy woman. A woman shaped like a bag of potatoes, tied around the middle. She stepped back to see Mrs. Red Connor, Little Finn's mother and Mrs. Geraghty. But it was herself.

At the table again with her tea, Conna May looked at the fineness of the glass and its frame. She wished she had had a picture made of her as the girl in the pleated dress. Then she was glad she had not. But she did wish that when she had held the paudeens up—starting with that Michael whose face now was so faint—that she had had the good glass, the new one. It would have made remembering so much better. But now, leastways, she had her glass.

That night when Pat came home, he saw that Conna May had washed and fluffed her hair and that it had been wound in two neat coils over her ears—like the German fisherman's wife. And Conna May was full of praise of the mirror. But, like a man, Pat did not see that the knotted lace was gone from her one shoe and that now both had the same lacings of fishing twine.

For many nights Conna May talked of the mirror and the new things it was bringing to them. She noticed more neatness in Bid and less bashfulness in Francie. Then one night she said, thoughtfully, that it was fairly big for the kitchen and she was afraid of bumping it and sending it to break in bits on the floor. So they moved it into the front room, near the foot of the stairs.

Pat would go in nights after washing to see if he was neat. Mornings, Bid and Francie would pause before it to look over themselves, wash and then go in to comb before it. Sometimes Pat found it easier, as he had before, to use the little splinter that still hung in the kitchen. But Bid often took to playing with her doll before the big glass and visiting with her playmate on the other side of it.

So Conna May finally said, "Pat, the children take such pride in the glass and it has given them a pride in themselves. I think it should go in their room—if you don't mind?"

And Pat, fearful that some moving of his foot might snag it leaning there at the foot of the stairs, said, "If you don't mind, Conna, it would be a grand thing for them."

The mirror went upstairs into the room of Bid and Francie. There, sometimes, Conna May caught a glimpse of herself making the bed. And, sometimes, scrubbing the floor, she would come face to face with a woman on her knees.

301

CAVEAT EMPTOR

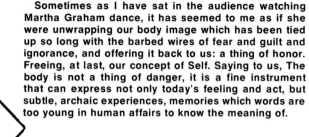

Sometimes as I have sat in the audience watching Martha Graham dance, it has seemed to me as if she were unwrapping our body image which has been tied up so long with the barbed wires of fear and guilt and ignorance, and offering it back to us: a thing of honor. Freeing, at last, our concept of Self. Saying to us, The body is not a thing of danger, it is a fine instrument that can express not only today's feeling and act, but subtle, archaic experiences, memories which words are too young in human affairs to know the meaning of.

The world is too much with us; late and soon,
Getting and spending, we lay waste our powers:
Little we see in Nature that is ours;
We have given our hearts away, a sordid boon!
This Sea that bares her bosom to the moon;
The winds that will be howling at all hours,
And are up-gathered now like sleeping flowers;
For this, for everything, we are out of tune;
It moves us not. —Great God! I'd rather be
A Pagan suckled in a creed outworn;
So might I, standing on this pleasant lea,
Have glimpses that would make me less forlorn;
Have sight of Proteus rising from the sea;
Or hear old Triton blow his wreathéd horn.

demanding a moral answer

"Much of our valuable energy is drained away to support our illusions of independence and separateness. As we experience our interdependence with our total environment, this formerly wasted energy becomes available to us. Living ecologically doesn't mean a life of deprivation or denial—it is a life full of meaning and the enjoyment of real wealth."

302

SYMBOLS

Create an appropriate title for each of these posters. Later explore the
effects of giving titles to pictures.

303

True or false: 1. Life is an image which must be activated
by each perceiver. 2. "I" am a catalyst.

FABLE IX*

The Tribulations of the Simple Husband Who Wanted Nothing More than to Eat Goose but was Denied this Delight by His Unfaithful Wife and Her Arrogant but Probably Handsome Lover.

haut couture

haut   pants

A simple husband one morning took his wife a goose and said, Cook this bird for me; when I come home in the evening I shall eat it.

The wife plucked the bird, cleaned it, and cooked it. In the afternoon her lover came. Before going away he asked what food he could take with him to his friends. He looked into the oven and saw the roasted goose.

That is for my husband, the wife said.

I want it, the lover said. If you do not let me take it, I shall never love you again.

The lover went off with the goose.

In the evening the husband sat at the table and said, Bring me the goose.

What goose? the wife said.

The goose I brought you this morning, the husband said. Bring it to me.

Are you serious? the wife said. You brought me no goose. Perhaps you dreamed it.

Bring me the goose, the husband shouted.

The wife began to scream, saying, My poor husband has lost his mind. My poor husband is crazy. What he has dreamed he imagines has happened.

The neighbors came and believed the wife, so the husband said nothing and went hungry, except for bread and cheese and water.

The following morning the husband brought his wife another goose and said, Is this a goose?

Yes, the wife said.

Am I dreaming?—No.

Is this the goose's head?—Yes.

Wings?—Yes.

Feathers?—Yes.

All right, the husband said, cook it. When I come home tonight I'll eat it.

The wife cooked the goose. The lover came.

There is another goose today, he said. I can smell it.

You cannot take it, the wife said. I had a terrible scene with my husband last night, and again this morning. It is too much, I love you but you cannot have the goose.

Either you love me or you don't love me, the lover said. Either I take the goose or not.

So he took the goose.

Bring the goose, the husband said.

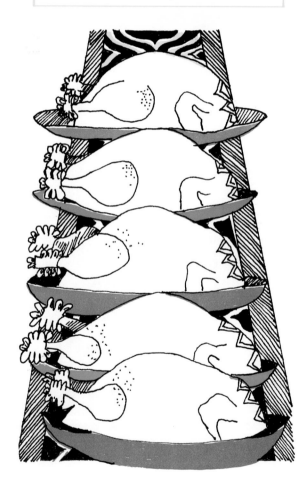

304

The smell of stars

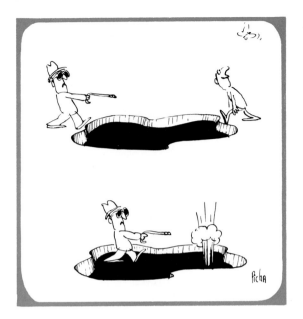

Heisenberg, Einstein, and Buddha really messed up Newton and Darwin.

Now cook the God Damned thing, he said, and when I come home in the evening I will eat it.

The wife cleaned the bird and cooked it. The lover came. There was a tender scene, tears, kisses, running, wrestling, more tears, more kisses, and the lover went off with the goose.

In the city the husband saw an old friend and said, Come out to the house with me tonight; the wife's roasting a goose; we'll take a couple of bottles of *rakki* and have a hell of a time.

So the husband and his friend went out to the house and the husband said, Have you cooked the goose?

Yes, the wife said. It's in the oven.

Good, the husband said. You were never really a bad wife. First, my friend and I will have a few drinks: then we will eat the goose.

The husband and his friend had four or five drinks and then the husband said, All right, bring the goose.

The wife said, There is no bread; go to your cousin's for bread; goose is no good without bread.

All right, the husband said.

He left the house.

The wife said to the husband's friend, My husband is crazy. There is no goose. He has brought you here to kill you with this enormous carving knife and this fork. You had better go.

The man went. The husband came home and asked about his friend and the goose.

Your *friend* has run off with the goose, the wife said. What kind of a friend do you call that, after I slave all day to cook you a decent meal?

The husband took the carving knife and the fork and began running down the street. At length in the distance he saw his friend running and he called out, Just a leg, my friend, that's all.

My God, the other said, he is truly crazy.

The friend began to run faster than ever. Soon the husband could run no more. He returned wearily to his home and wife. Once again he ate his bread and cheese. After this plain food he began to drink *rakki* again.

As he drank, the truth began to come to him little by little, as it does through alcohol.

When he was very drunk he knew all about everything. He got up and quietly whacked his wife across the room.

If your lover's got to have a goose every day, he said, you could have told me. Tomorrow I will bring *two* of them. I get hungry once in a while myself, you know.

My poor husband, the wife screamed. He's stark raving mad. Goose, goose, goose. What goose? There is no goose. My poor, poor husband.

The neighbors came and again believed the wife.

The husband went hungry.

The following morning he bought another goose in the city. He hired a tall man to carry the goose on a platter on his head. He hired an orchestra of six pieces, and with the musicians in a circle around the tall man carrying the goose, he walked with them through the streets to his house, calling to his neighbors.

When he reached his house there were many people following him.

He turned to the people and said, Mohammedans, neighbors, the world, heaven above, fish in the sea, soldiers, and all others, behold, a goose.

He lifted the bird off the platter.

A goose, he cried.

He handed the bird to his wife.

---

*Ed. note: *Fable IX* is supposed to have pedagogical value. The fact is, though, I couldn't resist putting it in. I get hungry once in a while myself.

ENGLISHMEN ARE worried about the ways they speak English.

The quaint rural dialects spoken throughout the countryside with little change from generation to generation are beginning to disappear under the influence of education, radio, television and shifts in population.

And so, the University of Leeds is attempting to record the vanishing dialects by taping the speech patterns of the older country people.

Researchers discovered that country folk were so sensitive about dialects that villagers with strong dialects often denied they spoke in dialect at all and pointed out other villages as the best place to hear country English. Young people also made conscious efforts to lose their dialect. But the researchers discovered an astonishing variety in spoken English.

* * *

IN THE WEST Midlands pigs are called to the food trough 23 different ways, including suss, usk, chack, pee-oo, piggy, coo-ey and hoy. Sheep also have 23 different summonses. There are 16 calls for getting cows in for milking, a dozen for ducks, eight for hens, four for horses. West Midland chickens answer to "oop;" "eek" brings in the ducks.

Cows are kept in a best house, cattle shed, cow bing, cow boosing, byre, cowhouse, cow pen or cow shud. The man who looks after them is a bungey, cattleman, cowman, herdsman, stockman or fogger. He might pitch hay with a haypick, pike, pikel, hayprong, sheppeck, pitching-fork, stacking-fork, reacher, handfork, tedding-fork, five-foot-prong, ruching-ikel or two-tine fork.

* * *

A SCARECROW IN some places is a dud-man or a mawkin though more common in the West Midlands is mommet which is seen as derivation of Mahomet, the Great Turk, the frightening villain of medieval mummers' plays staged in villages by traveling players.

And the influence in different regions of foreign languages will be shown. Scandinavian "loan" words, a surviving legacy of the Nordic invaders, are common in northern England.

"In Leeds I have heard children use 'laiking'—'Is Tom laiking out today?'—for 'Is Tom playing out today?' Leka is standard Norwegian for to 'play.' Other loan words we have in the north include the Scandinavian 'lop' for a flea and 'gigot' for a leg of lamb," a researcher said.

* * *

NORTH AMERICANS should not stand corrected by Britons when they call this time of year the fall. It originated in South Devon, Cornwall and Somerset where it is still used. Eastern and southern English call it autumn but in most of Lancashire and Yorkshire it's "backend."

Left-handers can trace the origins of "southpaw" to northeast Durham where it survives as "suthpod." Boils are "pushes" in East Anglia and scattered parts of the southwest and northeast. A goose's mate is a "steg" in the far north but a gander elsewhere. And widespread as ever is "ain't" which Webster loathed and tried to scrub in America.

Da com of more   under mist-hleothum
Grendel gongan.   Godes yrre bær;
mynte se man-scatha   manna cynnes
summe besyrwan·   in sele tham hean . . . .

Whan that Aprill with his
*   shoures soote*
The droghte of March hath
*   perced to the roote,*
And bathed every veyne
*   in swich licour*
Of which vertu engendred
*   is the flour . . . .*

A lovely Ladie rode him
    faire beside,

Upon a lowly Asse more
    white then snow,
Yet she much whiter,
    but the same did
    hide
Under a vele, that
    wimpled was full low . . . .

There is no past; the only tense is *now*.

PREENING, LOVEMAKING,

Cindy blushed but was not deflected; she continued, "Also he says, Misteh Bech, that they have thinneh *skulls,* thet's whah so many dah in the prahz ring? We used to be told they had *thick*eh!"

Puzzled by the intensity of her blush, Bech saw that for this excited young convert to liberalism anthropology was as titillating as pornography. He saw that even in an age of science and unbelief our ideas are dreams, styles, superstitions, mere animal noises intended to repel or attract. He looked around the ring of munching females and saw their bodies as a Martian or a mollusc might see them, as pu py stalks of bundled nerves oddly pinched to a bud of concentration in the head, a hairy bone knob holding some pounds of jelly in which a trillion circuits, mostly dead, kept records, coded motor operations, and generated an excess of electricity that pressed into the hairless side of the head and leaked through the orifices, in the form of pained, hopeful noises and a simian dance of wrinkles. Impossible mirage! A blot on nothingness. And to think that all the efforts of his life—his preening, his lovemaking, his typing—boiled down to the attempt to displace a few sparks, to bias a few circuits, within some random other scoops of jelly that would, in less time than it takes the Andreas Fault to shrug or the tail-tip star of Scorpio to crawl an inch across the map of Heaven, be utterly dissolved. The widest fame and most enduring excellence shrank to nothing in this perspective. As Bech ate, mechanically offering votive bits of dead lamb to the terror enthroned within him, he saw that the void should have been left unvexed, should have been spared this trouble of matter, of life, and, worst, of consciousness.

TYPING . . .

And, if he then should dare to think
Of the fewness, muchness, rareness,
Greatness of this endless only
Precious world in which he says
He lives . . .

Survival Hints for an Encounter Weekend

Learn these words and phrases. Sprinkle them judiciously.

1. That's garbage.
2. You're mind-f------.
3. You're not comin' on straight, man. (To male *or* female.)
4. You're intellectualizing.
5. You're on a mind trip; tell me what you're *feel*ing.
6. You're coming across like a human being.
7. That's a real gut reaction.
8. Self-actualizing
9. Peaking
10. Where your head's at
11. _____
12. _____
13. _____
14. _____
15. _____

Or, start right off with: "Take your filthy, f------, faggot hands off me!"

List here survival phrases for the real world:

SCENE LARGE

ALL AT ONCENESS

You cannot see your way.
I have no way, and therefore want no eyes;
I stumbled when I saw. Full oft 'tis seen,
Our means secure us, and our mere defects
Prove our commodities.

—While with an eye made quiet by the power
Of harmony, and the deep power of joy
We see into the life of things.

Title: _____

Plato . . . could never have seen a bunch of flowers shining with their own inner light and all but quivering under the pressure of the significance with which they were charged; could never have perceived that what rose and iris and carnation so intensely signified was nothing more and nothing less than what they were—a transience that was yet eternal life, a perpetual perishing that was at the same time pure Being, a bundle of minute, unique particulars in which, by some unspeakable and yet self-evident paradox, was to be seen the divine source of all existence.

Subtitle: _____

"You've been a swimmer on the surface," Piaget said. "You haven't even seen the struggle. You haven't yet developed the innocent eye that sees the universe uncluttered by past assumptions. You were programmed and sent here to break us up."
Dasein paled.
"To be programmed is to be prejudiced," Piaget said. "Because prejudice is selecting and rejecting and that is programming." He sighed . . .

He has a new
Leash on
Life

308

Sale

EATING

A dietician at a veteran's hospital in Martinez, California, has observed that World War I veterans prefer a meat-and-potatoes diet. World War II and Korean veterans like a balanced diet including vegetables, fruits and milk. But Vietnam veterans don't eat meals at all. "They don't eat breakfast, just pull the blankets up over their heads and go back to sleep. Late in the morning they start getting hungry and begin munching hamburgers, hot dogs, French fries and soft drinks."

According to the British Medical Journal:

"The frequency of orgasm is related to social class upbringing, education and previous attitudes. The better the education and the higher the social class the greater the frequency of orgasm is the usual pattern."
Reuters

True or False: All moods are punishment for one's self or for others.

"EVERY SOCIETY HAS ITS OWN ESSENTIAL CHEMISTRY, ITS OWN AROMA, A THING OF PROFOUND IMPORTANCE, BUT LEAST APPARENT TO ITS OWN MEMBERS."

HONG KONG

Hans and Erna W. from Zurich took their pet poodle Rosa into a restaurant here today and asked the waiter to feed her.

Though they do not speak Chinese, they used gestures to convey the idea, and the waiter finally picked up the pet and took her into the kitchen.

Eventually he returned carrying a dish. When the couple removed the silver lid, they found Rosa nicely roasted and garnished with pepper sauce and bamboo shoots.

"No man is a hypocrite in his pleasures."

Shotover: How much does your soul eat?
Ellie Dunne: Oh, a lot. It eats music and pictures and books and mountains and lakes and beautiful things to wear and nice people to be with. In this country, you can't have them without lots of money: that is why our souls are so horribly starved.

Seeking means to have a goal; but finding means:
to be free, to be perceptive, to have no goal.
A seeker striving toward a goal, does not see many things that are under his nose.

309

GIVIAK

She ate, and she watched Bill Hastings eat. Bill, dressed in a dark-gray well-cut suit, was talking about Beethoven, his warm voice enthusiastic without sounding eager, and she watched his fingers adroitly manipulate the two wooden chopsticks, raise a morsel of dripping food to his mouth, insert it between words; she watched the rhythmic motions of his jaw as he chewed, saw his bobbing Adam's apple as he swallowed, and she wondered, for the first time in her life, why this obscene ritual was undergone in company, surrounded by elegant manners and habits of fond association: The Sunday dinner, etiquette, the customary preliminary gesture of affection on a date; when in fact, and with only a little imagination *eating* was *filthy.*

She conceived instantly, while Bill talked about the adaptation of Schiller's poem to music, a turnabout society in which people ate privately in tiny closets, obliged to eat by the needs of the body, but necessarily ashamed of it, due to the implications of the act: *the grinding up and swallowing of garbage* (indeed, the plate of heaped vegetables, meats and sauce in front of Bill very much resembled garbage); while in the same society going to the toilet was a public function, to be undergone whenever possible in company, and accompanied with gay conversation, comparison of feces, urine color, et cetera. Her mind raced out of control. In such a society we wear masks over our mouths and kissing is the final act of sensuality; our genitals are exposed, and when a baby sucks its mother's breast it is not the breast we cover but the baby's mouth.*

AUTOMAT

BLUEBERRY PIE 35c

DEPOSIT COINS

FRESH BLUEBERRY PIE 35c

(This actually appeared in a N.Y. automat.)

*See 'The Great Safeway Caper,' Chapter IV, page 238

310

"No one is lonely while eating spaghetti."

"What do you mean he's not a materialist? Look at all the cars he has, the houses, the clothes, the TVs."

"That just proves it. If he truly believed in the material world he wouldn't need so many instances of it around. A materialist spends a long time shaving. It takes him a long time to know a pebble. By that time most of its hair is rubbed off."

"Wine of California: Inimitable fragrance of soft fire."

THINKING

Time and chance happeneth to all men.

He went straight to the window to have another look at the alley. There was much for him to think about that he wanted to get to as slowly as possible, but at the same time get to in the next hour or two. Time had always fascinated him. He knew he didn't understand it, but he also knew that anything you ever got—anything that ever mattered—any thought — any truth — you got *instantly*. You could wait forever if you wanted to, and let it go at that, or you could get moving—moving *into* time and *with* time—working at the thought to be received, and then suddenly, from having moved into time and with time, and from having worked at the thought, get it, get it whole, get it clean, get it instantly.

But you had to stay slow somewhere inside of yourself, too, to give the arrival a place to stop. You had to be going swiftly and you had to be almost not moving at all at the same time.*

"If you don't think, you only need to learn to argue."

"Every belief is a pain pill — to kill the pain of being alive."

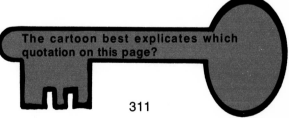

The cartoon best explicates which quotation on this page?

311

*For a good way to stand still and move fast, see page 87.

WAITING FOR THE BARBARIANS

What are we waiting for, gathered in the market-place?
    The barbarians are to arrive today.
Why so little activity in the Senate?
Why do the Senators sit there without legislating?
    Because the barbarians will arrive today.
    Why should the Senators bother with laws now?
    The barbarians, when they come, will do the law-making.
Why has our emperor risen so early,
and why does he sit at the largest gate of the city
on the throne, in state, wearing the crown?
    Because the barbarians will arrive today.
    And the emperor is waiting to receive
    their leader. He has even prepared
    a parchment for him. There
    he has given him many titles and names.
Why did our two consuls and our praetors go out
today in the scarlet, the embroidered, togas?
Why did they wear bracelets with so many amethysts,
and rings with brilliant sparkling emeralds?
Why today do they carry precious staves
splendidly inlaid with silver and gold?
   Because the barbarians will arrive today;
    and such things dazzle barbarians.
And why don't the worthy orators come as always
to make their speeches, say what they have to say?
   Because the barbarians will arrive today;
    and they are bored by eloquence and public speaking.
What does this sudden uneasiness mean,
and this confusion? (How grave the faces have become.)
Why are the streets and squares rapidly emptying,
and why is everyone going back home so lost in thought?
    Because it is night and the barbarians have not come.
    And some men have arrived from the frontiers
    and they say that there are no barbarians any longer.
And now, what will become of us without barbarians?
Those people were a kind of solution.

    Once you're there, where are
    you?

"fresh fish fry"

I've got it all together now. Power, control, skill, clarity. I've got the world by the gluteus maximus. Now what!

312

To be is to
Be relaxed

Fraudulent Forties

Seen any barbarians lately?

"On climbs which nearly approach the vertical, it must be realized that to hold oneself against the wall it is not necessary to cling on vigorously with the hands, because one's center of gravity is through the feet and they are enough to carry the entire weight of the body."

WELL USED

"A man in his late 30s may resume extra-marital dating behavior more characteristic of his earlier 20s and enjoy the relative comfort of behavior already learned, perhaps to avoid the pain of advancing to another developmental level."

"I don't mind rehearsing at all. It gives you good discipline. You get the feeling that you're making good use of yourself, and nothing makes you feel better than that."

Lauren Bacall

JOURNAL ENTRY

PROGRESS REPORT ON A ROCK KOAN

About my rock. It's remarkably warm—I mean it was warm to the touch when you handed it to me. It is still warm. I expected it to be cold, having been in a bag with other rocks. I could go into the rock's composition, but for some reason I don't like the idea or want to. Maybe later when I get to know it better.

I can see already that just getting to know its appearance is going to be tough. Pink, white, brown and black are its colors. It is small, 3 x 1½ inches, about ¾ to 1 inch thick and shaped somewhat like an egg. I used to pick up a stone every now and then and carry it in my pocket, just to feel with my fingers. I would get very attached to each rock. It would become my lucky piece.

I carried this rock home in my pocket and occasionally felt it. I had already become possessive of it. I don't want to with this rock, though, so I just gave it its freedom, although I will continue to maintain its surroundings for a while. Doing this, I have acknowledged its place in the circle of things, and it gave me in return a small insight: Man can't truly possess things, he can only maintain them. It's no longer my rock. I *could* be the rock's human.

This rock might be inanimate, but it has character and definite individuality. It even has scars. Some look like tiny sharp teeth marks, as though an animal has bitten into it. This rock must have suffered. It has accepted its experiences well, though, and it seems to have dignity.

Myself in the rock's place: "I look up at that person, and I'm a little grateful that he gave me my freedom to be just me and not his lucky piece or his gem."

RECONCILE "WE" AND "I"...

"It is not men's minds that are at stake, but their consciousness, their awareness. This isn't a struggle over a market area. Make no mistake about it. This is a struggle over what's to be judged valuable in our universe. Outside they value whatever can be measured, counted or tabulated. Here, we go by different standards."

"Every man is his own bureau of standards."

"Then why did Socrates allow the Greeks to kill him?"

Keep pesticides out of the reach of pets and children.

ORPHEUS

Sergeant Sunshine is sitting in the sun these days. Basking with his three children and a pretty blonde wife who works so he can do his thing.

His thing is to find the way to make the whole world happy.

And that's a noble undertaking which nobody except those who feel they have tormented themselves enough seem to be ready for.

"I look back on myself as a big loudmouth with a big ego," he says now.

And that's the way Sergeant Sunshine looked to a lot of people a few years ago.

Now he's changed, he says.

"Ego is like a pair of shoes. They always pinch. When you wear the shoes out and throw them away you feel better. It's the same with ego."

Sergeant Sunshine is Richard Bergess, an ex-San Francisco cop who rocked the law and order industry a few years ago by smoking marijuana on the steps of San Francisco's City Hall one bright Saturday morning.

Those were the days of San Francisco's famous — and now evidently departed — Flower Children.

Sergeant Sunshine dug them. He was working the Haight-Ashbury at the time as a squad car police officer. The Flower Children got to him in the gentlest of all ways. They loved him.

So Sergeant Sunshine, in some mood of resurrection, decided to blow the minds of the whole Establishment. He would walk to the temple of the Establishment and show everybody in the world that life can be beautiful when you're a little stoned.

He smoked pot on the steps of City Hall and the multitudes who came with him cheered.

And then Sergeant Sunshine started suffering.

First he was stripped of his job and uniform. Then he was thrown in the can.

When all this began, Sergeant Sunshine at the time was living in a good, solid suburban home in Walnut Creek. With a swimming pool, a wife who was bugging him and a couple of devoted neighbors. Today he's living in a very modest Berkeley tract house which he rents. He has a portable typewriter that works fine, an old car which doesn't run very well, a new blonde wife who wants what he wants. He also has two sons who are with him because his former wife is dead.

And then there's a happy little blonde daughter who toddles around getting in trouble.

"The cops had to climb over my six-foot cyclone fence in Walnut Creek. They took the dog away. Among my charges was possession of marijuana, possession of LSD—and not having a dog license. They gave me five days in the hole for not having a dog license . . ."

Sergeant Sunshine is laughing and tiny little Terra (that means earth) is sticking her fingers in his tea.

"Actually they threw me in the hole because I refused to wear their jail overalls. So I sat in the hole for the entire five days. I refused to eat anything. I was curious to see what state that would put my head in. Jesus fasted and Moses fasted and I wanted to see what it would do. You know, meditate. Boy there's nothing like that place to meditate. Nothing to disturb you but the clanging of the door as they let people in or out."

Sergeant Sunshine has just finished 178 pages of a book which could blow the lid off the law and order business and make him a little money.

Then he's going to buy a piece of land in Oregon and set up a cooperative for lost souls.

Among the things he's going to be saying in his book are things like this:

"This is how the soul learns (in jail). Through negative actions sometimes. All the time I was in jail—maybe six months—I practiced the mental discipline of observing my own thoughts. This is a practice of detaching from yourself and observing. It's like kitten watching, except you're one of the kittens. Anytime I got to feeling something negative, I'd just cast it out.

Knowing is not a sequential process, and it never was, though Newtonian physics and Euclidian geometry turned our eyes away from a rich and vital world which has remained intact in each of us.

"That's why this whole system is failing."

Sergeant Sunshine went through his own private inquisition on purpose. He went to City Hall with a roach because he wanted to do something about what he thought was an injustice.

"We all do what we think is right. That's what I did, at the time. Today, I would not do that. I'm a little wiser. I probably would take my superiors to task...but I'd still keep my sergeant's job. I was angry. I just didn't think smoking pot was that immoral.

"I figured 'I'm going to show those bastards what I think of them. I'm going to show them what I think of their uniform and their whole cop trip.' Putting people in rotten cages for smoking pot. They shouldn't do that. They should be out there protecting people like their law enforcement code of ethics says they should be."

Sergeant Sunshine isn't angry anymore. Even his kids don't irritate him. He lost almost everything defending himself through the courts. But he still has his children and his wife and his hopes.

"I've changed completely. I used to get a hell of a lot of fun out of beating up niggers, you know. And getting paid for it. I carried two guns—two of them! And at home I had a hell of a lot more. I loved guns."

He chuckled and shook his head in wonderment. His wife scooted over closer to him. Adoring.

"You know what this law and order industry is don't you?"

He paused for effect.

"It's authority! A cop wants power...I wanted power. So I got into the police force. It was great sport pushing people around. You can build a whole new ego phase for yourself that way. The Americans seem to be the least masculine of all people on earth. We need power. We chase the wrong things. We chase prestige. We chase all these illusions. We're confused. We don't know where the real things are."

His wife touched his hand.

"I went from being the master of ceremonies in a jail down to a point where I was an inmate in the jail. Certain causes were moved toward me and certain effects were produced.

"I wanted to overthrow the government. I'm an expert in explosives too. I had a lot of hate in me. Those cops came over my fence with guns — twelve of them..."

He put his arm around his new wife. She looked down at the plate.

"She made me realize I was indeed a man. I didn't have to go around stomping people anymore just so I could look like a man."

His wife looked up at him and smiled.

For the first time that evening, the ten people at the dinner party fell silent.

Now Sergeant Sunshine sees a whole new life ahead. When he gets the money, he's moving back to the forests where he spent much of his childhood.

And that's what San Francisco's famous Sergeant Sunshine is all about these days; love is starting to work for him.

All my life I had tried to turn life into fiction, to hold reality away; always I had acted as if a third person was watching and listening and giving me marks for good and bad behavior—a god like a novelist...

One student take the role of Sergeant Sunshine. Another be the author of "A Problem of Making Connections." Improvise a conversation between you. Afterward, reflect on the results with your group.

The Great Figure

Among the rain
and lights
I saw the figure 5
in gold
on a red
firetruck
moving
tense
unheeded
to gong clangs
siren howls
and wheels rumbling
through the dark city.

"What good is your reality, when justice fails and dishonesty is glossed over and the ones who keep faith suffer. Helene kept her bargain about Ellis and so did I. What good is your reality then?"

"Look here," Furii said. "I never promised you a rose garden. I never promised you perfect justice . . ." (She remembered Tilda suddenly, breaking out of the hospital in Nuremburg, disappearing into the swastika-city, and coming back laughing that hard, rasping parody of laughter. "Sholom Aleichem, Doctor, they are crazier than I am!") . . .and I never promised you peace or happiness. My help is so that you can be free to fight for all of these things. The only reality I offer is challenge, and being well is being free to accept it or not at whatever level you are capable. I never promise lies, and the rose-garden world of perfection is a lie . . .and a bore, too!"

"Will you bring it up at the meeting—about Helene?"

"I said I would and I will, but I promise nothing."

Sometimes, I have dared to dream to myself that one day, history may even say that my voice—which disturbed the white man's smugness, and his complacency—that my voice helped to save America from a grave, possibly even a fatal catastrophe.

Malcolm X

ONLY CONNECT

"Within the mountaineer, as he gets to know himself and to develop his propensities, the man is born."

317

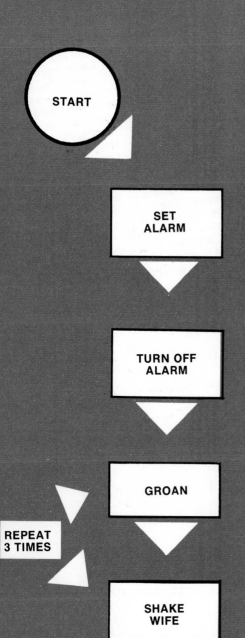

START

SET
ALARM

TURN OFF
ALARM

GROAN

REPEAT
3 TIMES

SHAKE
WIFE

318

WITHIN YOU

FERN HILL

Now as I was young and easy under the apple boughs
About the lilting house and happy as the grass was green,
   The night above the dingle starry,
     Time let me hail and climb
   Golden in the heydays of his eyes,
And honoured among wagons I was prince of the apple towns
And once below a time I lordly had the trees and leaves
     Trail with daisies and barley
   Down the rivers of the windfall light.

And as I was green and carefree, famous among the barns
About the happy yard and singing as the farm was home,
   In the sun that is young once only,
     Time let me play and be
   Golden in the mercy of his means,
And green and golden I was huntsman and herdsman, the calves
Sang to my horn, the foxes on the hills barked clear and cold,
     And the sabbath rang slowly
   In the pebbles of the holy streams.

All the sun long it was running, it was lovely, the hay
Fields high as the house, the tunes from the chimneys, it was air
   And playing, lovely and watery
     And fire green as grass.
   And nightly under the simple stars
As I rode to sleep the owls were bearing the farm away,
All the moon long I heard, blessed among the stables, the nightjars
   Flying with the ricks, and the horses
     Flashing into the dark.

Chicory and daisies ... seem hardly
flowers alone but the color and
the movement — or the shape
perhaps — of restlessness.

WITHOUT YOU

And then to awake, and the farm, like a wanderer white
With the dew, come back, the cock on his shoulder: it was all
    Shining, it was Adam and maiden,
        The sky gathered again
    And the sun grew round that very day.
So it must have been after the birth of the simple light
In the first, spinning place, the spellbound horses walking warm
    Out of the whinnying green stable
        On to the fields of praise.

And honoured among foxes and pheasants by the gay house
Under the new made clouds and happy as the heart was long,
    In the sun born over and over,
        I ran my heedless ways,
    My wishes raced through the house high hay
And nothing I cared, at my sky blue trades, that time allows
In all his tuneful turning so few and such morning songs
    Before the children green and golden
        Follow him out of grace,

Nothing I cared, in the lamb white days, that time would take me
Up to the swallow thronged loft by the shadow of my hand,
    In the moon that is always rising,
        Nor that riding to sleep
    I should hear him fly with the high fields
And wake to the farm forever fled from the childless land.
Oh as I was young and easy in the mercy of his means,
        Time held me green and dying
    Though I sang in my chains like the sea.

The whole of this inner me, this inner territory, is marked by one distinct difference from the outer me. The life of the inner arises spontaneously, showing surprising twists and turns. The outer me is guided by circumstances of what I choose to do and think. The border of the inner is reached when spontaneous thoughts, feelings, or images arise, perhaps related to the outer situation at hand, but still autonomously surprising in their nature. The surprise may be a little one, where one can see the associative link. Or it may be like a dream where the messages of the inner is not really understandable. To the conscious outer self the inner, or l'autre moi, is marked by this spontaneous unaccountability.

319

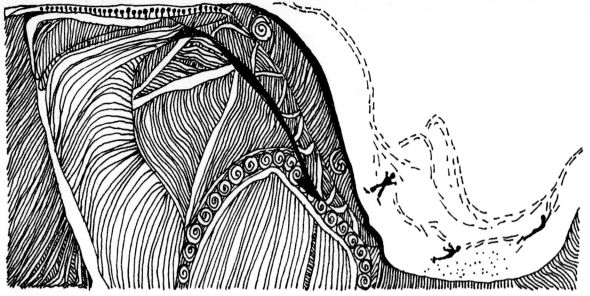

L'AUTRE MOI

Fritz: You see how you can use *everything* in a dream. If you are pursued by an ogre in a dream, and you *become* the ogre, the nightmare disappears. You re-own the energy that is invested in the demon. Then the power of the ogre is no longer outside, alienated, but inside where you can use it.

Chuck: (assured confident voice) Would you say the thing about the ogre again? I don't quite get all of it. The ogre outside and the ogre inside.

F: Do you have any nightmare?

C: Yes...(laughter)...(he comes up to work) The nightmare is not recurrent, but it has happened two or three times where—once I recall *very* vividly, when I was driving down the hill from my house—

F: You remember our agreement?

C: Yes. I'm sorry. We're in the present. I'm sorry. O.K. Here we come. I am driving down the hill in my car, on my way to work, and my little boy runs in front of the car and I hit him, and this is pretty frightening. This has happened two or three times.

F: Now play the car.

C: O.K. Over here or where I am?

F: Just play the car—as if you were this car.

C: I'm driving—giving the car a life of its own, that it doesn't have?

F: Yah.

C: I have the life. The car does what I tell it to.

F: Say this to the car.

C: Car, you do what I tell you to. When I turn the wheel, you—when I turn the wheel, you turn, and when you—when I hold the wheel straight, you go straight.

F: What does the car answer?

C: The car answers, "Yes, sir." (laughter) What else can it answer? I run it; it doesn't run me.

F: Say this to the car.

C: Car, I run you, and you don't run me.

F: Now play this boy. Dream the dream from

320

the point of view of the boy.

C: O.K. Here comes Daddy's car down the road, and I love Daddy and I want to run out and—uh, say hello to Daddy, and all of a sudden the car—all of a sudden this car is hitting me. Why?

F: (wryly) Funny boy. The moment the car hits him, he asks "Why?" (laughter)

C: Well, I—mind you, I'm second-guessing the boy. And I don't *know* what he thinks, this is just what—what's coming back to me that he thinks.

F: Okeh. Play the boy once more.

C: O.K. All right. Here comes Daddy in the car, and I love him and I want to talk to him—and he's gonna hit me! He hates me!

F: And?

C: Shall I do this dream, when he hits? Because this doesn't happen—this doesn't happen. I don't hit him. I'm awake before I hit him.

F: So, at what moment do you interrupt the dream?

C: The front wheels are about six inches away.

F: So what are you avoiding?

C: I'm avoiding killing the boy.

F: Yah. Now kill the boy.

C: O.K. All right. I'm driving down the hill in the car, and when I see the boy coming, I'm not going to stop.

F: And?

C: We hit him.

F: And?

C: He's dead.

F: Close your eyes. Look at him. He's dead...Talk to him, now.

C: (cries) I didn't mean to do it. I didn't mean to do it. I couldn't stop.

F: Go on talking to him.

C: There's no more to say...except I'm sorry.

F: Tell him all the things you're sorry about.

C: I'm sorry I pushed him away when he wanted to—come and be with Daddy and I was too busy to talk to him.

F: Say this to him, now.

C: I'm sorry that I pushed you away—all the times that I pushed you away when I was doing something that was—I felt was very very important to me, and the really important thing was not what I was doing, but the fact that you wanted to—be with Daddy.

F: Now play him.

C: O.K. Ah...ah...

F: Go back to the time when he wanted to talk to you.

C: O.K. Daddy,—I'm—I'm the boy. Daddy, why is so-and-so—Daddy, what's the mouse when he spins? Things like this.

F: Okeh. Now—

C: Daddy, I want to talk to you. I'll ask anything if you'll just talk to me and notice that I'm here. This is—this is the boy.

F: Okeh. Now, change over. Talk like this to *your* father.

C: All right. For Christ's sake, why do you sit there writing sermons all evening when *I'm* here?

F: Now go on with the dialogue. Let him talk back.

C: Son, you know I've got a service tomorrow. You know every Saturday afternoon is Sermon day. So would you please go away and don't bother me, because I've got to get the thing done... I'm projecting—I'm projecting in my own thoughts because I don't remember the exact words, but it was something like this.

F: Now, go on. Insist that he should talk to you.

C: Daddy, *please* talk to me or let's go—take me to the movies or something. *Anything.* I want to talk to you about what's important to me, and you won't listen. You *won't listen!* (shouts angrily) *You're too goddamn busy to listen!* And *I'm* here.

F: Make him listen.

C: (shouts louder) *For Christ's sake, listen, you son-of-a-bitch.* That'll teach you, that I'm here too.

F: Okeh. Now go back to your son.

C: Who am I? Am I him or—

F: You are you, and he is sitting there. Talk to him now.

C: What I'm doing isn't all that big. Let's go to the beach.

F: You are all the time looking at me. What do you want from me?

C: I want you to help me finish a few scenes.

F: Put Fritz in that chair.

C: O.K.

F: "Fritz, I want you to help me."

C: Fritz, I've got scenes that are unfinished and

321

shy = coy
humble = resentful
proud = impotent

they've been unfinished for years, and I want some help.

F: Change seats. Play Fritz.

C: From me, you want help? Look, Chuck, this is something *you've* got to do. If you know, if you know what the—if you know what the unfinished scene is, and you know what you ought to do to finish it, what in hell's stopping you? You—all you're—all you're doing is just—uh—playing games with yourself. All you—all you want to do is lay out flat and let me do it for you. Well, I'm not going to. *You're* going to.

F: Yah. You see how you want my support.

C: Yeah, of course I do.

F: Now *this* Fritz in the empty chair is going to give you all the support you need. Now change seats.

C: O.K. This Fritz is—there's a Fritz there, now, and I'm me.

F: Yah.

C: O.K....uh...Fritz, for Christ's sake help me, will you?—I'm not getting any feedback from you. (laughter) Because I already know what the feedback is, I just gave it...

F: You're not going to suck me in. (laughter) You can play helpless 'til doomsday with me. I'm a very good frustrator.

C: O.K. Um...Fritz, this Fritz, isn't really going to help me.

F: Oh, yes.

C: No, he isn't. He told me he wasn't. This Fritz just told me to pull my own red wagon. So that's what I've gotta do, is pull my own red wagon.

F: Are you willing to listen to him?

C: Certainly I'll listen to him.

F: Okeh. Find out.

C: I'm him?... He hasn't said anything, yet. Except what he's already said, which we all know about.

F: You feel that you are stuck?

C: I'm pretty stuck, right now.

F: Now describe the experience of being stuck.

C: You can go—it's very simple, you can go neither forward nor back. You're there. You're stuck. You don't move. You—ah—I feel—in — in the situation where you're stuck, whatever you do is wrong. Whatever you do is—is—if—if it moves you, it's gonna move you in deeper, not—not out

again. So best—best stay stuck and stay very very still... And so you're still leaving me stuck. Stuck. You're stuck, I'm stuck. So, you're not gonna unstick me, are you?

F: Certainly not. (laughter) I am a frustrator. I am certainly *not* an alpine rescuer.

C: All right. Where are we stuck at?

F: Ask him.

C: Well, he's being pretty uncommunicative right now. He's not telling me much. Uhh—O.K. I'm gonna be him. You still have to unstick yourself. You still have to decide for yourself what you're gonna do, and what's — what's — meaningful and what isn't. And you're the only one who knows that, so why don't you get off your ass and do it?

Now *me* again. Fritz, you—of course I know what I gotta do, but—if I—if I do something about it, one way or the other somebody's gonna get hurt.

F: Ahah. So you get already the first message. Somebody gets hurt.

C: Because it's like this: If I give up what I—what is meaningful and important to me, to—ah—well, let us say this: I've got a term paper due, Fritz, and it's Sunday afternoon, the thing is due on Monday morning and I haven't gotten it done. If I don't—if I drop this and take you to the beach, or whatever, and don't do the term paper, *I* get hurt, and I have a right not to be hurt, too. If I—if I *don't* do the term paper and do take him to—or if I *do* the term paper and don't take him to the beach, *he's* hurt. So whatever I do is wrong. Whatever I do, somebody's gonna get some pain out of it—either me or him, and sometimes I just take the pain myself, and sometimes I give it back to him, but neither one of us—but neither solution is very satisfactory. So what happens next? What do I do, dump them all over the side? What do I do, give up what's important to me so that you all won't be hurting any more? I can't be Fritz again.

F: Right now, I experience myself as a wailing wall.

C: Eh?... O.K. I'll buy it. I'm still looking for support from the environment—like crazy.

F: Yah.

C: *Why* isn't it *out* there? Why do I have to do it *all* myself? Why don't I get a little help?

F: Nyahhhnyahnyah. Say this in gibberish.

C: (does so) Yeah, that's what I'm doing. O.K.

I'll buy it.

F: Go on. Go on.

C: O.K. (makes the same gibberish sounds with more crying in them, like a small child, then carries the same sounds into words) Nobody loves me. Nobody'll help me. Nyanyahnhhnyah.

F: How old are you in this role?

C: About three.

F: Three. It's about time that you hit *that* child.

C: Yeah!

F: Now talk to that child, to the three-year-old child. The nyanhnyanh child.

C: Nyah, go peddle your own potatoes somewhere, I'm busy. Pull your own wed ragon—red wagon—go and play with your friends, I've got things to do. And if you get hurt, I'm sorry. I'm sorry. But I count too.

F: Say this again.

C: I'm sorry—but I *count too,* and don't you forget it.

F: Say this, "I count too."

C: I count too, goddammit, and *remember* it from now on!

F: Say this to the audience.

C: I count too, goddammit, and I—remember it, all of you, from now on. The lot of you!

F: Say it to more people—your wife, your father, and so on. Say this to your whole environment.

C: Remember one thing and dig this real good and wrap onto this real good and hold on tight because this is the way it's gonna be. *I count too!* as much as you do—not any more and not any less, but just as much, and remember it! Now, peddle that. Grab onto them apples and see how you like 'em. *I count too,* goddammit, and *remember it!*

F: Say this to me, too.

C: I count too! I'm just as important as anybody in this room, and don't *you* forget it...(as if asking for permission) O.K.? (laughter) And I can finish my own scenes. Can I say that again? (laughter) Because *I* want to remember that. I can finish my own scenes.

F: Yah. Now, I went along with you to quite an extent, except that I don't believe you in your tailored rules, that you have *either* to finish a term paper *or* go out with the boy. I think that's a lie.

C: O.K.... Of course it's a lie. Because as a matter of fact, in the case that—that I'm generalizing this from, this is exactly what happened. I did go out to the beach with him, and term papers are written—let's face it—at four o'clock in the morning, anyway. They're no good if they're not. And so it—it wasn't either/or, it was both/and, and there's no reason why it shouldn't be this all the time.

F: Exactly... Well, I see the existential message from the dream as, "You don't have to wait until you hit your boy, to get in touch with him." You don't have to copy your father.

"Carmen could have made it, that's all. She had a good, healthy sickness."

"That's a contradiction in terms!"

"That's impossible!"

"No, it isn't—think about it for a minute—a sickness with a good, hard hurt that's direct and doesn't cover with an appealing surface or exercises in normal-faking the doctors."

There was an embarrassed silence and without meaning to, Deborah found herself looking at Linda, the "psychological authority," who had read everything and gave jargon like currency, recklessly improvident because she hoped never to be touched by the pain that was wrapped in the words. Linda, frightened of the look and the definition, came back angrily. "Ridiculous—you're just rationalizing your own defensive system!"

Deborah tried to say it better, and make it more real. "Look at the bunch from the Men's Admitting—they're all very rational and 'sane' and witty. The staff likes them, even as people, but they're here and they've been here for years and they aren't helped by anything or anybody. They don't seem to suffer much because they don't feel anything much. That's sick-sickness. Miss Coral up on D may be sick, but she's feeling and fighting and alive..." Her voice petered out in the face of their anger and disbelief, but suddenly she felt again the quiet power of the opening of the world which she had felt that evening on the D ward. Only now it came more urgently and passionately. "Alive *is* fighting," Deborah said. "It's the same thing. I still think that Carmen could have made it."

COMPREHENSIVE

"Give a little, take a little; work at it."
Chicago Traffic Cop, June 18, 1965, 2:00 P.M.

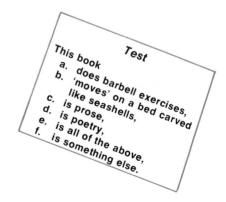

Love and Poetry

My girl the voluptuous creature
Was shaving her legs and saying, "Darling,
If poetry comes not as naturally
As the leaves to a tree
It had better not come at all."

"Och," I said, "and the sorra
Be takin your English Johnny!
What, is a poet a thing without brains in its head?
If wishing could do it, I'd compose
Poems as grand as physics,
Poems founded in botany, psychology, biology,
Poems as progressive as the effect
Of radiation on a foetus."

She turned on the switch of her razor
And said, "The art of poetry
Reminds me of a man in long underwear
Doing barbell exercises.
His biceps bulge. In the meantime
Outside in the gaslit street
His wife, a voluptuous lady,
Elopes with a "swell" who takes her
To Lindy's for oysters,
From there to the Waldorf, and there
On a bed carved like seashells
They move, while the man with the barbells
By gaslight is marching
And swinging his arms to the tune of the Washington Post."

I went to the window. It was night,
And the beautiful moon
Was stealing away to meet someone.
The bitches! They want to feel wanted,
And everything else is prose.

324

To begin, then, with Shakespeare. He was the man who of all modern, and perhaps ancient poets, had the largest and most comprehensive soul. All the images of nature were still present to him, and he drew them not laboriously but luckily: when he describes any thing, you more than see it, you feel it too. Those who accuse him to have wanted learning, give him the greater commendation: he was naturally learned; he needed not the spectacles of books to read nature; he looked inwards, and found her there. I cannot say he is every where alike; were he so, I should do him injury to compare him with the greatest of mankind. He is many times flat, insipid; his comic wit degenerating into clenches, his serious swelling into bombast. But he is always great, when some great occasion is presented to him; no man can say he ever had a fit subject for his wit, and did not then raise himself as high above the rest of poets,

Quantum lenta solent inter viburna cupressi.

Words both flesh and Thought... hold and hook my heart...

Test

This book
a. does barbell exercises,
b. 'moves' on a bed carved like seashells,
c. is prose,
d. is poetry,
e. is all of the above,
f. is something else.

YOU'RE IT

and that's not the half of it . . .*

What a Piece of Work Is Man!

Work in groups of three. Each group work out a description of man as some profession or group might define him. When you are ready, read your description aloud. The others must identify the profession or group you chose.

DO YOU KNOW THE WAY TO . . . OH, NEVER MIND.

SAN JOSE

Figure A
(An extension of the primary integral mechanism.)

A self-balancing, 28-jointed adapter-base biped; an electro-chemical reduction-plant, integral with segregated stowages of special energy extracts in storage batteries, for subsequent actuation of thousands of hydraulic and pneumatic pumps, with motors attached; 62,000 miles of capillaries; millions of warning signal, railroad and conveyor systems; crushers and cranes (of which the arms are magnificent 23-jointed affairs with self-surfacing and lubricating systems, and a universally distributed telephone system needing no service for 70 years if well managed); the whole, extraordinarily complex mechanism guided with exquisite precision from a turret in which are located telescopic and microscopic self-registering and recording range finders, a spectroscope, *et cetera*, the turret control being closely allied with an air conditioning intake-and-exhaust, and a main fuel intake.

Within the few cubic inches housing the turret mechanisms, there is room, also, for two sound-wave and sound-direction-finder recording diaphragms, a filing and instant reference system, and an expertly devised analytical laboratory large enough not only to contain minute records of every last and continual event of up to 70 years' experience, or more, but to extend, by computation and abstract fabrication, this experience with relative accuracy into all corners of the observed universe. There is, also, a forecasting and tactical plotting department for the reduction of future possibilities and probabilities to generally successful specific choice.

Finally, the whole structure is not only directly and simply mobile on land and in water, but, indirectly and by exquisite precision of complexity, mobile in air, and, even in the intangible, mathematically sensed electrical "world," by means of the extension of the primary integral mechanism to secondary mechanical compositions of its own devising, operable either by a direct mechanical hook-up with the device, or by indirect control through wired or wire-less electrical impulses.

True or false:

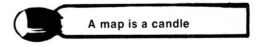

A map is a candle

* You will find the missing ingredient later in this chapter.

325

A man stands before a urinal _____ years of his life.

And I have felt
A presence that disturbs me with the joy
Of elevated thoughts; a sense sublime
Of something far more deeply interfused,
Whose dwelling is the light of setting suns,
And the round ocean and the living air,
And the blue sky, and in the mind of man:
A motion and a spirit, that impels
All thinking things, all objects of all thought,
And rolls through all things. Therefore am I still
A lover of the meadows and the woods,
And mountains; and of all that we behold
From this green earth; of all the mighty world
Of eye, and ear, —both what they half create,
And what perceive; well pleased to recognize
In nature and the language of the sense
The anchor of my purest thoughts, the nurse,
The guide, the guardian of my heart, and soul
Of all my moral being.

ITEM: A junior school in the West Riding of Yorkshire. A class of ten- and eleven-year-old boys and girls, most of them the children of coal miners, are taking a class in Movement. The teacher, with tweed suit and British walking shoes, looking like the American stereotype of a British headmistress, calls out the directions; their execution is left to each child's imagination and ability. "Move about in a small circle, as if your body were very heavy . . . Move about in a small circle as if your body were very light . . . Move very quickly . . . Move very slowly . . . Now find a partner and make your movements in response to his, so that you are aware of what he or she is doing as well as what you are doing. . . . Speed the movements up . . . Slow them down . . . Make them sharp and jerky . . . Move only your arms and body above the waist; move as if you felt very sad . . . Move only your fingers, hands and arms, as though they were very sad. . . . Now move them as though they were very happy. . . . Find a partner and move your fingers, hands, and arms as though you were talking to each other. . . . Move about the room as though you were a butterfly. . . . Move about the room as though you were an elephant. . . . Move about in your own space as though you were a snowflake. . . . Stay in the space around you, but try to use all of it, close to the floor, above your head. . . ." All this without music, then repeated with music of various kinds. (This same school, incidentally, has the best rugby team for miles around.)

326

fixated . . . at a stage that hasn't been successfully negotiated.

work on, age after age, nothing

is

to

be

lost.

GO BACK

AN ANCIENT LANGUAGE

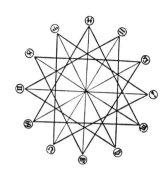

Hyt warneth alle and some
Of everych of her aventures
Be avisions, or be figures,
But that oure flessh ne hath no myght
To understonde hyt aryght,
For hyt is warned to derkly . . .

The house of
fame

WANTED

SPACIOUS PERSONALITY

"It is the mark of an educated man to look for precision in each class of things just so far as the nature of the subject admits; it is equally foolish to accept probable reasoning from a mathematician and to demand from a rhetorician scientific proofs."

*Work on, age after age, nothing is to be lost,
It may have to wait long, but it will certainly come
in use . . .*

327

THE MAP VS THE TERRITORY

I asked him to explain this point to me in more detail, or to describe the difference in effect between the two (peyote and mushrooms). He looked at me for a long time and laughed. He said that learning through conversation was not only a waste, but stupidity, because learning was the most difficult task a man could undertake. He asked me to remember the time I had tried to find my spot, and how I wanted to find it without doing any work because I had expected him to hand out all the information. If he had done so, he said, I would never have learned. But, knowing how difficult it was to find my spot, and, above all, knowing that it existed, would give me a unique sense of confidence. He said that while I remained rooted to my 'good spot' nothing could cause me bodily harm, because I had the assurance that at that particular spot I was at my very best. I had the power to shove off anything that might be harmful to me. If, however, he had *told* me where it was, I would never have had the confidence needed to claim it as true knowledge. Thus, knowledge was indeed power.

"Making compost is easy; almost any library has books or organic gardening to guide you."

When asked, "How are you going to make a true film [of Trotsky's life]? If it was true, how would any film company let you make it?" director Joseph Losey (*The Servant, The Accident, The Go-Between*) says, "I told him it couldn't be the complete truth. It's like the Trotskyite theory of revolution: if they couldn't have total world revolution, they wanted none at all. But I told him there would be as much truth as possible. Maybe even more. But that it is also necessary to just keep working."

328

Isolate, Set, Field

If ego and l'autre moi are seen as one, then the conception of self is enlarged. In spite of extensive training to express one's self in a language, one would need to accept an inner native ability and predilection for representing one's state in another primal and even archaic language. In this older language endless images of the world or phrases of the world language are used to faithfully represent one's state.

Here the difficulty lies. Can I speak a language not taught me, a rich language, faithfully showing myself even when I am relatively lost and ignorant? And how can I do this effortlessly?** To do this one has to let go of a conventional picture of the self to permit this effortless, wiser one to stand forth. Were I a primitive I might pray to the inner one, seeking its guidance in signs. But, as a psychologist, I stand in awesome respect for its richness and its spontaneous wisdom. It is appropriate perhaps simply to notice, describe and respect what lies beyond the bounds of struggling ego. Gabriel Marcel describes a mystery as what transcends its own data. Certainly this other side of us transcends the data given us. Is the innermost faculty a symbolic mirror which can but represent? This faculty deserves respect since it lies at the threshold of what we know ourselves to be, and it implies more than can be understood.

a mystery ← and I lost it

Cannonero II

A rich language faithfully showing me myself even when I am lost and ignorant? Do the matching test below and collate the results in your group. Reflect on these.

____ 1. Yellow

____ 2. Blue

____ 3. Green

____ 4. Black

____ 5. Red*
____ 6. Grey
____ 7. Brown

____ 8. Violet

A. Complete calm, tranquility, depth of feeling, femininity, oneness, truth, trust, surrender, devotion.
B. Fusion of conquest and surrender, subject and object, identification, erotic blending (or a need to blend and fuse the real and imaginary).
C. The 'no,' extinction, nothingness, renunciation, ultimate surrender.
D. Perseverance and tenacity, firmness, constancy, resistance to change, emphasis on the self, astringence, pride, dominance, control, power.
E. Warmth, cheerfulness, airiness, expansiveness, ease.
F. Passive, receptive vitality, sensuousness, home and hearth.
G. Uncommitted, uninvolved, insular, watching from the sidelines, neutral.
H. Vital force, activity, desire for results, sexual potency, productivity, force of will, intensity.

* The most colorful dressers among professional men are plastic surgeons.
** See universal grammar theory, p. 220

"HOME IS WHERE THE START IS"

HUNGER

How to study usage:

As to the poetical Character itself (I mean that sort of which, if I am any thing, I am a Member; that sort distinguished from the wordsworthian or egotistical sublime; which is a thing per se and stands alone) it is not itself—it has no self—it is every thing and nothing—It has no character—it enjoys light and shade; it lives in gusto, be it foul or fair, high or low, rich or poor, mean or elevated—It has as much delight in conceiving an Iago as an Imogen. What shocks the virtuous philosopher, delights the camelion Poet. It does no harm from its relish of the dark side of things any more than from its taste for the bright one; because they both end in speculation. A Poet is **the most unpoetical of any thing in existence; because he has no Identity—he is continually infor (ming) and filling some other Body—The Sun, the Moon, the Sea and Men and Women who are crea**tures of impulse are poetical and have about them an unchangeable attribute—the poet has none; no identity—he is certainly the most unpoetical of all God's Creatures. If then he has no self, and if I am a Poet, where is the Wonder that I should say I would write no more? Might I not at that very instant have been cogitating on the Characters of Saturn and Ops? It is a wretched thing to confess; but is a very fact that not one word I ever utter can be taken for granted as an opinion growing out of my identical nature—how can it, when I have no nature? When I am in a room with People if I ever am free from speculating on creations of my own brain, then not myself goes home to myself: but the identity of every one in the room begins to press upon me that I am in a very little time an(ni)hilated—not only among Men; it would be the same in a Nursery of children: I know not whether I make myself wholly understood: I hope enough so to let you see that no dependence is to be placed on what I said that day.

330

I HAVE A WEAK TEMPER

Master. I think you are devoting your whole life to one big koan.

Student. What if I don't like the answer I get.

Master. Then it is not the right answer.

Student. I'm getting the hell out of here. I don't like that answer.

"The most fundamental premise of our constitutional scheme may be that every adult bears the freedom to nurture or neglect his own moral and intellectual growth."

A computer study showed that for every 100 verbs in theatrical plays there were 11 adjectives. In doctoral theses there were 88 adjectives for every 100 verbs. Business letters had fewer adjectives than laws. Poetry contained fewer adjectives than ads.

GROK

The Saturday before, Deborah had gone to sleep looking forward to telling Carla about a new boarder and the landlady's son-in-law. She had a dream.

In the dream it was winter and night. The sky was thick blue-black and the stars were frozen in it, so that they glimmered. Over the clean white and windswept hills the shadows of snowdrifts drew long. She was walking on the crust of snow, watching the star-glimmer and the snow-glimmer and the cold tear-glimmer in her own eyes. A deep voice said to her, "You know, don't you, that the stars are sound as well as light?"

She listened and heard a lullaby made by the voices of the stars, sounding so beautiful together that she began to cry with it.

The voice said, "Look out there."

She looked toward the horizon. "See, it is a sweep, a curve." Then the voice said, "This night is a curve of darkness and the space beyond it is a curve of human history, with every single life an arch from birth to death. The apex of all of these single curves determines the curve of history and, at last, of man."

"Can I know about my curve?" she said, begging the voice. "Will I hold part of the sweep of the age?"

"I cannot show you yours," the voice said, "but I can show you Carla's. Dig here, deep in the snow. It is buried and frozen—Dig deep."

Deborah pushed the snow aside with her hands. It was very cold, but she worked with a great intensity as if there were salvation in it. At last her hand struck something and she tore it up from burial. It was a piece of bone, thick and very strong and curved in a long, high, steady curve.

"Is this Carla's life?" she asked. "Her creativity?"

"It is bone-deep with her, though buried and frozen." The voice paused a moment and then said, "It's a fine one—a fine solid one!"

Deborah wanted to plead again for the shape that her art would draw in time, but the dream faded and the voices of the stars became dim and died out entirely at last.

The child: like the adult, he is an active being whose action, controlled by the law of interest or need, is incapable of working at full stretch if no appeal is made to the autonomous motive forces of that activity.

In the morning the vividness was still with her, so that when Carla came and they sat idly and talked, Deborah was distracted and her mind was still hung with heavy stars and her hands were still gripping the smooth curve of bone.

"Please don't be angry," she said; and then told Carla the dream. When she got to the part about digging in the snow for the curve, Carla was with her; when she pulled up what was buried, Carla said, "Do you see it? What is it like!" moving a little whenever Deborah moved as if to brush the snow away from it. When she described it to Carla and told what the voice said, Carla began to cry.

"Do you think it's true—do you really think it's true?"

"I told you as it happened."

"You didn't make it up—I mean you really dreamed it that way—"

"Yes, I did."

She wiped her eyes. "It was only a dream, your dream..."

"It's true anyway," Deborah said.

"The one place I could never go..." Carla said musing, "...the one hunger I could never admit."

When Deborah finished, Furii said, "You always took your art for granted, didn't you? I used to read in the ward reports all the time how you managed to do your drawing in spite of every sort of inconvenience and restriction. You were rich in your gift, even at your sickest, and now you see how it can be with others who are not so lucky to have a creative calling into which they can grow and grow. The healthy friendship you had to bury in forgetfulness, and the times of sunlight you banished from your memory. I think this dream was to remind you of another joy as well; it was the understanding of Carla. There may be many who envy you a little—yes, yes, I know it sounds like the old 'lucky girl' business, but it isn't. You have been taking for granted this rich and prolific gift of yours that so many others would give so much to have themselves. By this dream you were perhaps awakening to it a little. It is part of the call of the world."

"On the other hand, where cortical-thalamic integration has been established, the nervous system can withstand almost any shock."

331

Instant astronomy: circa 1969

Twinkle, twinkle little star
We know exactly what you are:
Nuclear furnace in the sky,
You'll burn to ashes by and by.

But tick, tick, tick pulsating star,
Now we wonder what *you* are:
Magneto-nucleo-gravity ball,
Making monkeys of us all!

And twinkle, twinkle quasi-star,
You're the limit, yes you are:
With such indecent energy,
Did God not say you couldn't be?

Anon

332

"Those who prepare for all the emergencies of life beforehand may equip themselves at the expense of joy. It is necessary to prepare for an examination, or a dinner party, or a possible fall in the price of stock; those who attempt human relations must adopt another method, or fail."

ONLY CONNECT
shelley

Horatio. If your mind dislike anything, obey it. I will forestall their repair hither, and say you are not fit.

Hamlet.   Not a whit; we defy augury. There's a special providence in the fall of a sparrow. If it be now, 'tis not to come; if it be not to come, it will be now; if it be not now, yet it will come; the readiness is all.

"But it is also necessary to just keep working...."

333

WRAP SESSION

Which character or point of view in this chapter most resembles you? Reflect on that.

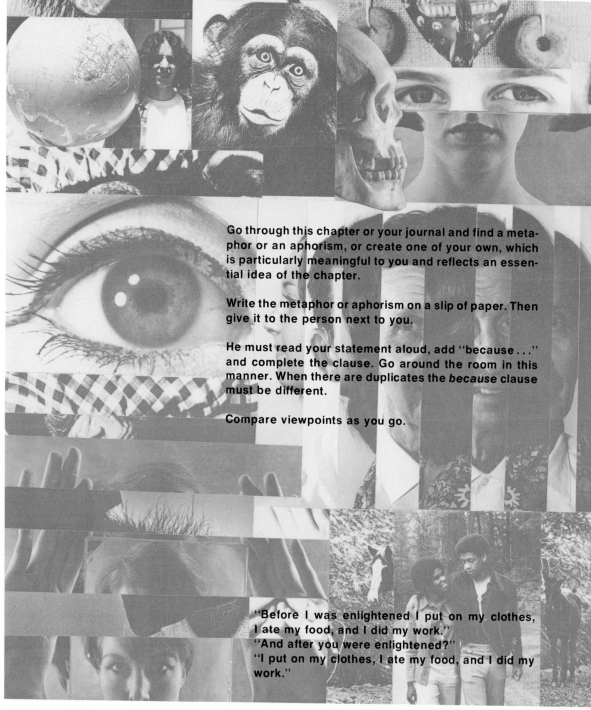

Go through this chapter or your journal and find a metaphor or an aphorism, or create one of your own, which is particularly meaningful to you and reflects an essential idea of the chapter.

Write the metaphor or aphorism on a slip of paper. Then give it to the person next to you.

He must read your statement aloud, add "because..." and complete the clause. Go around the room in this manner. When there are duplicates the *because* clause must be different.

Compare viewpoints as you go.

"Before I was enlightened I put on my clothes, I ate my food, and I did my work."
"And after you were enlightened?"
"I put on my clothes, I ate my food, and I did my work."

BEYOND

..discovery...jawbone fragment...appears to stretch history of race five million years.

From Eno's scrapbook:

The Rosicrucians * represented a group of human beings who had reached a higher state than the mass of humanity and thus possessed similar internal characteristics which enabled them to recognize one another at all times.

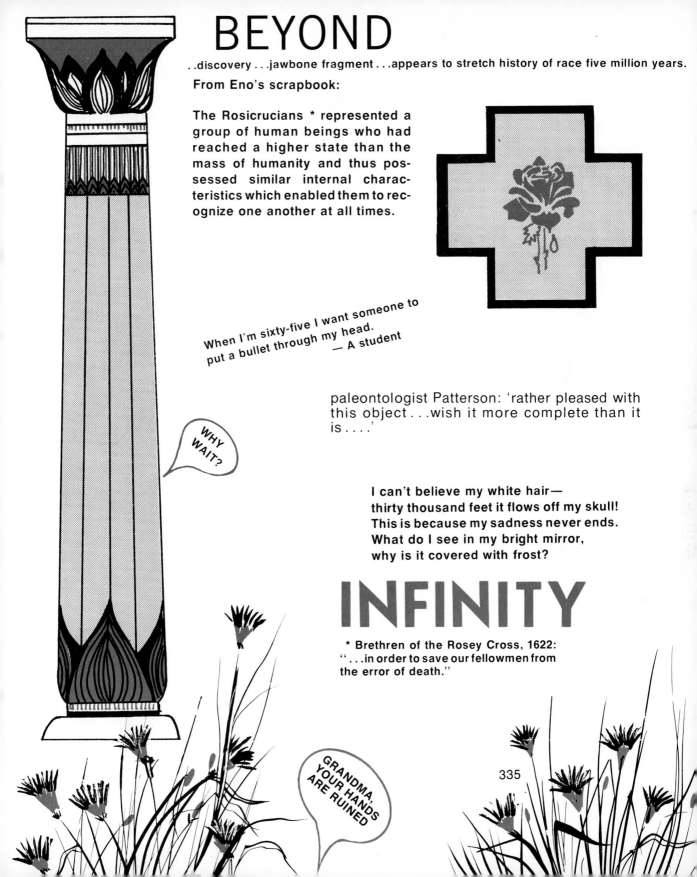

When I'm sixty-five I want someone to put a bullet through my head.
— A student

paleontologist Patterson: 'rather pleased with this object...wish it more complete than it is....'

WHY WAIT?

I can't believe my white hair—
thirty thousand feet it flows off my skull!
This is because my sadness never ends.
What do I see in my bright mirror,
why is it covered with frost?

INFINITY

* Brethren of the Rosey Cross, 1622:
"...in order to save our fellowmen from
the error of death."

335

GRANDMA, YOUR HANDS ARE RUINED

And yonder all before us lie
Deserts of vast eternity.

There's something more that I sense about old people that I haven't crystallized yet. Something about *me* as an old person, *already* old, carrying age in me now. The value of that, the value of being 'old' now, in my present body. Getting the *feel* of age. 'I was not young long; I met the soul early.' Something is on the verge of coming now. The soul *is* old. To know old people, to *be* old, ancient, is to come in contact with the eternal. Age suggests agelessness, whereas it is youth which is transient. Age stands for the eternal ground of being. With the withering away of the camouflage of flesh and leaves, we get a glimpse of the structure, the skeleton, the medium in which we are the message. Thus, when I get the feel of agedness, I get the feel of the now, that which *is*. To want to be rid of 'antiques' is to want to be rid of the eternal and all reminders of it. Not only that but I cannot really get an accurate picture of myself without this dimension. It becomes more than merely a matter of enrichment; it is a matter of truth. Without the dimension of the aged, I get a distorted picture of reality. I am confused and incomplete.

Walking from the opéra to Parc de Montsouris, I realized that Paris was built for eternity, and New York only for the present. A documentary film on Egypt portrayed their obsession with eternity.
—June 1935

'O sages standing in God's holy fire
As in the gold mosaic of a wall,
Come from the holy fire, perne in a gyre,
And be the singing-masters of my soul.'

336

There was a young fellow named Wright,
Whose speed was much faster than light.
He set out one day
In a relative way
And returned on the preceding night.

'More than a hundred thousand books and manuscripts on alchemy are known to exist. This vast literature, to which the finest minds have contributed and which solemnly affirms its attachment to facts and practical experiments, has never been systematically explored. The current intellectual climate...has always maintained in regard to these texts an attitude of ignorance or scorn.'

I will pour out my spirit upon all flesh; and your sons and your daughters shall prophesy, and your old men shall dream dreams, your young men shall see visions.

A bullet through the head.

WHO'S HEAD?

BASE METAL

Hundreds of thousands of 'alchemists' are now filed away in rest homes, retirement communities, and convalescent hospitals. The current intellectual climate maintains in regard to these texts an attitude of ignorance or scorn.

... and in this desert we will trace a road that will lead to God

"The man will be, by then, at the end of his journey of learning, and almost without warning he will come upon the last of his enemies: Old age! This enemy is the cruelest of all, the one he won't be able to defeat completely, but only fight away.

"This is the time when a man has no more fears, no more impatient clarity of mind—a time when all his power is in check, but also the time when he has an unyielding desire to rest. If he gives in totally to his desire to lie down and forget, if he soothes himself in tiredness, he will have lost his last round, and his enemy will cut him down into a feeble old creature. His desire to retreat will overrule all his clarity, his power, and his knowledge.

"But if the man sloughs off his tiredness, and lives his fate through, he can then be called a man of knowledge, if only for the brief moment when he succeeds in fighting off his last, invincible enemy. That moment of clarity, power, and knowledge is enough."

4:OLD AGE

● Omniplastic mastery — the old-age period, from 60 or so until death, when a person who has successfully met the tests of earlier periods often turns his attention to broader concerns

3:POWER

But he grew old —
This knight so bold —
And o'er his heart a shadow
Fell as he found
No spot of ground
That looked like Eldorado.

338

And one clock stopped
And knew the meaning of time.

0 0 0 0 0 0 0 0 0 0 0 0

AMALGAMATED STEEL

Monuments of unageing intellect.

The solace of such work as I do with brain and heart lies in this—that only there, in the silences of the painter or the writer can reality be reordered, reworked and made to show its significant side. Our common actions in reality are simply the sackcloth covering which hides the cloth-of-gold, the meaning of the pattern. For us artists there waits the joyous compromise through art with all that wounded or defeated us in daily life; in this way, not to evade destiny, as the ordinary people try to do, but to fulfill it in its true potential, the imagination.

2:CLARITY

1: FEAR

339

Why do you seek rest? You were only created for labor.
—Thomas Aquinas

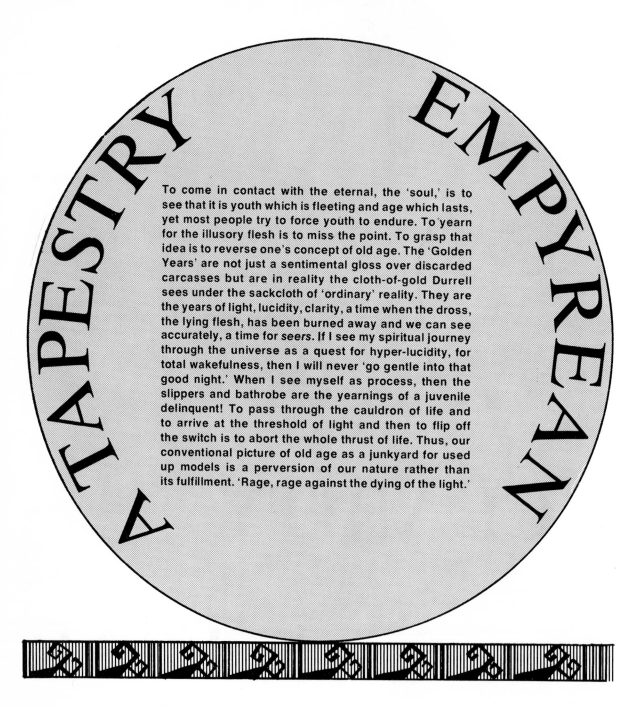

A TAPESTRY EMPYREAN

To come in contact with the eternal, the 'soul,' is to see that it is youth which is fleeting and age which lasts, yet most people try to force youth to endure. To yearn for the illusory flesh is to miss the point. To grasp that idea is to reverse one's concept of old age. The 'Golden Years' are not just a sentimental gloss over discarded carcasses but are in reality the cloth-of-gold Durrell sees under the sackcloth of 'ordinary' reality. They are the years of light, lucidity, clarity, a time when the dross, the lying flesh, has been burned away and we can see accurately, a time for seers. If I see my spiritual journey through the universe as a quest for hyper-lucidity, for total wakefulness, then I will never 'go gentle into that good night.' When I see myself as process, then the slippers and bathrobe are the yearnings of a juvenile delinquent! To pass through the cauldron of life and to arrive at the threshold of light and then to flip off the switch is to abort the whole thrust of life. Thus, our conventional picture of old age as a junkyard for used up models is a perversion of our nature rather than its fulfillment. 'Rage, rage against the dying of the light.'

...how Love fled
And paced upon the mountains overhead
And hid his face amid a crowd of stars.

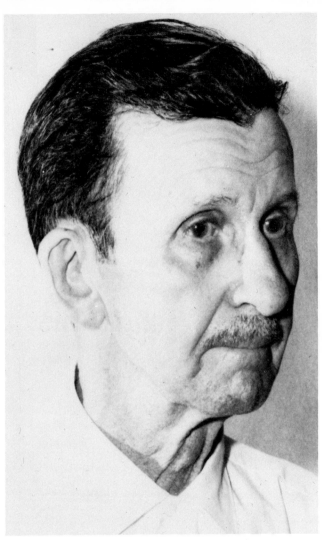

EARTH

A crucible for transmuting base metals into gold.

"Here, everything is open: the techniques of thought, logical processes and 'ensembles'—all this is alive and constantly renewed, while the strangest and most transparent conceptions are formed in the mind, one leading to another and being transformed, like the movements of a symphony; we are in the divine domain of the imagination. But an abstract imagination, so to speak, for these images arising out of mathematical techniques have nothing in common with those pertaining to the illusory world in which we are bogged down, *although they contain the key which can unlock the latters' hidden meaning.*"

mathematics

341

THE MOST SINCERE FORM OF SELF-CRITICISM IS **SUICIDE!**

THOUGH LEAVES ARE MANY, THE ROOT IS ONE:

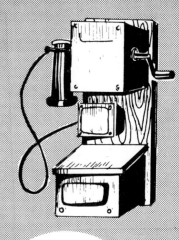

To decipher certain manuscripts found on the shores of the Black Sea, all the knowledge of the best linguists in the world was not enough. An electronic calculating machine was then set up in the Vatican and presented with an appalling scrawl, the debris of a parchment dating from time immemorial covered in every direction with indecipherable signs. The machine was being asked to do what hundreds and hundreds of brains, working for hundreds and hundreds of years could not have done: to compare the sign-traces; reconstruct all the possible series of similar signs; choose between all the possible probabilities; discover a common factor of resemblance between all imaginable terms of comparison; and finally having exhausted the infinite number of possible combinations, constitute an alphabet from the one acceptable similitude, recreate a language, restore and translate it. The machine, cold and motionless, opened its green and glassy eye; began to hum and click; its electronic brain was traversed by innumerable rapid waves; and at last from this poor rotting scrap of parchment a message emerged, a voice from an ancient world that vanished long ago. The machine translated. Those shadowy letters on that dusty parchment came to life again, reunited and refecundated; and from this shapeless carcass of what had once been the Word there issued a voice full of promise. The machine said: "And in this desert we will trace a road that will lead to God."

Le Martin des Magiciens

342

"The experience of our century is going to be something considerably more than the birth of Buddhism! It is no longer a question of endowing such and such a god with human faculties. The religious power of the Earth will undergo in us a final crisis: that of its own discovery. We are beginning to understand, and for ever, that the only acceptable religion for man is the one that will teach him first of all to recognize, love and passionately serve this universe of which he is the most important element."

**Through all the lying days of my youth
I swayed my leaves and flowers in the sun;**

In his *Ballad of Reading Goal* Oscar Wilde makes the discovery that mental inattention is the worst crime, and that intense mental concentration reveals not only the complete coherence of all the events in a man's life, but also, no doubt, on a vaster scale, the complete concordance and harmony between everything in Creation. And he exclaims: "Everything understood is good." I know of no finer saying.

Now I may wither into the truth.

Of hammered gold and gold enamelling

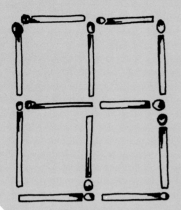

Make one
less square by

moving only three
matches.

OVERHUNGRY CHIMPS GET NO BANANAS

It would seem reasonable that the stronger the drive, the more efficient the problem solving. However, this principle holds true only to a point. Birch varied the hunger drive in chimps by depriving them of food for varying amounts of time. He observed the effects on the efficiency of solving problems to get bananas. As expected, the chimps performed progressively better as they got hungrier; but they reached a peak, after which they got steadily worse. Overhungry chimps get no bananas. This curvilinear relationship between motivation and performance is called the **Yerkes-Dodson law**. It is reflected in the comment by actors that it is good to be a little, but not too, nervous before a performance. There is a corollary to this law. A psychologist asked two groups of students to solve a series of problems. Members of the first group (low drive) were asked simply for their anonymous contribution in establishing norms for the test. Members of the second group (high drive) were told that it was a test of intelligence, innate decency, sense of humor, and sexual potency; that they must write their name on it; and that, incidentally, the university was a little over-crowded. The first group did better on the difficult tasks; the second group did better on the easy tasks.

A clue to the explanation of this finding is found through a qualitative analysis of Birch's study. The chimps did worse at low and high levels of drive than at medium levels. They did worse for different reasons: at low levels, because they just fooled around and were easily distracted; at high levels, because they persisted with an inappropriate strategy and could not break the set to try alternative strategies. Gleitman suggests that a difficult task is one in which the obvious thing to do is the wrong thing and an easy task is one in which the obvious thing to do is the correct thing. Thus highly motivated students, who tend to persist with the obvious solution, will do well on easy tasks and poorly on difficult tasks. When you take an examination, sweat if it is easy, but relax if it is difficult.

SERMONS IN STONES

It is therefore not surprising that language which can only relfect the world as it appears to our consciousness in its normal waking state becomes obscure as soon as it has to express those profound structures or anything to do with light, eternity, time, energy, the essence of Man, etc. Nevertheless we can distinguish two kinds of obscurity.

One is due to the fact that language is the vehicle of an intelligence that endeavors to examine these sructures without ever being able to assimilate them. It is the vehicle of one kind of Nature that is in conflict with another kind of Nature. At best, it can only demonstrate an impossibility and convey an impression of frustration and isolation. Its obscurity is real and positive; in fact, it is nothing but obscurity.

The other kind of obscurity occurs when the man who is trying to express himself has had, by a flash of intuition, a brief glimpse of another state of consciousness. He has *lived* for an instant in the intimacy of those profound structures. He has *known* them. I am thinking of mystics like St. John of the Cross, or intuitional scientists like Einstein, or inspired poets like William Blake, or enraptured mathematicians like Galois, or visionary philosophers like Meyrink.

On returning to Earth, the "seer" fails to communicate what he has experienced. But in doing so he expresses the certitude that the Universe could be controlled and manipulated if Man succeeded in establishing as close an association as possible between his ordinary waking state and a state of hyperwakefulness. Such a language could be really efficient, a sovereign instrument. Fulcanelli, speaking of the mystery of the Cathedrals; Wiener on the structure of Time, are obscure; but this is not real obscurity, but a sign that something is shining elsewhere.

The language of modern mathematics is the only one, no doubt, that can give some account of certain results of analogical thinking. There exist in mathematical physics regions of the "Absolute Elsewhere" and of "*continus de mesure nulle*," that is to say measurements applied to Universes that are inconceivable and yet real. We may wonder why it is that the poets have not yet turned to this science to catch an echo of the music of those spheres of fantastic reality—unless it be for fear of having to accept this evidence—that the magic art lives and flourishes outside their study walls.

346

Once out of nature, I shall never take
My bodily form from any natural thing.

time

was like

fire,

burning

as it

passed.

FIRE

THE RETREAT

Happy those early days, when I
Shined in my angel infancy;
Before I understood this place
Appointed for my second race,
Or taught my soul to fancy aught
But a white, celestial thought;
When yet I had not walked above
A mile or two from my first Love,
And looking back, at that short space,
Could see a glimpse of His bright face;
When on some gilded cloud or flower
My gazing soul would dwell an hour,
And in those weaker glories spy
Some shadows of eternity;
Before I taught my tongue to wound
My conscience with a sinful sound,
Or had the black art to dispense
A several sin to every sense,
But felt through all this fleshly dress
Bright shoots of everlastingness.
    Oh, how I long to travel back,
And tread again that ancient track!
That I might once more reach that plain
Where first I left my glorious train;
From whence the enlightened spirit sees
That shady city of palm trees.
But, ah! my soul with too much stay
Is drunk, and staggers in the way.
Some men a forward motion love;
But I by backward steps would move,
And when this dust falls to the urn,
In that state I came, return.

Summon the eyes and hidden mouths of stone and light and water

BEYOND

Sailing to Byzantium

I

That is no country for old men. The young
In one another's arms, birds in the trees,
—Those dying generations—at their song,
The salmon falls, the mackerel-crowded seas,
Fish, flesh, or fowl, commend all summer long
Whatever is begotten, born, and dies.
Caught in that sensual music all neglect
Monuments of unageing intellect.

II

An aged man is but a paltry thing,
A tattered coat upon a stick, unless
Soul clap its hands and sing, and louder sing
For every tatter in its mortal dress,
Nor is there singing school but studying
Monuments of its own magnificence;
And therefore I have sailed the seas and come
To the holy city of Byzantium.

III

O sages standing in God's holy fire
As in the gold mosaic of a wall,
Come from the holy fire, perne in a gyre,
And be the singing-masters of my soul.
Consume my heart away; sick with desire
And fastened to a dying animal
It knows not what it is; and gather me
Into the artifice of eternity.

IV

Once out of nature I shall never take
My bodily form from any natural thing,
But such a form as Grecian goldsmiths make
Of hammered gold and gold enamelling
To keep a drowsy Emperor awake;
Or set upon a golden bough to sing
To lords and ladies of Byzantium
Of what is past, or passing, or to come.

All the same, I can tell you this much: you are aware that in the official science of today the role of the observer becomes more and more important. Relativity, the principle of indeterminacy, shows the extent to which the observer today intervenes in all these phenomena. The secret of alchemy is this: there is a way of manipulating matter and energy so as to produce what modern scientists call 'a field of force.' This field acts on the observer and puts him in a privileged position *vis-à-vis* the Universe. From this position he has access to the realities which are ordinarily hidden from us by time and space, matter and energy. This is what we call 'The Great Work.' "

"But what about the philosopher's stone? The fabrication of gold?"

"These are only applications, particular cases. The essential thing is not the transmutation of metals, but that of the experimenter himself. It's an ancient secret that a few men re-discover once in a century."

"And what becomes of them then?"

"I shall know, perhaps, one day."

BEYOND

On the island

    in the fruit

Blocks   *of*   *slate*   *about*

        his   *head*

BEYOND

Ordinarily, we get along with conscious, superficial thinking: "To get to the bus station, go to the third traffic light, turn left and go one half block. It's on the left." When we need to satisfy several variables in a housing problem or in a complex mathematics problem, such thinking can become extremely taxing. Even the most complicated problem involving only known formulae, though it requires much energy and effort, requires the same *kind* of thinking. But another kind is uniquely distinctive of human beings. Although as far as we know it is exclusively our own, it is generally neglected and ignored. This thinking is what makes us human, but few are aware of it. The mixture of spirit and flesh we find embodied in a metaphor, once understood, is a model for this supralogical thinking, coupling the reservoir of unconscious, irrational knowledge with the conscious, logical mind. It does not make 'sense' to see one thing in terms of another, yet this process is the basis of all culture: the bridging of distinctions, the developing of a single concept for the entire universe.

ONE, TWO, THREE, INFINITY
1 2 3
1 2 3

By examining each instance of it in a systematic, step-by-step manner, we could never comprehend anything so infinitely variable; we would soon break down under the weight. (Most schools seem designed to do just that, however, and continue dishing up basket after basket of plastic-coated facts, never mixing chemistry and poetry, algebra and German.) We become human only by jumping to the conclusion of *language*. The bench mark for membership is the capacity to make this leap. Any who fall short must be cared for by the others.

As those who study language soon realize, such a complex system could never be mastered by step-by-step analysis alone. Indeed, no mature mind has yet been able to explain all the complexities of language which even young children can handle with absolute assurance. It is only through symbolic thinking, metaphoric thinking, that we can grapple with such complexity. But as Keats put it:

> Now it appears to me that almost any Man may like the spider spin from his own inwards his own airy Citadel—the points of leaves and twigs on which the spider begins her work are few, and she fills the air with a beautiful circuiting. Man must be content with a few points to tip with the fine Web of his Soul, and weave a tapestry empyrean . . . .

In ordinary analogical thinking, images and words are stripped of their ambiguity and are used to compare one thing with another in detail-for-detail parallels. In symbolic analogy, however, there is an instantaneous blurt of association, compressing awareness of the totality of a situation in one immediate flash of insight. The mind leaps over all the intervening steps and details and arrives at a solution allatonce. Point-for-point identification takes a long time for all the nuances to be seen, but symbolic thinking travels at electronic speed, establishing thousands of connections in a flash. Becoming consciously aware of this process and mastering its use is the work of the maturing mind. Those who stop at logical thinking might as well retire at forty, but symbolic thinkers travel a thrilling road on into the years of light.

348

AIR

'It is in fact nothing short of a miracle that the modern methods of instruction have not yet entirely strangled the holy curiosity of inquiry...It is a very grave mistake to think that the enjoyment of seeing and searching can be promoted by means of coercion and a sense of duty.'

—Einstein

I must point out, my thought is not far removed from that of Novalis who wrote: 'We are really living inside an animal whose parasites we are. What we are, our constitution, depends on this animal, and vice-versa.' I also find myself in agreement with William James, who asked: 'Who knows but that we may occupy in Nature as small a place by the side of beings of whom we know nothing as the cats and dogs who live beside us in our houses?' Scientists themselves would not contradict this point of view: 'All round us there may be beings, built on the same model as ourselves, but different—men, for example, whose albumins may be straight.'

"A new myth? Should we try to persuade these beings that they are nothing but a mirage, or give them an opportunity to reveal themselves?"

André Breton

This energy exists outside man, and must be captured. The Roman Catholic swallows the host—a ritual way of intercepting this energy. But if you have no faith? In that case, have a fire—that is all the alchemy is. A real fire. Everything begins and everything happens through contact with matter.

"I suppose a retired printer must have lots of memories."

LOOK 7-14-70

Is this man an alchemist?

TO KEEP A DROWSY EMPEROR AWAKE

For the alchemist, it must never be forgotten that power over matter and energy is only a secondary reality. The real aim of the alchemist's activities . . .is the transformation of the alchemist himself, his accession to a higher state of consciousness . . .towards his fusion with the divine energy.

'' 'Matter is everything; contact with matter, working with matter, working with the hands.' He made a great point of this:

'' 'Are you fond of gardening? That's a good start; alchemy is like gardening. Do you like fishing? Alchemy has something in common with fishing. Woman's work and children's games.' ''

Grave men, near death, who see with blinding sight
Blind eyes could blaze like meteors and be gay,
Rage, rage against the dying of the light.

Come from the holy fire, perne in a gyre,
And be the singing-masters of my soul.

350

Our bent for language is as much a part of us as our mating instincts. Evidence suggests that all languages are alike in their deep grammar and different only on the surface, in the more or less accidental paths along which inner forms link themselves and make their way to the top. As with sexual behavior, linguistic activity can be modified by social restrictions but never seriously changed.

TO EARTHWARD

Love at the lips was touch
As sweet as I could bear;
And once that seemed too much;
I lived on air

That crossed me from sweet things,
The flow of—was it musk
From hidden grapevine springs
Down hill at dusk?

I had the swirl and ache
From sprays of honeysuckle
That when they're gathered shake
Dew on the knuckle.

I craved strong sweets, but those
Seemed strong when I was young;
The petal of the rose
It was that stung.

Now no joy but lacks salt,
That is not dashed with pain
And weariness and fault;
I crave the stain

Of tears, the aftermark
Of almost too much love,
The sweet of bitter bark
And burning clove.

When stiff and sore and scarred
I take away my hand
From leaning on it hard
In grass and sand,

The hurt is not enough:
I long for weight and strength
To feel the earth as rough
To all my length.

...not eternal life
but eternal vivacity.

—Nietzche

At any given instant, a youth, an old man, and a rock have exactly the same age. They have exactly the same amount of history behind them. We are all in the same boat.

MATTER

351

Some 80 games have been identified in this painting.   What is your score?

Play generates energy
because it is a pleasure in
itself, an intrinsic end.

You won't find a leaf from an olive tree or
a single grape left of the ones I saw in Attica.
I even miss the grass that grew there in my
day. I haven't had the strength to make a
patch of heather grow.

—Chateaubriand to Ampère
departing for Greece

WHO ARE YOU ?

IMAGE

UNE MANIFIQUE

Like a Photograph Negative

"We are both middle-aged," she said. "Middle-aged."

She would never change. Oliver himself rather liked the idea of getting old; if he managed it right he'd be venerable, like the pope, and people would think him very wise . . . .

Helen Ware said "middle-aged," as if it were a charm that held back time. How foolish women were, how silly. *Middle-aged*. Not any more. And not for a long time past. You could see age in her body, could see every one of her years clearly marked on her skin. Hollows on the inside of her thighs, little caves where the flesh had fallen away. That wasn't middle-aged, he thought with a silent laugh. That was old. Like those bulges along her jaw that she smoothed and pressed and treated with creams each day. And the way her skin felt thin and dry and brittle and scorched . . . .Sometimes it seemed to him that time was like fire, burning as it passed. The heat of the blood dried and withered the flesh it supported.

Now, lying in her bed, he held one of his arms straight up into the air and looked at it. Sometimes it seemed to him that he wasn't really connected to himself. The memories of the person he'd been didn't seem possible. This arm now. He had a hard time believing that it belonged to him as a boy. The arm that had been with him forty years ago in the alleys of Singapore and the streets of Manila was sunburned and thick with light hair. This arm now—the one he held over his head—had white skin and dark hair. Like a photograph negative . . . .Feelings went that way too. Things important to the boy, the man never thought about.

He turned his arm about, staring at the corded veins along the inner side, trying to see the blood running inside them. When a man was cut, the blood pumped out in squirts, just like a pump emptying a boat. He'd seen that when he was little, back in the Ohio Valley; a saw slashed his thigh, his blood pumped red into the snow, steaming. Oliver remembered thinking that it was like hogs' blood at slaughtering time.

Now, here was his arm, again, stuck up in the air. He whistled through his teeth at it. Old man's arm, old man's body.

In 1948 the war was over, and new battles—atomic ones, this time—were threatening. Nevertheless he considered the disquieting and painful times to be no more than the negative of a magnificent image.

353

COMPOSITION:

Which writer would you kick out of bed?

'Turn on the prudent Ant thy heedless eyes,
Observe her labours, Sluggard, and be wise;
No stern command, no monitory voice,
Prescribes her duties, or directs her choice;
Yet, timely provident, she hastes away
To snatch the blessings of a plenteous day;
When fruitful Summer loads the teeming plain,
She crops the harvest and she stores the grain.
How long shall sloth usurp thy useless hours,
Unnerve thy vigour, and enchain thy powers?
While artful shades thy downy couch enclose,
And soft solicitation courts repose,
Amidst the drowsy charms of dull delight,
Year chases year with unremitted flight,
Till want now following, fraudulent and slow,
Shall spring to seize thee, like an ambushed foe.'

A

C

"Go to the Ant, thou Sluggard, consider her ways, and be wise: which having no guide, overseer, or ruler, provideth her meat in the summer, and gathereth her food in the harvest. How long wilt thou sleep, O Sluggard? when wilt thou arise out of thy sleep? Yet a little sleep, a little slumber, a little folding of the hands to sleep. So shall thy poverty come as one that travaileth, and thy want as an armed man."

B

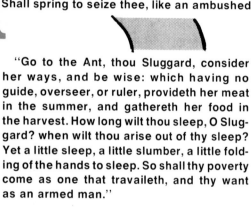

CLOTH of GOLD

RELATIONSHIP

Let me wither and wear out mine age in a discomfortable, in an unwholesome, in a penurious prison, and so pay my debts with my bones, and recompense the wastefulness of my youth, with the beggary of mine age; Let me wither in a spittle under sharp, and foul, and infamous diseases, and so recompense the wantonness of my youth, with that loathsomeness in mine age; yet, if God withdraw not his spiritual blessings, his Grace, his Patience, If I can call my suffering his Doing, my passion his Action, All this that is temporal, is but a caterpillar got into one corner of my garden, but a mildew fallen upon one acre of my Corn; The body of all, the substance of all is safe, as long as the soul is safe. But when I shall trust to that, which we call a good spirit, and God shall deject, and empoverish, and evacuate that spirit, when I shall rely upon a moral constancy, and God shall shake, and enfeeble, and enervate, destroy and demolish that constancy; when I shall think to refresh my self in the serenity and sweet air of a good conscience, and God shall call up the damps and vapours of hell itself, and spread a cloud of diffidence, and an impenetrable crust of desperation upon my conscience; when health shall fly from me, and I shall lay hold upon riches to succour me, and comfort me in my sickness, and riches shall fly from me, and I shall snatch after favour, and good opinion, to comfort me in my poverty; when even this good opinion shall leave me, and calumnies and misinformations shall prevail against me; when I shall need peace, because there is none but thou, O Lord, that should stand for me, and then shall find, that all the wounds that I have, come from thy hand, all the arrows that stick in me, from thy quiver; when I shall see, that because I have given my self to my corrupt nature, thou hast changed thine; and because I am all evil towards thee, therefore thou hast given over being good towards me; when it comes to this height, that the fever is not in the humours, but in the spirits, that mine enemy is not an imaginary enemy, fortune, not a transitory enemy, malice in great persons, but a real, and an irresistible, and an inexorable, and an everlasting enemy, The Lord of Hosts himself, The Almighty God himself, the Almighty God himself only knows the weight of this affliction, and except he put in that *pondus gloriae*, the exceeding weight of an eternal glory, with his own hand, into the other scale, we are weighed down, we are swallowed up, irreparably, irrevocably, irrecoverably, irremediably.

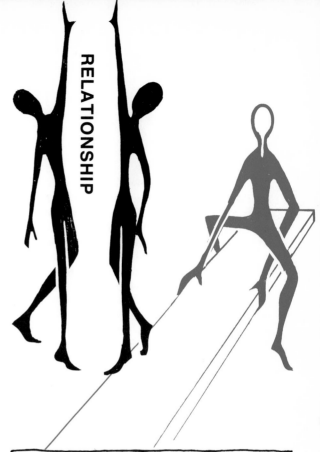

355

2001

SPACE FOR HIS

My dear Reynolds—I had an idea that a Man might pass a very pleasant life in this manner—Let him on a certain day read a certain page of full Poesy or distilled Prose, and let him wander with it, and muse upon it, and reflect from it, and bring home to it, and prophesy upon it, and dream upon it: until it becomes stale—But when will it do so? Never—When Man has arrived at a certain ripeness in intellect any one grand and spiritual passage serves him as a starting-post towards all 'the two-and-thirty Palaces.' How happy is such a voyage of conception, what delicious diligent indolence! A doze upon a sofa does not hinder it, and a nap upon Clover engenders ethereal finger-pointings— the prattle of a child gives it wings, and the converse of middle-age a strength to beat them—a strain of music conducts to 'an odd angle of the Isle,' and when the leaves whisper it puts a girdle round the earth.—Nor will this sparing touch of noble Books be any irreverence to their Writers—for perhaps the honors paid by Man to Man are trifles in comparison to the benefit done by great works to the 'spirit and pulse of good' by their mere passive existence. Memory should not be called Knowledge—Many have original minds who do not think it—they are led away by Custom. Now it appears to me that almost any Man may like the spider spin from his own inwards his own airy Citadel—the points of leaves and twigs on which the spider begins her work are few, and she fills the air with a beautiful circuiting. Man should be content with as few points to tip with the fine Web of his Soul, and weave a tapestry empyrean—full of symbols for his spiritual eye, of softness for his spiritual touch, of space for his wandering, of distinctness for his luxury. But the minds of mortals are so different and bent on such diverse journeys that it may at first appear impossible for any common taste and fellowship to exist between two or three under these suppositions.

It is however quite the contrary. Minds would leave each other in contrary directions, traverse each other in numberless points, and at last greet each other at the journey's end. An old man and a child would talk together and the old man be led on his path and the child left thinking. Man should not dispute or assert, but whisper results to his Neighbour, and thus by every germ of spirit sucking the sap from mould ethereal every human might become great, and humanity instead of being a wide heath of furze and briars, with here and there a remote Oak or Pine, would become a grand democracy of forest trees ... Now it is more noble to sit like Jove than to fly like Mercury—let us not therefore go hurrying about and collecting honey, bee-like, buzzing here and there impatiently from a knowledge of what is to be arrived at. But let us open our leaves like a flower, and be passive and receptive; budding patiently under the eye of Apollo and taking hints from every noble insect that favours us with a visit—Sap will be given us for meat, and dew for drink. I was led into these thoughts, my dear Reynolds, by the beauty of the morning operating on a sense of Idleness. I have not read any Books—the Morning said I was right—I had no idea but of the Morning, and the Thrush said I was right.

WANDERING

Reading Lesson

Agon, it happede me for to beholde
Upon a bok, was write with lettres olde,
And therupon, a certeyn thing to lerne,
The longe day ful faste I redde and yerne.

For out of olde feldes, as men seyth,
Cometh al this newe corn from yer to yere,
And out of olde bokes, in good feyth,
Cometh al this newe science that men lere.

True or False

1. An old man is a history book.
2. All history is now.
3. All history is me.

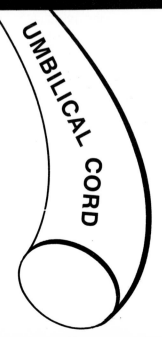

UMBILICAL CORD

Art is embedded in nature. He that can extract it hath it.

Swiss Charred Poodle*

The Chinese Poodle story goes back at least as far as 1939 according to *The San Francisco Chronicle's* Herb Caen. He printed it in that year with a Chinatown setting. It cropped up again in 1949 from New York and again in 1959 it took place in Honolulu.

After the story appeared in his own newspaper in 1971 by way of Reuters, Caen pointed out that the Zurich couple not wanting their names published was a telltale sign of the true fable. Robert Reynolds of the Hong Kong Tourist Association completed the debunking:

"First of all, that alleged Swiss couple couldn't have been tourists because pets are quarantined for six months before they're allowed into Hong Kong. And in the second place pets are forbidden in Hong Kong restaurants, just as they are here."

In his column, Caen quoted the following dialogue about the tale:
"Now there's the original Chinese Doggy Diner."
"Nope, it's chow mein."
"You're both wrong. That's a Swiss charred poodle."

* See story on page 309

357

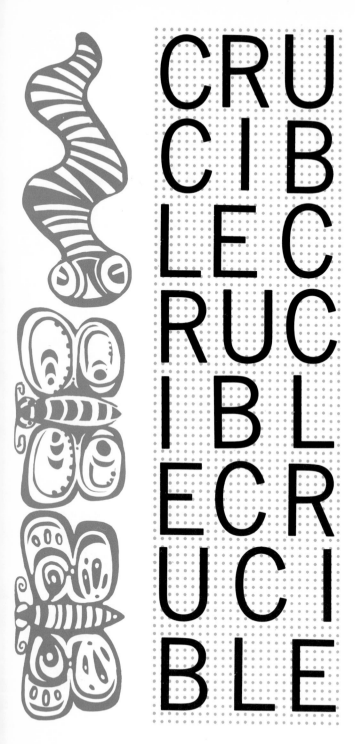

CRU
CIB
LEC
RUC
IBL
ECR
UCI
BLE

...The seventieth birthday! It is the time of life when you arrive at a new and awful dignity; when you may throw aside the decent reserves which have oppressed you for a generation and stand unafraid and unabashed upon your seven-terraced summit and look down and teach—unrebuked. You can tell the world how you got there. It is what they all do. You shall never get tired of telling by what delicate arts and deep moralities you climb up to that great place. You will explain the process and dwell on the particulars with senile rapture. I have been anxious to explain my own system this long time, and now at last I have the right.

I have achieved my seventy years in the usual way: by sticking strictly to a scheme of life which would kill anybody else. It sounds like an exaggeration, but that is really the common rule for attaining old age. When we examine the programme of any of these garrulous old people we always find that the habits which have preserved them would have decayed us; that the way of life which enabled them to live upon the property of their heirs so long, as Mr. Choate says, would have put us out of commission ahead of time. I will offer here, as a sound maxim, this: That we can't reach old age by another man's road.

I will now teach, offering my way of life to whomsoever desires to commit suicide by the scheme which has enabled me to beat the doctor and the hangman for seventy years. Some of the details may sound untrue, but they are not. I am not here to deceive; I am here to teach.

We have no permanent habits until we are forty. Then they begin to harden, presently they petrify, then business begins. Since forty I have been regular about going to bed and getting up—and that is one of the main things. I have made it a rule to go to bed when there wasn't anybody left to sit up with; and I have made it a rule to get up when I had to. This has resulted in an unswerving regularity of irregularity. It has saved me sound, but it would injure another person.

In the matter of diet—which is another main thing — I have been persistently strict in sticking to the things which didn't agree with me until one or the other of us got the best of it. Until lately I got the best of it myself. But last spring I stopped frolicking with mince pie after midnight; up to then I had always believed it wasn't loaded. For thirty years I have taken coffee and bread at eight in the morning, and no bite nor sup until seven-thirty in the evening. Eleven hours. That is all right for me, and is wholesome, because I have never had a headache in my life, but headachy people would not reach seventy comfortably by that road, and they would be foolish to try it. And I wish to urge upon you this — which I think is wisdom — that if you find you can't make seventy by any but an uncomfortable road, don't you go. When they take off the Pullman and retire you to the rancid smoker, put on your things, count your checks, and get out at the first way station where there's a cemetery.

I have made it a rule never to smoke more than one cigar at a time. I have no other restriction as regards smoking. I do not know just when I began to smoke, I only know that it was in my father's lifetime, and that I was discreet. He passed from this life early in 1847, when I was a shade past eleven; ever since then I have smoked publicly. As an example to others, and not that I care for moderation myself, it has always been my rule never to smoke when asleep, and never to refrain when awake. It is a good rule. I mean, for me; but some of you know quite well that it wouldn't answer for everybody that's trying to get to be seventy.

I smoke in bed until I have to go to sleep; I wake up in the night, sometimes once, sometimes twice, sometimes three times, and I never waste any of these opportunities to smoke. This habit is so old and dear and precious to me that I would feel as you, sir, would feel if you should lose the only moral you've got — meaning the chairman — if you've got one: I am making no charges. I will grant, here, that I have stopped smoking now and then, for a few months at a time, but it was not on principle, it was only to show off; it was to pulverize those critics who said I was a slave to my habits and couldn't break my bonds.

To-day it is all of sixty years since I began to smoke the limit. I have never bought cigars with life belts around them. I early found that those were too expensive for me. I have always bought cheap cigars — reasonably cheap, at any rate. Sixty years ago they cost me four dollars a barrel, but my taste has improved, latterly, and I pay seven now. Six or seven. Seven, I think. Yes, it's seven. But that includes the barrel. I often have smoking parties at my house; but the people that come have always just taken the pledge. I wonder why that is?

As for drinking, I have no rule about that. When the others drink I like to help; otherwise I remain dry, by habit and preference. This dryness does not hurt me, but it could easily hurt you, because you are different. You let it alone.

Since I was seven years old I have seldom taken a dose of medicine, and have still seldomer needed one. But up to seven I lived exclusively on allopathic medicines. Not that I needed them, for I don't think I did; it was for economy; my father took a drug store for a debt, and it made cod-liver oil cheaper than the other breakfast foods. We had nine barrels of it, and it lasted me seven years. Then I was weaned. The rest of the family had to get along with rhubarb and ipecac and such things, because I was the pet. I was the first Standard Oil Trust. I had it all. By the time the drug store was exhausted my health was established and there has never been much the matter with me since. But you know very well it would be foolish for the average child to start for seventy on that basis. It happened to be just the thing for me, but that was merely an accident; it couldn't happen again in a century.

I have never taken any exercise, except sleeping and resting, and I never intend to take any. Exercise is loathsome. And it cannot be any benefit when you are tired; and I was always tired. But let another person try my way, and see whence he will come out.

I desire now to repeat and emphasize that maxim: We can't reach old age by another man's road. My habits protect my life, but they would assassinate you.

I have lived a severely moral life. But it would be a mistake for other people to try that, or for me to recommend it. Very few would succeed: you have to have a perfectly colossal stock of morals; and you can't get them on a margin; you have to have the whole thing, and put them in your box....

I've wrestled with reality for thirty-five years, and I'm happy to say I've won out over it. —HARVEY

"Mind at Large has to be funneled through the reducing valve of the brain and nervous system. What comes out at the other end is a measly trickle of the kind of consciousness which will help us to stay alive on the surface of this particular planet."

Morals are of inestimable value, for every man is born crammed with sin microbes, and the only thing that can extirpate these sin microbes is morals. Now you take a sterilized Christian — I mean, you take *the* sterilized Christian, for there's only one. Dear sir, I wish you wouldn't look at me like that.

Threescore years and ten!

It is the Scriptural statute of limitations. After that, you owe no active duties; for you the strenuous life is over. You are a time-expired man, to use Kipling's military phrase: You have served your term, well or less well, and you are mustered out. You are become an honorary member of the republic, you are emancipated, compulsions are not for you, nor any bugle call but "lights out." You pay the time-worn duty bills if you choose or decline if you prefer — and without prejudice — for they are not legally collectable.

The previous-engagement plea, which in forty years has cost you so many twinges, you can lay aside forever; on this side of the grave you will never need it again. If you shrink at thought of night, and winter, and the late home-coming from the banquet and the lights and the laughter through the deserted streets — a desolation which would not remind you now, as for a generation it did, that your friends are sleeping, and you must creep in a-tiptoe and not disturb them, but would only remind you that you need not tiptoe, you can never disturb them more — if you shrink at thought of these things, you need only reply, "Your invitation honors me, and pleases me because you still keep me in your remembrance, but I am seventy; seventy, and would nestle in the chimney corner, and smoke my pipe, and read my book, and take my rest, wishing you well in all affection, and that when you in your turn shall arrive at pier No. 70 you may step aboard your waiting ship with a reconciled spirit, and lay your course toward the sinking sun with a contented heart."

1910

"They say that age kills the fire inside of a man. He hears death coming, he opens the door and says, 'Come in, give me rest.' That is a pack of lies. I've got enough fight in me to devour the world. So, I fight!"

—Zorba

Mary Steiner

Mary Kern Steiner, 75, 115 Front Street, Boswell, died yesterday. Born August 15, 1886, Aidel, Austria, daughter of Joseph and Esther Kern.

Her husband, John Steiner, who died six years ago, was a PRR conductor until his retirement. He was a member of the Boswell Volunteer Fire Department and the Dutch Club for many years. Mary Steiner was a member of Faith Lutheran Church, the Ladies' Auxiliary of the Brotherhood of Railroad Trainmen, and the Golden Age Club.

Surviving are a sister, Anna Kern Shultz, 80, of Blacklick, a daughter, Mrs. Clara Steiner Pohland, 225 Front Street, and a granddaughter, Mary.

Family will receive friends at Cole Brothers' Funeral Home, 10 A.M. to 10 P.M., with services at the Faith Lutheran Church 2 P.M. Friday, the Reverend Victor Sleigh in charge. Interment at Youngstown Cemetery.

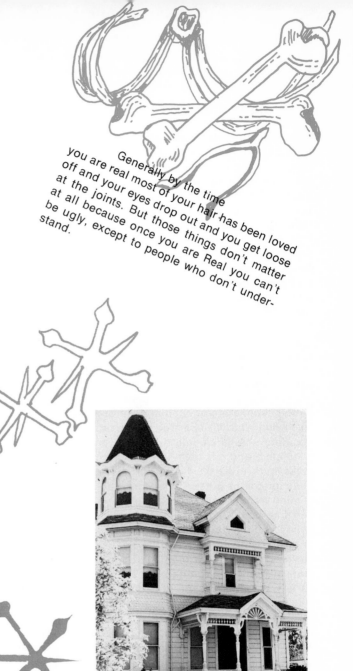

Generally by the time you are real most of your hair has been loved off and your eyes drop out and you get loose at the joints. But those things don't matter at all because once you are Real you can't be ugly, except to people who don't understand.

PRISM

Late green afternoons shimmered through
the mulberry bush where I sat
Shifting damp, cool dirt between my
Toes. I had the berries in a
Pan until my fingers, mouth, tongue,
Were juiced purple and maybe I
Had six left. "I picked these for you,"
I'd yell, pulling a mint garnish.
You wiped your hands on your apron
Roses, and oh — I loved you so.
Because of the secret wine at
Bedtime, taken in a cheese-glass,
Illicit and watered down. And
A green tray so "Howdy Doody"
And dinner-time could coincide.
Because of the folded dollar
For birthdays and Christmas, and your
Wrinkled, soft cheek; your vague, violet
Smell. For a million reasons that
Wander sadly through summer nights
And fly down dark cellar stairs.

HEART-WOOD

Warning to Children

The earliest Poets of all nations generally wrote from passion excited by real events; they wrote naturally, and as men: feeling powerfully as they did, their language was daring, and figurative. In succeeding times, Poets, and men ambitious of the fame of Poets, perceiving the influence of such language, and desirous of producing the same effect, without having the same animating passion, set themselves to a mechanical adoption of those figures of speech, and made use of them, sometimes with propriety, but much more frequently applied them to feelings and thoughts with which they had no natural connection whatsoever. A language was thus insensibly produced, differing materially from the real language of men in *any situation.* The Reader or Hearer of this distorted language found himself in a perturbed and unusual state of mind: when affected by the genuine language of passion he had been in a perturbed and unusual state of mind also: in both cases he was willing that his common judgment and understanding should be laid asleep, and he had no instinctive and infallible perception of the true to make him reject the false; the one served as a passport for the other. The agitation and confusion of mind were in both cases delightful, and no wonder if he confounded the one with the other, and believed them both to be produced by the same, or similar causes. Besides, the Poet spake to him in the character of a man to be looked up to, a man of genius and authority. Thus, and from a variety of other causes, this distorted language was received with admiration; and Poets, it is probable, who had before contented themselves for the most part with misapplying only expressions which at first had been dictated by real passion, carried the abuse still further, and introduced phrases composed apparently in the spirit of the original figurative language of passion, yet altogether of their own invention, and distinguished by various degrees of wanton deviation from good sense and nature.

362

It is indeed true that the language of the earliest Poets was felt to differ materially from ordinary language, because it was the language of extraordinary occasions; but it was really spoken by men, language which the Poet himself had uttered when he had been affected by the events which he described, or which he had heard uttered by those around him. To this language it is probable that metre of some sort or other was early superadded. This separated the genuine language of Poetry still further from common life, so that whoever read or heard the poems of these earliest Poets felt himself moved in a way in which he had not been accustomed to be moved in real life, and by causes manifestly different from those which acted upon him in real life. This was the great temptation to all the corruptions which have followed: under the protection of this feeling succeeding Poets constructed a phraseology which had one thing, it is true, in common with the genuine language of poetry, namely, that it was not heard in ordinary conversation; that it was unusual. But the first Poets, as I have said, spake a language which, though unusual, was still the language of men. This circumstance, however, was disregarded by their successors; they found that they could please by easier means: they became proud of a language which they themselves had invented, and which was uttered only by themselves; and, with the spirit of a fraternity, they arrogated it to themselves as their own. In process of time metre became a symbol or promise of this unusual language, and whoever took upon him to write in metre, according as he possessed more or less of true poetic genius, introduced less or more of this adulterated phraseology into his compositions, and the true and the false became so inseparably interwoven that the taste of men was gradually perverted and this language was received as a natural language: and at length, by the influence of books upon men, did to a certain degree really become so. Abuses of this kind were imported from one nation to another, and with the progress of refinement this diction became daily more and more corrupt, thrusting out of sight the plain humanities of nature by a motley masquerade of tricks, quaintnesses, hieroglyphics, and enigmas.

It would be highly interesting to point out the causes of the pleasure given by this extravagant and absurd language; but this is not the place; it depends upon a great variety of causes, but upon none perhaps more than its influence in impressing a notion of the peculiarity and exaltation of the Poet's character, and in flattering the Reader's self-love by bringing him nearer to a sympathy with that character; an effect which is accomplished by unsettling ordinary habits of thinking, and thus assisting the Reader to approach to that perturbed and dizzy state of mind in which if he does not find himself, he imagines that he is *balked* of a peculiar enjoyment which poetry can and ought to bestow.

—1802

A newspaper philosopher says the three most difficult words to pronounce consecutively are "I was mistaken." The philosopher is himself mistaken; the most difficult are "I deliberately lied." These are not only more difficult than the others, but they are more frequently true.

73

That time of year thou may'st in me behold
When yellow leaves, or none, or few, do hang
Upon those boughs which shake against the cold,
Bare ruined choirs, where late the sweet birds sang.
In me thou see'st the twilight of such day
As after sunset fadeth in the west;
Which by and by black night doth take away,
Death's second self, that seals up all in rest.
In me thou see'st the glowing of such fire,
That on the ashes of his youth doth lie,
As the death-bed whereon it must expire
Consumed with that which it was nourished by.
  This thou perceiv'st, which makes thy love more
     strong,
To love that well which thou must leave ere long.

WAKE UP, STUPID

"Take a watch," we were told, "and look at the big hand while trying to remain conscious of yourself and concentrate on the thought: 'I am Louis Pauwels, and I am here now, at this moment.' Try to think of nothing else but that; simply follow the movement of the big hand and go on being conscious of yourself, your name, your existence and the place where you are now."

At first this seemed simple, and rather ridiculous. Of course I could concentrate on the idea that my name was Louis Pauwels and that I was there, at that moment, watching the big hand of my watch moving slowly round. Soon I had to admit that this idea did not remain stable within me for long; it began to take on a thousand shapes and to flow about in every direction, like those objects that Dali paints in mud. But I had to remember, too, that I had not been asked to keep alive and fixed in my mind an idea, but a perception. I had not only to think that I existed, but to know it and to have an absolute knowledge of that fact. I felt that that would be possible, and that it could happen in me and bring me something new and important. I discovered, however, that I was perpetually being distracted by a thousand more or less vague thoughts, sensations, images and associations of ideas that had nothing to do with the object of my efforts, and indeed prevented me from pursuing it. Sometimes it was the watch-hand that absorbed all my attention, and while gazing at it I lost sight of myself. Sometimes it was my body — a twitching muscle in my leg, a sensation in my stomach that took my attention away from both the watch and myself. Sometimes, again, I thought I had closed down my little internal cinema and eliminated the external world; but I soon found then that I had sunk into a kind of sleep in which the watch-hand as well as myself had disappeared, while images, sensations and ideas continued to be mixed up in my mind behind a kind of veil, as if in a dream unfolding itself independently of me while I slept. Sometimes, for a fraction of a second, while looking at the watch-hand, I was totally and completely conscious that I was I. But in the same fraction of a second, I was congratulating myself on having achieved this state; my mind, so to speak, was applauding, whereupon my intelligence, by expressing satisfaction at my success, ruined it irremediably. Finally, disappointed, but above all thoroughly exhausted, I gave up the experiment, because it seemed to me that I had just been through the most difficult few minutes in the whole of my existence and deprived of air to a degree that had taxed my endurance to its extreme limits. How interminable it had seemed! And yet it had lasted scarcely more than a couple of minutes; and in those two minutes I had only had a real perception of myself in three or four imperceptible flashes. I was then forced to admit that we are practically never conscious of ourselves, and that we are hardly ever conscious of the difficulty of being conscious.

The state of consciousness, we were told, is at first the state of a Man who, having at last discovered that he is hardly ever conscious then begins gradually to learn what, in himself, are the obstacles to what he is trying to do. In the light of this little experiment one knows now that a Man may, for example, read a book, approve or be bored by it, protest or be enthusiastic, without ever being conscious for a moment of the fact that He himself "is" and that consequently nothing of what he has read has really impinged on the Man he "is." His reading is another dream added to his own dreams — a flux in the perpetual flux of the unconscious. For our real consciousness may be — and almost always is — completely absent from everything we do, think, desire or imagine.

I understood then that there is very little difference between our normal waking and sleeping states. Our dreams when we are awake have become invisible, as it were, like the stars in daytime; but they are still there, and we continue to live under their influence. We have merely acquired on waking a critical attitude towards our own sensations; our thoughts are better coordinated, our actions more controlled, our impressions, sensations and desires more lively; but we are still in a state of non-consciousness. We are not now discussing the real "awakened state" but what could be called a "waking sleep"; and it is in that state that we spend practically the whole of our lives. We were taught that it is possible to become completely awake, and to be conscious of oneself. In this state, as I discovered during the experiment with the watch, I was able to have an objective knowledge of my thoughts and of a succession of images, ideas, sensations, sentiments and desires. While in that state, I could try to make a real effort to examine and even halt from time to time, or change this flow of sensations. And the very fact of making this effort, so I was told, created in me a certain subsistence. It did not actually result in anything definite. The mere fact of its having been made was enough to call into being and accumulate in me the very substance of my being. I was assured that I could then, having a fixed "being," acquire an "objective consciousness," and that I would then be in a state to have a completely objective and total knowledge not only of myself, but of other men and things and of the whole world.*

Rules for the More Formal Type of Friendly Letter

Use appropriate stationery and ink.
Make the letter neat.
Make the margins equal.
Make the five parts of the letter conform to standard practice.

The Thank-You Note

The thank-you note is a "must" after you have received a thoughtful gift. It should be written promptly. Make the person from whom you received the gift feel you appreciate it. Be specific. The ability to make your feelings known in a letter is a skill you will enjoy all your life.

FUN

Study this example of a thank-you letter.

PINOLE SENIOR CITIZENS HOME
316 Alhambra Way
Danville, California

December 28, 1973

Mr. Marvin L. Sloan
Executive Director

Dear Mr. Sloan

I want to thank you so very much for your lovely Christmas gift of a table radio. It's just wonderful that an absolute stranger such as yourself remembers people like us.

I am 82 years old and have been here at the home for 16 years. They treat us very well, but the loneliness is sometimes hard to bear.

My room-mate, Mrs. Manley, is a very nice person but she is very stingy. She has a table model radio but she won't let me use it and she turns it off when I come into the room. Now I have my very own.

My son and daughter-in-law are very nice and they come to visit me once a month. I appreciate it, but I also understand their sense of obligation. This makes your gift all the more wonderful because it was given not from a sense of duty, but from a feeling of compassion for a fellow human being.

Today Mrs. Manley's radio went out of order and she asked me if she could listen to mine. I told her to go ▉▉▉ herself.

Yours sincerely,

Hattie Lasell

Hattie Lasell

8 9

GETTING

THERE

4

365

OUT OF OLDE FELDES

While passing near Tiberias in Galilee, the emperor Hadrian observed an old man digging a large trench in order to plant some fig trees.

"If you had properly employed the morning of your life," remarked Hadrian, "you would not have to work so hard in the evening of your days."

"I have well employed the morning of my early days, nor will I neglect the evening of my life; and let God do what he thinks best," replied the man.

"How old are you, good man?"

"A hundred years."

"What!" exclaimed Hadrian, "a hundred years old, and you are still planting trees? Do you hope to enjoy the fruits of your labor?"

"Great king," rejoined the hoary-headed elder, "yes, I do hope so; if God permit, I may even eat the fruit of these very trees; if not, my children will. Did not my forefathers plant trees for me, and shall I not do the same for my children?"

Hadrian, pleased with the old man's reply, said,

"Well, old man, if you ever live to see the fruit of these trees, let me know. Yes, let me know. Do you hear, old fellow?" and with these words he left him.

The old man did live long enough to see the fruits of his labor. The trees flourished, and bore excellent fruit. As soon as they were sufficiently ripe, he gathered the choicest figs, put them in a basket, and marched off toward the emperor's residence. Hadrian happened to be looking out of one of the windows of his palace, and noticed the old man, bent with age, with a basket on his shoulders, standing near the gate. He ordered him to be admitted to his court.

"What is your pleasure, old man?"

"May it please your majesty to recollect seeing some years ago a very old man planting some trees; you commanded him, if he ever should gather the fruit, to let you know. I am that old man, and this is the fruit of those very trees. May it please you graciously to accept them as a humble tribute of gratitude for your great condescension."

Hadrian, surprised and gratified to see so extraordinary an example of old age crowned with the full use of all faculties and honest effort, asked the old man to be seated, and ordering the basket to be emptied of fruit, and to be filled with gold, gave it to him as a present. Some courtiers who witnessed this remarkable scene, exclaimed,

"Is it possible that our great emperor should show so much honor to a miserable Jew!"

"Why should I not honor him whom God has honored?" replied Hadrian. "Look at his age, and imitate his example!"

The emperor then very graciously dismissed the old man, who returned home highly pleased and delighted. When he reached his village and exhibited the present he had received, the people were all astonished. Amongst the neighbors whom curiosity had brought to his house, there was a silly covetous woman, who, seeing so much treasure obtained for a few figs, imagined that the emperor must be very fond of this fruit. She therefore hastily ran home, and shouted at her husband.

"You wretch, why are you tarrying here? Have you not heard that Caesar is very fond of figs? Go, take some to him, and you may become as rich as your neighbor."

The foolish fellow, unable to bear the reproaches of his wife, took a large sack, filled with figs, on his shoulders, and after a strenuous journey, arrived, much fatigued, at the palace-gate, and demanded admittance to the emperor. Being asked what he wanted, he answered that, understanding that his majesty was very fond of figs, he had brought a whole sack full, for which he expected a great reward. The officer on duty reported this to the emperor. Hadrian smiled at the man's folly and impertinence.

"Yes," he said to the officer, "the fellow shall have his reward. Let him remain where he is, and let everyone who enters the gate take one of his figs and throw it at his face until they are all gone: then let him depart."

The order was immediately executed. The wretched man, abused, pelted, derided, instead of wishing for gold, prayed only to see the bottom of his bag. After much patience, and still more pain, his prayer was answered. The bag being empty, the poor fellow was dismissed. Dejected and sorrowful, he hastened home. His wife, who was all the while considering how to spend the unexpected treasure, how many fine gowns and cloaks and jewels she would purchase and relishing the thought of how attractive she would look, how the neighbors would stare to see her dressed in silk and gold—most impatiently awaited her husband's return. He came finally, and though she saw the bag was empty, she imagined that his pockets at least were full. Without even greeting him, or permitting him to take breath, she hastily asked him what good luck he had.

"Have patience," replied the enraged husband, "have patience, and I will tell you. I have both great and good luck. My great luck was that I took to the emperor figs and not peaches, else I should have been stoned to death. And my good luck was that the figs were ripe, else I should have left my brains behind me."

"Are you fond of gardening? That's a good start; alchemy is like gardening. Do you like fishing? Alchemy has something in common with fishing."

WATER

I fish because I love to; because I love the environs where trout are found, which are invariably beautiful, and hate the environs where crowds of people are found, which are invariably ugly; because of all the television commercials, cocktail parties, and assorted social posturing I thus escape; because, in a world where most men seem to spend their lives doing things they hate, my fishing is at once an endless source of delight and an act of small rebellion; because trout do not lie or cheat and cannot be bought or bribed or impressed by power, but respond only to quietude and humility and endless patience; because I suspect that men are going along this way for the last time, and I for one don't want to waste the trip; because mercifully there are no telephones on trout waters; because only in the woods can I find solitude without loneliness; because bourbon out of an old tin cup always tastes better out there; because maybe one day I will catch a mermaid; and, finally, not because I regard fishing as being so terribly important but because I suspect that so many of the other concerns of men are equally unimportant—and not nearly so much fun.

Maybe I will catch a mermaid

367

I never met a self I didn't like.

FEATS OF REBELLION

One asked him, "Suh, do you feel there is any place left in modern poetry for *rhaam?*"

"For what?" Bech asked, and educed a gale of giggles.

The girl blushed violently, showing blood suddenly as a wound. "For rhy-em," she said. She was a delicate creature, with a small head on a long neck. Her blue eyes behind glasses felt to be on stalks. The sickness in Bech bit deeper as he apologized, "I'm sorry, I simply didn't hear what you said. You ask about rhyme. I write only prose — "

A sweet chorus of mutters protested that No, his prose was a poet's, was poetry.

He went on, stooping with the pain inside him, dazed to hear himself make a kind of sense, " — but it seems to me rhyme is one of the ways we make things hard for ourselves, make a game out of nothing, so we can win or lose and lighten the, what?, the *indeterminacy* of life. Paul Valéry, somewhere, discusses this, the first line that comes as a gift from the gods and costs nothing, and then the second line that we make ourselves, word by word, straining all our resources, so that it harmonizes with the supernatural first, so that it *rhymes*. He thought, as I remember, that our lives and thoughts and language are all a 'familiar chaos' and that the arbitrary tyranny of a strict prosody goads us to feats of, as it were, rebellion that we couldn't otherwise perform. To this I would only add, and somewhat in contradiction, that rhyme is very ancient, that it marks rhythm, and that much in our natural lives is characterized by rhythm."

THE TRANSMUTATION OF THE ALCHEMIST HIMSELF

The first line comes as a gift from the gods and costs nothing.

The second we make ourselves...straining all our resources.

THE NAUGHTY PREPOSITION

I lately lost a preposition;
    It hid, I thought, beneath my chair;
And angrily I cried, "Perdition!
    Up from out of in under there!"

Correctness is my vade mecum,
    And straggling phrases I abhor,
And yet I wonder, "What should he come
    Up from out of in under for?"

Communicating — shaking one's world awake.

DO NOT GO GENTLE INTO THAT GOOD NIGHT

Do not go gentle into that good night,
Old age should burn and rave at close of day;
Rage, rage against the dying of the light.

Though wise men at their end know dark is right,
Because their words had forked no lightning they
Do not go gentle into that good night.

Good men, the last wave by, crying how bright
Their frail deeds might have danced in a green bay,
Rage, rage against the dying of the light.

Wild men who caught and sang the sun in flight,
And learn, too late, they grieved it on its way,
Do not go gentle into that good night.

Grave men, near death, who see with blinding sight
Blind eyes could blaze like meteors and be gay,
Rage, rage against the dying of the light.

And you, my father, there on the sad height,
Curse, bless, me now with your fierce tears, I pray.
Do not go gentle into that good night.
Rage, rage against the dying of the light.

ENGLAND
Clifford Lewis

"You're going to be a difficult man
to replace, Hoskins! They don't
grovel like you any more."

"Life is trouble; only death
is not. To be alive is to undo
your belt and look for trouble."

—Zorba

369

EVERYTHING!

When a situation arises which cannot be grasped directly and by ordinary methods, a symbolic model sometimes comes to mind whereby we can discover in an instant the answers to all our questions about the original situation. For most people such symbols arise haphazardly, but researchers have established that such symbolic solutions can be induced deliberately. Symbolic models enable us to grasp situations of mathematical or physical reality completely beyond our ordinary sensate world.

Symbol models are not small-scale replicas of actual objects, however. On the contrary, they are always summoned when we cannot grasp ideas or situations through ordinary physical or logical means. Certain attitudes are necessary in order to release the mechanism of such metaphors. Attempts to understand metaphoric thinking with ordinary logic produce ludicrous results. Symbols are not ordinary schematics which can be interpreted by conventional, rational thinking.

Einstein, with his sublime intelligence, was able, in a flash of illumination, to catch a glimpse of the space-time relationship, but without completely understanding or integrating it into his scheme of things. To communicate his discovery at a communicable and intelligible level, and to help him to recapture his own illuminating vision, he drew the sign λ representing the trihedral angle. This sign is not a schema of reality and means nothing to the mass of mankind.

In order to comprehend such models and thus gain practical answers, the mind has to be functioning on its supralogical plane. Working very hard on the logical plane, one sometimes finds another level of intelligence has been set in motion and for a brief instant base metal has been transformed into metaphoric gold. When the thinker allows himself to enter into the feel of the metaphor, becomes in a sense the metaphor itself, he finds tens of thousands of connections are established with electronic speed. The processes of comparisons, classifications, deductions are enormously accelerated, and the entire situation is illuminated. The brief flashes of light everyone has experienced at one time or another, as at the instant of seeing through a riddle, are instances of such illumination. Functioning in this lucid state the mind can use models, images, symbols to 'see into the life of things,' 'the Universe in a grain of sand, and eternity in an hour.'

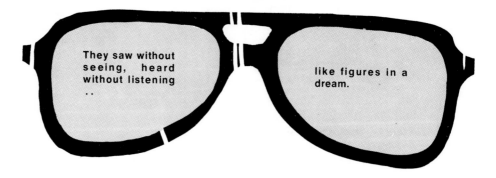

They saw without seeing, heard without listening ..

like figures in a dream.

THE OTTER'S SONG TO US

Press against the bars of my cage, and I will pass
My sleek warm head, my long belly and back over you.
I will wrap my webbed forefeet around your fingers.
Ten memories of wildness,
Each a cold stream.

BRAHMA

If the red slayer thinks he slays,
    Or if the slain think he is slain,
They know not well the subtle ways
    I keep, and pass, and turn again.

Far or forgot to me is near;
    Shadow and sunlight are the same;
The vanished gods to me appear;
    And one to me are shame and fame.

They reckon ill who leave me out;
    When me they fly, I am the wings;
I am the doubter and the doubt,
    And I the hymn the Brahmin sings.

The strong gods pine for my abode,
    And pine in vain the sacred Seven;
But thou, meek lover of the good!
    Find me, and turn thy back on heaven.

AND NOON

THE LAKE ISLE OF INNISFREE

I will arise and go now, and go to Innisfree,
And a small cabin build there, of clay and wattles made:
Nine bean-rows will I have there, a hive for the honey-bee,
And live alone in the bee-loud glade.

And I shall have some peace there, for peace comes dropping
    slow,
Dropping from the veils of the morning to where the cricket
    sings;
There midnight's all a glimmer, and noon a purple glow,
And evening full of linnet's wings.

I will arise and go now, for always night and day
I hear lake water lapping with low sounds by the shore:
While I stand on the roadway, or on the pavements grey,
I hear it in the deep heart's core.

A PURPLE GLOW

And while thy willing soul transpires
At every pore with instant fires,
Now let us sport us while we may,
And now, like amorous birds of prey,
Rather at once our time devour
Than languish in his slow-chapped power.
Let us roll all our strength and all
Our sweetness up into one ball
And tear our pleasures with rough strife
Thorough the iron gates of life:
Thus, though we cannot make our sun
Stand still, yet we will make him run.

"Could you give us an example?" the girl asked.

"For example, lovemaking," Bech said, and to his horror beheld her blush surging up again, and beheld beyond her blush an entire seething universe of brainless breeding, of moist interpenetration, of slippery clinging copulation, or courtship dances and come-on signals, of which her hapless blush, unknown to her, was one. He doubted that he could stand here another minute without fainting. Their massed fertility was overwhelming; their bodies were being broadened and readied to generate from their own cells a new body to be pushed from the old, and in time to push bodies from itself, and so on into eternity, an ocean of doubling and redoubling cells within which his own conscious moment was soon to wink out.

When I heard the Earth-song,
I was no longer brave;
My avarice cooled
Like lust in the chill of the grave.

True or False?

PRE FACE

TO THE VIRGINS, TO MAKE MUCH OF TIME

Gather ye rosebuds while ye may,
  Old Time is still a-flying;
And this same flower that smiles today,
  Tomorrow will be dying.

The glorious lamp of heaven, the sun,
  The higher he's a-getting,
The sooner will his race be run,
  And nearer he's to setting.

That age is best which is the first,
  When youth and blood are warmer;
But being spent, the worse, and worst
  Times still succeed the former.

Then be not coy, but use your time;
  And while ye may, go marry:
For having lost but once your prime,
  You may for ever tarry.

A GOOD ADVENTURE NEEDS A TERRIBLE DRAGON

ON SITTING DOWN TO READ KING LEAR ONCE AGAIN

O golden tongued romance, with serene lute!
    Fair-plumèd Syren, Queen of far-away!
    Leave melodizing on this wintry day,
Shut up thine olden pages, and be mute:
Adieu! for, once again, the fierce dispute
    Betwixt damnation and impassioned clay
    Must I burn through; once more humbly assay
The bitter-sweet of this Shakespearian fruit:
Chief poet! and ye clouds of Albion,
    Begetters of our deep eternal theme!
When through the old oak Forest I am gone,
    Let me not wander in a barren dream,
But, when I am consumèd in the fire,
Give me new Phoenix wings to fly at my desire.

It is not growing like a tree
    In bulk, doth make man better be;
Or standing long an oak, three hundred year,
To fall a log at last, dry, bald, and sear:
    A lily of a day
    Is fairer far, in May,
    Although it fall and die that night;
    It was the plant and flower of light.
In small proportions we just beauties see,
And in short measures life may perfect be.

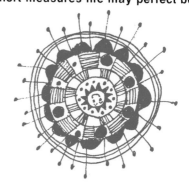

To speculate about dying doesn't disturb me as it might some people. I never have felt that I would live to become an old man. To come right down to it, if I take the kind of things in which I believe, then add to that the kind of temperament that I have, plus the one hundred per cent dedication I have to whatever I believe in—these are ingredients which make it just about impossible for me to die of old age.

— Malcolm X

If you have only two pennies left in the world, buy a loaf of bread with one and a lily with the other.
—Old Chinese proverb

374

LIGHT

As soon as he saw me, Cephalus greeted me. You don't often come down to the Piraeus to visit us, Socrates, he said. But you ought to. If I still had the strength to walk to town easily, you would not have to come here; we would come to you. But, as things are, you really ought to come here oftener. I find, I can assure you, that in proportion as bodily pleasures lose their savour, my appetite for the things of the mind grows keener and I enjoy discussing them more than ever. So you must not disappoint me. Treat us like old friends, and come here often to have a talk with these young men.

To tell the truth, Cephalus, I answered, I enjoy talking with very old people. They have gone before us on a road by which we too may have to travel, and I think we do well to learn from them what it is like, easy or difficult, rough or smooth. And now that you have reached an age when your foot, as the poets say, is on the threshold, I should like to hear what report you can give and whether you find it a painful time of life.

I will tell you by all means what it seems like to me, Socrates. Some of us old men often meet, true to the old saying that people of the same age like to be together. Most of our company are very sorry for themselves, looking back with regret to the pleasures of their young days, all the delights connected with love affairs and merry-making. They are vexed at being deprived of what seems to them so important; life was good in those days, they think, and now they have no life at all. Some complain that their families have no respect for their years, and make that a reason for harping on all the miseries old age has brought. But to my mind, Socrates, they are laying the blame on the wrong shoulders. If the fault were in old age, so far as that goes, I and all who have ever reached my time of life would have the same experience; but in point of fact, I have met many who felt quite differently. For instance, I remember someone asking Sophocles, the poet, whether he was still capable of enjoying a woman. 'Don't talk in that way,' he answered; 'I am only too glad to be free of all that; it is like escaping from bondage to a raging madman.' I thought that a good answer at the time, and I still think so; for certainly a great peace comes when age sets us free from passions of that sort. When they weaken and relax their hold, most certainly it means, as Sophocles said, a release from servitude to many forms of madness. All these troubles, Socrates, including the complaints about not being respected, have only one cause; and that is not old age, but a man's character. If you have a contented mind at peace with itself, age is no intolerable burden; without that, Socrates, age and youth will be equally painful.

I was charmed with these words and wanted him to go on talking; so I tried to draw him out. I fancy, Cephalus, said I, most people will not accept that account; they imagine that it is not character that makes your burden light, but your wealth. The rich, they say, have many consolations.

That is true, he replied; they do not believe me; and there is something in their suggestion, though not so much as they suppose. When a man from Seriphus taunted Themistocles and told him that his fame was due not to himself but to his country, Themistocles made a good retort: 'Certainly, if I had been born a Seriphian, I should not be famous; but no more would you, if you had been born at Athens.' And so one might say to men who are not rich and feel old age burdensome: If it is true that a good man will not find it easy to bear old age and poverty combined, no more will riches ever make a bad man contented and cheerful.

WHEN YOU ARE OLD

When you are old and grey and full of sleep,
And nodding by the fire, take down this book,
And slowly read, and dream of the soft look
Your eyes had once, and of their shadows deep;

How many loved your moments of glad grace,
And loved your beauty with love false or true,
But one man loved the pilgrim soul in you,
And loved the sorrows of your changing face;

And bending down beside the glowing bars,
Murmur, a little sadly, how Love fled
And paced upon the mountains overhead
And hid his face amid a crowd of stars.

A   sad   tense,

the   past   tense

The volox invented death. There is no reason intrinsic in the plasmic substance why life should ever end. Amoebas never die; and those male sperm cells which enjoy success become the cornerstone of new life that continues beyond the father. But the volox, a rolling sphere of flagellating algae organized in somatic and reproductive cells, neither plant nor animal — under a microscope it looks just like a Christmas ball — by pioneering the new idea of *cooperation* rolled life into the kingdom of certain — as opposed to accidental — death. For — hold tight kids, just seven minutes more of torture — while each cell is potentially immortal, by volunteering for a specialized function within an organized society of cells, it enters a compromised environment. The strain eventually kills it. It dies sacrificially, for the good of the whole. The first cells who got tired of sitting around forever in a blue-green scum and said, "Let's get together and make a volox," were the first altruists.

Being invisible and without substance, a disembodied voice, as it were, what else could I do? What else but try to tell you what was really happening when your eyes were looking through? And it is this which frightens me: Who knows but that, on the lower frequencies, I speak for you?

STOP

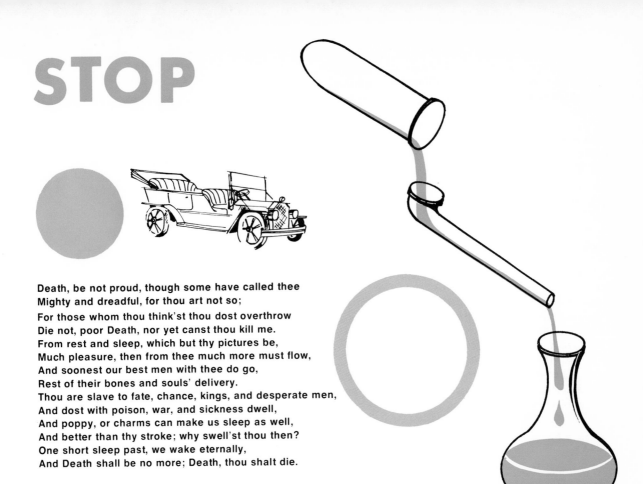

Death, be not proud, though some have called thee
Mighty and dreadful, for thou art not so;
For those whom thou think'st thou dost overthrow
Die not, poor Death, nor yet canst thou kill me.
From rest and sleep, which but thy pictures be,
Much pleasure, then from thee much more must flow,
And soonest our best men with thee do go,
Rest of their bones and souls' delivery.
Thou are slave to fate, chance, kings, and desperate men,
And dost with poison, war, and sickness dwell,
And poppy, or charms can make us sleep as well,
And better than thy stroke; why swell'st thou then?
One short sleep past, we wake eternally,
And Death shall be no more; Death, thou shalt die.

Back of the wine is the vintner
and back through the years, his skill
and back of all the vines is the sun
                and the rain
                and the master's will.

Death in Samarra

In the city of Ispahan, in Persia, a certain man's servant came to him and said, "I was in the market place and there I saw Death and he made a threatening gesture to me." The man said, "Let us flee," and he and his servant set out posthaste for Samarra. No sooner had they entered that city than they encountered Death, to whom the man said, "Why did you threaten my servant in the market place in Ispahan?" Death replied, "My gesture was not one of threat but of surprise, for I had an appointment to meet you in Samarra, and I was surprised to learn from seeing your servant, that you were still in Ispahan."

He advised me to keep a journal of my life, fair and undisguised. He said it would be a very good exercise, and would yield me infinite satisfaction when the ideas were faded from my remembrance. I told him that I had done so ever since I left Scotland. He said he was very happy that I pursued so good a plan. And now, O my journal! art thou not highly dignified? Shalt thou not flourish tenfold? No former solicitations or censures could tempt me to lay thee aside; and now is there any argument which can outweigh the sanction of Mr. Samuel Johnson? He said indeed that I should keep it private, and that I might surely have a friend who would burn it in case of my death. For my own part, I have at present such an affection for this my journal that it shocks me to think of burning it. I rather encourage the idea of having it carefully laid up among the archives of Auchinleck. However, I cannot judge fairly of it now. Some years hence I may. I told Mr. Johnson that I put down all sorts of little incidents in it. "Sir," said he, "there is nothing too little for so little a creature as man. It is by studying little things that we attain the great knowledge of having as little misery and as much happiness as possible." (16 JULY 1763)

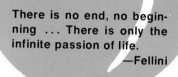

There is no end, no beginning ... There is only the infinite passion of life.
—Fellini

WATER

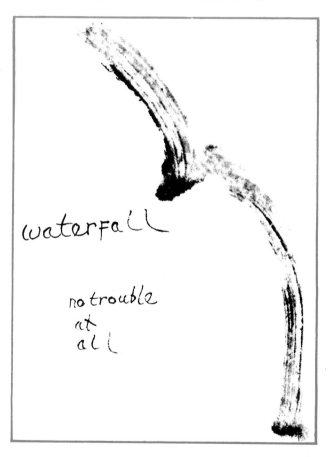

waterfall

no trouble
at
all

NOTICE

The new audio-visual
department is on the ground
floor. Enter on the north.
You will find your self in
the listening-viewing lab.

In all cases, please exit
by the same door by which
you entered.

379

AUTHOR INDEX

Legend: P=poem; E=essay; S=story; EX=excerpt; Q=quotation; A=artwork; F=photograph;
C=cartoon or drawing; G=game
See Acknowledgments for further information on the works.